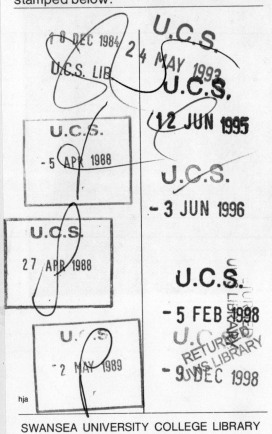

EXERCISES IN MACROECONOMICS

EXERCISES IN MACROECONOMICS: DEVELOPMENT OF CONCEPTS

WILLIAM E. MITCHELL
Associate Professor of Economics
University of Missouri–St. Louis

JOHN H. HAND
Associate Professor of Finance
Ohio University

INGO WALTER
Professor of Economics and Finance
New York University

McGRAW-HILL BOOK COMPANY
New York   St. Louis   San Francisco   Düsseldorf   Johannesburg
Kuala Lumpur   London   Mexico   Montreal   New Delhi
Panama   Rio de Janeiro   Singapore   Sydney   Toronto

Library of Congress Cataloging in Publication Data

Mitchell, William E   1936–
    Exercises in macroeconomics.

    Includes bibliographical references.
    1. Macroeconomics–Problems, exercises, etc.
I. Hand, John H., 1940–   joint author.   II. Walter,
Ingo, joint author.   III. Title.
HB171.5.M664   339   73–4794
ISBN 0–07–042511–6   (pbk.)

EXERCISES IN MACROECONOMICS:
Development of Concepts

1 2 3 4 5 6 7 8 9 0 V H V H 7 9 8 7 6 5 4 3

This book was set in Press Roman by Allen-Wayne Technical Corp.
The editors were Jack R. Crutchfield and Sally Mobley;
the designer was Nicholas Krenitsky;
and the production supervisor was Ted Agrillo.
The drawings were done by Danmark & Michaels, Inc.
The printer and binder was Von Hoffmann Press, Inc.

TO LEE, ROBERTA, AND JUTTA

CONTENTS

Courses in intermediate macroeconomics require the student to master a considerable amount of rather formalistic subject matter. An understanding of such material as the multiplier, the *IS–LM* diagram, liquidity preference, marginal efficiency of capital, and aggregate supply and demand requires intense concentration and repetition that is usually not appropriate in the classroom. Class time is best devoted to the study of general concepts and policy applications, while the formal apparatus is mastered by the student working at his own pace. *EXERCISES IN MACROECONOMICS: Development of Concepts* is designed to assist such self-study.

Each exercise concentrates on several central concepts which will provide a better background for understanding the institutional material and the more detailed and refined discussion of theory covered in a typical intermediate macro text. Extensive use is made of numerical and graphical applications to emphasize principal concepts. A self-contained format is used, whereby the major concepts and tools are developed independently in the book. The student will not need to refer back and forth from textbook to exercise book. All answers are conveniently included in the volume, providing immediate reinforcement or correction in the learning process.

The exercises in this book can be used with any standard textbook in intermediate macroeconomics. A list of references to these textbooks, following the preface, indicates which exercises relate to the subject matter of the regular textbook being used. Depending on the objectives of the course, the instructor may omit some exercises or assign them in a different order.

The book is divided into nine parts, each corresponding to a fairly broad topic in much the same way that standard books are divided into chapters. Each part has an introduction which explains and emphasizes the principal objectives of that part, including policy issues and theoretical controversies illustrated in the exercises, and relates these objectives to material covered elsewhere in the text. The introductions are not substitutes for textbook material but should help the student coordinate his use of this book and a regular text. Each part is divided into individual exercises which provide intensive study of a limited number of macroeconomic concepts and tools. Finally, each part has a Review Test. These self-test questions are designed to further strengthen the learning process and to provide the student with a check on his progress. The true-false and multiple-choice questions test for understanding of vocabulary and the ability to apply principles. The answers to the Review Tests are provided at the back of the book.

Most exercises have two components, development of concepts and applied problems. The important tools and concepts of macroeconomic analysis are presented in a modified programmed learning format. The student must play an active role in the development of this material by filling in blanks (inserting the proper word or phrase, completing a statement, or solving a numerical problem), choosing correct answers from two or more alternatives, or constructing, using, and interpreting graphical materials. When the text provides a multiple-choice option, the student should underline or circle the correct answer or cross out the incorrect options. Since the solutions are given at the end of each exercise, the student can determine at once whether or not his response is correct. He can correct any errors before proceeding to new material. The answers to graphical problems are designated with an A following the graph number.

The applied problems for each exercise provide the student with the opportunity to test his understanding of the material developed in the first section of the exercise. In certain instances, depending on the importance and difficulty of the material, more than one problem is provided for a particular concept or topic. Most problems are geared to the presentation level of a typical intermediate macro text. Occasionally, however, problems of a more complex nature are offered and are identified as optional. The continuity of the material will not be lost if they are omitted.

The authors wish to express special thanks to Professor Duncan M. McDougall for his innumerable suggestions which greatly improved the book. Thanks are also due to Olive Fanghanel, Vickie Landrum, Marion Epps, Mary Boyd, Katherine Peterman, Kathleen Shelley, Eileen Wiegert, Patricia Clegg, and Jane Kleszczewski for handling the various manuscript tasks. Final responsibility for the contents rests with the authors.

William E. Mitchell
John H. Hand
Ingo Walter

REFERENCES TO SELECTED
STANDARD MACROECONOMICS TEXTBOOKS

Nancy S. Barrett, *The Theory of Macroeconomic Policy*, Prentice-Hall, 1972.

Chapter 1, *Exercise 1*; Chapters 2 and 3, *Exercises 4 to 7 and 21 to 24*; Chapter 4, *Exercise 9*; Chapter 5, *Exercise 8*; Chapter 6, *Exercises 10 and 11*; Chapter 7, *Exercises 12 and 13*; Chapter 8, *Exercises 14 to 18*; Chapter 9, *Exercises 19 and 20*; Chapter 12, *Exercise 25*; Appendix B, *Exercises 2 and 3*.

Thomas F. Dernburg and Duncan M. McDougall, *Macroeconomics*, 4th ed., McGraw-Hill Book Company, 1972.

Chapter 1, *Exercise 1*; Chapter 2, *Exercise 2*; Chapter 4, *Exercise 3*; Chapter 5, *Exercises 4 to 8*; Chapter 6, *Exercise 9*; Chapter 7, *Exercises 10 and 11*; Chapter 8, *Exercises 12 and 13*; Chapter 9, *Exercises 14 to 16*; Chapter 10, *Exercise 17*; Chapter 11, *Exercises 18 to 20*; Chapter 13, *Exercises 21 to 24*; Chapter 15, *Exercise 25*.

Norman F. Keiser, *Macroeconomics*, Random House, 1971.

Chapter 2, *Exercises 2 and 3*; Chapter 3, *Exercise 1*; Chapter 4, *Exercises 4 to 6*; Chapter 5, *Exercise 7*; Chapters 6 and 7, *Exercise 8*; Chapters 8 and 9, *Exercises 10 and 11*; Chapters 12, 14 and 15, *Exercise 9*; Chapter 13, *Exercises 21 to 24*; Chapter 16, *Exercises 12 to 15*; Chapter 17, *Exercises 16 to 18*; Chapters 19 and 20, *Exercises 19 and 20*; Chapter 24, *Exercise 25*.

John Lindauer, *Macroeconomics*, John Wiley & Sons, Inc., 1968.

Chapter 1, *Exercises 1 to 3*; Chapter 2, *Exercises 4, 5, and 8*; Chapter 3, *Exercises 10, 11, and 21 to 24*; Chapter 4, *Exercises 6, 7, and 14*; Chapter 5, *Exercise 9*; Chapter 6, *Exercises 12 and 13*; Chapter 7, *Exercises 15 to 17;* Chapter 8, *Exercise 18*; Chapter 9, *Exercise 19*; Chapter 11, *Exercise 25*; Chapter 14, *Exercise 20*.

Joseph P. McKenna, *Aggregate Economic Analysis*, 4th ed., The Dryden Press, 1972.

Chapter 1, *Exercise 1*; Chapter 2, *Exercises 2 and 3*; Chapter 4, *Exercises 4 to 7*; Chapter 5, *Exercise 9*; Chapter 6, *Exercise 8*; Chapter 7, *Exercises 10 and 11*; Chapter 8, *Exercise 14*; Chapter 9, *Exercises 12, 13, and 15*; Chapter 10, *Exercises 16 and 17*; Chapter 11,

Exercises 21 to 24; Chapter 12, *Exercise 18*; Chapter 13, *Exercise 19*; Chapter 14, *Exercise 20*; Chapter 17, *Exercise 25*.

Wallace C. Peterson, *Income, Employment, and Economic Growth*, rev. ed., W. W. Norton, 1967.

Chapter 1, *Exercise 1*; Chapters 2 and 3, *Exercises 2 and 3*; Chapter 6, *Exercises 4 to 8*; Chapter 7, *Exercises 10 and 11*; Chapter 9, *Exercise 9*; Chapter 10, *Exercises 21 to 24*; Chapter 11, *Exercises 12 and 13*; Chapter 12, *Exercises 14 to 16*; Chapter 13, *Exercises 17 to 20*; Chapter 15, *Exercise 25*.

D. D. Rowan and Thomas Mayer, *Intermediate Macroeconomics*, W. W. Norton, 1972.

Chapters 2 and 3, *Exercises 2 and 3*; Chapter 6, *Exercise 1*; Chapters 7 and 8, *Exercises 4 to 7*; Chapter 9, *Exercise 8*; Chapter 10, *Exercises 10 and 11*; Chapter 12, *Exercises 12 and 13*; Chapter 13, *Exercises 14 to 18*; Chapter 14, *Exercises 9 and 21 to 24*; Chapters 15 to 17, *Exercises 19 and 20*; Chapter 18, *Exercise 25*.

Edward Shapiro, *Macroeconomic Analysis*, Harcourt, Brace & World, 1970.

Chapters 2 to 5, *Exercises 2 and 3*; Chapter 6, *Exercise 1*; Chapter 7, *Exercises 4 to 6*; Chapter 8, *Exercise 7*; Chapter 9, *Exercise 8*; Chapter 11, *Exercise 10*; Chapter 12, *Exercise 11*; Chapter 14, *Exercise 9*; Chapter 15, *Exercises 21 to 24*; Chapter 16, *Exercise 19*; Chapter 17, *Exercise 20*; Chapter 18, *Exercises 12 and 13*; Chapter 19, *Exercises 14 to 18*; Chapter 22, *Exercise 25*.

Barry N. Siegel, *Aggregate Economics and Public Policy*, 3d ed., Richard D. Irwin, 1970.

Chapter 1, *Exercise 1*; Chapter 2, *Exercises 2 and 3*; Chapter 4, *Exercises 4 to 7*; Chapter 5, *Exercises 9 and 21 to 24*; Chapter 6, *Exercise 8*; Chapter 8, *Exercises 10 and 11*; Chapter 10, *Exercises 12 to 16*; Chapter 11, *Exercises 17 and 18*; Chapter 12, *Exercises 19 and 20*; Chapter 14, *Exercise 25*.

Gerald Sirkin, *Introduction to Macroeconomic Theory*, 3d ed., Richard D. Irwin, 1970.

Chapter 1, *Exercises 2 and 3*; Chapter 2, *Exercise 1*; Chapter 3, *Exercises 4 to 7 and 9*; Chapter 4, *Exercise 8*; Chapter 5, *Exercises 10 and 11*; Chapter 7, *Exercises 12 to 16*; Chapter 9, *Exercises 17 to 20*; Chapter 10, *Exercise 25*; Chapter 11, *Exercises 21 to 24*.

EXERCISES IN MACROECONOMICS

INTRODUCTION TO MACROECONOMIC ANALYSIS

Macroeconomics is the study of the utilization level of resources—employment, output, and the level and rate of growth of potential output—and the general level of prices. The macroeconomic approach ultimately seeks to examine the simultaneous interdependence of all markets through the simplifying device of aggregation. Individual markets are combined by adding together, for example, all the demand functions for consumer goods and services in the household sector, all the demand functions for investment goods in the business sector, or all the supply functions for consumer and investment goods in the production sector. After variables in the individual markets are reduced to a manageable number through aggregation, their contributions to overall resource utilization can be studied, as can the interrelationships between the variables in the several markets. Thus it can be said that the macroeconomic framework is a general equilibrium system.

Although the number of variables is drastically reduced through aggregation, in the study of something as intricate as a national economy, there still remains a considerable degree of complexity. This book presents a set of analytical techniques and devices that can be used to facilitate understanding of the general equilibrium macroeconomic approach. Mastery of these tools requires only simple algebra and geometry. The economic relationships, such as the aforementioned demand and supply functions for different markets, can be expressed in the form of equations. These equations can be represented by either an algebraic or a geometric form; each has its expository advantages. The purpose of this Exercise is to briefly review the basic concepts that will be needed to complete the other exercises.

1 If the value of an item is subject to systematic change in the economy or in a simplified framework set up for study of the economy, that item is called a *variable*. For example, national income is a variable, for, as everyone knows, it is always changing under the influence of a variety of economic processes. If an item is subject to arbitrary and irregular change rather than to systematic change, it is called a *parameter*. The marginal propensity to consume, defined as the amount by which consumption changes if income changes by one unit, is a *parameter*. Changes in parameters are believed to be infrequent and irregular. Finally, if an item never changes in value, it is called a *constant*. The speed of light is a constant. There are no true constants in economics. While some parameters can be treated as if they were constant for some purposes, ultimately everything is subject to change—even if that change is infrequent and arbitrary.

2 A functional relationship is one in which one variable depends on another in a systematic way. If it is proposed that the amount of investment expenditures I depends on the value of the interest rate i, the functional relationship can be expressed with the following equation:

(1) $I = f(i)$

The letter f is a functional notation symbol. Equation (1) states that for each and every value assigned to i there corresponds a value of I. The variable to which values are assigned is called the *independent* variable and the variable for which corresponding values are determined is called the dependent variable.

3 Consider another functional relationship. The amount of consumption expenditures C depends on the level of income Y.

(2) $C = f(Y)$

The letter C is the (dependent, independent) variable and the letter Y is the (dependent, independent) variable. The letter f is a (multiplication, functional notation) symbol.

4 Equations (1) and (2) state the general form of a relationship between variables. There are two additional aspects of a functional relationship which are important in order to describe the specific form of the function: (*a*) whether the relationship is positive or inverse; (*b*) whether the relationship between the independent and the dependent variable is 1:1—that is, whether a value of one variable corresponds to only one value of the other—or is more complicated. Let us consider a more descriptive form of Eq. (1).

(3) $I = \$250 \text{ bil} - 10i$

The letter (I, i) represents the independent variable. The negative sign before the independent variable indicates that the functional relationship is *inverse*; that is, if the interest rate rises, the amount of investment will (rise, fall). The value of the number preceding the variable i is a parameter (see paragraph 1 above) called the *coefficient of the functional relationship*. This parameter describes the specific numerical relationship between the independent and dependent variable. In Eq. (3), if $i = 5$ percent,

$I = \$$_____ bil. If $i = 6$ percent, $I = \$$_____ bil. When the interest rate increases by

1 percentage point, investment (increases, decreases) by $\$$_____ bil. Thus the coefficient of the functional relationship describes the degree of response of the dependent variable to changes in the independent variable. The value of this parameter is fixed for the discussion represented by Eq. (3), but can change from one discussion to another.

5 If the value of i in Eq. (3) is zero, $I = \$$_____ bil. Thus it is said that $250 bil of investment spending is *autonomously* determined, that is, not determined by the value of the independent variable. The amount, $250 bil, is another parameter value in Eq. (3). The autonomous value may represent the quantitative effects on the value of I of other variables in the economic system which are ignored in the equation. Alternatively, the value may represent spending that is not affected by anything. For the discussion represented by Eq. (3), the quantitative effects of these other variables are fixed at $250 bil. But we can consider arguments which introduce a change in the effect of these variables on I. Let the value of the parameter—autonomous investment—increase to $400 bil. If i does not change, the value of the dependent variable I will increase by

$_____$ bil. A shift in the value of the autonomous variable (does, does not) alter the functional relationship between the dependent and the independent variable.

The general form of Eq. (3) can be written as follows:

(4) $I = I_0 - di$

The letter I represents the $_____$ variable; i is the $_____$

variable; I_0 is a $_____$ and represents the value of $_____$

investment; d is a $_____$ and represents the value of the $_____$

$_____$ of the functional relationship.

6 Now assume that we have more complete information about the form of the functional relationship stated in Eq. (2). Specifically, assume that consumption expenditures are $100 bil, regardless of the income level, and additionally, consumption changes—in the same direction—by $75 bil whenever income changes by $100 bil. Write the consumption function

(5) $C = _____$

The relationship in Eq. (5) is (positive, inverse). The letter C is the (dependent, independent) variable and Y is the (dependent, independent) variable. The value of the coefficient of the functional relationship is $_____$. The value of autonomous consumption is $_____$. The letters C and Y (are, are not) called parameters.

7 Graphing a function is quite helpful for visualizing the specific shape of the function. Most of the equations used in this book, including the preceding ones, are called *linear* equations. The locus or graph of a linear equation in two variables is a straight line. A line drawn through any two plotted points is sufficient to graph a linear equation. It is advisable for accuracy, however, that the two points not be too close, and, as a check, a third point should be plotted.

Consider the previously discussed investment function

(3) $I = \$250 \text{ bil} - 10i$

Using Eq. (3), let the independent variable i assume the values 0, 10, and 20. Solve for the resulting values of I, the dependent variable, and complete Table 1-1. Plot these

Table 1-1

$i, \%$	I
0	$_____$ bil
10	$_____$ bil
20	$_____$ bil

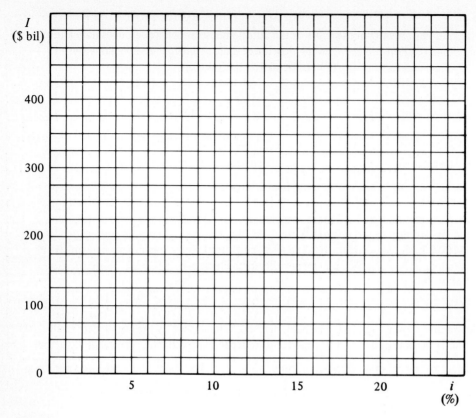

FIGURE 1-1

three pairs of values in Fig. 1-1. Draw a line connecting these three points. Label the curve I_1. (Note: A straight line is a special case of the general class of "curves.") The point where the curve intersects the vertical axis is equal to the value of the (I_O, d, i) variable. The graph of a function always intersects the axis of the dependent variable at the autonomous variable. The graph of the investment function falls from left to right, indicating that I and i are (positively, inversely) related.

8 The I_1 curve is reproduced in Fig. 1-2. We now want to examine the characteristic of the slope or "steepness" of the curve. Assume we are initially at point 1 and now move to point 3. The distance from point 1 to point 2 measures the (increase, decrease) of

_____ . Label this distance ΔI, where the symbol Δ represents *change*. The term ΔI is read as "the change in investment." The distance from point 2 to point 3

measures the (increase, decrease) of the _____ _____ .

Label this distance Δi. When we move from point 1 to point 3, $\Delta I = \$$ _____ bil, and

$\Delta i =$ _____ percent. Compute the value of the ratio of these two changes, $\Delta I/\Delta i =$

_____ . This value is equal to (I_O, d, i) in Eq. (3). The ratio $\Delta I/\Delta i$ measures the value

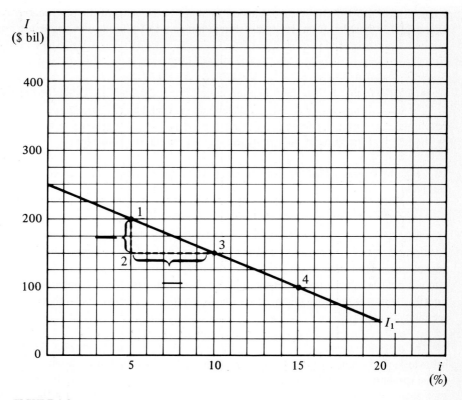

FIGURE 1-2

of the *slope* of the investment curve. The slope of a curve is a measure of the change in the amount of the dependent variable for a one-unit change in the independent variable. The slope of a curve (is, is not) equal to the coefficient of the functional relationship. This fact can be demonstrated algebraically. Using the symbol Δ to indicate change, we can restate Eq. (4) as

(6) $\quad \Delta I = \Delta I_O - d\Delta i$

We assume that d will remain constant for this discussion. If we also assume that $\Delta I_O = 0$, then Eq. (6) reduces to

(7) $\quad \Delta I = -d\Delta i$

Solve for d

(8) $\quad d = $ _____

Thus the value of d is equal to the slope of the graphed function and can be measured by the ratio $\Delta I / \Delta i$, the change in the dependent variable divided by the change in the independent variable. Since the value of d is a constant, the slope of the I_1 curve (is also, need not be) a constant. Compute the value of the slope of I_1 over the distance from point 3 to point 4. The slope of I_1 is a (constant, variable).

9 Let us now introduce into the discussion a change in the value of the parameters. Using Eq. (3), now let autonomous investment increase *to* $400 bil. The new equation can be written as

(9) $I =$ _____

Graph Eq. (9) in Fig. 1-2 for the following values of i: 0, 10, and 20. Label the new curve I_2. The curve I_2 has shifted to the (right, left) and is (parallel, nonparallel) to I_1. The functional relationship between I and i (has, has not) changed. This feature is indicated by the fact that the slope of the investment curve (has, has not) changed.

10 Let us now assume that the slope of Eq. (9) changes to $d = 5$. The new equation will be

(10) $I =$ _____

Graph Eq. (10) in Fig. 1-2 for the following values of i; 0, 10, and 20. Label the new curve I_3. Compared to I_2, I_3 has shifted to the (right, left); autonomous investment (has, has not) changed. The curve I_3 (is, is not) parallel to I_2. A one-unit change in the interest rate in Eq. (10) will result in a (larger, smaller) change in investment, compared to Eq. (9). Thus it is said that the interest-rate *elasticity* or responsiveness of investment spending has declined.

11 The preceding equations represent hypotheses about economic behavior. These behavioral relationships can be grouped together to form a *model* of economic behavior. A macroeconomic *model* is designed to describe the behavior of groups in the economy, such as households, business firms, and the government. A model allows for the systematic study of interrelationships between these groups, and assists in explaining the determination of levels of and changes in aggregate income, employment, and prices for specified changes in the parameters of the model.

There are two types of equations used in models, *behavioral* and *definitional* equations. Equations (3) and (5) are examples of behavioral equations. They describe the aggregate expenditure behavior of consumers and businessmen. The most common definitional equation used in this book is the *equilibrium condition.* This equation describes the condition under which opposite forces for change will be in balance, so that further change does not occur. The most familiar equilibrium condition in economics is that quantity demanded equals quantity supplied. When this condition holds, an equilibrium price and quantity is determined. When a single parameter of the model changes, the balance is upset and the system is said to be in *dis*equilibrium. After all adjustments have taken place and the system again meets the condition of the equilibrium equation, a new equilibrium price and quantity will be obtained.

There are other types of definitional equations, often known as *identities*. For example, the statement "the demand for money M_d is composed of two components, the transactions demand M_1 and the speculative demand M_2" can be written as the following equation:

(11) $M_d = M_1 + M_2$

12 The set of equations which comprises an economic model must be solved to obtain the unique equilibrium values. What this procedure requires is that we consider a system of two or more simultaneous equations and their solution. To solve a system of two equations in two unknowns, for example, means that we must find the values of the two unknowns that will satisfy *both* of the equations simultaneously. One algebraic method of solving for the equilibrium values is as follows: Locate the equilibrium-condition equation and substitute all other equations into it; solve for the desired equilibrium value. For example, one of the most elementary macroeconomic models is the following one comprising three equations:

(12) $Y = C + I$

(13) $C = a + bY$

(14) $I = I_O$

Equation (12) is the equilibrium condition. Equations (13) and (14) are behavioral equations. Note that, for this discussion, all investment is assumed to be autonomously determined. Solve for Y. Substitute Eqs. (13) and (14) into (12).

(15) $Y = $ _____

Transpose all terms that include the variable Y to the left-hand side of Eq. (15).

(16)   _____ = _____

Factor out the variable Y from both terms on the left-hand side of Eq. (16).

(17)   _____ = _____

Divide both sides of Eq. (17) by the term $(1 - b)$.

(18) $Y = $ _____

Equation (18) represents the equation for computing equilibrium Y. Assume that the following parameter values hold: $a = \$100$ bil; $b = 0.75$; $I_O = \$200$ bil. Substitute these values into Eq. (18). Equilibrium $Y = \$$ _____ bil. Now substitute the values for a, b, and equilibrium Y into Eq. (13). Equilibrium $C = \$$ _____ bil. Now substitute the values for Y and C that you have found, along with the value for I_O, into Eq. (12). The sum of $C + I = \$$ _____ bil. Is the condition for the equilibrium equation satisfied (yes, no)?

ANSWERS FOR EXERCISE 1

3 dependent, independent, functional notation
4 i, fall, 200, 190, decreases, 10
5 250, 150, does not, dependent, independent, parameter, autonomous, parameter, coefficient

6 Eq. (5) $C = \$100$ bil $+ 0.75Y$,
positive, dependent, independent, 0.75, $100 bil, are not

7 250, 150, 50, Fig. 1-1A, I_O, Fig. 1-1A, inversely

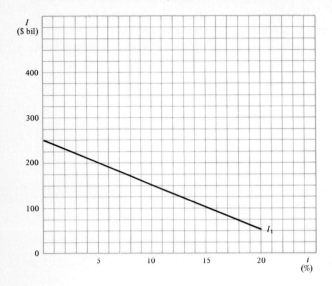

FIGURE 1-1A

8 decrease, investment, Fig. 1-2A, increase, interest rate, Fig. 1-2A, 50, 5, 10, d, is,
Eq. (8) $d = \Delta I / \Delta i$, is also, constant

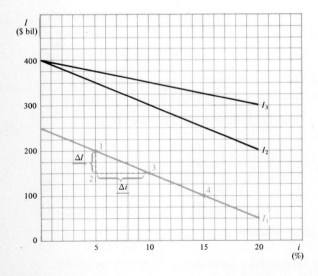

FIGURE 1-2A

9 Eq. (9) I = \$400 bil – $10i$,
Fig. 1-2A, right, parallel, has not, has not

10 Eq. (10) I = \$400 bil – $5i$,
Fig. 1-2A, right, has not, is not, smaller

12 Eq. (15) $Y = a + bY + I_O$,
Eq. (16) $Y - bY = a + I_O$,
Eq. (17) $Y(1 - b) = a + I_O$,
Eq. (18) $Y = (a + I_O)/(1 - b)$,
1,200, 1,000, 1,200, yes

PART ONE

THE NATIONAL ACCOUNTS

The economy is composed of individual producers, consumers, manufacturing firms, financial institutions, governmental units, and so forth, all going about the task of improving their own or someone else's social and economic welfare, however defined. It is not hard for an individual to gauge when he is better off: He can usually tell you whether or not he is and what yardstick he is using to measure his own welfare. It is infinitely more difficult to tell when society is better off, for three main reasons. First is the problem of measurement—of devising concepts that can be expressed as numbers, which in turn can be generated by observing various developments in the real world of the national economy. Measurement systems are in need of constant review, and there is the issue of whether what we are measuring is really what we *think* we are measuring. Second is the problem of aggregation—of lumping together large numbers of individual businesses, governments, and institutions, and trying to assess changes in their collective welfare. Even though the economy "improves" this year, I as an individual may very well have lost my job and may be substantially worse off than last year. Reading about the rosy national economic outlook is small consolation. When the overall economic picture improves, chances are that the individual will be better off—but not necessarily. Aggregate measures cannot reach down to describe much beyond the very general. Third is the issue of whether what we are measuring is what we really *ought* to be measuring. Do total output of goods and services, total production of automobiles or steel, or total tax receipts by government really measure contributions to national welfare? What about environmental despoliation and the other "spillover" effects that are not costed-out in the marketplace and never enter the data? What about the *distribution* of income and product? These issues of social accounting continue to raise questions about the adequacy of the yardsticks we are using to measure economic performance and call for their continual reassessment.

There are a variety of important concepts used in measuring economic activity, and it is important to know precisely what each of these means if they are to be interpreted correctly. Moreover, aggregate economic measurement is a complex business. The objective of the two exercises in Part 1 is to present the data as they are in the real world, not as they might be if things were simpler and more elegant. Development and interpretation of economic indicators is messy and often tedious. The student should fully appreciate this fact before coming to grips with the theoretical foundations of macroeconomics, which often abstract from much of the detail studied here.

AGGREGATE INCOME, PRODUCT, AND FINANCIAL FLOWS

1 The purpose of productive activity is to contribute something, on net, which will lead to an improvement in material well-being. Suppose an individual owns a corporation that is in the hamburger business. He buys meat and other ingredients, called *intermediate products.* He sells hamburgers. If he does things right, his total sales in dollars will exceed his total intermediate purchases of goods in dollars from others. The difference between sales and purchases is the *net value added* (NVA) by his hamburger business, and represents the contribution the firm has made to national output. The firm's supplier, the meat company, also contributed some NVA, which is the difference between the dollar value of its purchases from others—sides of beef, etc.,—and the dollar value of its sales. So did all the other suppliers of intermediate products down the line to the suppliers of basic industrial and agricultural raw materials. If we add up all the NVA's directly or indirectly related to the final sale of the firm's burgers to the public—including its own NVA—then that sum will equal its total receipts from or sales to the public. Suppose the firm's total sales for the year to the public were $500,000 and its purchases from suppliers were

$450,000. The firm's net contribution to the economy is $ _____ . The net contribution to the total output of the economy by the firm and all its suppliers is $ _____ . The meat company sells only on a wholesale basis. Its total sales for the year were $2.0 mil and its purchases from suppliers were $1.0 mil. Its net contribution to output is

$ _____ . The net contribution to the economy of the burger company *and* the meat

company is $ _____ . The burger company's total sales (can, cannot) be added to other final sales to consumers in determining the overall output of the national economy. The total sales of the meat company (can, cannot) be added to the final sales total. What

is the reason for the difference? _____

_____

_____

2 We can easily move from this very simple example to a more realistic one. Refer to the data given in Table 2-1 representing a simplified income statement for a hypothetical

Table 2-1 Financial Statement for Corporation A, Calendar Year 1972

Disbursements and profits			Receipts and output	
1 Purchases from other firms		$ 500	10 Sales to other firms	$ 1,500
2 Wages and salaries		1,000	11 Sales to final consumers	500
3 Social security contributions		50	12 Change in value of inventories (+)	500
4 Rent		60		
5 Net interest		8		
6 Depreciation		100		
7 Indirect business taxes		60		
8 Pretax profits		722		
Corporate profits tax	$350			
Dividends paid	150			
Undistributed profit	222			
9 Total disbursements		$ 2,500	13 Total output	$ 2,500

corporation. The right-hand side gives monetary receipts and the left-hand side gives monetary disbursements. Total production during 1972 was $ _____ , and a total of

$ _____ was sold. The remainder of $ _____ represents a(n) (investment, disinvestment, production cost) by the firm—in effect, a sale by the firm to (other firms, consumers, the government, itself). Considering only the right-hand side of Table 2-1, item 10 (can, cannot) be considered a contribution by that firm in estimating total national

product. Why or why not? _____

_____

    Looking at the left-hand side of the table, the first item appears as item _____ in

the corresponding production statements of other firms. The firm paid $ _____ in wages, salaries, and social security contributions for the services of labor, with additional

expenses for rent and net interest—interest paid less interest received—of $ _____ . At the same time, provision was made to replace capital equipment—depreciation—that was

worn out in the amount of $ _____ . This amount is not an out-of-pocket expense, but it is a very real cost of production. Additional costs were contributed by sales, property,

and other indirect taxes, which added another $ _____ to operating costs, for a total

of $ _____ in direct and indirect expenses, leaving a profit of $ _____ before taxes.

Of this latter amount $ _____ went for taxes, $ _____ was paid out in dividends to

stockholders, and $ _____ was retained within the firm for future expansion. The

firm's NVA is $ _____ .

3 Now consider Fig. 2-1. Assume Firm 1 buys no intermediate goods at all, while Firm 9 sells all of its output to final consumers. Compute the following information:

Firm	Value of sales ($)	Net value added ($)
1	_____	_____
2	_____	_____
3	_____	_____
4	_____	_____
5	_____	_____
6	_____	_____
7	_____	_____
8	_____	_____
9	_____	_____
Total	$ _____	$ _____

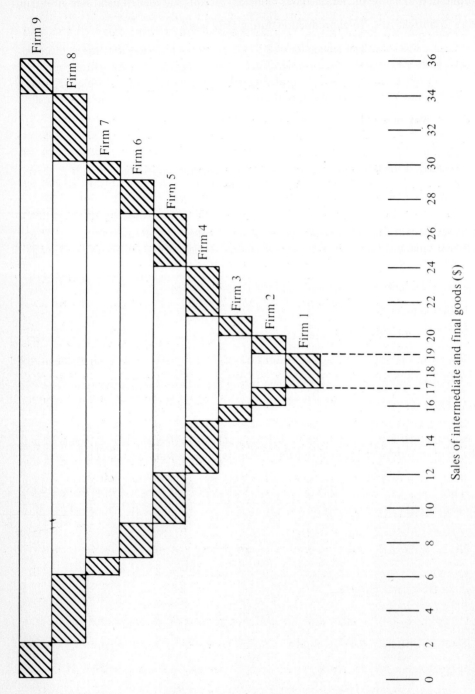

FIGURE 2-1

Note that the value of sales to final consumers by Firm 9, in the amount of $ _____ , equals the sum of the NVA's of all suppliers of intermediate goods plus its own NVA. This amount represents the total contribution of all firms to the national product with respect to $36 worth of sales of this particular product. We can either count the final sales to consumers by Firm 9 *or* add all the NVA's of Firms 1 to 9, i.e., the shaded areas

in Fig. 2-1. We (do, do not) count intermediate sales of $ _____ , the unshaded area.

4 The most frequently used measure of aggregate economic activity is the *Gross National Product* **(GNP)**. This measure is the sum total of all sales to final purchasers at market prices. In terms of Fig. 2-1, we simply add up all Firm 9 sales that go on in the economy over a specified period of time—month, quarter, year, etc. This measure automatically gives us the (GNP, NVA, intermediate sales) for the economy as a whole. Since the NVA equals all payments to the factors of production—direct and indirect labor costs, interest, rents, and profits—we can also arrive at GNP by simply adding up all payments to the factors of production during the period of time under consideration. The two measures will be identical. The former is called *GNP at market prices*, the latter is called *GNP at factor cost*. Table 2-2 presents the GNP accounts both ways.

Considering first GNP at market prices, we find that final demand by consumers in

1971 was $ _____ bil, composed of durable goods, nondurable goods, and services.

The largest consumption goods item in 1971 is _____ . Final demand by the business sector consists of investment in plant and equipment as well as net change in value of inventories. The only type of investment undertaken by the household sector is in residential structures. According to Table 2-2, 1971 gross private domestic invest-

ment was $ _____ bil, of which $ _____ bil was in the form of factories, office

buildings, and other business plants; $ _____ bil was business equipment; $ _____

bil was business inventories; and the remaining $ _____bil was residential structures. Exports represent foreign expenditures for products and services produced in the United States, while imports represent domestic spending for products produced abroad. Net exports of goods and services—exports minus imports—indicates whether, on net, the foreign sector added to or subtracted from domestic demand. In 1970, net exports

represented a(n) (addition, subtraction) of $ _____ bil; and in 1971 $ _____ bil. The final expenditure for the goods and services component in 1971 originates in the

government sector, of which $ _____bil was at the federal level and $ _____ bil at the state and local level.

5 Turning to GNP at factor cost, the main categories are compensation of employees—

direct and indirect labor costs—of $ _____ bil in 1971, income of unincorporated

proprietorships and partnerships of $ _____ bil, rents paid to individuals of $ _____

bil, corporate profits of $ _____ bil, as well as an adjustment in the valuation of

inventory stocks held by business of $_____bil. Note that corporate profits are

distributed in 1971 as $_____bil to the government in the form of taxes, $_____

Table 2-2 United States Gross National Product, 1970 and 1971 (Billions of Dollars)

A At market prices	1970	1971
Personal consumption expenditures	615.8	662.1
Durable goods	88.6	100.5
Nondurable goods	264.7	278.6
Services	262.5	282.9
Gross private domestic investment	135.3	151.6
Fixed investment	132.5	149.3
Nonresidential	102.1	108.7
Structures	36.8	38.2
Producers' durable equipment	65.4	70.5
Residential structures	30.4	40.6
Nonfarm	29.7	40.1
Farm	0.6	0.5
Change in business inventories	2.8	2.2
Nonfarm	2.5	1.7
Farm	0.3	0.5
Net exports of goods and services	3.6	0.0
Exports	62.9	65.3
Imports	59.3	65.3
Government purchases of goods and services	219.4	233.0
Federal	97.2	97.6
National defense	75.4	71.4
Other	21.9	26.2
State and local	122.2	135.5
Gross National Product	974.1	1,046.8

B At factor cost	1970	1971
Compensation of employees	601.9	641.9
Wages and salaries	541.4	574.2
Private	426.6	450.4
Military	19.4	18.6
Government civilian	95.5	105.2
Supplements to wages and salaries	60.5	67.7
Employer contributions for social insurance	29.6	34.0
Other labor income	30.8	33.7
Proprietors' income	66.9	68.3
Business and professional	51.0	52.1
Farm	15.8	16.3
Rental income of persons	23.3	24.3
Corporate profits and inventory valuation adjustment	70.8	81.0
Profits before tax	75.4	85.4
Profits tax liability	34.1	37.8
Profits after tax	41.2	47.6
Dividends	25.0	25.5
Undistributed profits	16.2	22.1
Inventory valuation adjustment	-4.5	-4.4
Net interest	33.0	35.6
Capital consumption allowances	87.6	95.2
Indirect business tax and nontax liability	92.9	102.1
Statistical discrepancy	-4.5	-4.9
Subsidies (net)	1.7	1.0
Gross National Product	974.1	1,046.8

SOURCE: U.S. Department of Commerce, *Survey of Current Business*, May 1972.

bil to shareholders in the form of dividends, and $ _____ bil retained within the firms to increase their capital base.

6 Another useful yardstick of economic performance is *Net National Product* (NNP). Gross national product includes an allowance for depreciation, or the using up of productive capital, as a charge against current output. If we let CCA stand for depreciation, or capital consumption allowances, then

$$NNP = GNP - CCA$$

In 1970, according to Table 2-2, NNP was $ _____ bil, while in 1971 it was $ _____ bil. The difference between GNP and NNP (increased, decreased) from 1970 to 1971 by

$ _____ bil.

7 Another frequently used measure of economic performance is *national income* (NI), which measures income actually earned by the factors of production during the time period in question. National income represents gross output or income of the national economy, adjusted for depreciation (CCA), *less* (1) the nonfactor costs of indirect business taxes (IBT) and (2) the business transfer payments (BTP) for pensions, unemployment insurance, etc., which represent indirect labor costs to firms of $3.9 bil in 1970 and $4.3 bil in 1971, *plus* (3) net subsidies paid by the government to the *business sector* (SUB), and *adjustments for* (4) statistical discrepancies (SD) in the data collected on the factor-cost side of the GNP accounts. In summary

$$NI = GNP - CCA - IBT - BTP + SUB \pm SD$$

$$= NNP - IBT - BTP + SUB \pm SD$$

Indirect business taxes are excluded from national income because they do not accrue to productive factors, but are included in prices of goods and services. From the data in

Table 2-2, U.S. national income was $ _____ bil in 1970 and $ _____ bil in 1971.

8 For many purposes it is useful to know how much income actually accrues to individuals. Not all NI goes to individuals since *corporate profits taxes* (CPT), *corporate retained earnings* (RE), and social security contributions (SS) by businesses on behalf of their employees do not reach the individual during the time period in question. These payments were $49.3 bil in 1970 and $56.0 bil in 1971. Revaluation of inventories recorded in the *inventory valuation adjustment* (IVA) item of the GNP account in Table 2-2 also must be taken into consideration, with increases in inventory values deducted and decreases added in deriving personal income. Finally, although not given separately in Table 2-2, wages that have accrued to employees but are not yet paid out (accruals less disbursements) must be deducted if they are positive (WA), since any net accruals of this type have not yet reached the public in the time period under study: These were nil in 1970 and 1971. After deducting CPT, RE, and SS, and adjusting for IVA and WA, we need to add back incomes that were *not earned* during the current time period but *have* been paid out. These include government payments such as social security, unemployment and veterans' benefits in the form of *government transfer payments* (GTP) which were $75.6 bil in 1970 and $90.4 bil in 1971, as well as pensions and other currently unearned benefits paid out by businesses–*business transfer payments* (BTP)–which we deducted earlier in deriving NI. Also added is *net interest* (NR) paid by government and consumers. Hence income actually going to individuals, called *personal income* (PI), is defined as

$$PI = NI - CPT - RE - SS + GTP + BTP + NR \pm IVA \pm WA$$

$$= GNP - CCA - IBT - CPT - RE - SS + GTP + NR \pm SD \pm IVA \pm WA$$

Note that in deriving PI from GNP, business transfer payments do not appear, since they are subtracted out in deriving NI and added back again to derive PI. United States personal income was $ _____ bil in 1970 and $ _____ bil in 1971.

9 A final measure that is commonly used is *Disposable Personal Income* (DPI)–what the household sector actually has left, after paying federal, state, and local income taxes, to spend on goods and services or to save. If we let YT stand for taxes on personal income, then

$$DPI = DI - YT$$

$$= GNP - CCA - IBT - CPT - RE - SS + GTP + NR - YT$$

$$\pm SD \pm IVA \pm WA$$

The average tax rate on personal income was 14.5 percent in 1970 and 13.8 percent in 1971. Disposable personal income was $ _____ bil in 1970 and $ _____ bil in 1971.

10 It is sometimes useful to know in greater detail where DPI comes from and–apart from income taxes–where it goes. Hence a separate statement is generally published giving personal income and its disposition. This statement for 1970 and 1971 data is presented in Table 2-3 (p. 22) which contains the following major headings as *sources* of personal income:

1971 Amount

(a) _____ $ _____ bil

(b) _____   _____

(c) _____   _____

(d) _____   _____

(e) _____   _____

(f) _____   _____

(g) _____   _____

Total _____   _____

In 1971, the largest share of personal income was contributed by the manufacturing industry, $_____bil of a total of $_____bil in wages and salaries. Transfer payments rose
by $_____bil from 1970 to 1971. Personal income is allocated as follows:

	1971 Amount
(a) _____	$ _____ bil
(b) _____	_____
(c) _____	_____
(d) _____	_____
(e) _____	_____
(f) _____	_____
Total _____	_____

About _____ percent of disposable personal income in 1971 was allocated to consumption and _____ percent to savings.

11 A considerable portion of GNP is allocated to the government sector through taxation.
Indirect business taxes, social security taxes, corporate profits taxes, and taxes on personal
incomes in 1971 total to $ _____ bil, representing about _____ percent of GNP.
These taxes are collected by federal, state, and local levels of government. By far the
largest single taxing and spending agent in the public sector is the federal government. It
is the most important not only because of its sheer magnitude, but also because changes
in taxes and spending of the federal government are used to stabilize the entire economy.
For this reason, the federal budget as an accounting statement is an important analytical
device. Table 2-4A presents a statement of federal government receipts and expenditures
for the years 1970 and 1971. State and local receipts and expenditures are presented in
Table 2-4B.
In 1971 the federal government collected $ _____ bil in taxes and $ _____ bil
in social security contributions, for total receipts of $ _____ bil. During that same
year it spent $ _____ bil, of which $ _____ bil was for purchases of goods and
services and $ _____ bil was in the form of transfer payments. Expenditures for
national defense in 1971 were $ _____ bil, representing _____ percent of total
federal government expenditure and _____ percent of U.S. GNP for that year. When
the government takes in more revenue than it spends, it is said to have a budgetary *surplus;* when it spends more than it takes in, it has a budgetary *deficit*. According to
Table 2-4A, the federal government had (deficits, surpluses) of $ _____ bil in 1970

Table 2-3   United States Personal Income and Its Disposition, 1970 and 1971
(Billions of Dollars)

	1970	1971
Personal income	803.6	857.0
Wage and salary disbursements	541.4	574.2
Commodity-producing industries	200.7	205.7
Manufacturing	158.3	160.8
Distributive industries	129.1	138.8
Service industries	96.7	105.9
Government	114.8	123.8
Other labor income	30.8	33.7
Proprietors' income	66.9	68.3
Business and professional	51.0	52.1
Farm	15.8	16.3
Rental income of persons	23.3	24.3
Dividends	25.0	25.5
Personal interest income	64.7	67.5
Transfer payments	79.6	94.7
Old age, survivors, disability, and health insurance benefits	38.5	44.8
State unemployment insurance benefits	3.9	5.8
Veterans benefits	9.7	11.5
Other	27.4	32.6
Less: Personal contributions for social insurance	28.0	31.2
Less: Personal tax and nontax payments	115.9	115.8
Equals: Disposable personal income	687.8	741.3
Less: Personal outlays	633.7	680.7
Personal consumption expenditures	615.8	662.1
Interest paid by consumers	16.9	17.7
Personal transfer payments to foreigners	0.9	0.9
Equals: Personal saving	54.1	60.5

SOURCE: U.S. Department of Commerce, *Survey of Current Business,* May 1972.

and $_____bil. in 1971. Grants-in-aid to state and local governments in 1971 were

$_____bil, which show up on the (receipts, expenditures) side of Table 2-4B. Note that government transfers and interest payments, presenting shifts in income from one set of individuals to another, do not appear in the GNP accounts as net current contributions to output but necessarily appear in the federal government budget in Table 2-4A.

These items can, however, be ascertained once we know what _____ is. For that reason government budgets that include these important items are said to be calculated on a *national income account* (NIA) basis. If we were to draw up a consolidated NIA budget for all United States governmental units from Table 2-4, the one item that would not appear in such a budget is _____ .

Table 2-4 United States Governmental Receipts and Expenditures, 1970 and 1971 (Billions of Dollars)

A Federal government receipts and expenditures	1970	1971
Federal government receipts	191.5	198.8
Personal tax and nontax receipts	92.2	89.0
Corporate profits tax accruals	30.6	33.6
Indirect business tax and nontax accruals	19.3	20.2
Contributions for social insurance	49.3	56.0
Federal government expenditures	205.1	221.9
Purchases of goods and services	97.2	97.6
National defense	75.4	71.4
Other	21.9	26.2
Transfer payments	63.4	75.9
To persons	61.2	73.4
To foreigners (net)	2.2	2.5
Grants-in-aid to state and local governments	24.4	29.6
Net interest paid	14.6	13.7
Subsidies less current surplus of government enterprises	5.5	5.1
Less: Wage accruals less disbursements	0.0	0.0
Surplus or deficit (−), national income and product accounts	−13.6	−23.1

B State and local government receipts and expenditures	1970	1971
State and local government receipts	133.4	151.7
Personal tax and nontax receipts	23.6	26.8
Corporate profits tax accruals	3.5	4.3
Indirect business tax and nontax accruals	73.6	81.8
Contributions for social insurance	8.3	9.2
Federal grants-in-aid	24.4	29.6
State and local government expenditures	132.9	148.9
Purchases of goods and services	122.2	135.5
Transfer payments to persons	14.4	17.1
Net interest paid	0.1	0.5
Less: Current surplus of government enterprises	3.8	4.1
Less: Wage accruals less disbursements	0.0	0.0
Surplus or deficit (−), national income and product accounts	0.5	2.8

SOURCE: U.S. Department of Commerce, *Survey of Current Business*, May 1972.

In 1970, federal government expenditures amounted to _____ percent of GNP and in 1971 they (rose, fell) to _____ percent of the GNP. State and local government expenditures (rose, fell) from _____ percent of GNP in 1970 to _____ percent in 1971. Note that the receipts by the federal government from social security contributions is (larger, smaller) than its receipts from corporate profits taxes. It is also interesting that state and local receipts from indirect taxes are almost as large as federal government receipts from personal income taxes.

12 Another measurement that is frequently used in aggregate economic analysis is the *balance of payments:* a census of all financial transactions between residents of one country, such as the United States, and the rest of the world. Discussion of the balance of payments is deferred to Exercise 22.

13 Note that to a very large extent our discussion has focused on national income and product, or on accounting, in money terms, for physical economic transactions that determine how much has been produced by the economy in the current year. As we shall see, the financial system plays a very important role in the determination of real income and output, and for this reason a more detailed accounting of national financial flows is often very useful. This information is provided by the *flow of funds accounts,* presented in Table 2-5. This table is categorized according to uses of funds U and sources of funds S. The transaction category column gives all possible types of transactions that are recorded as sources or uses of funds on the part of individual sectors indicated by the individual column headings. Table 2-5 is divided into two basic *types* of sectors,

_____ and _____ . The nonfinancial sector is divided into the following *domestic* sectors:

(i)   _____

(ii) _____

(iii) _____

to which are added transactions with the *rest of the world* and transactions of the *federal government.*

The financial sector is divided into

(i)   _____

(ii) _____

(iii) _____

(iv) _____

all of which are composed of financial intermediaries.

Transactions categories 1 to 9 in Table 2-5 represent financial flows arising out of real income and product accounts. The second largest nonfinancial sector source of funds is

_____ , of which a major part is charged against replacements of depreci-

Table 2-5 Summary of Flow-of-Funds Accounts for First Quarter 1972 (Seasonally Adjusted Annual Rates in Billions of Dollars)

Line	Transaction category / Sector	Private domestic nonfinancial sectors								Rest of the world		U.S. government		Financial sectors										All sectors		Discrepancy	National savings and investment
		Households U	Households S	Business U	Business S	State and local governments U	State and local governments S	Total U	Total S	U	S	U	S	Total U	Total S	Sponsored credit agencies U	Sponsored credit agencies S	Monetary authority U	Monetary authority S	Commercial banking U	Commercial banking S	Private nonbank finance U	Private nonbank finance S	U	S	U	
1	Gross saving	182.4			102.5			282.2		10.0				6.8			0.1					3.6		3.1	284.3			274.3
2	Capital consumption		97.2		86.6				183.9					2.8			0.1					1.1		1.7		186.6		186.6
3	Net saving (1-2)	85.2			15.9		-2.7		98.3	10.0			-14.7	4.0								2.5		1.5		97.7		87.7
4	Gross investment (5+10)	183.2		83.9		-5.5		261.7		11.4		-16.7		2.4		-1.3					2.4		1.3		258.8		25.5	264.5
5	Private capital expenditures	144.0		128.9				272.9						3.0							1.2		1.8		275.9		8.4	275.9
6	Consumer durables	107.6						107.6																	107.6			107.6
7	Residential construction	30.7		18.3				49.0																	49.0			49.0
8	Plant and equipment	5.7		110.0				115.7						3.0							1.2		1.8		118.7			118.7
9	Inventory change			0.6				0.6																	0.6			0.6
10	Net financial investment (11-12)	39.2		-44.9		-5.5		-11.2		11.4		-16.7		-0.6		-1.3					1.2		-0.5		-17.1		17.1	-11.4
11	Financial uses	98.3		27.2		11.7		137.2		18.9		-13.4		139.1		7.0		2.1		42.9		87.0			281.9			7.6
12	Financial sources		59.1		72.1		17.3		148.5	7.6			3.3		139.7		8.3		2.1		41.7		87.5		299.0		18.9
13	Gold, SDR's, and official foreign exchange									2.2	-0.3	-0.2						-2.2						-0.3			
14	Treasury currency and SDR certificates												0.7	1.0				1.0						1.0	0.7	-0.4	
15	Demand deposits and currency	10.2						29.2						18.5				4.0		14.5		-0.5		18.5		14.6	
16	Private domestic			6.3		2.7								29.9		-0.3		7.3		22.6		-0.5		29.9		28.4	
17	U.S. government											-12.2		-9.8				-2.5		-7.4				-9.8		-12.2	
18	Foreign									-1.6				-1.6				-0.8		-0.7		0.7		-1.6			
19	Time and savings accounts	84.6						86.8			1.4			88.8							31.3		57.4		88.8			
20	At commercial banks	27.9		0.8		1.4		30.2						31.3							31.3				31.3			
21	At savings institutions	56.7						56.7						57.4		0.7							57.4		57.4			
22	Life insurance reserves	7.2						7.2						7.2									7.2		7.2			
23	Pension fund reserves	14.9						14.9						14.9									13.6		14.9			
24	Interbank items		-10.0					-10.0		2.7	-0.1			-25.5		-2.8		-0.6	NS	-24.0		15.4		-25.5		-2.8	
25	Corporate shares	-19.1		3.0			16.8	11.0		13.4	4.3		3.0	-2.8				3.9		4.2		60.4		8.1		1.5	
26	Credit market instruments	-21.3		6.7		7.2	16.5	122.9		11.4	11.4		3.6	129.3		7.2	6.6	4.3		-4.1		10.8		140.5	140.5	2.4	
27	U.S. government securities	-2.2		-4.5		7.7	16.5	18.1		-1.0		-12.2	3.7	9.7		5.6	6.3	4.3		17.3		0.5		10.0	10.0		
28	State and local obligations	13.9		1.0		-0.1		13.5						6.3						3.4		16.5		16.5			
29	Corporate and foreign bonds			14.2		-0.4		14.2		1.7			-0.1	7.2		4.8				6.7		10.6	3.8	23.1			
30	Home mortgages	0.2		1.3				2.8						0.2		2.0				4.1		16.7	0.2	27.0			
31	Other mortgages		1.5			3.0		3.0					0.4	18.4						5.6		12.4		21.6			
32	Consumer credit		2.8		20.1			21.4	13.9					18.4						26.1		5.3		21.6		13.9	
33	Bank loans n.e.c.	6.5		15.0			0.3	7.7		3.0	0.4			10.9		4.2				2.2		4.1		26.1			
34	Other loans	-12.4		6.1			2.8	8.7			2.3	3.4		0.5		-8.2		-0.5		5.8	0.8	7.8		1.7			
35	Security credit	1.3		7.2			0.1							13.6		6.2	0.3			4.9		4.1		14.9			
36	To brokers and dealers	1.3						1.3						6.2		6.2						6.2		6.2			
37	To others	8.7						8.7			0.1			4.9						0.9		7.8		6.2			
38	Taxes payable	8.7		2.1		0.5		8.7				-1.6		8.7						-0.9				0.4		-1.1	
39	Trade credit		0.6	7.7	4.9		0.5	0.5	7.7	0.1	0.2		-1.7	0.5								0.5		4.6		6.7	
40	Equity in noncorporate business	-3.2			-3.2			-3.2																-3.2			
41	Miscellaneous claims	2.4	0.5	5.5	0.6	0.6		8.0	1.1	0.7	3.4	0.1	1.7	6.9	4.4	0.1		1.0		4.1		2.6	1.9	15.2	7.6	14.3	
42	Sector discrepancies (1-4)	-0.8		18.6		2.8		20.5		-1.4		2.0		4.4		1.4				1.1				25.5		25.5	9.8

SOURCE: *Federal Reserve Bulletin*, June 1972.

ating assets and hence is deducted from GNP to get NNP, but nevertheless gives rise to a
financial source of funds.

In the first quarter of 1972, sources of funds attributed to *all* sectors amounted to

$_____$bil, of which _____percent was from nonfinancial sources and _____
percent from financial sources. These funds were used for (*a*) private expenditures on

(i) _____

(ii) _____

(iii) _____

(iv) _____

and for (*b*) net investment in financial assets—item 11 in Table 2-4. Note that item

_____ above is considered "investment" in the flow of funds accounts but not in the
national income and product accounts. This is because of the importance of consumer
credit for installment buying in financial flows.

14 Thus far, the flow of funds accounts have not told us very much that we could not
already have derived from the GNP accounts. Its real contribution consists of dissecting
net financial investment to see whether and how financial transactions, *on net*, absorbed
or contributed financial resources. Net financial investment in 1972 (I) consisted of

financial uses of $ _____ bil and financial sources of $ _____ bil. The largest

sectoral source of funds was _____ , while the

largest single user of funds was _____ . Lines
13 and 14 give official—treasury and central bank—transactions. Lines 15 to 18 record
net changes in cash balances held by each of the sectors. Lines 19 to 24 record the
savings functions of banks and other financial institutions, such as life insurance companies and pension funds, while line 25 records financial flows into and out of—
purchases and sales of—corporate stocks. In 1972 (I) the largest net sellers of corporate

shares were _____ , and _____

_____ , in that order, and the largest single buyer was _____

_____ . Lines 26 to 34 present financial flows involving credit
instruments such as bonds, mortgages, and bank loans. Lines 35 to 41 record other
items, as indicated, while line 42 and the next-to-last column indicate statistical discrepancies. We shall return to the flow of funds statement for analytical purposes later on.

15 Finally, we will examine an input-output (I/O) table. This device permits us to look
inside the national economy to actually see how industries relate to one another. Table
2-6 presents the schematic for an I/O table based on 1966 data.[1] If we compare knowledge
of GNP or one of the other macroeconomic statistics with a physical examination, then

---

[1] For the 1966 input-output table for the United States, see U.S. Department of Commerce, Bureau
of Economic Analysis, Staff Paper in Economics and Statistics, no. 19, *Input-Output Transactions:
1966*, February 1972.

Table 2-6 Schematic for Input-Output Table Based on 1966 Data (Millions of Dollars)

Output of				Purchased by					
	(1) Livestock products	(2) Other farm products	(3) Forestry & fisheries	. . .	(86) Household industry	(87) Inventory valuation adjustment	(TA) Total sales of intermediate outputs	(TB) Final demand
1 Livestock products	5,508	1,833	199		0	0	30,075	2,528
2 Other farm products	8,673	811	113		0	0	22,954	5,041
3 Forestry & fisheries	0	0	48		0	0	1,767	529
. .								
86 Household industry	0	0	0		0	0	0	4,028
87 Inventory valuation adjustment	0	0	0		0	—	—	−2,173
Total purchases of intermediate inputs	22,035	12,971	1,479		0	—	—	746,833

I/O analysis is like a thorough x-ray examination of the national economy. Each entry in the columns and rows of Table 2-6 represents an industry, 86 in all, ranging from livestock products to household industry. Each entry in the body of the table represents sales by the industry listed in the left-hand column to the industry listed in the top row. The 87th column gives inventory valuation adjustment, if any, for the industry in question, while the TA column gives total sales of that industry to all other industries and the TB column gives total sales of that industry to final consumers. The bottom row gives total purchases of the indicated industry from each of the other industries presented in the table. In 1966 sales of the livestock industry to itself, intra-industry transactions,

were $ _____ mil, with $ _____ mil of its output sold to the *other farm products*

industry, $ _____ mil to the forestry and fisheries industries, and $ _____ mil to

all other industries combined, for total sales of intermediate output of $ _____ mil.

When added to sales of $ _____ mil to final consumers, total sales of that industry to

all buyers were $ _____ mil, but only $ _____ mil of this found its way into 1966 GNP accounts.

16 The I/O table can be made more or less detailed, depending on the need, but it is extremely expensive and time-consuming to tabulate—hence the 1966 I/O table only became available in 1972. We can convert an I/O table such as Fig. 2-5 into ratio form by calculating what portion of each industry's intermediate sales went to each of the

other industries. The entry under 1:1 in the table would be _____, for 1:2

_____, for 1:3 _____, and so forth. These values are called *flow coefficients*, and can also be calculated the other way—i.e., the proportions of each industry's *purchases* of intermediate inputs from each industry *per dollar* of gross output for each industry, as well as the *direct and indirect* input requirements per dollar of gross output. Hence it becomes an extremely useful analytical device. It can tell us how forecast changes in aggregate economic activity, as measured by GNP, are likely to affect a particular industry in which we are interested. It can also tell us something about interdependence of industries and how what happens in one invariably affects others.

PROBLEMS FOR EXERCISE 2

You are given the following data for 1950:

Personal consumption expenditures	191.0
Durable goods	30.5
Nondurable goods	98.1
Services	62.4
Gross private domestic investment	54.1
Fixed investment	47.3
Nonresidential	27.9

Structures 9.2

Producers' durable equipment 18.7

Residential structures 19.4

Nonfarm 18.6

Change in business inventories 6.8

Nonfarm 6.0

Net exports of goods and services 1.8

Exports 13.8

Imports 12.0

Government purchases of goods and services 37.9

Federal 18.4

National defense 14.1

Other 4.3

State and local 19.5

Compensation of employees 154.6

Wages and salaries 146.8

Private 124.4

Military 5.0

Government civilian 17.4

Supplements to wages and salaries 7.8

Employer contributions for social insurance 4.0

Other labor income 3.8

Proprietors' income 37.5

Business and professional 24.0

Farm 13.5

Rental income of persons 9.4

Corporate profits and inventory valuation adjustment 37.7

Profits before tax 42.6

Profits tax liability 17.8

Profits after tax 24.9

Dividends 8.8

Undistributed profits 16.0

Inventory valuation adjustment 5.0

Net interest 2.0

Capital consumption allowances 18.3

Indirect business tax and nontax liability 23.3

Business transfer payments 0.8

Statistical discrepancy 1.5

Subsidies less current surplus of government enterprises 0.2

Corporate profits and inventory valuation adjustment 37.7

Personal contributions for social insurance 2.9

Excess of wage accruals over disbursements 0

Government transfer payments 14.3

Net interest paid by government and consumers 7.2

Dividends 8.8

Business transfer payments 0.8

Personal tax and nontax payments 20.7

Personal outlays 193.9
   Personal consumption expenditures 191.0
   Consumer interest payments 2.4
   Personal transfer payments to foreigners 0.5

Calculate the following:

  1 GNP =

  2 NNP =

  3 GDP =

  4 NDP =

  5 NI =

  6 PI =

  7 DPI =

  8 Personal saving =

  9 Consolidated government receipts =

  10 Consolidated government expenditures =

  11 Consolidated government budget = _____ (surplus) (deficit)

12 The values you have calculated above are for 1950 data expressed in 1950 dollars. Suppose prices of all goods and services that make up GNP are twice as high in 1971 as in 1950. If we let 1950 = 100, then the price index for 1971 = _____ .

13 1950 GNP expressed in 1971 prices would be $ _____ bil.

14 Suppose 1971 GNP is $1,139.2 bil. The GNP increase from 1950 to 1971 in *current dollars* has been _____ percent.

15 The GNP increase from 1950 to 1971 in real terms has been _____ percent

ANSWERS FOR EXERCISE 2

1 50,000, 500,000, 1.0 mil, 1.05 mil, can, cannot, his sales are exclusively to other producers or distributors, and will be counted in full when they are finally sold to consumers; hence adding his sales would be double-counting

2 2,500, 2,000, 500, investment, itself, cannot, they are intermediate sales and will be counted again further along the production-distribution chain, 10, 1050, 68, 100, 60, 1,778, 722, 350, 150, 222, 2,000

3

Firm	Value of Sales	Net value added
1	$ 2	$ 2
2	4	2
3	6	2
4	12	6
5	18	6
6	22	4
7	24	2
8	32	8
9	36	4
Total	$156	$ 36

36, do not, 120

4 GNP and NVA, 662.1, services, 151.6, 38.2, 70.5, 2.2, 40.6, addition, 3.6, 0, 97.6, 135.5

5 641.9, 68.3, 24.3, 85.4, −4.4, 37.8, 25.5, 22.1

6 886.5, 951.6, increased, 7.6

7 786.9, 841.3

8 804.3, 860.1

9 687.8, 741.3

		1971 Amount
10 (a)	Wages and salaries	$ 574.2 bil
(b)	Other labor income	33.7
(c)	Proprietors' income	68.3
(d)	Rental income	24.3
(e)	Dividends	25.5
(f)	Personal interest income	67.5
(g)	Transfer payments	94.7
	Total	$ 888.2 bil

160.8, 574.2, 15.1

		1971 Amount
(a)	Taxes	$ 115.8 bil
(b)	Personal contributions for social insurance	31.2
(c)	Consumption	662.1
(d)	Interest	17.7
(e)	Transfers to foreigners	.9
(f)	Savings	60.5
	Total	$ 888.2 bil

89.3, 8.2

11 320.9, 31, 142.8, 56.0, 198.8, 221.9, 97.6, 75.9, 71.4, 32.2, 6.8, deficits, 13.6, 23.1, 29.6, receipts, national income, grants-in-aid to state and local governments, 21.1, rose, 21.2, rose, 13.6, 14.2, larger

13 nonfinancial, financial
  (i) households
  (ii) business
  (iii) state and local government

  (i) sponsored credit agencies
  (ii) monetary authorities
 (iii) commercial banking
 (iv) private nonbank finance
business gross saving, 583.3, 48.7, 51.3
  (i) consumer durables
  (ii) residential construction
 (iii) plant and equipment
 (iv) inventories
  (i)

14 281.9, 299.0, private nonbank finance, households, business, households, private nonbank finance

15 5,508, 1,833, 199, 22,585, 30,075, 2,528, 32,603, 2,528

16 0.183, 0.061, 0.007

ANSWERS TO PROBLEMS FOR EXERCISE 2

1 $284.8 bil	**6** $227.6 bil	**11** $11.1 bil surplus
2 $266.5 bil	**7** $206.9 bil	**12** 200
3 $283.0 bil	**8** $13.1 bil	**13** $569.6
4 $264.7 bil	**9** $68.7 bil	**14** 400
5 $241.1 bil	**10** $57.6 bil	**15** 200

THE SECTOR ACCOUNTS: RECEIPTS AND OUTLAYS

1 The previous exercise dealt with aggregate income and product as well as financial flows within the economy and interindustry relationships. We will now examine the receipts and outlays of individual sectors which go to make up the national economy. These sectors are

(a) Personal
(b) Business
(c) Foreign
(d) Government

They contribute to final demand through their respective expenditures, and each receives payment for its services in the form of wages, rent, interest, and profits. Table 3-1 reproduces the United States national income and product account for 1971. Note that it is slightly revised vis-à-vis Table 2-2. Final demand originating in the personal

sector—consumption expenditures—is $ _____ bil, in the government sector $ _____

bil, in the foreign sector $ _____ bil, and investment expenditures in the business

sector $ _____ bil. The sectoral distribution of final demand includes $42.6 bil of investment in residential structures. Although this expenditure item originates in the

_____ sector, it is classified as investment and listed with business
sector investment. If we let

    C = consumer expenditures (except for residential structures)
    I = investment expenditures
    G = government expenditures
    X = exports
    Z = imports
then

    GNP = _____

Table 3-1 United States National Income and Product, 1971 (Billions of Dollars)

Line			Line		
1	Compensation of employees	644.1	24	Personal consumption expenditures (2–3)	664.9
2	Wages and salaries	573.5	25	Durable goods	103.5
3	Disbursements (2–7)	572.9	26	Nondurable goods	278.1
4	Wage accruals less disbursements (3–7+6–4)	0.6	27	Services	283.3
5	Supplements to wages and salaries	70.7	28	Gross private domestic investment (6–1)	152.0
6	Employer contributions for social insurance (3–15)	34.1	29	Fixed investment	148.3
7	Other labor income (2–8)	36.5	30	Nonresidential	105.8
8	Proprietors' income (2–9)	70.0	31	Structures	38.4
9	Rental income of persons (2–10)	24.5	32	Producers' durable equipment	67.4
10	Corporate profits and inventory valuation adj.	78.6	33	Residential structures	42.6
11	Profits before tax	83.3	34	Change in business inventories	3.6
12	Profits tax liability (3–12)	37.3	35	Net exports of goods and services	0.7
13	Profits after tax	45.9	36	Exports (4–1)	66.1
14	Dividends (2–11)	25.4	37	Imports (4–3)	65.4
15	Undistributed profits (6–5)	20.5	38	Government purchase of goods and services (3–1)	232.8
16	Inventory valuation adjustment (6–6)	−4.7	39	Federal	97.8
17	Net interest (2–13)	38.5	40	National defense	71.4
18	National income	855.7	41	Other	26.3
19	Business transfer payments (2–17)	4.6	42	State and local	135.0
20	Indirect business tax and nontax liability (3–13)	101.9			
21	Less: Subsidies less current surplus of government enterprises (3–6)	0.9			
22	Capital consumption allowances (6–7)	93.8			
23	Statistical discrepancy (6–10)	−4.8			
	Charges against Gross National Product	1,050.4		Gross National Product	1,050.4

Note: Numbers in parentheses refer to sector account tables that follow.
SOURCE: *Survey of Current Business,* July 1972.

(If necessary, the student should review Exercise 2, paragraph 4.) Or, in numbers from Table 3-1,

GNP = $ _____ + _____ + _____ + _____ - _____ bil

GNP = $ _____ bil

Each source of final demand gives rise to factor payments which comprise: compensation of employees of $ _____ bil, rental income of $ _____ bil, business income—proprietorships and corporations—of $ _____ bil, and net interest of $ _____ bil. National income to productive factors is $ _____ bil. To this are added nonincome items totaling $ _____ bil for a GNP of $ _____ bil on the factor-cost side.

2 Let us develop a sector account for personal income and outlays. Principal outlays of the personal sector are taxes and other payments to government, consumption expenditures, interest, transfer payments to foreigners, and personal saving. Principal sources of income are: wages, salaries, and other returns to labor; business income of proprietorships; rents; dividends and interest; transfer payments received, minus contributions by individuals for social insurance. Table 3-2 presents the United States personal income and outlay sector-account for 1971. Complete this table by filling in the blanks from data presented in Table 3-1. In addition to households, the personal sector includes all nonbusiness organizations such as universities and charities. Since there is no "market price" for their services, we implicitly assume that the value of their contribution to national product is equal to the salaries and wages paid by them. Sometimes households are also employers, as in the case of gardeners and chauffeurs. If, in 1971, households paid $30 bil in salaries for this purpose, the value would appear on *both* the income and

outlay sides of Table 3-2 under _____ and

_____ .

Indicate below the appropriate sectors, identified at the beginning of this exercise, to whom personal outlays are paid and from whom income is received as presented in Table 3-2.

Table 3-2 item	To whom paid	From whom received
1	_____	_____
3	_____	_____
4	_____	_____
5	_____	_____
7	_____	_____
8	_____	_____

Table 3-2 The Personal Income and Outlay Account, 1971 (Billions of Dollars)

Line		Line	
1 Personal tax and nontax payments (3–11)	117.0	7 Wage and salary disbursements (1–3)	
2 Personal outlays	683.4	8 Other labor income (1–7)	
3 Personal consumption expenditures (1–24)		9 Proprietors' income (1–8)	
4 Interest paid by consumers (2–15)	17.6	10 Rental income of persons (1–9)	
5 Personal transfer payments to foreigners (net) (4–5)	1.0	11 Dividends (1–14)	1.0
6 Personal saving (6–3)	60.9	12 Personal interest income	69.6
		13 Net interest (1–17)	13.5
		14 Net interest paid by government (3–5)	17.6
		15 Interest paid by consumers (2–4)	93.6
		16 Transfer payments to persons	
		17 From business (1–19)	
		18 From government (3–3)	89.0
		19 Less: Personal contributions for social insurance (3–16)	31.2
Personal Taxes, Outlays, and Savings		Personal Income	

Note: Numbers in parentheses indicate accounts and items of counterentry in other accounts.
SOURCE: *Survey of Current Business*, July 1972.

Table 3-2 item	To whom paid	From whom received
9	_____	_____
10	_____	_____
11	_____	_____
13	_____	_____
14	_____	_____
15	_____	_____
17	_____	_____
18	_____	_____
19	_____	_____

Note that the item *omitted* from the above list is _____ , which is
on the (income, outlay) side of Table 3-2. This item is called a residual. We know
that personal income is $ _____ bil. We know that $ _____ bil of this total has
been spent for taxes, consumption, interest, and net transfers to foreigners. Hence the
remaining $ _____ bil must have been saved. And the assets owned by the personal
sector must have (increased, decreased) during 1971 by $ _____ bil. It (is, is not)
possible for saving to be negative during a given year. We shall return to the question
of saving later.

3 A second sector of the national economy is government: federal, state, and local.
A *consolidated* government receipts and expenditures account is presented in
Table 3-3. Complete this table by filling in the blanks using the data of Tables 3-1
and 3-2. Government receipts take the form of *taxes* in three main categories,

_____ , _____ ,

and _____ . A fourth category of government

receipts is _____ _____ , which are, in a sense,
insurance premiums. Together, these four governmental receipt items represent the
"sales" of public services to the public. Since there is no market for public services,
national income accountants arbitrarily assume that the value of services rendered by
government equals the wage and salary costs incurred in producing these services.
The higher the direct and indirect wage and salary disbursements by government, the
larger its assessed contribution to national product.

Table 3-3 Government Receipts and Expenditures Account, 1971 (Billions of Dollars)

Line		Line	
1 Purchases of goods and services (1–38)		11 Personal tax and nontax payments (2–1)	
2 Transfer payments	91.6	12 Corporate profits tax liability (1–12)	
3 To persons (2–18)		13 Indirect business tax and nontax liability (1–20) . . .	
4 To foreigners (net) (4–4)	2.6	14 Contributions for social insurance	65.3
5 Net interest paid (2–14)		15 Employer (1–6)	
6 Subsidies less current surplus of government enterprises (1–21)		16 Personal (2–19)	
7 Less: Wage accruals less disbursements (1–4)	0.2		
8 Surplus or deficit (–), national income and product accounts (6–8)			
9 Federal			
10 State and local	4.8		
Government Expenditures and Surplus		Government Receipts	

Note: Numbers in parentheses indicate accounts and items of counterentry in other accounts.
SOURCE: *Survey of Current Business*, July 1972.

Indicate below the appropriate sectors, identified at the beginning of this exercise, to whom government expenditures are "paid" and from whom government receipts originate.

Table 3-3 item	To whom paid	From whom received
1	_____	_____
3	_____	_____
4	_____	_____
5	_____	_____
6	_____	_____
11	_____	_____
12	_____	_____
13	_____	_____
15	_____	_____
16	_____	_____

Note that we have again left out two items. Item 7, wage accruals less disbursements of $200 mil, represents governmental wages not actually paid during 1971 and hence must be deducted from the expenditure side. Item 8, government surplus or deficit, is a residual item. If government spends more than it takes in—items 1 to 7 and 11 to 16—then a deficit has been incurred which must be financed, either by borrowing from the private sector or printing new money. In case of a government surplus, some of these borrowings can be repaid. In 1971, the federal government had a (surplus, deficit) of

$ _____ bil, while state and local governments had a (surplus, deficit) of $ _____

bil, for a combined (surplus, deficit) of $ _____ bil.

In 1971, the largest item in government receipts was _____

_____ , followed closely by _____ .

The largest item of government expenditure was _____ , of which $108.0 bil was for the purchase of goods and services from the business sector.

4 Some income originating in the United States accrues to foreign residents for the services of their labor, capital, and land employed here. At the same time, income originating abroad and earned by United States-owned factors of production employed there represents a current receipt from abroad. In 1971, *net* payments to the United States approximately equaled net payments to residents of foreign countries.

Goods and services produced in the United States and sold to foreigners—exports—represent income earned here, while goods and services produced abroad and sold in the United States—imports—represent income earned abroad. Exports represent (receipts from, payments to) foreigners, while imports represent (receipts from, payments to) foreigners.

In addition, there are various capital transactions. The United States gives to and receives from the rest of the world capital grants, and makes public and private international transfer payments through foreign aid grants, pensions, private gifts, and so on. From the data in Tables 3-1 to 3-3, complete the foreign transactions account in Table 3-4. Indicate below the appropriate sectors identified at the beginning of this exercise from whom payments are made to foreigners and by whom payments are received from foreigners.

Table 3-4 item	To whom paid	From whom received
1	_____	_____
3	_____	_____
4	_____	_____
5	_____	_____

The second and sixth items are transactions for which it is impossible to tell from the information available their distribution with respect to the other sectors. The latter represents the balancing item in the foreign transactions account and shows whether or not the international creditor position of the United States was increased or decreased during the course of the year, with respect to current transactions only.

5 We have considered thus far the personal, government, and foreign sectors of the national economy. The business sector includes all incorporated, unincorporated, and government enterprises producing goods and services for sale on the open market for profit, including financial institutions. Table 3-5 presents the consolidated—incorporated and unincorporated—business income and product account for 1971. From the data in Tables 3-1 to 3-4, fill in the missing blanks of Table 3-5. Gross business product in 1971

was $ _____ bil. Note that all of the data in Table 3-5 can be derived from the previous tables *except* item 5-1. This is because item 2-7 includes wages, salaries, and supplements paid by government and household sectors which must first be subtracted to derive business payments for labor services. Note also that, in addition to selling goods and services to consumers, government, and foreigners, business also sells to itself—in the

form of investment in capital assets of $ _____ bil and inventories of $ _____ bil.

Table 3-4 Foreign Transactions Account, 1971 (Billions of Dollars)

Line		Line	
1 Exports of goods and services (1-36)	....	3 Imports of goods and services (1-37)	....
2 Capital grants received by the United States (6-9)	0.7	4 Transfer payments from U.S. government to foreigners (net) (3-4)	....
		5 Personal transfer payments to foreigners (net) (2-5)	....
		6 Net foreign investment (6-2)	-2.1
Receipts from Foreigners	....	Payments to Foreigners	....

Note: Numbers in parentheses indicate accounts and items of counterentry in the accounts.
SOURCE: *Survey of Current Business,* July 1972.

Indicate below the appropriate sectors identified at the beginning of this exercise from whom revenues are received and to whom payments are made by the business sector.

Table 3-5 item	To whom paid	From whom received
1	_____	_____
2	_____	_____
3	_____	_____
4	_____	_____
5	_____	_____
6	_____	_____
7	_____	_____
8	_____	_____
9	_____	_____
10	_____	_____
12	_____	_____
14	_____	_____
16	_____	_____
17	_____	_____
18	_____	_____
19	_____	_____
20	_____	_____

6 We have now considered all four economic sectors, and have detailed the interrelationships among them and how each is related to the national income and product account. We have yet to discuss savings and investment. The personal sector saved $ _____ bil in 1971. There are various other sources of savings as well. Table 3-6 gives the United States gross saving and investment account for 1971. Complete that table by filling in the missing data.

Gross private domestic investment is composed of business purchases of plant and equipment, residential construction, and any net business build-up of inventories. Net foreign investment is the residual item in the foreign sector account. The principal source of saving is _____ , done by the personal sector, to which is added the "forced" saving of accrued but as yet unpaid wages. *Gross* saving by the business sector comprises depreciation, net revaluation of inventories, and undistributed corporate profits. *Net* saving excludes depreciation, or capital consumption allowance (CCA). Any saving

Table 3-5 The Consolidated Business Income and Product Account, 1971 (Billions of Dollars)

Payments		Receipts	
1 Wages, salaries and supplements (ex 2–7)	$561.5	16 Sales to consumers (2–3)	$____
2 Social security payments (3–15)	____	17 Sales to government (3–1)	____
3 Proprietors' income (2–9)	____	18 Sales (net) abroad (1–35)	____
4 Rental income of persons (2–10)	____	19 Sales to business (capital) (1–28)	____
5 Net interest (2–13)	____	20 Sales to business (inventory) (1–34)	____
6 Corporate profits and inventory valuation adjustment (1–10)	____		
7 Profits tax liability (3–12)	$____		
8 Dividends (domestic) (2–11)	____		
9 Undistributed profits (1–15)	____		
10 Inventory valuation adjustment (1–16)	____		
11 Income originating (subtotal)	(____)		
12 Indirect business taxes (3–13)	____		
13 Charges against net business product	____		
14 Depreciation (1–22)	____		
15 Charges against gross business product	$____	21 Gross business product	$____

Note: Numbers in parentheses indicate accounts and items of counterentry in the accounts.
SOURCE: Tables 3–1 to 3–4.

43

done by the government takes the form of budgetary surpluses, while budgetary deficits represent governmental *dis*-saving. Fill in the missing information below.

Table 3-6 item	Sector investing or saving
1	_____
2	_____
3	_____
4	_____
5	_____
6	_____
7	_____
8	_____
9	_____

The last item in Table 3-6 is the statistical discrepancy that arises between payments for goods and services and payments to productive factors. This item can be quite large, depending on the net errors and omissions in accounting for payments to productive factors.

7 Suppose we define the following variables ($ bil):

Gross national product = GNP = 1,218
Net national product = Y = 1,110.1
National income = NI = 997.6
Disposable income = Yd = 838.8
Consumption spending = C = 772.5
Government spending = G = 273.8
Net exports = $X - Z$ = 3.8
Net foreign investment = If = 1.3
Net domestic investment = Ir = 60.0
Personal receipts = Rp = 903.8
Transfer payments (domestic) = Tr = 113.8
Transfer to foreigners = Tf = 2.5
Personal saving = Sp = 66.3
Government saving = Sg = -17.5
Business saving = Sb = 12.5
Direct taxes (on individuals) = Tp = 178.8
Direct taxes (on business) = Tb = 81.3

Table 3-6 The Gross Saving and Investment Account (Billions of Dollars)

Line		Line	
1 Gross private domestic investment (1–28) . . . . $\_\_\_\_$		3 Personal saving (2–6)	
2 Net foreign investment (4–6)	$\_\_\_\_$	4 Wage accruals less disbursements (1–4)	
		5 Undistributed corporate profits (1–15)	
		6 Corporate inventory valuation adjustment (1–16)	
		7 Capital consumption allowances (1–22)	
		8 Government surplus or deficit (–), national income and product accounts (3–8)	
		9 Capital grants received by the United States (4–2) . . .	
		10 Statistical discrepancy (1–23)	
Gross Investment . . . . $\_\_\_\_$		Gross Saving and Statistical Discrepancy . . . . $\_\_\_\_$	

Note: Numbers in parentheses indicate accounts and items of counterentry in the accounts.
SOURCE: *Survey of Current Business,* July 1972.

Indirect taxes = Ti = 112.5
Depreciation = D = 108.7

From the data contained in Tables 3-1 to 3-6, fill in the 1971 values for the United States on the receipts and payments matrix in Fig. 3-1. Recall that, from Exercise 2,

(1)   GNP = $C + Ir + X - Z + G + D$

From the data in Fig. 3-1

GNP = \$ _____ + _____ + _____ - _____ + _____ + _____ bil

GNP = \$ _____ bil

We also know that

(2) $Y = GNP - D$

or

(3) $Y = C + Ir + X - Z + G$

Hence

Y = \$ _____ bil - \$ _____ bil

or

Y = \$ _____ + _____ + _____ - _____ + _____ bil

Y = \$ _____ bil

The above calculations are based on aggregate product or expenditures. To calculate GNP by adding all payments to factors of production, we have

(4)   GNP = $Rp + Tb + Ti + Sb + D$

GNP = \$ _____ + _____ + _____ + _____ + _____ bil

GNP = \$ _____ bil

But we know that personal receipts must equal personal expenditures, such that

(5) $Rp + Tr = C + Tp + Sp$

or

• (6) $Rp = C + Tp + Sp - Tr$

Rp = \$ _____ + _____ + _____ + _____ bil

Rp = \$ _____ bil

We also know that taxes received by the government from all sources must equal government expenditures for all purposes *plus* the net deficit or surplus in the government budget at the end of the year. That is,

(7) $Tb + Tp + Ti = G + Tr + Tf + Sg$

or

Figure 3-1 Receipts and Expenditures Matrix for the United States, 1971 (Billions of Dollars)

Payments	Business	Persons	Government	Net foreign payments	Net saving	National income	Indirect business taxes	Depreciation	Total
Business		$R_p =$ ___	$T_b =$ ___		$S_b =$ ___	$NI =$ ___	$T_i =$ ___	$D =$ ___	___
Persons	$C =$ ___		$T_p =$ ___		$S_p =$ ___				___
Government	$G =$ ___	$T_r =$ ___		$T_f =$ ___	$S_g =$ ___				___
Net exports	$X - Z =$ ___								___
Net investment	$I_r =$ ___			$I_f =$ ___					___
Net national product	$Y =$ ___								
Indirect business taxes			$T_i =$ ___						
Depreciation	$D =$ ___								
Totals	$GNP =$ ___								

(8) $Tb + Ti = G + Tr + Tf + Sg - Tp$

$Tb + Ti = \$ \_\_\_\_\_ + \_\_\_\_\_ + \_\_\_\_\_ + \_\_\_\_\_ - \_\_\_\_\_$ bil

$Tb + Ti = \$ \_\_\_\_\_$ bil

We can now substitute Eqs. (6) and (8) into Eq. (4), so that

(9) $GNP = C + Tp + Sp - Tr + G + Tr + Tf + Sg - Tp + Sb + D$

$= C + Sp + G + Tf + Sg + Sb + D$

$= \$ \_\_\_\_\_ + \_\_\_\_\_ + \_\_\_\_\_ + \_\_\_\_\_ + \_\_\_\_\_$

$+ \_\_\_\_\_ + \_\_\_\_\_$ bil

$= \$ \_\_\_\_\_$ bil

We know that Eqs. (1) and (9) add up to the same thing, so that

(10) $C + Ir + X - Z + G + D = C + Sp + G + Tf + Sg + Sb + D$

and

(11) $X - Z + Ir + D = Sp + Sg + Tf + Sb + D$

But we know that net foreign investment If equals net exports $X - Z$ minus transfer to foreigners Tf:

(12) $X - Z - Tf = If$

Hence

(13) $If + Ir + D = Sp + Sg + Sb + D$

and

$\$ \_\_\_\_\_ + \_\_\_\_\_ + \_\_\_\_\_$ bil = $\$ \_\_\_\_\_ + \_\_\_\_\_ + \_\_\_\_\_$

$+ \_\_\_\_\_$ bil

$\$ \_\_\_\_\_$ bil $= \$ \_\_\_\_\_$ bil

So gross savings and gross investment must be equal, and if we subtract depreciation from both sides we have

(14) $If + Ir = Sp + Sg + Sb$

$\$ \_\_\_\_\_ + \_\_\_\_\_$ bil $= \$ \_\_\_\_\_ + \_\_\_\_\_ + \_\_\_\_\_$ bil

$\$ \_\_\_\_\_$ bil $= \$ \_\_\_\_\_$ bil

or net savings equals net investment.

8 We know from the top row in Fig. 3-1 that

(15) $NI = Rp + Tb + Sb$

$NI = \$ \_\_\_\_\_$ bil

We also know that

(16) $PI = Rp + Tr = \$$ _____ bil

which is disposed of as

(17) $PI = C + Tp + Sp = \$$ _____ bil

So

(18) $Rp + Tr = C + Tp + Sp$

and

(19) $Yd = Rp + Tr - Tp = C + Sp$

$Yd = \$$ _____ bil

Yd can also be derived directly from Y by adding government transfers and subtracting income in Fig. 3-1 that does not accrue to persons.

(20) $Yd = Y - Ti - Tp - Tb + Tr - Sb$

$= \$$ _____ - _____ - _____ - _____ + _____ - _____ bil

$= \$$ _____ bil

Define net taxes T as

(21) $T = Ti + Tp + Tb - Tr$

$= \$$ _____ + _____ + _____ - _____ bil

$= \$$ _____ bil

Hence

(22) $Yd = Y - T - Sb$

$= \$$ _____ - _____ - _____ bil

$= \$$ _____ bil

Lastly, we find that we can calculate the government surplus or deficit by subtracting from net taxes total government expenditures and transfers to foreigners

(23) $Sg = T - G - Tf$

$= \$$ _____ - _____ - _____ bil

$= \$$ _____ bil

PROBLEMS FOR EXERCISE 3

You are given the following data for the United States economy in 198_ :

		$ bil
1	Wages and salaries	1,367.4
2	Dividends	70.5

  3 Business transfer payments 9.4
  4 Employer contribution for social insurance 63.1
  5 Undistributed corporate profits 81.6
  6 Personal consumption expenditures 1,635.5
  7 Net interest from government 37.3
  8 Other labor income 67.2
  9 Corporate profits tax liability 113.2
 10 Net interest from business 62.3
 11 Personal transfers to foreigners 2.5
 12 Net interest from consumers 41.0
 13 Proprietors' income 209.5
 14 Rental income 74.6
 15 Inventory valuation adjustment . . . .   - 1.2

 16 Total compensation of employees . . . .   _____

 17 Corporate profits before taxes . . . .   _____

 18 Personal outlays . . . .   _____

 19 Interest paid by government and consumers . . . .   _____

 20 Interest income from all sources . . . .   _____

 21 National income . . . .   _____

 22 Personal saving . . . .   _____
 23 Total contribution to social insurance 114.0
 24 Disposable income 1,784.7
 25 Capital consumption allowance 228.4
 26 Personal tax payments 242.7
 27 Indirect business taxes 237.8
 28 Government transfer payments to persons 140.2
 29 Statistical discrepancy . . . .   - 1.2
 30 Gross private domestic investment 380.9
 31 Exports of goods and services 151.7
 32 Subsidies (net) of government enterprises 4.9
 33 Government purchases of goods and services 526.4
 34 Import of goods and services 116.9

 35 Personal contributions to social insurance . . . .   _____
 36 United States government transfers to foreigners 9.0

A Fill in the missing data above.

B Calculate the following:

   GNP =
   NNP =
   NI =

PI   =
DPI =

C From the information given above, set up the following sector accounts:

National Income and Product Account

Allocations	Receipts
Gross national product	Gross national product

Personal Income and Outlay Account

Allocations	Receipts
Personal outlays, taxes, and saving	Personal income

Government Receipts and Expenditures Account

Allocations	Receipts
Expenditures and surplus/deficit	Government receipts

Foreign Transactions Account

Receipts	Allocations
Receipts from foreigners	Payments to foreigners

Gross Saving and Investment Account

Investment	Saving
Gross investment	Gross saving

ANSWERS FOR EXERCISE 3

1 664.9, 232.8, 0.7, 152.0, personal, Eq. (1) GNP = $C + I + G + X - Z$,
   GNP = \$664.9 + 152.0 + 232.8 + 66.1 - 65.4, GNP = 1,050.4, 664.1, 24.5, 148.6, 38.5,
   855.7, 194.7, 1,050.4

2 Item: 2–3 = 664.9
            2–7 = 572.9
            2–8 = 26.5
            2–9 = 70.0
           2–10 = 24.5
           2–11 = 25.4
           2–13 = 38.5
           2–17 =   4.6

personal outlays, wage and salary disbursements

Table 3-2 item	To whom paid	From whom received
1	Government	
3	Business	
4	Business	
5	Foreign	
7		Business, government
8		Business, government
9		Business, government
10		Business, government
11		Business
13		Business
14		Government
15		Consumers
17		Business
18		Government
19	Government	

personal saving, outlay, 861.4, 800.5, 60.9, increased, 60.9, is

3 Table 3-3
   Item: 3–1 = 232.8
            3–3 = 89.0
            3–5 = 13.5
            3–6 =   0.9
            3–8 = –16.9
            3–9 = –21.7
           3–11 = 117.0
           3–12 = 37.3
           3–13 = 101.9
           3–15 = 34.1
           3–16 = 31.2

personal taxes, corporate profits taxes, indirect business taxes, contributions for social insurance

Table 3-3 item	To whom paid	From whom received
1	Business	
3	Persons	
4	Foreign	
5	Persons	
6	Business	
11		Persons
12		Business
13		Business
15		Business
16		Persons

deficit, 21.7, surplus, 4.8, deficit, 16.9, personal taxes, indirect business taxes, purchases of goods and services

4 receipts from, payments to

Table 3-4

Item: 4-1 = 66.1
      4-3 = 65.4
      4-4 = 2.6
      4-5 = 1.0

Table 3-4 item	To whom paid	From whom received
1	Business	
3		Business
4		Government
5		Persons

5 Table 3-5

Item: 5-2 =   34.1
      5-3 =   70.0
      5-4 =   24.5
      5-5 =   38.5
      5-6 =   78.6
      5-7 =   37.3
      5-8 =   25.4
      5-9 =   20.5
     5-10 =   -4.7
     5-11 =   807.2
     5-12 =   101.9
     5-13 =   909.1
     5-14 =   93.8
     5-15 = 1,002.9
     5-16 =   664.9
     5-17 =   232.8
     5-18 =   0.7
     5-19 =   152.0
     5-20 =   3.6

5–21 = 1,002.9
1,002.9, 152.0, 3.6

Table 3-5 item	To whom paid	From whom received
1	Persons	
2	Government	
3	Persons	
4	Persons	
5	Persons	
6	Persons	
7	Government	
8	Persons	
9	Business	
10	Business	
12	Government	
14	Business	
16		Persons
17		Government
18		Foreign
19		Business
20		Business

6 60.9
Table 3-6
Item: 6–1 = 152.0
6–2 = –2.1
6–3 = 60.9
6–4 =   0.4
6–5 = 20.5
6–6 = –4.7
6–7 = 93.8
6–8 = –16.9
6–9 =   0.7
6–10 = –4.8
personal saving

Table 3-6 item	Sector investing or saving
1	Business
2	Foreign
3	Persons
4	Persons
5	Business
6	Business
7	Business
8	Government
9	Foreign

7   Eq. (1) GNP $= C + Ir + X - Z + G + D$
$\qquad = 772.5 + 60.0 + 3.8 + 273.8 + 108.7$
$\qquad = 1{,}218.8$

Eq. (2) $Y = GNP - D$

Eq. (3) $Y = C + Ir + X - Z + G$
$\qquad = 1{,}218.8 - 108.7$
$\qquad = 772.5 + 60.0 + 3.8 + 273.8$
$\qquad = 1{,}110.1$

Eq. (4) GNP $= Rp + Tb + Ti + Sb + D$
$\qquad = 903.8 + 81.3 + 112.5 + 12.5 + 108.7$
$\qquad = 1{,}218.8$

Eq. (5) $Rp + Tr = C + Tp + Sp$

Eq. (6) $Rp = C + Tp + Sp - Tr$
$\qquad = 772.5 + 178.8 + 66.3 - 113.8$
$\qquad = 902.8$

Eq. (7) $Tb + Tp + Ti = G + Tr + Tf + Sg$

Eq. (8) or $Tb + Ti = G + Tr + Tf + Sg - Tp$
$\qquad = 273.8 + 113.8 + 2.5 + (-17.5) - 178.8$
$\qquad = 193.8$

Eq. (9) GNP $= C + Tp + Sp - Tr + G + Tr + Tf + Sg - Tp + Sb + D$
$\qquad = C + Sp + G + Tf + Sg + Sb + D$
$\qquad = 772.5 + 66.3 + 273.8 + 2.5 + (-17.5) + 12.5 + 108.7$
$\qquad = 1{,}218.8$

Eq. (10) $C + Ir + X - Z + G + D = C + Sp + G + Tf + Sg + Sb + D$

Eq. (11) and $X - Z + Ir + D = Sp + Sg + Tf + Sb + D$

Eq. (12) $X - Z - Tf = If$

Eq. (13) $If + Ir + D = Sp + Sg + Sb + D$
$\qquad 1.3 + 60.0 + 108.7 = 66.3 + (-17.5) + 12.5 + 108.7$
$\qquad 170.0 = 170.0$

Eq. (14) $If + Ir = Sp + Sg + Sb$
$\qquad 1.3 + 60.0 = 66.3 + (-17.5) + 12.5$
$\qquad 61.3 = 61.3$

8   Eq. (15) NI $= Rp + Tb + Sb$
$\qquad = 903.8 + 81.3 + 12.5$
$\qquad = 997.6$

Eq. (16) PI $= Rp + Tr = 903.8 + 113.8 = 1{,}017.6$

Eq. (17) PI $= C + Tp + Sp = 772.5 + 178.8 + 66.3 = 1{,}017.6$

Eq. (18) $Rp + Tr = C + TP + Sp$

Eq. (19) $Yd = Rp + T - Tp = C + Sp$
$\qquad 903.8 + 113.8 - 178.8 = 772.5 + 66.3 = 838.8$

Eq. (20) $Yd = Y - Ti - Tp - Tb + Tr - Sb$
$\qquad = 1{,}110.1 - 112.5 - 178.8 - 81.3 + 113.8 - 12.5$
$\qquad = 838.8$

Eq. (21) $T = Ti + Tp + Tb - Tr$
$\qquad = 112.5 + 178.8 + 81.3 - 113.8$
$\qquad = 258.8$

Eq. (22) $Yd = Y - T - Sb$
$$= 1{,}110.1 - 258.8 - 12.5$$
$$= 838.8$$
Eq. (23) $Sg = T - G - Tf$
$$= 258.8 - 273.8 - 2.5$$
$$= -17.5$$

ANSWERS TO PROBLEMS FOR EXERCISE 3

A 16 #1 + #4 + #8 = 1,497.7
17 #9 + #2 + #5 = 265.3
18 #6 + #12 + #11 = 1,679.0
19 #7 + #12 = 78.3
20 #7 + #10 + #12 = 140.6
21 #16 + #13 + #17 + #14 + #10 + #15 = 2,108.2
22 #24 - #18 = 105.8
35 #23 - #4 = 50.9

B GNP = #6 + #30 + #33 + #31 - #34 = 2,577.7
NNP = #6 + #30 - #25 + #33 + #31 - #34 = 2,349.3
NI = NNP - #27 - #3 - #29 + #32 = 2,108.2
PI = #26 + #18 + #22 = 2,027.5
DPI = #18 + #22 = 1,784.7

National Income and Product Account

Allocations		Receipts	
Compensation of employees	$1,497.7	Personal consumption expenditures	$1,635.5
Proprietors' income	209.5		
Rental income	74.6	Gross private domestic investment	380.9
Corporate profits before taxes	265.3		
Inventory valuation adjustment	-1.2	Government purchases of goods and services	526.4
Net interest	62.3		
National income	$2,108.2	Net exports of goods and services	34.9
Indirect business taxes	237.8		
Business transfer payments	9.4		
minus: Subsidies less current surplus of government enterprises	4.9		
Statistical discrepancy	-1.2		
Net national product	2,349.3		
Capital consumption allowances	228.4		
Gross national product	$2,577.7	Gross national product	$2,577.7

Personal Income and Outlay Account

Allocations		Receipts	
Personal outlays	$1,679.0	Wages and salaries	$1,367.4
Personal taxes	242.7	Other labor income	67.2
Personal saving	105.8	Proprietors' income	209.5
		Rental income	74.6
		Dividends	70.5
		Interest income	140.6
		Transfer payments (from business and government)	149.7
		Minus: Personal contributions for social insurance	52.1
Personal outlays, taxes, and saving	$2,027.5		$2,027.5

Government Receipts and Expenditures Account

Allocations		Receipts	
Purchases of goods and services	$ 526.4	Personal tax payments	$ 242.7
Transfer payments	149.2	Corporate profit tax liability	113.2
To persons 140.2		Indirect business taxes	237.8
To foreigners 9.0		Contributions for social	
Net interest paid	37.3	insurance	114.0
Subsidies less current surplus		Employer 61.9	
of government enterprises	4.9	Personal 52.1	
Surplus (+) or deficit (−) on			
income and product account	−10.3		
Government expenditures and			
surplus or deficit	$ 707.7	Government receipts	$ 707.7

Foreign Transactions Account

Receipts		Allocations	
Exports of goods and services	$ 151.7	Imports of goods and services	$ 116.8
		Transfer payments from	
		United States government (net)	9.0
		Personal transfer payments (net)	2.5
		Net foreign investment	23.4
Receipts from foreigners	$ 151.7	Payments to foreigners	$ 151.7

Gross Saving and Investment Account

Investment			Saving		
Gross private domestic investment	$	380.9	Personal saving	$	105.8
Net foreign investment		23.4	Undistributed corporate profits		81.6
			Capital consumption allowances		228.4
			Government surplus (+) or deficit (−) on income and product account		−10.3
			Statistical discrepancy		−1.2
Gross investment	$	404.3	Gross saving	$	404.3

You are given the following information:

Undistributed corporate profits	$122.5 bil
Personal taxes	140.0
Interest paid by consumers	14.0
Net private domestic investment	175.0
Personal consumption expenditures	875.0
Social Security contributions	52.5
Corporate income taxes	140.0
Transfer payments	77.0
Indirect business taxes	70.0
Exports	84.0
Government purchases of goods and services	315.0
Gross private domestic investment	262.5
Imports	77.0

1 Disposable personal income is
   (a) 1,151.5
   (b)   826.0
   (c)   924.0
   (d) 1,407.0
   (e)   997.5

2 Personal income is
   (a) 1,529.5
   (b) 1,211.0
   (c) 1,428.0
   (d) 1,498.0
   (e) 1,064.0

3 National income is
   (a) 1,564.5
   (b) 1,302.0
   (c) 1,634.5
   (d) 1,274.0
   (e) 1,337.0

4 Net national product is
   (a) 1,634.5
   (b) 1,704.5
   (c) 1,372.0
   (d) 1,295.0
   (e) 1,407.0

5 Gross national product is
   (a) 1,365.0
   (b) 1,477.0
   (c) 1,722.0
   (d) 1,459.5
   (e) 1,792.0

6 Personal saving is
   (a)   77.0
   (b)   59.5
   (c) 115.5
   (d)   94.5
   (e)   35.0

Government purchases of goods and services	$ 213.4 bil
Undistributed corporate profits	24.2
Corporate taxes	50.6
Corporate profits	103.4
Net private domestic investment	70.4
Indirect business taxes	92.4
Interest	35.2
Dividends	28.6
Social Security contributions	22.0
Exports	50.6
Personal consumption expenditures	690.8
Transfer payments	59.4
Imports	52.8
Personal taxes	101.2
Capital consumption allowances	90.2
Proprietors' income	101.2

7 Net national product is
   (a) 1,137.4
   (b) 1,126.4
   (c)   972.4
   (d)   880.0
   (e) 1,062.6

8 Personal income is
   (a)   741.4
   (b)   482.6
   (c)   706.2
   (d)   818.4
   (e) 1,062.6

9 National income is
   (a)   880.0
   (b)   972.4
   (c)   917.4
   (d) 1,126.4
   (e)   948.2

10 Disposable income is
   (a)   706.2
   (b)   482.6
   (c)   818.4
   (d)   741.4
   (e) 1,062.6

11 Gross national product is
   (a)   880.0
   (b) 1,137.4
   (c)   972.4
   (d) 1,062.6
   (e) 1,126.4

Gross private domestic investment	$100.8 bil
Personal taxes	41.4
Indirect business taxes	57.6
Proprietors' income	81.0
Undistributed corporate profits	27.0
Net private domestic investment	59.4
Personal saving	18.0
Exports	36.0
National income	500.4

Net exports. 10.8
Disposable income 396.0
Interest paid by consumers. 9.0

12 Imports are
  (a) 25.2
  (b) 46.8
  (c) 43.2
  (d) 28.8
  (e) insufficient data

13 Personal income is
  (a) 437.4
  (b) 493.2
  (c) 412.2
  (d) 455.4
  (e) insufficient data

14 Capital consumption allowance is
  (a) insufficient data
  (b) 57.6
  (c) 25.2
  (d) 41.4
  (e) 46.8

15 Government purchases of goods and services are
  (a) insufficient data
  (b) 127.8
  (c) 118.8
  (d) 185.4
  (e) 154.8

16 Personal consumption expenditures are
  (a) 329.4
  (b) 369.0
  (c) 415.8
  (d) insufficient data
  (e) 405.0

17 Personal income will be larger
  (a) the larger the fraction of after-tax corporate profits retained in business firms
  (b) the larger the amount of personal contributions for social insurance
  (c) the larger the amount of interest paid by consumers
  (d) the larger the amount of government transfer payments to persons

18 The total income earned in any given year by the owners of productive resources
is measured by
(a) DI
(b) PI
(c) GNP
(d) NI
(e) NNP

19 Interest on the national debt is included in
(a) GNP
(b) NNP
(c) PI
(d) NI

20 Which of the following is a true statement about the national income accounts?
(a) They allow for changes in the quality of goods and services .
(b) They include the value of leisure.
(c) They measure social costs.
(d) They measure economic and social values.
(e) None of the above.

21 When gross investment is positive, net investment
(a) is negative
(b) is zero
(c) is positive
(d) can be either positive or negative

22 If prices rise during a given year, inventory valuation adjustment
(a) must be positive
(b) must be negative
(c) must be negative if there is a drop in the amount of inventories
(d) must be negative if there is a rise in the amount of inventories

23 If capital consumption allowances exceed gross private domestic investment, it can
be concluded that
(a) the economy is exporting more than it imports
(b) the economy is expanding
(c) net investment is negative
(d) money GNP is rising but real GNP is declining

24 The following government expenditure does not appear in the sector accounts as a
receipt of persons:
(a) government interest payments
(b) wages and salaries
(c) subsidies
(d) transfer payments

25 In an economy whose productive capacity is expanding
  (a) DPI exceeds PI
  (b) gross private domestic investment exceeds depreciation
  (c) NNP exceeds GNP
  (d) money GNP is rising
  (e) exports exceed imports

26 Net domestic investment refers to
  (a) the total production of capital equipment, construction, and additions to inventories
  (b) the total investment less the amount of investment goods used up in accomplishing the year's production
  (c) exports minus imports
  (d) the total domestic investment less net exports

27 Interest on the public debt
  (a) is part of NNP but not a part of NI
  (b) is treated like any other form of interest income
  (c) is not part of NI but is included in PI
  (d) is part of NI but not part of PI

28 The smallest national income accounting aggregate is usually
  (a) PI
  (b) GNP
  (c) DPI
  (d) NI
  (e) NNP

29 Disinvestment occurs when
  (a) inventories expand
  (b) the prices of investment goods rise
  (c) businesses sell machinery and equipment to domestic buyers
  (d) the capital consumption allowance exceeds gross private domestic investment

30 Corporate profits included in disposable personal income are
  (a) dividends
  (b) indirect business taxes
  (c) capital consumption allowances
  (d) corporate income taxes
  (e) undistributed corporate profits

31 A negative contribution to aggregate demand is sometimes made by the following sector:
  (a) business
  (b) household
  (c) foreign
  (d) government

32 The volume of sales is actually several times as large as the GNP because
   (a) GNP excludes corporate taxes
   (b) total sales are in money terms and GNP is always stated in real terms
   (c) GNP excludes intermediate transactions
   (d) GNP understates the value of output

33 The term "subsidies" includes
   (a) transfer by government or by business firms
   (b) transfer in business firms to individuals
   (c) payments in exchange for which no goods or services are provided
   (d) payments to business, in exchange for which no goods or services are provided by the government

34 The purchase of a new home is included in the GNP as a part of
   (a) capital consumption allowance
   (b) personal consumption expenditures
   (c) investment
   (d) personal saving

35 Net foreign investment equals
   (a) the excess of purchases from foreigners over purchases from foreigners
   (b) the net exports of goods and services
   (c) net disinvestment by foreigners in the domestic economy during the period
   (d) imports minus exports

36 Which of the following would be included in current NNP?
   (a) the receipt of $1,000 by a welfare client
   (b) replacement of a wornout drill press
   (c) milk purchased by a housewife
   (d) the purchase of milk by a dairy

37 The net contribution to GNP by the government sector is measured by
   (a) government purchases of goods and services
   (b) wages and salaries and supplements as paid by the government
   (c) intergovernmental transfer
   (d) the size of the government surplus

38 In calculating GNP which of the following should be excluded?
   (a) rental incomes
   (b) interest payments
   (c) dividends
   (d) government transfer payments

39 The total sales of all firms in an economy in a given year is
   (a) the same as gross national product
   (b) equal to that of national income
   (c) more than gross national product
   (d) less than gross national product

40 *NI* is less than NNP by the amount of
   (a) transfer payments
   (b) capital consumption allowance.
   (c) indirect business taxes
   (d) personal taxes

41 In the sector accounts, government purchases of imports appear in part as a receipt of
   (a) the household sector
   (b) the government sector
   (c) the business sector
   (d) the foreign sector

42 Net exports are negative when
   (a) net investment is positive
   (b) exports are exceeded by imports
   (c) exports exceed private transfer to foreigners
   (d) imports are exceeded by exports

43 Which of the following is *not* a source of aggregate demand?
   (a) X-M
   (b) C
   (c) G
   (d) S

44 Which social accounting statement will tell you what amount has been invested in corporate securities?
   (a) Input-output table
   (b) Flow of funds
   (c) National income and product
   (d) Balance of payments

45 Net national product excludes
   (a) interest
   (b) profits
   (c) rents
   (d) wages
   (e) replacement investment

46 Which of the following is *not* included in disposable income?
   (a) business transfer payments
   (b) social security benefits
   (c) corporate dividends
   (d) personal income taxes

47 Real GNP is greater than it would otherwise be if
- **(a)** imports exceed exports
- **(b)** prices are falling
- **(c)** exports exceed imports
- **(d)** prices are rising

48 The consolidated government budget differs from the federal budget by
- **(a)** imports
- **(b)** state and local government expenditures
- **(c)** federal tax receipts
- **(d)** intergovernmental transfers

49 Which of the following is counted in determining GNP?
- **(a)** a do-it-yourself roof-repair job
- **(b)** a housewife's work at home
- **(c)** an operation performed in a hospital
- **(d)** vegetables grown by a farmer for his own use

50 Which social accounting statement can tell you what are the interrelationships between specific industries?
- **(a)** flow of funds
- **(b)** balance of payments
- **(c)** input-output table
- **(d)** national income and product

PART TWO

CONSUMPTION, SAVING,
AND INCOME DETERMINATION

At this time our attention passes from *measurement* of GNP and its components to an effort to explain *why* GNP reaches a particular level. Naturally, analysis of a complicated economy must begin with some drastic simplifications in order to facilitate understanding. Thus, an extremely simple model of income determination is introduced first. It is hoped that this model is simple enough to be understood with a little effort, but realistic enough to capture the essence of how the economy actually works. After this elementary model is mastered, it is not difficult to add complicating factors which improve the relationship between model and reality. These additions are made one by one until, at length, the student is furnished with a framework which can provide sensible, rigorous answers to some extremely complicated questions about the economic impact of private and public actions.

It is usually convenient to approach a problem in economics with supply and demand analysis. Aggregate income determination is no exception. We first simplify by assuming that the supply side, that is, the production decisions of business, are completely passive. Business is assumed to produce precisely what consumers demand at all times. Thus, for the time being, we abstract from independent behavior by producers. This highly unrealistic assumption will be dropped later (see, e.g., Part 7).

By ignoring supply considerations, we are assuming that income and output are determined solely by demand factors. Thus, the first task in building the model is to identify and study the sources of demand. The basic framework follows the income and product accounts of the United States. There, the economy is divided into four sectors: personal, business, government, and foreign. Each of these sectors can be regarded as a source of demand for goods and services. We initially ignore the government and foreign sectors (they are replaced in Parts 3 and 8 respectively), and further assume that only goods and services are demanded. The latter assumption implies that income not spent is simply left in idle cash.

At this point, therefore, only consumption and investment demand are introduced. Detailed discussion of business (investment) demand will be made in Part 3, Exercises 10 and 11. For now, we will consider this variable to be independently determined. An arbitrary amount will be assigned to investment expenditures. The determinants of consumption demand, particularly the relationship between consumption and income, will be explored at length in this part.

Two important concepts are central to the analysis that follows. First, an economy is said to be in *equilibrium* when no decision-maker has an incentive to change his behavior. When this condition is not satisfied, all economic variables are subject to change as individuals adjust their behavior. Second, it is necessary to make a distinction between *intended* and *realized* behavior. The former represents *plans* and the latter represents actual *results*, which may or may not coincide with the plans. A discrepancy between plans and their realization can arise for a number of reasons. For example, because plans are formulated on the basis of forecasts of the future, an individual or firm will have to abandon the plan and change his behavior if the forecasts prove to be incorrect.

The theory of income determination proceeds by examining *intended* and *realized* positions. An equality between intended and realized, or actual, positions will produce an equilibrium income level; an inequality causes disequilibrium to occur, resulting subsequently in a new income level. Thus macroeconomic models seek to explain *levels* of and *changes* in aggregate income.

In the simple two-sector model presented here, a consumption function of intended behavior, together with a given amount of (intended) investment spending, combine to produce an equilibrium level of aggregate income when intentions are realized. Changes in intended spending, i.e., changes in aggregate demand, will lead to changes in the equilibrium level of aggregate income.

THE CONSUMPTION FUNCTION

1 Aggregate consumption expenditures in our economy depend on a number of things, the most important being disposable income. In Table 4-1 we have a hypothetical *schedule* of data for consumption and income. This *schedule* represents (intended, realized) consumption expenditures since it shows the amount of such expenditures for

Table 4-1

Consumption C ($ bil)	Income Y ($ bil)
100	0
175	100
250	200
325	300
400	400
475	500
550	600
625	700
700	800

different levels of income. Thus, consumption in this sense is (a single numerical figure, an entire set of possible figures) and is an (ex ante, ex post) concept. In contrast, consumption data from the national income accounts is a(n) (intended, realized) figure and (does, does not) represent a single numerical amount. Consumption in this sense is an (ex ante, ex post) concept.

2 In the simple two-sector model presented here—personal and business sectors—we introduce just two types of spending—consumption and investment—which fully determine income. We further simplify by assuming that investment is independently determined, thus eliminating the role of business saving—depreciation and retained earnings—from the analysis. The effect of eliminating the depreciation component of business saving is to make ($Y = \text{GNP}$, $Y = \text{NNP}$, $Y = \text{PI}$). The effect of eliminating the government sector is to make ($Y = \text{NI}$, $Y = \text{PI}$, $Y = \text{DPI}$). The foreign sector will also be omitted. (For review of the relationship between the principal measures of national income, see Exercise 2.)

3 Plot the data in Table 4-1 on Fig. 4-1 and connect the points with a line. Label this line C_1.

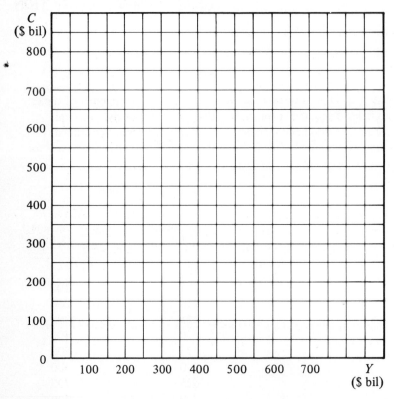

FIGURE 4-1

4 The following equation conveniently summarizes the information given in Table 4-1:

(1) $C_1 = \$100 \text{ bil} + 0.75Y$

This equation is a(n) (function, identity) which states that intended consumption expenditures C are (directly, inversely) related to income levels Y and that a part of C ($\$100$ bil) is determined autonomously—i.e., by factors other than income. The general form of this equation can be written as

(2) $C = a + bY$

Using Eq. (1), we find that at an income level of $\$500$ bil, $\$_____$ bil of consumption is determined by income and $\$_____$ bil by other factors. Thus consumption is always

$100 bil + 0.75 of the amount of income received. When income is $520 bil, consumption is $_____ bil.

5 The coefficient 0.75 expresses the relationship between changes in Y and changes in C. This coefficient, known as the *marginal propensity to consume* (MPC), is defined as $\Delta C/\Delta Y$, where the symbol Δ represents change. The MPC shows how much consumption expenditures *change* when income changes. Again using Eq. (1), if income is $500 bil, consumption is $_____ bil. If income is $600 bil, consumption is $_____ bil. Thus, as a result of a change in income of $_____ bil, consumption (increases, decreases) by $_____ bil. In this case the value of the MPC is (positive, negative) and is equal to (0.6, 0.75, 0.9). The ratio of $\Delta C/\Delta Y$ measures the slope of the consumption schedule and (is, is not) equal to the value of the b coefficient in our consumption function. Since our consumption function is a straight line, its slope is a (constant, variable). If $b = 0.6$ in Eq. (2), then a change in income of $100 bil would produce a change in consumption of $_____ bil. As a result of this change in income, the a component of Eq. (2) will change by $_____ bil. (Note: If necessary, the student should review Exercise 1 on functions and graphs.)

6 Considering C_1 in Fig. 4-1, an increase in income causes intended consumption to increase. This represents a (movement along, shift of) the consumption function and can be considered an (autonomous, induced) change in intended consumption behavior. If the a coefficient in the consumption function changes, such as from $C = \$100$ bil $+ 0.75Y$ to

$$(3) \qquad C_3 = \$200 \text{ bil} + 0.75Y$$

then (intended, actual) consumption changes at every level of income. This represents a (movement along, shift of) the consumption function and can be considered an (autonomous, induced) change in intended consumption behavior; i.e., it is not based on a change in income.

7 In Fig. 4-1 plot Eq. (3). Label this curve C_3. Since C_3 is parallel to C_1, the MPC has (increased, decreased, not changed).

8 If the consumption function changes from $C = \$100$ bil $+ 0.75$ to

$$(4) \qquad C_4 = \$100 \text{ bil} + 0.5Y$$

this (does, does not) represent a change in the MPC. The slope of the consumption function has (increased, decreased, not changed), which produces a (parallel, nonparallel) shift (upward, downward) of the consumption function.

9 Plot Eq. (4) on Fig. 4-1. Label this curve C_4. Thus a change of either the autonomous consumption component a or the MPC b represents a shift in the consumption function.

PROBLEMS FOR EXERCISE 4

1 Complete Table 4-2, assuming the following consumption function:

(5) $C = \$100 \text{ bil} + 0.6Y$

Table 4-2

Income ($ bil)	Consumption ($ bil)	MPC
200	————	————
500	————	————
800	————	————

2 As income increases in Table 4-2, the absolute level of consumption expenditures (increases, decreases, does not change), while the MPC (increases, decreases, does not change).

3 What is the value of the slope of the consumption schedule in question 1? ————.

4 In Fig. 4-2 plot consumption function 5 for income levels $0 to $1,000 bil. Label this curve C_1. Illustrate the MPC on the graph for a change in income from $500 to $750 bil.

5 Plot a new consumption schedule on Fig. 4-2 for income levels $0 to $1,000 bil, where autonomous consumption is $100 bil and the MPC is 0.8. Label this curve C_2.

6 Write the equation for C_2 in question 5. ————————————————.

7 Assume autonomous consumption spending increases by $100 bil. The new consumption function will be ———————————————————.

8 Plot the function in question 7 on Fig. 4-2 and label it C_3.

9 In Fig. 4-2 the slopes of the consumption functions are such that (answer yes or no)

The slope of C_1 < the slope of C_2 ————

The slope of C_1 < the slope of C_3 ————

The slope of C_2 < the slope of C_3 ————

10 For any given level of income, (C_1, C_2, C_3) will produce the largest amount of consumption spending.

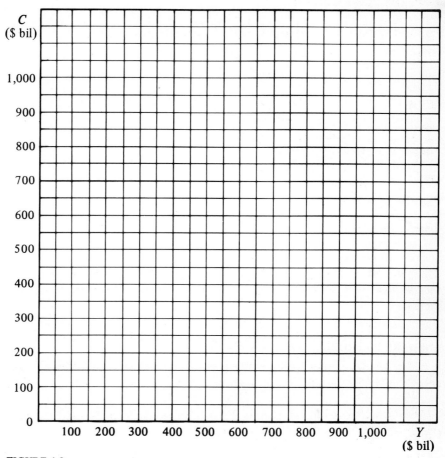

FIGURE 4-2

ANSWERS FOR EXERCISE 4

1 intended, an entire set of possible figures, ex ante, realized, does, ex post
2 Y = NNP, Y = DPI
3 Fig. 4-1A
4 function, directly, 375, 100, 490
5 475, 550, 100, increases, 75, positive, 0.75, is, constant, 60, zero
6 movement along, induced, intended, shift of, autonomous
7 Fig. 4-1A, not changed
8 does, decreased, nonparallel, downward
9 Fig. 4-1A

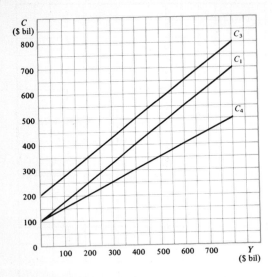

FIGURE 4-1A

ANSWERS TO PROBLEMS FOR EXERCISE 4

1 220   0.6
  400   0.6
  580   0.6
2 increases, does not change
3 0.6
4 Fig. 4-2A

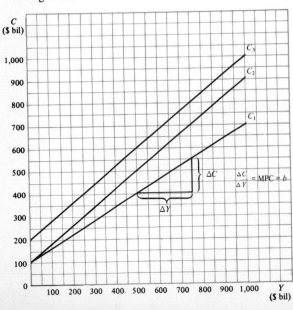

  5 Fig. 4-2A
  6 $C = \$100$ bil $+ 0.8Y$
  7 $C = \$200$ bil $+ 0.8Y$
  8 Fig. 4-2A
  9 yes, yes, no $(C_2 = C_3)$
 10 C_3

THE SAVING FUNCTION

1 There are only two ways to dispose of income: spend it or save it. Continuing the simple model of Exercise 4, saving—which is confined to the personal sector—is defined simply as the difference between disposable income and consumption. Since $Y = C + S$,

then $S = $ _____ . (Note: Remember that $Y = Y_d$.)

In Exercise 4 we expressed the general form of the consumption function as

(1) $C = a + bY$

Since saving can be expressed as

(2) $S = Y - C$

then by substituting (1) into (2), we have

(3) $S = Y - ($_____$)$

Eliminate the parenthesis from Eq. (3):

(4) $S = Y$ _____

Collect the terms that contain Y:

(5) $S = $ _____

Factor out Y:

(6) $S = $ _____

Equation (6) is a (function, identity) which states that intended saving is (directly, inversely) related to income levels and that a part of saving is determined

_____ .

2 If consumption has the following relationship to income:

(7) $C = \$100 \text{ bil} + 0.75Y$

then the relationship between saving and income may be expressed as

(8) $S = $ _____

At an income level of $500 bil, $_____ bil is determined by other–autonomous–factors.

Total saving is $_____ bil. When income is $520 bil, saving is $_____ bil.

3 *The marginal propensity to save* (MPS) measures how much saving will *change* when income *changes*. For example, when income rose from $500 bil to $520 bil in paragraph

2 above, saving rose from $_____ bil to $_____ bil. The change in saving was

$_____ bil. Thus, the ratio of the change in saving to the change in income (MPS) is

$\Delta S/\Delta Y = $ $_____ bil/$ $_____ bil = $ _____ . The MPS is (equal, not equal) to the value of the coefficient on income in Eq. (8). Because we have assumed a linear relationship between S and Y, the MPS is a (constant, variable). The value of the slope of the

saving function is _____ .

4 Add the right sides of Eq. (7) and (8) together.

(7) _____

+ (8) _____

= (9) _____

Do saving and consumption add up to income (yes, no)? What is the sum of the MPC and

the MPS in Eq. (9)? _____ . Is this always true (yes, no)? Why or why not? _____

_____

_____ .

5 Draw a straight line from the origin to the upper right-hand corner of Fig. 5-1. Each point on this line (is, is not) a point where the vertical distance from the income axis is equal to the horizontal distance from the consumption-saving axis. Since we are measuring consumption and saving on the vertical axis and income on the horizontal axis,

this line is a schedule of points where $Y = $ _____ . Label the line

$Y = C + S$. The slope of this line is equal to _____ . This 45° line, starting at the origin, is a graphical description of the identity that $Y = C + S$; i.e., whatever disposable income is, the personal sector can only either spend it or save it.

6 Plot Eq. (7) in Fig. 5-1 and label it C_1. Complete Table 5-1 on the basis of the information in Fig. 5-1. The amount of saving (can, cannot) be measured by the vertical distance between the $C + S$ and the C_1 lines in Fig. 5-1. When the $C + S$ line is above the C_1 line, saving is (positive, negative, zero). When the $C + S$ line is below the C_1 line,

saving is (positive, negative, zero). Saving is zero at income level $_____ bil.

7 The saving function can be graphed directly from Fig. 5-1. Plot the vertical distance between the $C + S$ and C_1 lines at $Y = $0 bil, $Y = $400 bil, and $Y = $800 bil. Connect

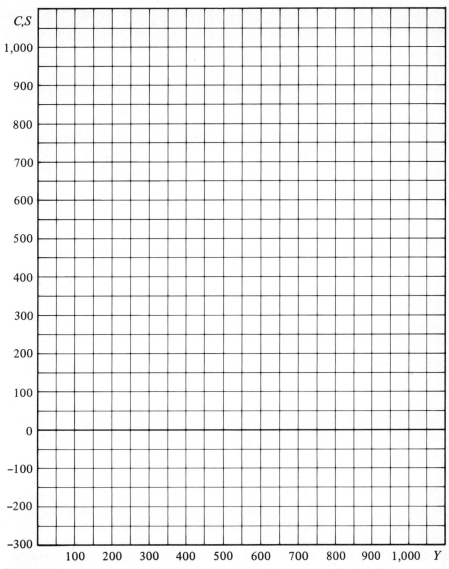

FIGURE 5-1

Table 5-1 Hypothetical Data on Income, Consumption, and Saving ($ bil)

Y	C	S
$100	$_____	$_____
200	$_____	$_____
400	$_____	$_____
600	$_____	$_____
800	$_____	$_____

the points with a straight line and label it S_1. The equation for the S_1 function is

(10) $S_1 =$ _____

Equations (8) and (10) are (different, identical).

8 Assume that the consumption function shifts to

(11) $C = \$200 \text{ bil} + 0.75Y$

Plot Eq. (11) in Fig. 5-1 and label it C_2. Draw the new saving function and label it S_2. As a result, the slope of the saving function has (increased, decreased, not changed). The S_2 function has shifted (upward, downward, not at all) and is (parallel, nonparallel) to the S_1 function.

PROBLEMS FOR EXERCISE 5

1 $C_1 = \$100 \text{ bil} + 0.6Y$

$C_2 = 0.6Y$

Given the foregoing consumption equations, derive the corresponding saving equations and compute the value of saving when $Y = \$800$ bil.

$S_1 =$ _____ $S = \$$____ bil

$S_2 =$ _____ $S = \$$____ bil

2 Assume that autonomous consumption increases by \$200 bil. As a result, the saving functions and saving in paragraph 1 would change to

$S_1' =$ _____ $S = \$$____ bil

$S_2' =$ _____ $S = \$$____ bil

These changes represent a(n) (upward, downward) (shift of, movement along) the saving functions (S_1, S_2, both S_1 and S_2). The MPS (has, has not) changed.

3 Suppose that, due to a change in consumer behavior, the slopes of both consumption functions in paragraph 1 increased to 0.8. As a result, when $Y = \$$____ bil, corresponding saving functions and saving will now be

$S_1'' =$ _____ $S = \$$____ bil

$S_2'' =$ _____ $S = \$$____ bil

These changes represent a(n) (upward, downward) (shift of, movement along) the saving functions (S_1, S_2, both S_1 and S_2). The MPS (has, has not) changed.

4 Using the consumption function contained in panel (1) of Fig. 5-2, graphically derive the corresponding saving function in panel (2) and label it S_1. (Be sure to first construct the $Y = C + S$ curve.)

(1)

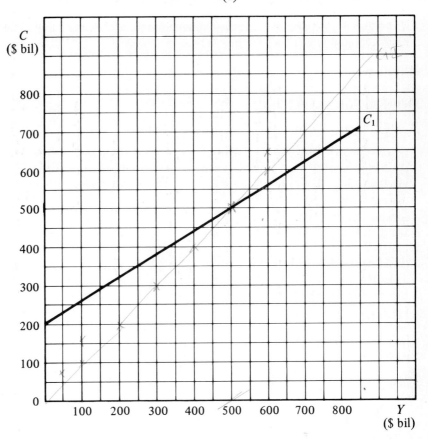

(2)

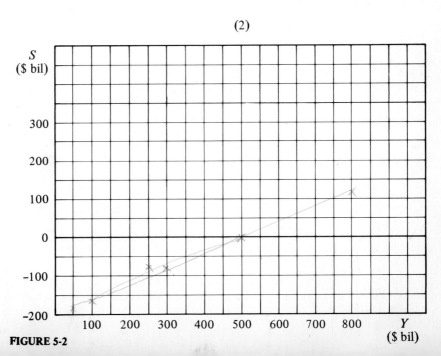

FIGURE 5-2

85

Now assume that autonomous consumption expenditures decrease by $150 bil. Draw the new consumption C_2 and saving S_2 curves.

ANSWERS FOR EXERCISE 5

1 $Y - C$,
   (3) $S = Y - (a + bY)$
   (4) $S = Y - a - bY$
   (5) $S = -a + Y - bY$
   (6) $S = -a + (1 - b)Y$
   function, directly, autonomously
2 $S = -\$100$ bil $+ 0.25Y - 100, 25, 30$
3 $25, 30, 5, 5/20, 0.25$, equal, constant, 0.25
4 (7) $\$100$ bil $+ 0.75Y +$ (8) $-\$100$ bil $+ 0.25Y =$ (9) Y, yes, 1, yes, since income is by definition divided up between consumption and saving any change in income must also be divided up between consumption and saving
5 Fig. 5-1A, is, $C + S$, 1

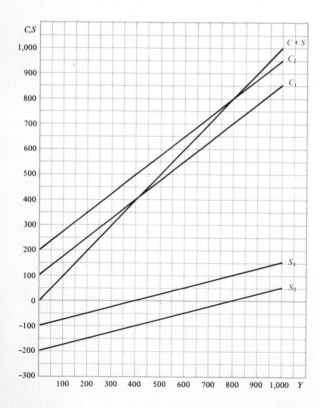

FIGURE 5-1A

6 Fig. 5-1A,

C	S
175	−75
250	−50
400	0
550	50
700	100

can, negative, positive, 400

7 Fig. 5-1A, $S_1 = -\$100$ bil $+ 0.25\,Y$, identical

8 Fig. 5-1A, not changed, downward, parallel

ANSWERS TO PROBLEMS FOR EXERCISE 5

1 $S_1 = -\$100$ bil $+ 0.4\,Y$, 220, $S_2 = 0.4\,Y$, 320

2 $S_1 = -\$300$ bil $+ 0.4\,Y$, 20, $S_2 = -\$200$ bil $+ 0.4\,Y$, 120, downward, shift of, both S_1 and S_2, has not

3 $S_1 = -\$100$ bil $+ 0.2\,Y$, 60, $S_2 = 0.2\,Y$, 160, downward, shift of, both S_1 and S_2, has

4 Fig. 5-2A

(1)

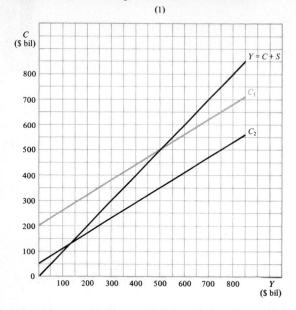

(2)

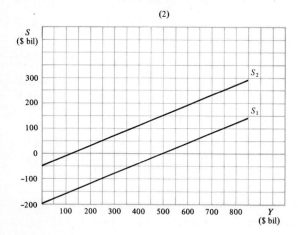

FIGURE 5-2A

INCOME DETERMINATION

1 In a simple two-sector model—personal and business—we assume that income is determined solely by two aggregate demand factors, _____

and _____ expenditures. Production is assumed to adjust passively to the level of aggregate demand. Thus, income is determined solely by demand factors. This condition can be symbolically described as $Y = C + I$. In this elementary model, therefore, the explanation of levels of and changes in income (Y) focuses on the determinants of the expenditure components C and I.

Exercise 4 emphasized that the major determinant of consumption expenditures was

_____ _____ .

The general form of the consumption function can be written as $C = a + bY$. The value

of Y in this equation is equal to disposable income because _____

_____ are initially omitted from study. (If necessary, the student should review Exercise 4, paragraphs 1 to 4.) At this point we will also assume that investment expenditures are independently determined.

2 The foregoing elements of a simple two-sector model can be summarized with the following equations, which we will assume are representative for an economy:

(1) $Y = C + I$

(2) $C = \$275 \text{ bil} + 0.50Y$

(3) $I = \$250 \text{ bil}$

Equation (1) states the condition or definition that there are two expenditure components of national income, consumption and investment. Equations (2) and (3) describe aggregate (intended, realized) expenditure behavior for the economy.

3 Plot Eq. (2) in Fig. 6-1. Label it C. Can we determine the current level of aggregate consumption expenditures from the C function (yes, no)? If yes, how much is it?

$_____ bil. If no, why not? _____

_____ .

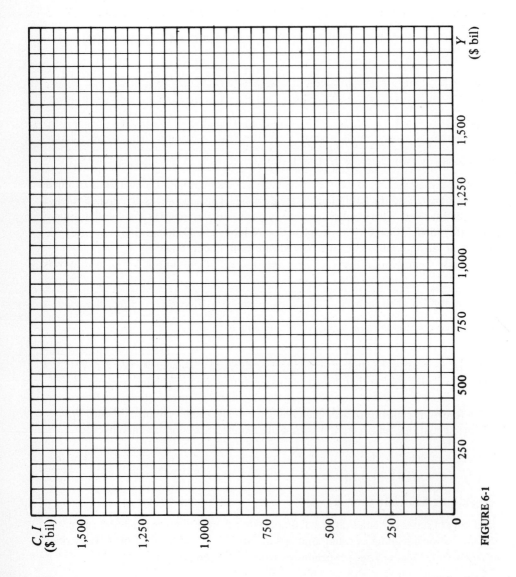

C, I
($ bil)

1,500

1,250

1,000

750

500

250

0

250   500   750   1,000   1,250   1,500

Y
($ bil)

FIGURE 6-1

4 In our model, the total aggregate expenditure function would be

(4) $C + I = $ _____

Plot Eq. (4) in Fig. 6-1 and label it $C + I$. The $C + I$ line is (parallel, nonparallel) to C, which means that the slope of $C + I$ (is, is not) equal to the slope of the C function. The fact that the $C + I$ line is positively sloped (does, does not) indicate that investment expenditures are related to income in this model. The $C + I$ line is higher than C at all income levels by $ \$$ _____ bil. This distance is equal to the value of intended _____ expenditures.

5 Since we are measuring consumption and investment on the vertical axis and income on the horizontal axis, the graph of Eq. (1) is a (straight, curved) line with a (positive, negative) slope equal to _____. Now plot Eq. (1) in Fig. 6-1. Label this line $Y = C + I$. The $Y = C + I$ line is a schedule of all points where _____ is equal to total _____ expenditures. Equation (1) can therefore be considered a schedule of (equilibrium, full employment) income conditions. The vertical distance of the $C + I$ line measures total intended expenditures for any given income level. In Fig. 6-1, find the point where income is just equal to the amount of total intended expenditures. Mark this point E. For the amount of intended expenditures given in Fig. 6-1, point E represents the _____ level of income.

Equilibrium occurs at the intersection of the _____ and _____ lines. If the amount of intended expenditures was higher, point E would be (higher, lower, unchanged). Thus, the equilibrium level of income (does, does not) depend on the level of intended expenditures.

6 At any given point in time, intended expenditures may not be realized because intentions are based upon forecasts and plans, whereas realized expenditures represent actual results. An inequality between intended and realized expenditures leads to *unintended* results. The discrepancy between intended and realized positions in the two-sector model occurs because businessmen must base production rates on their estimate of sales. If they misjudge, production will either exceed or fall short of sales. This factor leads to *unintended* inventory changes which businessmen will attempt to rectify in subsequent time periods. If inventories build up beyond their intended level, due to overproduction, firms will lay off workers and cut back output in order to regain their desired inventory level. This action, in turn, will lead to a decline in income. Conversely, if sales are initially underestimated, actual inventories will fall below desired levels. The resulting upward adjustment in the production rate will cause income to rise as employment and output expands. When unintended changes in inventory investment are eliminated, the economy will reach an equilibrium level of income. Only at equilibrium will there be no incentive for decision-makers to change their behavior to adjust for unintended results.

7 Refer again to Fig. 6-1. Assume that businessmen in the consumption goods industry estimate they will have $500 bil of sales during the next time period; the investment goods industry expects sales of $250 bil. The investment component consists of intended expenditure on producers' durable equipment, residential and commercial construction, and the net change in inventories. (If necessary, the student should review Exercise 2.) We will simplify here by assuming that the current inventory level is the intended one. Thus, at the beginning of the period, *intended* changes in inventory are zero. We will also assume that producers are able to accomplish their intentions for the production of consumer and investment goods.

Production and employment are set on the basis of these expenditure estimates. Total realized current output will be $_____ bil. Mark this point A_1 in Fig. 6-1. This level of income, however, actually results in $_____ bil of consumption expenditure, rather than the estimated $_____ bil. The current production rate of consumption goods cannot meet this unexpected demand. The excess demand is filled by drawing down consumption goods inventories in the amount of $_____ bil. Total expenditures for the current time period are $_____ bil. Mark this point A_2. It should be noted that the national income accountant will find that the income generated in producing the inventory goods now included in consumption expenditures occurred in (the current, a previous) time period and (does, does not) show up in the current level of income.

8 For the current time period, income is $750 bil and realized consumption expenditure is $650 bil, so that realized saving is $_____ bil. Since expenditures on the investment goods categories other than inventories—producers' durable equipment, residential and commercial construction—is $250 bil, and there is realized inventory (investment, disinvestment) of $_____ bil, net realized total investment for the period is $_____ bil. Realized saving (is, is not) equal to realized investment.

9 Under the conditions described in paragraph 7, aggregate demand is (greater than, equal to, less than) aggregate current output. The shortfall in output, resulting in unintended inventory disinvestment A_1A_2, will lead to a(n) (upward, downward) adjustment of production plans. Consequently, income in subsequent time periods will (rise, fall, not be affected).

10 Now assume that firms initially estimate that total sales will be $1,500 bil in the next period, and they base employment and production rates on this estimate. Total current output in that period will be $_____ bil and total income will be $_____ bil. Mark this point B_1 in Fig. 6-1. Total intended expenditures for the current time period will be $_____ bil. Mark this point B_2. Current output is (greater than, less than, equal to) intended expenditures. If investment expenditures are unchanged (see paragraph 7), realized consumption expenditures will be (greater than, less than) expected by producers in the amount of $_____ bil. This result will lead to (intended, unintended) inventory (investment, disinvestment) of $_____ bil, which is equal to the (excess, shortfall) of output over expenditures. This amount is equal to the distance _____ in Fig. 6-1.

Thus, income in subsequent time periods will (rise, fall, remain constant), due to a(n) (upward, downward) adjustment of production plans. By how much, if any, will income ultimately change when income returns to the equilibrium level? ($_____bil)

11 Under the conditions stated in paragraph 10, when income is $1,500 bil, realized saving will be $_____bil. Since realized inventory (investment, disinvestment) is $_____bil and sales of other investment goods were assumed to equal $250 bil, net realized total investment for the period is $_____bil. Realized saving (is, is not) equal to realized investment.

12 Now examine the equilibrium point, where $Y = C + I$ intersects $C + I$. The amount of unintended inventory investment at E is $_____bil. Consequently, for the conditions given in Fig. 6-1, income (will, will not) change in subsequent time periods. (If necessary, refer back to paragraph 6 above.) At point E, realized saving of $_____bil (is, is not) equal to realized investment of $_____bil.

Equilibrium income (will, will not necessarily) be the full employment level for an economy; thus it (must, may not) be the socially desirable level of income.

13 On the basis of the results in paragraphs 7 and 9 above, we can generalize that when expenditures actually made are greater than the expenditures expected by producers, income will (rise, fall); realized positions which exceed intentions will result in a (rise, fall) in income. On the basis of paragraphs 8, 11, and 12, realized investment (often, always, never) equals realized saving, but only at equilibrium income will realized positions equal intended positions.

14 The model developed in the early part of this exercise, utilizing the aggregate demand approach to explain the determination of aggregate income, is called a *total expenditure* model. An alternative model can be developed which concentrates on the factors that determine equilibrium income. In paragraph 7 above, businessmen *underestimated* intended expenditures for consumption goods by $150 bil. Since there are only two ways to dispose of income, spend it or save it, we could alternatively say that businessmen *overestimated* intended saving by $150 bil. Saving is a withdrawal or spending *leakage* from the income stream. In Fig. 6-1, what is the level of intended consumption expenditure when income is $750 bil? $_____bil. This amount is determined by the _____ _____sector. Mark this point A_3 on the C_1 line. The distance _____ measures the intended spending leakage (saving) at this income level. The intended spending injection (investment), however, equals the distance _____. This amount is determined by the _____ sector. At an income level of $750 bil, therefore, intended injections are (greater than, less than, equal to) intended leakages.

At an income level of $1,500 bil, the converse is true—intended saving is *underestimated*. In Fig. 6-1, for an income level of $1,500 bil, mark intended consumption point B_3. Intended leakages equal the distance _____, while intended injections are

_____; intended injections are (greater than, less than, equal to) intended leakages.

The equilibrium income of $1,050 bil is divided between consumption-good expenditures of $800 bil and investment-good expenditures of $250 bil. In equilibrium, the

spending leakage of $_____ bil is exactly balanced by the spending injection of

$_____ bil.

15 From the discussion in paragraph 14 above, we can conclude that an equality between intended leakages from and intended injections into the income stream is an alternative way of stating the equilibrium income condition. The equilibrium condition equation

for the total expenditure model was given as _____. We can rearrange this equation in the following way:

(5) $Y - C = I$

But since we defined saving S as $Y - C$, the left side of Eq. (5) is equal to _____

_____. Thus, by substituting the term S for the term $Y - C$, we can rewrite the equilibrium condition as

(6)   _____

According to Eq. (6), the economy is in equilibrium when intended saving S is equal to intended investment I.

16 In Fig. 6-2, construct an intended saving function from the information in Fig. 6-1. Label it S. (If necessary, refer back to Exercise 5, paragraphs 5 to 7.) Now plot the

investment function in Fig. 6-2 and label it I. These functions intersect at $Y = $_____ bil, which (is, is not) equal to equilibrium income in Fig. 6-1. Mark the equilibrium point E. The model shown in Fig. 6-2 is known as a *leakage-injection* model.

17 At income level $750 bil, mark intended saving A_1 and intended investment A_2. The distance A_1A_2 represents the (excess, shortfall) of intended injections relative to

intended leakages. This distance is identical to the distance _____ in Fig. 6-1. This condition results in (intended, unintended) inventory (investment, disinvestment) at $Y = $750 bil. As a result, the shortfall in output will lead to a(n) (upward, downward) adjustment of production plans. Income in subsequent time periods will (rise, fall, not be affected).

At an income level of $1,500 bil, mark intended saving B_1 and intended investment B_2. As a result of the (excess, shortfall) of intended injections relative to intended leakages—distance B_1B_2—income in subsequent time periods will (rise, fall, not be affected).

18 Using the values assumed in paragraph 2 above, we can summarize the elements of this simple two-sector leakage-injection model in the following way:

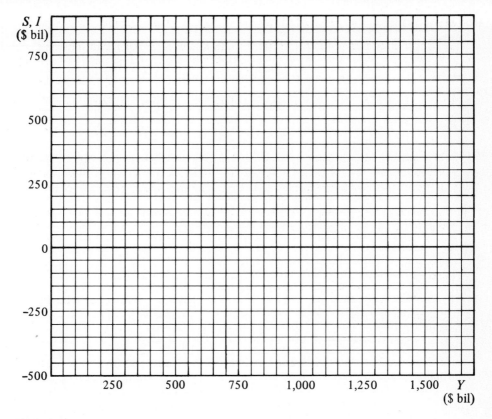

FIGURE 6-2

(6) $S = I$

(7) $S = -\$275 \text{ bil} + 0.50Y$

(3) $I = \$250 \text{ bil}$

PROBLEMS FOR EXERCISE 6

1 $C_1 = \$150 \text{ bil} + 0.50Y$

   $I_1 = \$250 \text{ bil}$

Plot the above equations in Fig. 6-3 for a total expenditure model. Label all axes and functions.

2 The equilibrium condition equation for this model is _____

_____ .

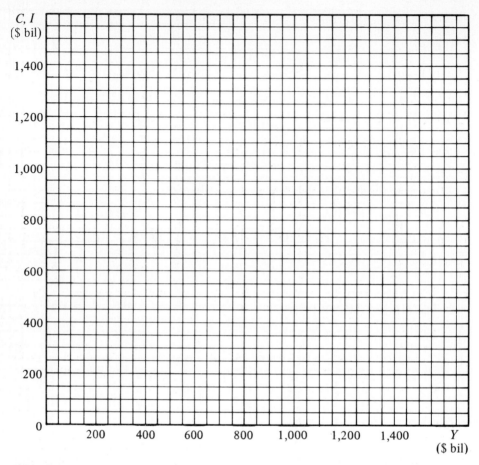

FIGURE 6-3

3 Label the equilibrium income and consumption points as Y_e and C_e respectively.

4 $Y_e = \$$_____ bil, $C_e = \$$_____ bil

5 Now assume that intended consumption increases by \$175 bil for all income levels. The MPC remains unchanged. The new consumption and total expenditure equations are

$$C_2 = \underline{\hspace{8cm}}$$

$$C_2 + I_1 = \underline{\hspace{7cm}}$$

Plot the new curves in Fig. 6-3 and label them properly.

6 Assume that businessmen do not correctly forecast this increase in intended consumer demand, but instead base their next-period production plans on the current aggregate demand level of $C_1 + I_1$. Compute the following amounts for the next time period:

Output . . . . $____bil

Income . . . . $____bil

Total intended expenditures . . . . $____bil

Intended consumption expenditures . . . . $____bil

Businessmen's expectations of consumption expenditures . $____bil

Unintended change in consumption goods inventories . . . $____bil

7 Label the new equilibrium income and consumption points to which the economy will move as Y'_e and C'_e respectively. At this new equilibrium position, the unintended change in consumption-good inventories is $____bil at Y'_e.

8 Using the information given in paragraph 1 above, now construct a leakage-injection model in Fig. 6-4. Label all axes and functions.

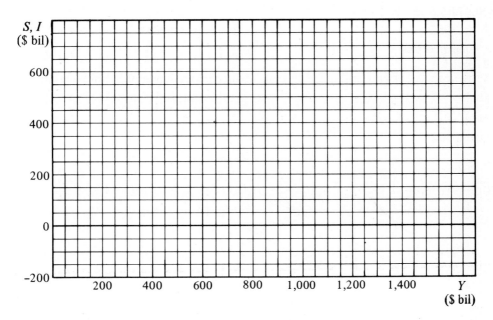

FIGURE 6-4

9 The equilibrium condition for the leakage-injection model is _____ .

10 Label the equilibrium income point as Y_e.

11 Y_e = \$_____ bil, C_e = \$_____ bil, S_e = \$_____ bil.

12 Now assume that intended investment increases by \$175 bil for all income levels. Demonstrate this change in Fig. 6-4. Label the new investment curve I_2 and equilibrium income as Y'_e.

13 As a result of an (autonomous, induced) increase in intended consumption expenditures of \$175 bil in paragraph 5, equilibrium income increased by \$_____ bil. (For a review of autonomous and induced changes, see Exercise 4, paragraph 6.) As a result of an (autonomous, induced) increase in intended investment expenditures of \$175 bil in paragraph 12, equilibrium income increased by \$_____ bil. Thus, we can conclude that, in the simple model presented here, equivalent changes in either autonomous

_____ or _____

expenditures lead to _____ changes in equilibrium income. The change in income, however, was (greater than, less than, equal to) the initial change in autonomous expenditures. This result is called a multiplier effect, the topic of Exercise 7.

ANSWERS FOR EXERCISE 6

1 consumption, investment, disposable income, depreciation and the government and foreign sectors
2 intended
3 Fig. 6-1A, no, the C function is a schedule of intended consumption expenditures for

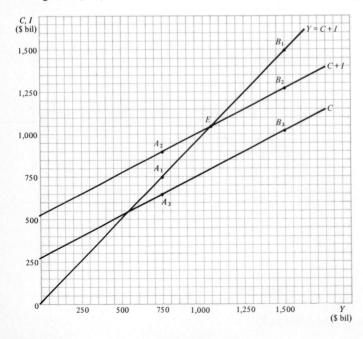

FIGURE 6-1A

all possible income levels but we cannot know the specific current consumption level until we find the current income level

4 $525 bil + 0.50 Y, Fig. 6-1A, parallel, is, does not, 250, investment

5 straight, positive, 1, Fig. 6-1A, income, intended, equilibrium, equilibrium, $Y = C + I$, $C + I$, higher, does

7 750, 650, 500, 105, 900, a previous, does not

8 100, disinvestment, 150, 100, is

9 greater than, upward, rise

10 1,500, 1,500, 1,275, greater than, less than, 225, unintended, investment, 225, excess, $B_1 B_2$, fall, downward, 450

11 475, investment, 225, 475, is

12 0, will not, 250, is, 250, will not necessarily, may not

13 rise, fall, always

14 650, personal, $A_1 A_3$, $A_2 A_3$, business, greater than, $B_1 B_3$, $B_2 B_3$, less than, 250, 250

15 $Y = C + I$, saving S, $S = I$

16 Fig. 6-2A, 1,050, is

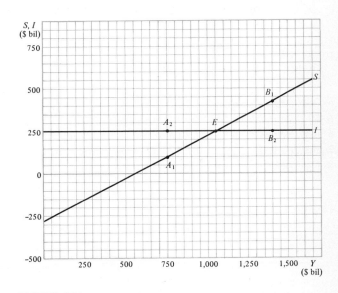

FIGURE 6-2A

17 Fig. 6-2A, excess, $A_1 A_2$, unintended, disinvestment, upward, rise, shortfall, fall

ANSWERS TO PROBLEMS FOR EXERCISE 6

1 Fig. 6-3A

2 $Y = C + I$

3 Fig. 6-3A

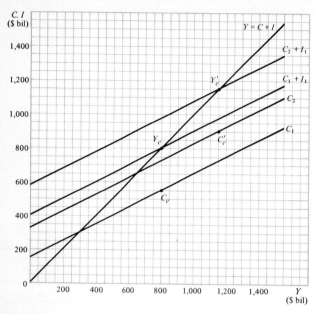

FIGURE 6-3A

4 800, 550
5 $325 bil + 0.50Y, $575 bil + 0.50Y, Fig. 6-3A
6 800, 800, 975, 725, 550, −175
7 Fig. 6-3A, 0
8 Fig. 6-4A

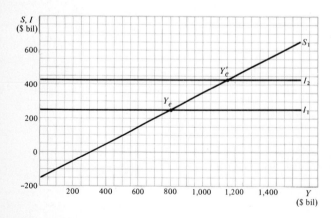

FIGURE 6-4A

9 $S = I$
10 Fig. 6-4A

11 800, 550, 250

12 Fig. 6-4A

13 autonomous, 350, autonomous, 350, consumption, investment, equivalent, greater than

THE INVESTMENT MULTIPLIER

1 Assume that the following equations are representative for an economy: $S_1 = -\$100$ bil $+ 0.50Y$; $I_1 = \$250$ bil. These equations are graphed in Fig. 7-1. As a result, $Y_e =$

$_____$bil. Mark the equilibrium point E_1. Assume that investment now permanently increases to \$500 bil. Graph the new investment equation in Fig. 7-1 and label it I_2. Y_e

has increased to \$$_____$bil. Mark the new equilibrium point E_2. Thus, for a change

in investment ΔI of \$$_____$bil, income changed ($\Delta Y$) in the (same, opposite) direction

by \$$_____$bil. ΔY is (greater than, less than, equal to) ΔI. This result is called a *multiplier* effect. Mark with an A the point on the I_2 curve directly above E_1. Designate the distance $E_1 A$ as ΔI. On the I_1 curve, mark with a B the point directly below E_2.

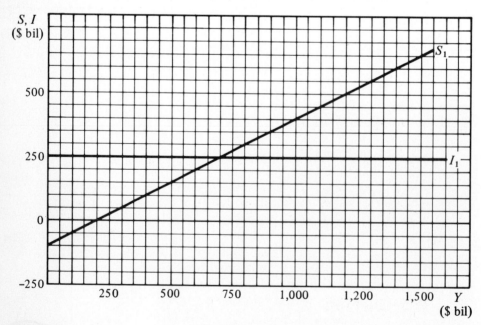

FIGURE 7-1

Designate the distance E_1B as ΔY. The distance E_1B or ΔY is _____(how many?) times greater than E_1A or ΔI. The value of this multiplier effect is ($\Delta C/\Delta Y$, $\Delta I/\Delta Y$, $\Delta Y/\Delta I$). In this example, the multiplier value is _____. Since it was the initial change in (C, I, S) which led to ΔY, the multiplier value associated with this change in income is called the *investment multiplier*.

2 The general form of the equations which comprise the (total expenditure, leakage-injection) model used above can be stated algebraically as follows:

(1) $S = I$

(2) $S = -a + (1 - b)\, Y$

(3) $I = I_O$

Equation (1) is the _____ condition. Equations (2) and (3) describe intended _____ and

_____ behavior. The coefficient of Y in Eq. (2), $1 - b$, is the (MPC, MPS, multiplier). The term I_O in Eq. (3) signifies that investment spending is autonomously determined.

In order to solve algebraically for equilibrium income, we must substitute Eq(s). (1, 2, 3) into Eq(s). (1, 2, 3), forming the following equation:

(4)   _____ = _____

Now transpose the a term to the right-hand side

(5)   _____ = _____

Now divide both sides of the equation by the term $1 - b$

(6)   _____ = _____

Equation (6) is the formula for equilibrium Y. We can rearrange Eq. (6) in the following way:

(7) $Y = \dfrac{1}{(1 - b)}\, (a + I_O)$

3 In our initial example, the values for the right-hand variables in Eq. (7) were $a =$

_____ ; $b =$ _____ ; $I =$ _____ .

By substituting these values into Eq. (7), we get

(7) $Y = \dfrac{1}{(1 - b)}\, (a + I_O)$

$Y = \dfrac{1}{(1 - 0.5)}\, (\$100\ \text{bil} + \$250\ \text{bil})$

$Y = 2(\$350\ \text{bil})$

$Y = \$700\ \text{bil}$

The value of equilibrium income is (identical to, different from) our graphical solution in Fig. 7-1. The term $1/(1-b)$ is equal to the _____ value computed in paragraph 1. The term in the denominator of the multiplier, $1-b$, is equal to the (MPC, MPS, induced I). We can alternatively state the multiplier as ($1/$MPS, $1-$MPS, $1/$MPC). Thus, the multiplier value is the reciprocal of the MPS. Equation (7) states that Y_e is equal to the _____ X

_____ expenditures.

4 We can rearrange Eq. (7) by multiplying the term $1/(1-b)$ by each of the autonomous expenditure variables, as follows:

$$(8) \qquad Y = \frac{1}{1-b} a + \frac{1}{1-b} I_o$$

In Eq. (8) we see that the *level of* income is determined by two components,

_____ and _____. Each component is the product of the multiplier term, $1/(1-b)$, and an autonomous expenditure variable. A *change in* equilibrium income can result from a change in the values of (a, b, I_o). If we assume that b, the MPC, is constant, the multiplier term $1/(1-b)$ (is, is not) a constant. Then ΔY can be caused by Δa or ΔI. This condition can be expressed as follows:

$$(9) \qquad \Delta Y = \frac{1}{1-b} \Delta a + \frac{1}{1-b} \Delta I_o$$

Equation (9) is the formula for *changes in* the level of equilibrium income.

5 We can use Eq. (9) to compute the change in income for a $250 bil increase in investment.

$$(9) \qquad \Delta Y = \frac{1}{1-b} \Delta a + \frac{1}{1-b} \Delta I_o$$

Now insert the values for Δa, ΔI, and b.

$$\Delta Y = \frac{1}{1-0.5} 0 + \frac{1}{1-0.5} \$250 \text{ bil}$$

$$\Delta Y = 0 + 2 (\$250 \text{ bil})$$

$$\Delta Y = \$500 \text{ bil}$$

The value of the change in income computed from Eq. (9) is (identical to, different from) our graphical solution in Fig. 7-1.

6 From Eq. (7), we found that $Y_e = \$$_____ bil. From Eq. (9), we found that $\Delta Y = \$$_____ bil. Thus, the new equilibrium income level $Y_e{}'$ will be $_____ bil. $Y_e{}'$ (does, does not) correspond to our graphical solution in Fig. 7-1. We can summarize the above relationship between *levels of* and *changes in* equilibrium income in the following way:

(10) $Y_e' = Y_e + \Delta Y$

7   Let us now examine the logic behind the multiplier concept. The existence of the multiplier effect is due to the nature of the circular flow process described in Exercise 2. For example, the increase in autonomous investment spending shown above initially causes an equivalent increase in income because this higher demand level leads to increased production and employment. This rising income, however, *induces* additional (consumption, investment) spending. Given that the consumption function is $C = a + bY$, and that a and b do not change, the induced consumption expenditure effect can be expressed as follows:

(11) $\Delta C = b \Delta Y$

Equation (11) states that any change in income causes a change in consumption expenditures in the (same, opposite) direction. The higher consumption-goods demand leads to a further increase of production, employment, *and* income, and thus expenditure-income expansion is repeated through further "rounds" in the circular flow. The increase in income (does, does not) lead to an equivalent increase in consumption spending. If the MPC is 0.75, then according to Eq. (11), a $1 bil change in income will lead to a

$_____$change in consumption spending. Thus, in this "round,"

$_____$ of income is drained off into saving. The rate at which income drains into saving is called the (MPC, MPS, multiplier). From our discussion in paragraph 3 above, we saw that the value of the multiplier was determined by the reciprocal of the MPS. Thus, for a given change in autonomous expenditures, the size of the MPS—the spending leakage rate in our model—controls how large the ultimate multiplier effect on income will be. As the value of the MPS increases, the value of the multiplier (increases, decreases).

8   The total amount of ΔY is thus determined by two factors, the amount of the initial change in spending—the (autonomous, induced) effect on income—and the MPS, which determines the size of the (autonomous, induced) effect on income. The autonomous and induced expenditure effects on changes in total income can be demonstrated in the following way:

(12) $\Delta Y = \Delta I + \Delta C$

where ΔI is autonomous expenditure and ΔC is induced expenditure. But Eq. (11) states that $\Delta C = b \Delta Y$, so that by substituting Eq. (11) into Eq. (12) we get

(13) $\Delta Y = $ _____

Now transpose all ΔY terms to the left-hand side:

(14)   _____ = _____

Factor out ΔY:

(15)   _____ = _____

Divide both sides by $(1 - b)$:

(16) $\Delta Y = \underline{\hspace{5cm}} = \dfrac{1}{1-b} \, \Delta I$

Equation (13) demonstrates that the total ΔY can be divided into an autonomous and an induced effect. Equation (16) shows that the sum of these two expenditure effects produces the total ΔY, which is a multiple of the initial ΔI. If the MPC = 0, then according to Eq. (13) the induced effect on income would be \$_____ bil. As the MPC increases, the induced effect on income (increases, decreases).

PROBLEMS FOR EXERCISE 7

1 Use the following equations to derive the algebraic expression of the equilibrium income level

(17) $Y = C + I$

(18) $C + a + bY$

(19) $I = I_O$

(20) $Y_e = \underline{\hspace{6cm}}$

Equation (20) is identical to Eq(s). (6, 7, 8) in Exercise 7. The (total expenditure, leakage-injection) model presented above yields an equilibrium income equation derived from the leakage-injection model in Exercise 7.

2 For questions 2 to 5, assume that the following values are representative for an economy: $a = \$75$ bil; $b = 0.75$; $I = \$125$ bil.

$Y_e = \$$_____ bil $C_e = \$$_____ bil $I_e = \$$_____ bil

Now assume that the level of investment expenditure permanently increases to \$200 bil. As a result, income increases by \$_____ bil, consumption expenditure increases by \$_____ bil, and the MPC (increases, decreases, remains constant). The induced expenditure effect on the change in income is \$_____ bil, which is equal to (ΔY, ΔI, ΔC). If the investment expenditure level decreases by \$75 bil, income would (increase, decrease) by \$_____ bil. The value of the multiplier in this example is _____. Its value depends on (MPS, Y, ΔY).

3 If autonomous consumption expenditures increase by \$75 bil, the change in income will be (greater than, less than, equal to) that in the case where investment increased by \$75 bil. This result implies that the multiplier value associated with autonomous C is (equal to, different from) the investment multiplier.

4 If autonomous C increases by $50 bil and autonomous I decreases by $50 bil, Y_e changes by $_____ bil. If autonomous C increases by $50 bil and autonomous I decreases by $75 bil, Y_e changes by $_____ bil.

5 By how much would autonomous I have to increase in order for income to rise by $60 bil? $_____ bil. How much would autonomous C have to increase? $_____ bil.

6 Complete the following blanks:

MPC	MPS	Multiplier value
0.90	_____	_____
0.80	_____	_____
_____	0.25	_____
_____	0.40	_____
_____	_____	2
_____	_____	1

7 In order to test your understanding of the basic equations used for determining the *level of* and *changes in* equilibrium income, compute the following values in your head *without* referring to the text or your notes.

(A) a = $100 bil
 b = 0.50
 I = $100 bil

 Y = $_____ bil

(B) a = $125 bil
 MPS = 0.25
 I = $275 bil

 Y = $_____ bil

(C) a = $100 bil
 b = 0.75
 ΔI = $50 bil

 ΔY = $_____ bil

(D) a = $100 bil
 MPC = 0.80
 I = $150 bil
 ΔI = $50 bil

 ΔY = $_____ bil

(E) a = $50 bil
 b = 0.90
 I = $150 bil
 Δa = $30 bil

 ΔY = $_____ bil

 ΔC = $_____ bil

(F) Δa = $25 bil
 ΔI = –$35 bil
 b = 0.80

 ΔY = $_____ bil

(G) $a = \$80$ bil
    $(1 - b) = 0.25$
    $\Delta Y = \$100$ bil

    $\Delta I = \$$_____ bil

ANSWERS FOR EXERCISE 7

1   700, Fig. 7-1A, 1,200, 250, same, 500, greater than, Fig. 7-1A, 2, $\Delta Y / \Delta I$, 2, I

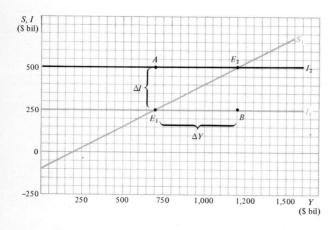

FIGURE 7-1A

2   leakage-injection, equilibrium, saving, investment, MPS, 2 and 3, 1, $-a + (1 - b)Y = I_O$, $(1 - b)Y = a + I_O$, $Y = (a + I_O)/(1 - b)$
3   $100 bil, 0.50, $250 bil, identical to, multiplier, MPS, 1/MPS, multiplier, autonomous
4   $1/(1 - b)a$, $1/(1 - b)I_O$, a or b or I_O, is
5   identical
6   700, 500, 1,200, does
7   consumption, same, does not, 750 mil, 250 mil, MPS, decreases
8   autonomous, induced
   (13) $\Delta Y = \Delta I + b\Delta Y$
   (14) $\Delta Y - b\Delta Y = \Delta I$
   (15) $\Delta Y(1 - b) = \Delta I$
   (16) $\Delta Y = \Delta I/(1 - b)$
   0, increases

ANSWERS TO PROBLEMS FOR EXERCISE 7

1 $Y_e = 1/(1 - b)a + 1/(1 - b)I_0$, 6, 7, and 8, total expenditure
2 800, 675, 125, 300, 225, remains constant, 225, ΔC, decrease, 300, 4, MPS
3 equal to, equal to
4 0, −100
5 15, 15
6

MPC	MPS	Multiplier value
0.90	0.10	10
0.80	0.20	5
0.75	0.25	4
0.60	0.40	2.5
0.50	0.50	2
0.00	1.00	1

7 (A) 400; (B) 1,600; (C) 200; (D) 250; (E) 300, 300; (F) −50; (G) 25

FACTORS AFFECTING THE LEVEL OF
AGGREGATE CONSUMPTION

1 Aggregate consumption functions estimated for short-run periods of time reveal that the consumption-income relationship is of the general form

(1) $\quad C = a + bY_d$

where Y_d represents disposable income (DPI). Recall that Exercises 4 to 7 assumed that $Y = Y_d$ because the government sector was not yet introduced. That simplifying assumption is no longer necessary.

For example, the following statistical consumption function was estimated for the time period 1946–57 (1954 dollars)[1] :

(1a) $\quad C = \$186.3 \text{ bil} + 0.81\,Y_d$

But when aggregate consumption data are plotted against aggregate disposable income for longer periods of time, the consumption function approaches the form

(2) $\quad C = bY_d$

where the value of b, the MPC, is approximately 0.9. We can consider Eqs. (1) and (1a) (short-run, long-run) functions, while Eq. (2) is a _____ function.

2 Equations (1) and (2) are graphed in Fig. 8-1 for the following hypothetical relationships: $C_{s_1} = \$60 \text{ bil} + 0.5Y_d$ and $C_L = 0.8Y_d$. The short-run and long-run functions are labeled C_{s_1} and C_L respectively. Complete Table 8-1, using these functions.

3 The ratio of consumption to income (C/Y_d), computed in columns 3 and 6 of Table 8-1, is called the *average propensity to consume* (APC). The APC indicates that, for the C_L function, the percentage of disposable income that is consumed (increases, decreases, does not change) as income increases. Thus, we can say that (short-run, long-run) consumption expenditures are (proportional, nonproportional) to disposable income.

4 For the C_{s_1} function, the APC (increases, decreases, does not change), whereas C_L

[1] Gardner Ackley, *Macroeconomic Theory*, New York: The Macmillan Company, 1961, p. 252.

Table 8-1 Hypothetical Data on Income and Consumption

(1)	(2)	(3)	(4)	(5)	(6)	(7)
Income ($ bil)	C_{S_1} ($ bil)	$(C/Y_d)_{S_1}$	$(S/Y_d)_{S_1}$	C_L ($ bil)	$(C/Y_d)_L$	$(S/Y_d)_L$
$200	$_____	_____	_____	$_____	_____	_____
$400	$_____	_____	_____	$_____	_____	_____
$600	$_____	_____	_____	$_____	_____	_____

suggests that, in the long run, there is (a, no) tendency for the proportion of income saved to increase at higher income levels.

5 Since the equations in Fig. 8-1 are representative of actual statistical functions in the United States, we can conclude that the basic consumption-saving behavior is related to disposable income, but that other factors have important short-run effects. According to Fig. 8-1, as disposable income increases from $200 bil to $400 bil, in the short-run aggre-

gate consumption will rise from $_____ bil to $_____ bil. Thus, consumers initially react to a change in income by moving along consumption function (C_{S_1}, C_L). But, as the length of period studied increases, consumption expenditures eventually rise from

$_____ bil to $_____ bil at income level $400 bil.

6 A primary objective in macroeconomic analysis is to build a national income determination model for short-run forecasting and public policy purposes. Consequently, we need to know how consumption expenditures will change in the immediate future in response to changes in disposable income. For these purposes, the long-run time-series data (are, are not) suitable. Conversely, short-run statistical studies, relying only on disposable income, do not adequately explain short-run deviations from the long-run trend. Moreover, as the time period studied shortens, the explanatory importance of disposable income diminishes. Thus, we must introduce additional variables to more accurately forecast the short-run changes in the APC noted above.

7 There has been a recognizable tendency for the short-run consumption function to shift upward over time—a phenomenon known as "consumption drift." In Fig. 8-1 draw a new short-run consumption function that will be consistent with $C = \$320$ bil and $Y = \$400$ bil. Assume that the MPC remains constant. Label the new curve C_{S_2}. The C_{S_2} curve (is, is not) parallel to C_{S_1}. The shift from C_{S_1} to C_{S_2} resulted from a change in the (autonomous component, slope) of the consumption function, that is, a change in intended consumption caused by (income, factors other than income).

8 One approach to explaining "consumption drift" is to identify additional variables whose changes cause a systematic tendency for consumers to spend more out of a given

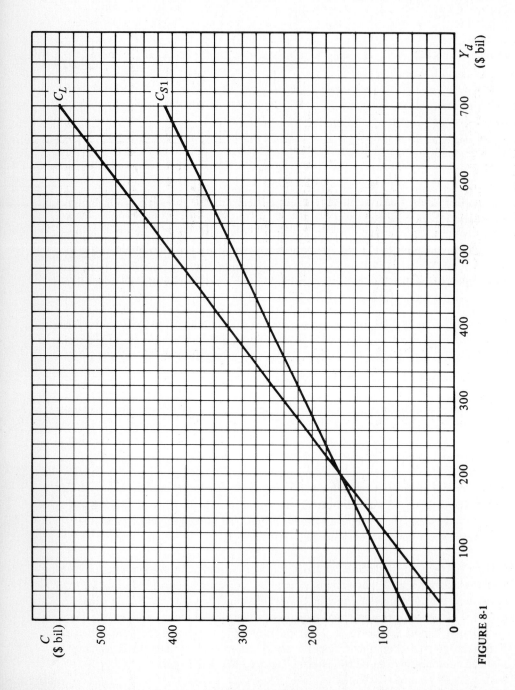

FIGURE 8-1

112

level of income as time passes. Wealth is a variable commonly used for this purpose. The use of wealth–actually net worth, not gross wealth–is justified on the ground that individuals plan their consumption expenditures partly on the basis of their *expectations* about the future, not only on the basis of current conditions. It would be most unusual if an individual's expected income corresponded every year to the amount he wanted and needed to spend. Peak spending years are not always the peak earning years. In order to obtain a more desirable consumption pattern over time, people find it useful to supplement low-income years by borrowing–or dissaving–and to put away surplus funds from high-income years. Naturally, the more wealth an individual currently owns, the more he can consume this year if he so desires.

The introduction of wealth provides a simple explanation of consumption drift. In the (short run, long run), wealth is constant and has no influence on (the level of, changes in) consumption expenditures. Only income is variable. In the long run, wealth increases, providing an additional source of funds for consumption changes. Thus, the short-run MPC is (smaller, larger) than the long-run MPC. If consumers tend to spend a constant proportion of their net worth, the constancy of net worth in the short run (does, does not) provide a constant term in the short-run consumption function. In the long run, when wealth is growing for the average person, there (is also a, is no) constant term.

9 Suppose that consumption depended on income and wealth as follows:

$$(3) \quad C = 0.6 Y_d + 0.05 W$$

where Y_d is current disposable income and W is net worth. Using Eq. (3), complete Table 8-2. Plot the data for aggregate consumption and income in Fig. 8-2 and label the function C_L. The equation for this "long-run consumption" function–as a function of disposable income–is

$$(4) \quad C_L = \underline{\hspace{4cm}}$$

Thus, although the MPC out of current disposable income in Eq. (3) is only 0.6, the effect of rising wealth over time on consumption increased the aggregate long-run MPC to 0.8. Thus wealth "explains" short-run changes in the APC.

10 The wealth effect can be illustrated in another way. Assume that the short run consumption function in the early 1950s is

$$(5) \quad C_{s_1} = \$75 \text{ bil} + 0.5 Y_d$$

Table 8-2 Hypothetical Data on Consumption, Income, and Wealth ($ bil)

Year	Disposable income	Wealth	Consumption
1953	$ 250	$1,000	$_____
1972	750	3,000	_____
1976	1,250	5,000	_____

Plot this equation in Fig. 8-2. If disposable income in 1953 is $250 bil, the C_{S_1} function will predict the same consumption level as the consumption function which explicitly introduced wealth as an explanatory variable of consumption—Eq. (3).

11   Assume that the procedure described in paragraph 10 is repeated for the early 1970s. That is, find a functional relationship between C and Y_d that will give the same C as Eq. (3) did for the data of 1972 in Table 8-2. Assume that the MPC is 0.5, as in paragraph 10. The short-run consumption function that is consistent with long-run behavior in 1972 is

(7) $C_{S_2} =$

Plot Eq. (7) in Fig. 8-2 and label it C_{S_2}.

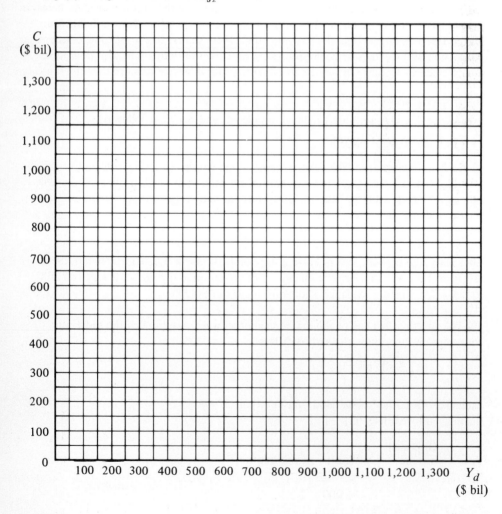

FIGURE 8-2

12 Repeat the step in paragraph 11 for the mid-1970s—i.e., 1976 in Table 8-2. Label the new curve C_{s_3}. Thus, the absolute income hypothesis (can, cannot) be made fully consistent with observed consumer behavior. In the short run, wealth is relatively constant, so that consumption varies with disposable income along the short-run function. Over the longer run, saving adds to wealth and causes the consumption function to shift upward, (raising, lowering) the APC above what the short-run consumption function would predict.

13 Another hypothesis of consumer behavior which is consistent with observed consumption-income data is the *relative income* hypothesis. One variation of this hypothesis, based on past living standards, proposes that the highest previous level of income is an important factor in consumer behavior. As income declines in the short run, consumers attempt to maintain their previous standard of living—i.e., consumption spending level— and sharply decrease saving to finance these expenditures. Subsequent increases in income are used by family units to replenish saving levels previously depleted. Once the highest previous income level is reached, the proportion of consumption out of further increases in income is restored to the customary long-run trend.

14 If the highest previous level of income is an important factor in consumer behavior, the consumption function might be modified as follows:

$$(8) \quad C_t = 0.6 Y_t + 0.2 Y_{max}$$

where C_t is aggregate consumption expenditures in the current time period, and Y_{max} is the highest previous disposable income level attained. Using Eq. (8), complete Table 8-3, column 3.

15 Plot each point in Table 8-3 on Fig. 8-3. Draw a small circle around the points where income declined from a previous high. Draw a line connecting all of the uncircled points. Do the uncircled points fall in a pattern? (yes, no)   If there is a pattern, what is it?

_____ .

If the economy has a general trend of income growth over time, the uncircled points represent (short-run, long-run) conditions.

16 The equation for the long-run consumption function is

$$(9) \quad C_t = \text{_____}$$

In Fig. 8-3 label the long-run consumption function C_L. If the economy experiences uninterrupted income growth, Y_{max} is always equal to (Y_t, Y_{t-1}), and Eq. (9) can be rewritten as

$$(10) \quad C_t = 0.6 Y_t + \text{_____} = \text{_____}$$

Thus, Eqs. (9) and (10) are identical under (short-run, long-run) income growth conditions.

17 Can you discern a pattern for the circled points? If so, what is it? _____

_____ . Connect the

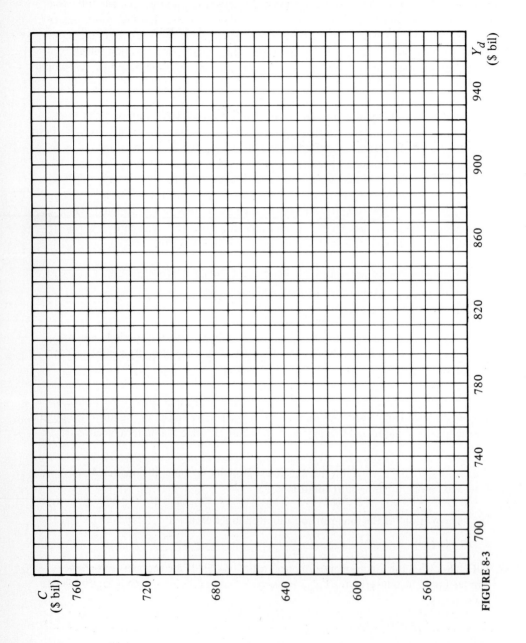

FIGURE 8-3

Table 8-3 Hypothetical Data on
Consumption and Income ($ bil)

Time period (1)	Disposable income (2)	Consumption	
		(3)	(4)
1	$700	$_____	$_____
2	740	_____	_____
3	780	_____	_____
4	800	_____	_____
5	760	_____	_____
6	740	_____	_____
7	780	_____	_____
8	820	_____	_____
9	860	_____	_____
10	900	_____	_____
11	840	_____	_____
12	800	_____	_____
13	860	_____	_____
14	900	_____	_____
15	940	_____	_____

circled points to show the pattern(s) they represent. Label these curves C_{S_1} and C_{S_2}. The short-run consumption functions are described by the equation

(11) $C_S =$ _____

18 The short-run functions produced by the relative income hypothesis are (similar to, different from) those produced by the wealth effect in the absolute income hypothesis.

19 An alternative theory, the *permanent income* hypothesis, can also explain consumption behavior over different time periods. This proposition contends that consumers base consumption and saving decisions on their expected level of long-run resources. Current consumption is based on "permanent" or *average-normal*, not current disposable income. "Transitory" or short-run deviations from "permanent" income do not greatly affect short-run consumption decisions.

20 Suppose that consumption depended on permanent income

$$(12) \quad C_t = 0.8 Y_p$$

where Y_p stands for permanent disposable income, and that consumers estimate permanent income by a weighted average of past incomes as follows:

$$(13) \quad Y_p = 0.75 Y_t + 0.25 Y_{t-1}$$

By substituting Eq. (13) into (12), the equation representing the relationship between consumption and income—past and present—is

$$(14) \quad C_t = \underline{\hspace{4in}}$$

21 Using Eq. (14), complete column 4 of Table 8-3. Plot the points in Fig. 8-4. Circle the points that do not represent an income maximum. Do the uncircled points fall into a

pattern? (yes, no) If so, what is it? _____

_____. If the economy has a general trend of long-run growth, the uncircled points represent (short-run, long-run) conditions. Label the long-run consumption function C_L.

22 Do the circled points fall in a pattern? (yes, no) This fact indicates that in the short run, according to the permanent income hypothesis, the consumption function and MPC are (stable, unstable).

23 Find the turning points—maximum and minimum incomes—in Table 8-3. The first change in income after the maximum or minimum produces a MPC that is (lower, higher) than is usual in the long run. This fact indicates that, at least in the beginning of a recession or a recovery, the permanent income hypothesis gives results that are (similar to, different from) (both, only) the (relative income hypothesis, the absolute income hypothesis with consumption drift characteristics).

PROBLEMS FOR EXERCISE 8

Figure 8-5 contains three consumption functions: OFJ, AFI, and BGJ. The following questions are based on these functions.

1 The MPC of OFJ is equal to (JZ/OZ, JI/FI, OJ/JZ).

2 At income level OZ, the APC of OFJ is equal to (JI/JZ, IZ/JZ, JZ/OZ).

3 The MPC (is, is not) equal to the APC for the consumption function OFJ.

4 The MPC of AFI is equal to (IZ/HZ, IH/OZ, FE/AE, IZ/OZ).

5 The APC of AFI is equal to (IZ/OZ at all levels of income, IZ/OZ only at income level OZ, IH/OZ only at income level OZ).

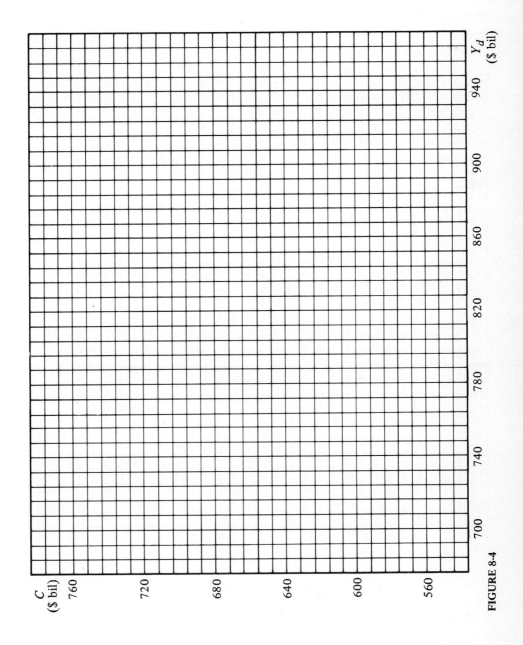

FIGURE 8-4

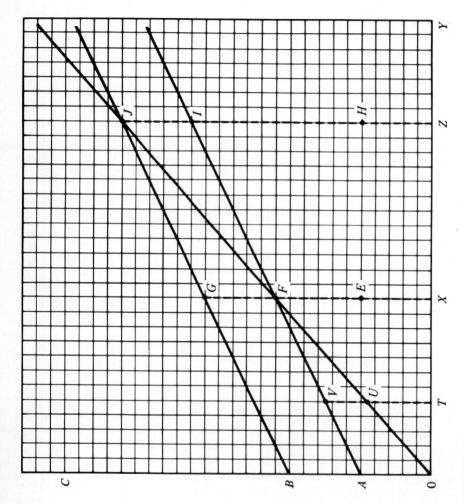

FIGURE 8-5

6 The MPC (is, is not) equal to the APC for the consumption function *AFI*.

7 The APC is a (constant, variable) for equation *AFI*; the APC is a (constant, variable) for equation *OFJ*.

8 The condition MPC = APC holds for equation (*OFJ*, *AFI*, both *OFJ* and *AFI*).

9 The MPC is (constant, variable) for *OFJ*: the MPC is (constant, variable) for *AFI*.

10 The MPC for *OFJ* is larger than the MPC for *AFI*. (true, false)

11 Suppose that national income has been at *OX* for a considerable period of time. Total consumption will likely be (*EX*, *FX*, *GX*).

12 Assume that the horizontal axis measures per capita income, not total income. If the average per capita income were *OX*, budget study data would probably indicate that an individual whose income was *OT* would probably consume (*OU*, *TU*, *TV*, none of these).

13 Following the assumptions in paragraph 12, an individual whose income was *OZ* would probably consume (*JZ*, *IZ*, *HZ*).

14 Following the assumptions in paragraph 12, if national income increased from *OX* to *OZ* in three months' time, total consumption would probably rise to (*JZ*, *IZ*, *HZ*, *FX*).

15 If national income increased from *OX* to *OZ* in three months' time and then remained at level *OZ* for two years, total consumption would probably then be (*JZ*, *IZ*, *HZ*, *FX*).

16 Consumption functions *AFI* and *BGJ* are (short-run, long-run) functions.

17 If total income had been at *OZ* for some time, an income decline to *OX* would probably cause consumption to fall to (*XG*, *XF*, *XE*). As a result, the aggregate APC will (increase, decrease).

18 A shift of the consumption function from *AFI* to *BGJ* could result from
  (a) a temporary increase in income
  (b) a permanent increase in income
  (c) an increase in wealth
  (d) an increase in taxes

ANSWERS FOR EXERCISE 8

1 short-run, long-run

2

(1)	(2)	(3)	(4)	(5)	(6)	(7)
$200	$160	8/10	2/10	$160	8/10	2/10
400	260	6.5/10	3.5/10	320	8/10	2/10
600	360	6/10	4/10	480	8/10	2/10

3 does not change, long-run, proportional

4 increases, no

5 160, 260, C_{S_1}, 260, 320

6 are not

7 Fig. 8-1A, is, autonomous component, factors other than income

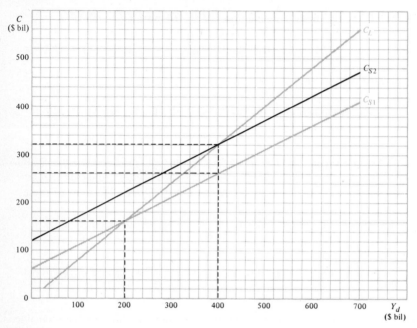

FIGURE 8-1A

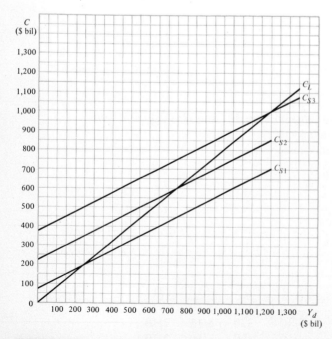

FIGURE 8-2A

8 short run, changes in, smaller, does, is no

9 200, 600, 1000, Fig. 10-2A, $0.8 Y_d$

10 Fig. 8-2A

11 $225 bil + $0.5 Y_d$, Fig. 8-2A

12 can, raising

14 —, 592, 624, 640, 616, 604, 628, 656, 688, 720, 684, 660, 696, 720, 752

15 Fig. 8-3A, yes, straight line with slope of 0.8, long-run

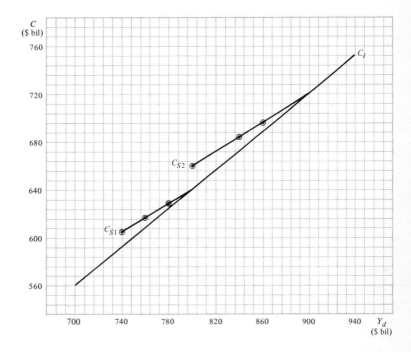

FIGURE 8-3A

16 $0.8 Y_d$, Y_t, $0.2 Y_t$, $0.8 Y_t$, long-run

17 yes, two parallel lines with slopes of 0.6, Fig. 8-3A, $0.6 Y_t + 0.2 Y_{max}$

18 similar to

20 $0.6 Y_t + 0.2 Y_{t-1}$, i.e.:

$C_t = 0.8 Y_p$ and
$Y_p = 0.75 Y_t + 0.25 Y_{t-1}$, so
$C_t = 0.8 (0.75 Y_t + 0.25 Y_{t-1})$
$C_t = 0.6 Y_t + 0.2 Y_{t-1}$

21 —, 584, 616, 636, 616, 596, 616, 648, 680, 712, 684, 648, 676, 712, 744, Fig. 8-4A, no (almost), not quite: all points but one fall on a straight line with slope of 0.8, long-run

22 no, unstable

23 lower, similar to, both, relative income hypothesis and the absolute income hypothesis with consumption drift characteristics

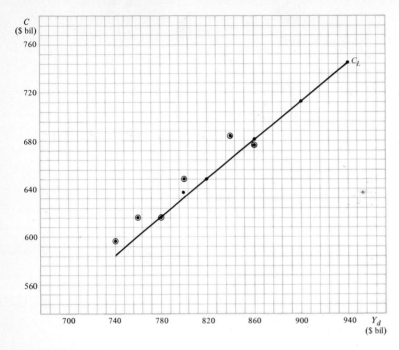

FIGURE 8-4A

ANSWERS TO PROBLEMS FOR EXERCISE 8

1 *JZ/OZ*
2 *JZ/OZ*
3 is
4 *IH/OZ* or *FE/AE*
5 *IZ/OZ* only at income level *OZ*
6 is not
7 variable, constant
8 *OFJ*
9 constant, constant
10 true
11 *FX*
12 *TV*
13 *IZ*
14 *IZ*
15 *JZ*
16 short-run
17 *XG*, increase
18 *b, c*

1 The slope of the consumption function measures the marginal propensity to consume (MPC).
(a) true
(b) false

2 The marginal propensity to consume is measured by the
(a) intercept of the consumption function
(b) ratio of C/Y
(c) slope of the consumption function
(d) ratio of $1/(1 - \text{MPC})$

3 If the MPC is a constant, then the consumption function will
(a) never shift
(b) be a straight line
(c) be a curved line
(d) intercept the vertical axis above zero

4 For a consumption function of the form $C = a + bY_d$, the MPC increases as disposable income increases.
(a) true
(b) false

5 For a consumption function of the form $C = a + bY_d$,
(a) the MPS is constant at all disposable income levels
(b) the a term is realized expenditures and the bY_d term is intended expenditures
(c) if disposable income is zero, consumption expenditures are zero
(d) an increase in the b term will increase consumption expenditures unless disposable income is zero

6 Autonomous consumption spending is
(a) directly related to disposable income
(b) inversely related to disposable income
(c) not related to disposable income
(d) a constant term which never changes

7 Intended consumption expenditures is an ex post concept.
(a) true
(b) false

8 A parallel upward shift of the consumption function represents an increase in the MPC.
(a) true
(b) false

9 An increase in consumption expenditures that is the result of an increase in income is
(a) an autonomous change in consumption
(b) an induced change in consumption
(c) represented by a shift of the consumption function
(d) represented by a movement along a consumption function

10 If a family spends $8,000 out of an annual disposable income of $10,000, its MPC is necessarily 0.8.
(a) true
(b) false

11 If disposable income increases from $800 bil to $850 bil and as a result, consumption expenditures increase by $40 bil, the change in consumption expenditures is
(a) an autonomous change
(b) an induced change
(c) an ex ante change
(d) none of these

12 Consumption expenditures from the national accounting data are
(a) intended consumption
(b) realized consumption
(c) potential consumption
(d) ex ante consumption

13 We may assume that disposable income Y_d and NNP Y are identical only if we simplify by assuming that there are no taxes or transfer payments,
(a) no corporate saving (retained earnings) and no business transfer payments
(b) total saving is zero and no business transfer payments
(c) no business sector and realized saving always equals realized investment
(d) no corporate saving (retained earnings) and capital consumption allowances are zero

14 The slope of the saving function can be measured by
(a) $(1 - MPS)$
(b) S/Y
(c) $\Delta S/\Delta Y$
(d) MPS
(e) none of these

15 When the MPC increases, the MPS also increases.
  (a) true
  (b) false

16 If the MPS increases
  (a) the MPC will increase
  (b) the MPC will decrease
  (c) autonomous consumption will decrease
  (d) consumption expenditures will likely decline
  (e) consumption expenditures will likely increase

17 If the MPS is constant
  (a) saving is constant at all income levels
  (b) saving is always positive
  (c) the same percentage will be saved of increments to income
  (d) saving as a percentage of income is approximately equal for different family-income classes

18 A decrease in the MPS is represented by a shift to a flatter curve.
  (a) true
  (b) false

19 For a consumption function of the form $C = a + bY_d$, it is possible for aggregate saving to be negative.
  (a) true
  (b) false

20 If the MPC is always constant, the MPS will
  (a) increase above "break-even" income
  (b) decrease above "break-even" income
  (c) always be constant
  (d) be indeterminate from the information given

21 If autonomous consumption expenditures increase,
  (a) autonomous saving will increase
  (b) autonomous saving will decrease
  (c) MPS will increase
  (d) MPS will decrease
  (e) consumption expenditures will rise

22 When the value of the MPC is 0.75, the
  (a) MPS is 0.75
  (b) MPS is 4.0
  (c) MPC is 4.0
  (d) MPS is 0.25
  (e) none of these

23 In the simple two-sector model—personal and business—if aggregate saving is zero, aggregate consumption must be
  (a) zero
  (b) less than income
  (c) equal to income
  (d) none of these

Answer questions 24 to 28 on the basis of Fig. A.

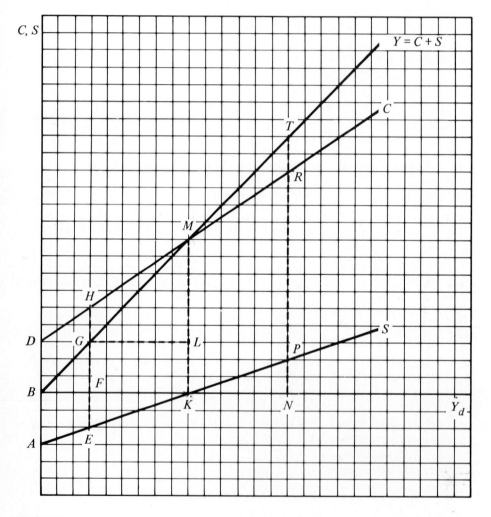

FIGURE A

24 At what disposable income level will aggregate saving be zero?
  (a) *B*
  (b) *F*

(c) K

(d) N

25 The MPS is measured on the graph as

(a) AB/AK

(b) NP/KN

(c) GH/GL

(d) ML/GL

(e) none of these

26 At disposable income level N

(a) intended saving is NP

(b) intended saving is PR

(c) intended consumption is KM

(d) intended saving is RT

(e) none of these

27 The MPC is measured on the graph as GH/GL.

(a) true

(b) false

28 The distances FH, KM, and NR all measure intended consumption expenditures.

(a) true

(b) false

29 An investment function of the form $I = \$140$ bil is interpreted to mean that intended investment expenditures are $140 bil at all income levels.

(a) true

(b) false

30 If realized saving is equal to realized investment, income must be in equilibrium.

(a) true

(b) false

31 The condition of equilibrium income in the simple two-sector model is met when

(a) realized saving equals realized investment

(b) intended saving equals intended investment

(c) full employment income is reached

(d) aggregate demand equals aggregate output

(e) consumption equals saving

32 A condition whereby intended investment exceeds intended saving will result in

(a) an inequality of realized saving and investment

(b) an increase in income in succeeding time periods

(c) aggregate demand exceeding aggregate output

(d) full employment eventually being reached

33 If we assume that consumption always equals $75 bil plus 60 percent of current income and investment is always $125 bil, equilibrium income in the two-sector model will be
(a) $200 bil
(b) $400 bil
(c) $500 bil
(d) $1,200 bil
(e) indeterminate

34 Assume that, under the assumptions of the two-sector model, investment expenditures permanently decline by $5 bil and the MPC is 0.6. As a result
(a) investment expenditures will decline by $12.5 bil
(b) consumption expenditures will decline by $12.5 bil
(c) income will decline by $12.5 bil
(d) consumption will decline by $7.5 bil
(e) income will temporarily decline by $5 bil, but will eventually return to the initial equilibrium level

35 In a simple two-sector model, if $C = \$60$ bil $+ 0.75\,Y$, an increase in investment of $5 bil will ultimately increase equilibrium *consumption* by
(a) $5 bil
(b) $15 bil
(c) $20 bil
(d) $25 bil
(e) indeterminate

36 Assume that $S = -\$80$ bil $+ 0.25Y$ and $I = \$70$ bil.
(a) Equilibrium income and saving are, respectively, $600 bil and $70 bil.
(b) Consumption expenditures are too high to maintain equilibrium income.
(c) Current consumption expenditures are $530 bil.
(d) Current period output must equal $600 bil.

37 Assume that $C = \$20$ bil $+ 0.8Y$, $I = \$120$ bil, and current period output is valued at $600 bil.
(a) Aggregate investment will likely increase in subsequent time periods.
(b) Unplanned inventory investment will likely rise.
(c) There is an excess of intended over actual expenditures.
(d) There is an excess of intended investment over intended saving.
(e) Aggregate saving will likely increase in subsequent time periods.

Answer questions 38 to 46, using Fig. B.

38 When $I = I_1$, equilibrium income is
(a) *OA*
(b) *OF*
(c) *OL*
(d) *FH*

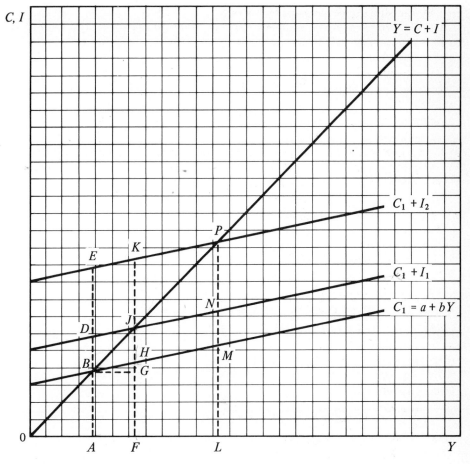

FIGURE B

39 When $I = I_1$, equilibrium consumption is
 (a) OA
 (b) AF
 (c) FH
 (d) FJ
 (e) GH

40 When $I = I_1$, dissaving will occur below income level
 (a) OA
 (b) OB
 (c) OC
 (d) AD
 (e) none of these

41 The MPC can be measured by the value of
    (a) *JF/AF*
    (b) *GH/BG*
    (c) *GJ/BG*
    (d) *BD/BG*
    (e) none of these

42 When $I = I_2$, equilibrium income is
    (a) *OA*
    (b) *OF*
    (c) *OL*
    (d) *LN*

43 When $I = I_2$, equilibrium consumption is
    (a) *LP*
    (b) *AB*
    (c) *FJ*
    (d) *LM*
    (e) *LN*

44 At income level *OL*, total investment is
    (a) *LM*
    (b) *MN*
    (c) *MP*
    (d) *NP*
    (e) *KP*

45 When $I = I_2$, total saving is
    (a) *LN*
    (b) *MN*
    (c) *MP*
    (d) *JP*
    (e) none of these

46 When $I = I_1$, if realized output is *OA*, unintended inventory investment is a minus
    (a) *AB*
    (b) *JK*
    (c) *DJ*
    (d) *BD*
    (e) none of these

47 Realized investment equals intended plus unintended investment.
    (a) true
    (b) false

48 When intended investment exceeds intended saving, the effect will be
   (a) an unintended accumulation of inventory investment
   (b) an eventual decrease in aggregate saving
   (c) a rise in income
   (d) none of these

49 Intended investment is that portion of output which is not consumed at the income
   level where aggregate demand equals aggregate supply.
   (a) true
   (b) false

50 If, during a given time period, there is an increase in *unintended* inventory investment,
   (a) aggregate saving will rise in subsequent time periods
   (b) the condition that realized saving equals realized investment will not be met
   (c) income will fall in subsequent time periods
   (d) income will rise in subsequent time periods

51 The existence of unintended inventory investment indicates that production and sales
   are not synchronized.
   (a) true
   (b) false

52 If unintended inventory investment is negative during a given time period, output will
   increase in subsequent time periods.
   (a) true
   (b) false

53 Assume that intended investment is $48 bil for plant and equipment and $2 bil for
   inventories. Intended consumption expenditures are $C = \$100$ bil $+ 0.8Y$. The
   current dollar value of output is $800 bil. Under these conditions
   (a) realized investment exceeds intended investment
   (b) the $800 bil represents a disequilibrium level of output
   (c) production equals sales
   (d) unintended inventory investment will be $10 bil for this time period
   (e) total inventory investment for the time period will be $12 bil

54 The full employment level of output must occur
   (a) at the intersection of the saving and investment lines
   (b) at the intersection of the $C + I$ and the $45°$ lines
   (c) when realized investment equals intended and unintended investment
   (d) all of these
   (e) none of these

55 As a result of a change in autonomous demand in the real world, the level of income
   usually adjusts immediately to the new equilibrium.
   (a) true
   (b) false

56 The value of the investment multiplier is equal to
(a) the MPC
(b) 1 − MPC
(c) the change in income divided by the change in investment
(d) the change in income divided by the change in consumption
(e) 1 − MPS

57 The value of the investment multiplier in a simple two-sector model is the reciprocal of the MPS.
(a) true
(b) false

58 If the value of the MPC is ½, the multiplier in the simple two-sector model will also be ½.
(a) true
(b) false

59 If the MPC is 0.75, the value of the investment multiplier in a simple two-sector model is
(a) ¼
(b) ¾
(c) 2
(d) 4
(e) 6

60 If intended investment expenditures change by $5 bil and, as a result, income changes by $20 bil, the investment multiplier is 4.
(a) true
(b) false

61 The additional rounds of spending and income get smaller and smaller in the multiplier process.
(a) true
(b) false

62 An increase in investment spending has a multiplied effect on income because the additional investment spending raises income, which, in turn, leads to additional consumption spending and thus further raises income.
(a) true
(b) false

63 A constant increase in intended saving at all levels of income will not decrease the size of the multiplier.
(a) true
(b) false

64 For a parallel shift upward of the consumption function, the value of the multiplier will increase.
   (a) true
   (b) false

65 If the consumption function does not shift, the multiplier process will not operate.
   (a) true
   (b) false

66 The larger the rate of leakage (MPS) from the circular income flow, the
   (a) smaller the multiplier
   (b) larger the multiplier
   (c) larger the MPC
   (d) greater the change in investment expenditures

67 Since, according to cross-sectional data, consumption increases more slowly than income at successively higher family income levels,
   (a) as aggregate income levels increase over time, the aggregate marginal propensity to consume will decline
   (b) aggregate consumption at all income levels will likely increase if income is redistributed toward lower income classes
   (c) these studies provide evidence that consumption expenditures are independent of "permanent" income
   (d) the short-run consumption function is more reliable for predictive purposes, since cross-sectional studies are more accurate than time-series studies

68 The long-run proportional consumption function derived from time-series data in the United States
   (a) can be consistent with a nonproportional consumption function that shifts upward over time
   (b) is probably misleading since cross-sectional data clearly show that the consumption function is of the form $C = a + bY_d$
   (c) suggests that the permanent income hypothesis is a more valid theory of consumer behavior than the relative income hypothesis
   (d) is approximately of the form $C = 0.9 Y_d$

69 The nonproportional consumption function $C = a + bY_d$ predicts that
   (a) saving will be zero at some income level
   (b) consumption will be zero at some income level
   (c) the average propensity to consume C/Y will be constant as disposable income changes
   (d) increases in disposable income will result in increases in aggregate saving
   (e) the MPC is constant

70 The relative income hypothesis of consumer behavior predicts that two families with similar incomes
   (a) will have the same relative levels of consumption expenditures

(b) may have dissimilar consumption levels if the average incomes in their neighbor-hoods are significantly different

(c) may have different consumption levels if one family was accustomed to higher consumption levels due to previously higher incomes

(d) who experience an unexpected increase in income will increase consumption proportionately to the level of income, but will change consumption expenditures nonproportionately if income unexpectedly declines

71 According to the relative income theory, aggregate consumption expenditures

    (a) depend on the absolute level of income except during time periods when income is rising relatively faster than the preceding period

    (b) are relatively constant if the changes in income are unexpected

    (c) are a higher percentage of income when income falls than when it rises

    (d) depend on current income and highest previous income

    (e) none of these

72 Under the relative income hypothesis, the empirical short-run and long-run consumption functions are reconciled by assuming that

    (a) increases in wealth have shifted the short-run consumption function upward over time

    (b) individuals base their consumption decisions on an estimate of life-cycle income, not current income

    (c) transitory changes in income have little effect on consumer expenditures

    (d) all of these

    (e) none of these

73 The permanent income hypothesis predicts that current consumption expenditures are partly determined by anticipated future income.

    (a) true

    (b) false

74 The permanent income hypothesis predicts that the MPC out of "transitory" income will be very high because such income is considered to be a "windfall" by families.

    (a) true

    (b) false

75 The permanent income hypothesis of consumer behavior predicts that

    (a) as current income increases, consumption will always increase proportionately

    (b) only permanent changes in income will change consumption proportionately

    (c) changes in current income will have large effects on a consumer's permanent income, but small effects on his consumption expenditures

    (d) consumption is related importantly to long-run consumption

76 The concept of permanent income

    (a) is the sum of "transitory" and "permanent" income

    (b) is conceptually measured by adjusting current income for "transitory" changes in income

    (c) can be estimated for measurement purposes as a weighted average of past and future income

    (d) is closer to average annual income for families with stable incomes than for families with variable incomes

    (e) assumes that individuals do make estimates of their future income

77 The permanent income theory predicts that an unexpected short-term decline in family income will

    (a) have little effect on consumption expenditures

    (b) lead to a large decrease in family saving

    (c) lead to a proportional increase in consumption expenditures

    (d) affect low-income families differently from middle- or high-income families

    (e) have similar but opposite effects for an unexpected short-term increase in family income

78 The long-run statistical consumption function can be explained by

    (a) the relative income hypothesis

    (b) the permanent income hypothesis

    (c) cross-section consumption data

    (d) changes in current disposable income

79 Both the permanent income and relative income theories

    (a) include wealth as an important determinant of consumption expenditures

    (b) include transitory income as the most important determinant of consumption expenditures

    (c) predict that the MPC *increases* as income increases past the highest previous income level

    (d) predict proportional long-run consumption functions for essentially *different* reasons

    (e) none of these

80 The absolute, relative, and permanent income hypotheses of consumer behavior help to explain the difference between cross-sectional and long-run consumption functions.

    (a) true

    (b) false

81 It is difficult to identify the "correct" factors accounting for consumer behavior because competing theories are consistent with data on observed behavior.

    (a) true

    (b) false

PART

INCOME DETERMINATION:
GOVERNMENT AND INVESTMENT

In this part we extend the study of the theory of income determination begun in Part 2. We will add the government-sector demand for goods and services (Exercise 9) and examine in more detail the determinants of business-sector investment demand (Exercises 10 and 11).

Spending and taxation decisions made by—or through—the federal, state, and local branches of government not only determine the public-private allocation of resources, but can also have an impact on the level of aggregate income. Taxation reduces aggregate demand of the personal and business sectors, transferring this purchasing power to the government sector. The displaced private spending can then be replaced by government spending.

In addition to the allocation of resources function, however, changes in the tax-expenditure process can alter aggregate demand, and thus employment and income. The set of budgetary adjustments made by the government sector which attempt to reach a full-employment, noninflationary income level is called *fiscal policy*.

Most theories proposed to explain investment expenditure begin with the hypothesis that investment occurs because a decision-maker wishes to eliminate the gap between the amount of capital he has—*actual* capital stock—and the amount he would like to have—*desired* capital stock. The theory then must explain the determination of the desired capital stock and the determination of the speed at which the gap is eliminated. The existence of a $1-bil gap does not necessarily produce $1 bil of investment spending in the same year; the gap might only be closed gradually over a period of several years. If that is the case, this year's gap will not produce an equal addition to this year's investment spending. In Exercises 10 and 11, however, the study of the investment problem is simplified by assuming that all gaps between desired and actual capital stock are eliminated in one year. This assumption reduces the problem of explaining investment spending for a particular year to one of explaining the desired capital stock for that year.

Two variables which are likely to affect the desired or "optimal" capital stock—and thus investment spending—are considered in this part. In Exercise 10 a model is used that assumes the interest rate has an inverse impact on investment: If the interest rate rises, the level of investment tends to fall. In Exercise 11 a model is used that assumes the size of the actual capital stock has an inverse impact on investment spending: the larger the actual capital stock with respect to a given level of output, the smaller the level of investment. The relationship between investment and the actual capital stock can be transformed to show that investment depends on the change of income, provided that the desired capital stock depends on the level of output (or income).

The theories described here, while reasonably realistic, abstract from a number of other factors which help to explain investment spending behavior. One of the more important of these factors is the assumption that the future returns of an investment are known with certainty. In reality, the future is always uncertain, and this uncertainty has important implications for behavior which are not explored here. Second, it is assumed that the prices of both the capital goods and the output they produce do not change. In reality, however, it is possible that so many firms will attempt to take advantage of investment opportunities that their efforts would raise the price of the capital goods and reduce the price of the output. Third, investment opportunities do not last forever. For simplicity, we assume that if, for example, a reduction of interest rates stimulated investment, the increased level of investment will last forever. This is not generally true. One by one, the newly profitable opportunities will be exhausted. A permanent stream of investment spending can exist only if new opportunities similar to the old ones are continuously generated. These three weaknesses of the theory point to the same conclusion: The theory of investment as described here makes the investment decision seem to be simpler and safer than it really is. As a result, we might be inclined to overestimate both the size and stability of investment spending.

Finally, it should be noted that the theory of investment presented in these exercises is not fully compatible with the Keynesian model being developed in the rest of the book. The major discrepancy is the assumption in the short-run Keynesian models that the capital stock is constant, despite continuous investment spending. Investment theory, we have seen, is based on the premise that investment occurs because firms wish to *change* the size of their capital stock. If the stock of capital is assumed not to change, it cannot enter into the investment decision. Hence, investment demand equations used in later parts will include only the interest rate as a determinant of investment.

THE GOVERNMENT SECTOR:
INCOME DETERMINATION AND FISCAL POLICY

1 The inclusion of the government sector in our model involves adding three variables, government spending G, taxes T and transfer payments Tr. For simplicity in presentation, let us initially assume that $Tr = 0$. Using the leakage-injection approach, we can state a simple three-sector model—personal, business and government—as follows:

(1) $S + T = I + G$

(2) $S = -a + s(Y - T)$

(3) $I = I_O$

(4) $G = G_O$

(5) $T = T_O$

In Eq. (1), S and T are both (leakage, injection) variables; I and G are both (leakage, injection) variables. Equation (1) is the _____ condition, and states that the economy is in equilibrium when (intended, realized) _____

_____ is/are equal to (intended, realized) _____.
   We can rearrange Eq. (1) as follows:

(6) $S - I = G - T$

The term $G - T$ represents the government budget. The equality $G = T$ (also must, need not) hold in order to satisfy the equilibrium condition. If, for example, G is greater than T, then in equilibrium S would have to (exceed, fall short of) I. Thus, a government budget deficit, $G > T$, must be "financed" by a private sector surplus, $S > I$.
   Equation (2) states that saving is a function of (net national, disposable) income. The

term $(Y - T)$ represents _____.
The coefficient of the disposable income variable s is the (MPC, MPS, multiplier). The value of s (is, is not) equal to the value of $(1 - b)$ used in Exercise 7. Equations (3), (4), and (5) state that I, G and T are autonomously determined.

2 In order to solve for equilibrium income, we must substitute Eq(s). $(1, 2, 3, 4, 5)$ into Eq(s). $(1, 2, 3, 4, 5)$, forming the following equation:

(7) _____ = _____

Multiply through to eliminate the parenthesis:

(8) _____ = _____

Now transpose the a, sT_O and T_O terms to the right-hand side:

(9) _____ = _____

Now divide both sides of Eq. (9) by the term s:

(10) _____ = _____

Equation (10) is the formula for equilibrium income for a simple three-sector model. We can rearrange Eq. (10) in the following way:

(11) $\quad Y = \dfrac{1}{s}\,(a - T_O + sT_O + I_O + G_O)$

The term $1/s$ is the _____ and is (the same as, different from) the multiplier value $1/(1 - b)$ derived in Exercise 7.

3 In Eq. (11) there are two terms which include the tax variable, T_O and sT_O. We can combine these two terms and factor out T_O as follows:

(12) $\quad -T_O + sT_O = 1 - s - T_O$

and since $1 - s = b$, we have

(13) $\quad -T_O + sT_O = -bT_O$

Substitute the term $-bT_O$ of Eq. (13) into Eq. (11):

(14) $\quad Y = \dfrac{1}{s}\,(a - bT_O + I_O + G_O)$

4 We can rearrange Eq. (14) by multiplying the term $1/s$ by each of the autonomous variables, as follows:

(15) $\quad Y = \dfrac{1}{s}\,a - \dfrac{b}{s}\,(T_O) + \dfrac{1}{s}\,I_O + \dfrac{1}{s}\,G_O$

Equation (15) demonstrates that the *level of* income is determined by the sum of the products of multiplier values and their respective autonomous components. If we assume that the marginal propensity to consume is constant, the multiplier term $1/s$ will (also, not necessarily) be constant. Hence, a *change in* equilibrium income can result from a change in which of the following values? (a, T_O, I_O, G_O) This relationship can be expressed as follows:

(16) $\quad \Delta Y = \dfrac{1}{s}\,\Delta a - \dfrac{b}{s}\,\Delta T + \dfrac{1}{s}\,\Delta I + \dfrac{1}{s}\,\Delta G$

Equation (16) is the formula for *changes in* the level of equilibrium income.

5 The tax multiplier, which essentially shows how income changes in response to a change in average tax rates ΔT is (larger, smaller) than the multiplier values associated with the other autonomous variables. This result derives from the fact that changes in taxes have an induced effect, but no autonomous effect on income. (For review of autonomous and induced effects, see Exercise 7, paragraph 7.) In the simple three-sector model, taxes affect income through its effect on _____ expenditures. Given the definition of disposable income

$$(17) \quad Y_d = Y - T$$

a $1 increase in taxes will lead to a ($1, less than $1) (increase, decrease) in disposable income. This relationship can be expressed as

$$(18) \quad \Delta Y_d = Y - \Delta T$$

But since the functional relationship between changes in consumption expenditures and changes in disposable income is

$$(19) \quad \Delta C = b \Delta Y_d$$

a $1 change in disposable income only changes consumption expenditures by $b \Delta Y_d$. If the MPC = 0.8, a $20 bil increase in taxes will initially (increase, decrease) consumption expenditures by $ _____ bil. Through the multiplier effect, the initial change in C will lead to a $ _____ bil (increase, decrease) in income. Thus the tax multiplier $\Delta Y / \Delta T =$ _____ . This value (is, is not) equal to b/s in Eq. (14). Alternatively, if autonomous G initially decreases by $20 bil, income will ultimately decline by $ _____ bil. The government expenditures multiplier $\Delta Y / \Delta G =$ _____ . This value (is, is not) equal to $1/s$ in Eq. (16). Hence, income changes by $ _____ bil more in the case of the autonomous ΔG, as compared to autonomous ΔT. This difference (is, is not) equal to the autonomous effect on income on ΔG.

6 The leakage-injection model presented in paragraph 1, including G and T, can be shown in graphical form by plotting the total leakage equation $S + T$ and the total injection equation $I + G$. The total leakage equation can be computed in the following way. Substitute Eqs. (2) and (5) into the left-hand side of Eq. (1)

$$(20) \quad S + T = \underline{\hspace{7cm}}$$

Multiply through to eliminate the parenthesis:

$$(21) \quad S + T = \underline{\hspace{7cm}}$$

Repeating the steps followed in paragraph 3, we can restate the terms T_O and $-sT_O$ as bT_O. By substituting the latter term into Eq. (21) and rearranging the order, we have

$$(22) \quad S + T = -a + bT_O + sY$$

The first two terms on the right-hand side of Eq. (22), $-a$ and bT_O, are (constants, variables) and thus constitute the value of the (vertical intercept, slope) of the total leakage equation.

7 Using the following values, plot the total leakage equation in Fig. 9-1: $a = \$255$ bil; $b = 0.50$; $T = \$200$ bil. Label the curve $(S + T)_1$.

8 The total injection equation can be computed in the following way. Substitute Eqs. (3) and (4) into the right-hand side of Eq. (1):

(23) $I + G = $ _____

Using the following values, plot the total injection equation in Fig. 9-1: $I = \$75$ bil; $G = \$175$ bil. Label the curve $(I + G)_1$. Equilibrium income is $\$$ _____ bil. Label this point E_1. The government budget is in (surplus, deficit) by $\$$ _____ bil. Saving (does, does not) equal investment. Saving plus taxes (does, does not) equal investment plus government spending.

9 Let us now consider a tax increase. A tax increase induces two separate shifts of the total leakage equation. Since saving is a function of disposable income, a tax increase leads to a decrease of disposable income and consequently leads to a(n) (increase, decrease) of saving. Refer to Fig. 9-2. The curve $S + T$ represents the total leakage equation *before* the tax increase. The distance AB represents the decrease of saving due to the tax increase. This distance is equal to the value (ΔT, $s\Delta T$, $b\Delta T$) and represents a change of the (autonomous component, slope) of the total leakage equation. Label the distance AB with the proper value. Label the new leakage equation $S' + T$ to indicate that it incorporates the *saving* effect of a tax increase.

The tax-drain effect of a tax increase, described by Eq. (18), would shift the $S' + T$ leakage function (upward, downward) by an amount equal to (ΔT, $s\Delta T$, $b\Delta T$). This shift represents a change of the (autonomous component, slope) of the total leakage equation. Let the distance BD represent the value ΔT. Label the distance BD with the proper value. Label the new leakage equation $S' + T'$ to indicate that it incorporates *both* the saving and the tax-drain effects.

The effect *on saving* of a tax increase is to (increase, decrease) leakages from the income stream and hence, for a given amount of injections, would have a(n) (expansionary, deflationary) effect on equilibrium income. The *tax-drain* effect of a tax increase has the (same, opposite) result as the saving effect on the total leakages from the income stream. Thus the net change of total leakages is the algebraic sum of the saving and the tax-drain effects. The value of this drain is equal to (ΔT, $s\Delta T$, $b\Delta T$). This effect can be measured by the distance (AB, AD, BD) in Fig. 9-2. Label the distance AD with the proper value.

10 An activity designed to alter either government expenditures or taxes to achieve a desired change of income is called *fiscal policy*. If current aggregate demand, measured at the full-employment, noninflationary income level Y_{FE}, is greater than the demand necessary to achieve Y_{FE}, an *inflationary gap* is said to exist. If aggregate demand falls short of Y_{FE}, the difference—again measured at Y_{FE}—represents a *deflationary gap*. Let us rewrite the basic equation for *changes in* equilibrium income:

(24) $\Delta Y = \dfrac{1}{s}(\Delta a) - \dfrac{b}{s}(\Delta T) + \dfrac{1}{s}(\Delta I) + \dfrac{1}{s}(\Delta G)$

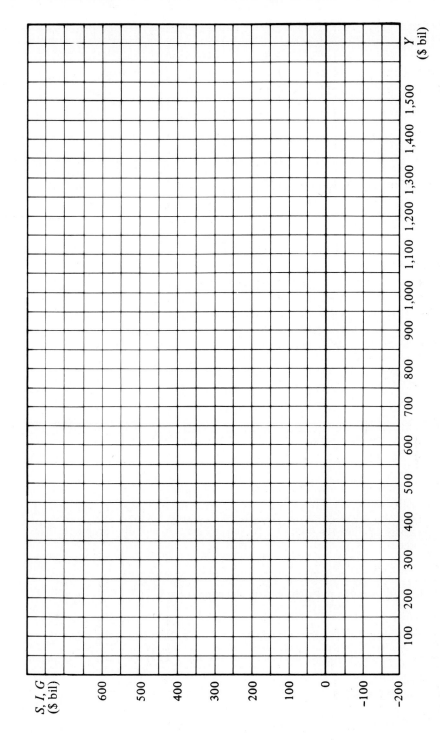

FIGURE 9-1

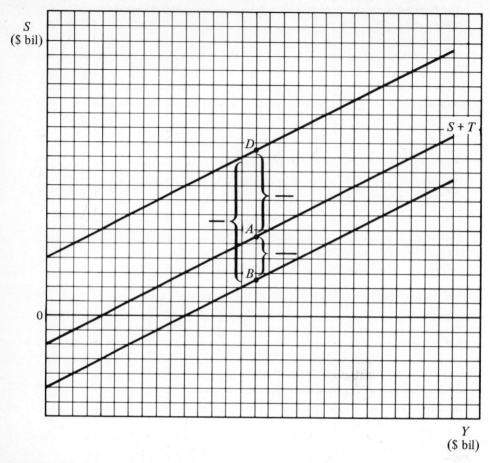

FIGURE 9-2

If only G and T change, then the terms Δa, ΔI and ΔG are zero and thus drop out. The change in income is

(25) $\Delta Y =$ _____

Any desired level of income can be reached by changing either G or T. First solve Eq. (25) for ΔG:

(26) $\Delta G =$ _____

If $s = 0.25$, the necessary (increase, decrease) of G to achieve a $100 bil increase of income

is $ _____ bil.
    Now solve Eq. (25) for ΔT:

(27) $\Delta T =$ _____

The necessary (increase, decrease) of T to achieve the specified increase of income is

$ _____ bil. Since the tax multiplier is (larger, smaller) than the government expenditures multiplier, it takes a (larger, smaller) change of autonomous taxes to achieve the same change of income.

11 Government activities often involve both ΔG and ΔT. ΔG is a(n) (leakage, injection) and ΔT is a(n) (leakage, injection). Thus the net result on the level of income from changes in both G and T will be the algebraic sum of the two changes. If the total injection effect $1/s$ (ΔG) is greater than the total leakage effect b/s (ΔT) income will (rise, fall). If $1/s$ (ΔG) is less than b/s (ΔT), income will (rise, fall). Let government expenditures increase by $300 bil and taxes increase by $200 bil. Assuming that $b = 0.50$,

equilibrium income will (increase, decrease) by $ _____ bil.

12 Beginning with the coefficient values of paragraph 7 and adding the changes of T in paragraph 11, the new leakage equation is

(28) $S + T =$ _____

Plot Eq. (28) in Fig. 9-1 and label it $(S + T)_2$.
   Using the same procedure, the new injection equation is

(29) $I + G =$ _____

Plot Eq. (29) in Fig. 9-1 and label it $(I + G)_2$. Label the new equilibrium income E_2.

Equilibrium income is $ _____ bil, which (is, is not) equivalent to the original amount plus the change computed in paragraph 11.

13 Return to the original conditions described by $(S + T)_1$ and $(I + G)_1$. Now let government expenditures increase by $200 bil, financed by a tax increase of $200 bil. Plot the new injection equation in Fig. 9-1 and label it $(I + G)_3$. The leakage equation will be $(S + T)_2$, which already includes a tax of $200 bil. Label the new equilibrium

point E_3. As a result, equilibrium income will (rise, fall) by $ _____ bil, which is equivalent to the increase of the government budget level. The result wherein equivalent changes of G and T lead to equivalent changes of Y is called the *balanced budget multiplier* effect. The net expansionary effect of a government balanced budget increase is due to the fact that the tax increase is partly paid out of saving, which is then spent by government. Recalling the two tax components in paragraph 9, ΔT and $s\Delta T$, the tax increase, ΔT, represents a dollar-for-dollar drain, but $s\Delta T$ dollars are paid out of saving, so that C is decreased by only $b\Delta T$ dollars. However, G ($=T$) dollars are spent, so that there is a net (increase, decrease) of expenditures. In effect, government spends the tax dollars that are paid out of saving, $s\Delta T$, which consumers would not otherwise have spent, and that money, when multiplied by the government expenditures multiplier, is equal to the net increase of equilibrium income. This relationship can be stated as follows:

(30) $(s\Delta T) \times (\frac{1}{s}) = \Delta Y$

Using Eq. (30) and the foregoing example wherein the government budget $G + T$ was increased by $200 bil, complete Eq. (31):

(31) $ _____ bil $\times$ _____ = $ _____ bil

The value of Eq. (31) (does, does not) measure the balanced budget multiplier effect.

14 Let us now consider a slightly more realistic three-sector model which incorporates the fact that many taxes in the United States, particularly personal and corporate income and social security tax collections, are based on income. The following model is identical to the one presented in paragraph 1, except that the tax equation has been altered:

(1) $S + T = I + G$

(2) $S = -a + s(Y - T)$

(3) $I = I_o$

(4) $G = G_o$

(5a) $T = T_o + tY$

Equation (5a) states that taxes are partly autonomously determined and are partly a function of the income level. For a given proportional tax rate t total taxes (rise, fall) as income rises and (rise, fall) as income falls. Following the same procedure as in paragraph 2, derive the formula for equilibrium income. Arrange the equation in the same form as Eq. (11).

(32) $Y = $ _____

15 The multiplier value is (greater than, equal to, less than) the one derived in Eq. (11). The tax rate t adds a new drain to the model similar to s, the saving drain. The multiplier value is now the reciprocal of the sum of two drain coefficients. The term $s + bt$ can be rearranged to show more clearly the two drain coefficients.
Since

(33) $S = -a + sY_d$

then s is the marginal propensity to save disposable income,
and

(34) $Y_d = Y - T$

and

(35) $T = tY$

Then by substituting Eqs. (34) and (35) into (33), we have

(36) $S = -a + s(Y - tY)$

$S = -a + sY - stY$

$S = -a + (s - st)Y$

$S = -a + s(1 - t)Y$

The term $s(1 - t)$ is the marginal propensity to save total income and represents the saving-drain coefficient. The term t, of course, is the tax-drain coefficient. Thus the multiplier value for the model is

$$\frac{1}{s(1-t) + t} = \frac{1}{s + bt}$$

In general, therefore, a multiplier value is the reciprocal of the sum of the drain coefficients.

16 Compared to the condition stated in Eq. (11), a change in autonomous I, for example, will now lead to a (greater, equivalent, smaller) change in income. Would the same comparative results follow if any of the other autonomous values changed? (yes, no) As a result of introducing taxes as a function of income in the model, initial changes in autonomous values will now lead to (larger, smaller) changes in income, compared to the model in paragraph 1. Thus, by making taxes a function of income, it is said that a *built-in stabilizer* has been introduced into the model.

The total leakage equation for the above model can be written as

(37) $S + T = $ _____

As a result of introducing taxes as a function of income, the (autonomous component, slope) of the total leakage equation has (increased, decreased), compared to the leakage Eq. (22), graphed in Fig. 9-1.

PROBLEMS FOR EXERCISE 9

1 (a) Given: $C = \$25$ bil $+ 0.75Y_d$

$Y_d = Y - T$

$I = \$150$ bil

$G = 0$

$T = 0$

$Y_e = \$$ _____ bil; $C_e = \$$ _____ bil

(b) Assume that federal, state, and local governments spend $300 bil for national security and domestic programs. The expenditures are financed by an increase of autonomous taxes. $Y_e = \$$ _____ bil; $C_e = \$$ _____ bil. The government budget is in (deficit, surplus, balance).

(c) Now assume that the full-employment, noninflationary level of income Y_{FE} is $1,400 bil. There is a(n) (inflationary, deflationary) gap of $ _____ bil.

(d) If the federal government wished to pursue a fiscal policy designed to raise Y_e to Y_{FE} through changing expenditures, leaving taxes unchanged, by how much should G be changed? $ _____ bil. As a result, at Y_{FE} the government budget would be in (deficit, surplus) by $ _____ bil.

(e) If the fiscal policy tool in Prob. 1d was taxes instead of expenditures, $\Delta T = \$$_____

bil. At Y_{FE} the government budget would be in (deficit, surplus) by $ _____ bil.

(f) If Y_{FE} was to be achieved while maintaining a balanced government budget (i.e.,

$G = T$), $\Delta G = \$$ _____ bil; $\Delta T = \$$ _____ bil.

2 (a) Given: $C = \$25$ bil $+ 3/6Y_d$

$I = \$250$ bil

$G = \$125$ bil

$T = 2/6Y$

$Y_e = \$$ _____ bil; $C_e = \$$ _____ bil; $S_e = \$$ _____ bil.

(b) The government budget is in (deficit, surplus) by $ _____ bil.

(c) Assume that $Y_{FE} = \$1,200$ bil. In order to reach the Y_{FE} target through

changing only autonomous government expenditures, $\Delta G = \$$ _____ bil. When $Y_e =$

Y_{FE}, $C_e = \$$ _____ bil; $T_e = \$$ _____ bil.

(d) As a result of Prob. 2c, the government budget is in (deficit, surplus) by

$ _____ bil.

(e) Assume that while the government authorities are carrying out the fiscal program described in Prob. 2c, the average propensity to consume increases, reflecting, perhaps, confidence in the success of the program to raise income. Consumption is now higher by $125 bil at every income level. What fiscal policy adjustment must be made to the

proposed plan in Prob. 2c? _____

_____

_____

3 (a) In Fig. 9-3 graph the equations listed in Prob. 2a, using the leakage-injection model. Label all axes and curves. Designate the initial curves with a subscript 1. Label the initial equilibrium point E_1.

(b) Draw the full-employment, noninflationary income level as a vertical line. Label it Y_{FE}.

(c) Now show the event described in Prob. 2c. Label the new curve $(I + G)_2$. Label the new equilibrium E_2.

(d) Now show the events described in Prob. 2e. Label the new curves $(I + G)_3$ and $(S + T)_3$, and the new equilibrium point E_3.

4 (Optional) Transfer payments are income payments that are not represented by current production of goods and services. Since transfer payments include those paid as relief by federal, state, and local governments to low-income and unemployed families, the volume of transfer payments tends to be somewhat inversely related to income levels. In the following model we introduce transfer payments Tr that are partly autonomously determined and are partly an inverse function of the income level. The term h represents the

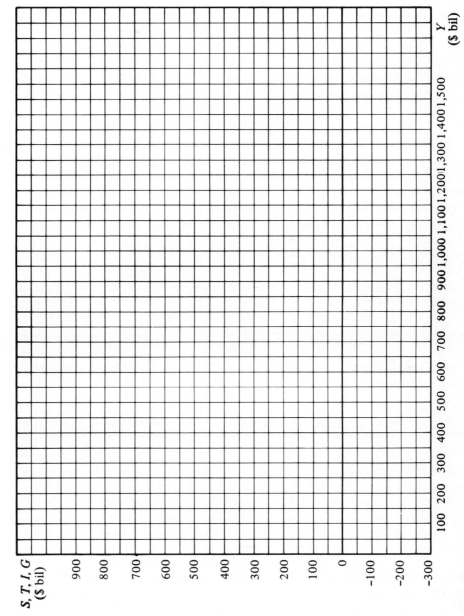

FIGURE 9-3

151

marginal propensity to pay transfer payments. (Note: With the introduction of transfer payments, $Y_d = Y - T + Tr$.)

(a) Given: $S = -a + sY_d$

$$I = I_O$$

$$G = G_O$$

$$T = T_O + tY$$

$$Tr = Tr_O - hY$$

Solve the foregoing model for equilibrium income, arranging the equation in the same form as Eq. (14) in Exercise 9.

$Y =$ _____

(b) The value of the multiplier associated with autonomous taxes (is, is not) equal in absolute value to the transfer payment multiplier, but of opposite sign. The different sign is due to the fact that transfer payments are (leakages from, injections into) the income stream.

(c) Following the steps in Exercise 9, paragraph 15, rearrange the multiplier value in Prob. 4a to show that it is the reciprocal of the sum of the drain coefficients.

$$\frac{1}{s + bt + bh} = \frac{1}{}$$

(d) Write the general form of the investment multipliers derived in Probs. 1a, 2a, and 4a in their order of magnitude.

$$\frac{1}{} > \frac{1}{} > \frac{1}{}$$

(e) If transfer payments represent an injection into the income stream, explain why the marginal propensity to pay transfer payments h enters as a drain coefficient and not as an injection coefficient. _____

_____

_____ .

(f) Since transfer payments are to some extent a discretionary variable, they can be used to achieve fiscal policy objectives. Assume the following values: $a = \$20$ bil; $T_O = \$30$ bil; $Tr_O = \$150$ bil; $I = \$100$ bil; $G = \$200$ bil; $b = 4/6$; $t = 2/6$; $h = 1/6$; $Y_e = \$600$ bil; $Y_{FE} = \$750$ bil. A fiscal policy program designed to raise income to Y_{FE} through changing only autonomous transfer payments would require a(n) (increase, decrease) of $Tr =$

\$ _____ bil. At Y_{FE} total transfer payments will have increased by \$ _____ bil, which is (more than, equal to, less than) the initial increase of autonomous transfer payments. Why? _____

_____

_____ . Do tax payments change (yes, no)? If yes, by how much? \$ _____ bil. If no, why not? _____

_____ .

At Y_{FE} the government budget is in (deficit, surplus) by \$ _____ bil. The budget deficit has increased by \$ _____ bil over what it was at Y_e, which is (more than, equal to, less than) the total increase of transfer payments. Why? _____

_____

_____

_____.

ANSWERS FOR EXERCISE 9

1 leakage, injection, equilibrium, intended, leakages, intended, injections, need not, exceed, disposable, disposable income, MPS, is

2 2, 3, 4, 5, into Eq. 1,
Eq. (7) $-a + s(Y-T_O) + T_O = I_O + G_O$
Eq. (8) $-a + sY - sT_O + T_O = I_O + G_O$
Eq. (9) $sY = a + sT_O - T_O + I_O + G_O$
Eq. (10) $Y = \dfrac{a + sT_O - T_O + I_O + G_O}{s}$

multiplier, the same as

4 also, $a\ T_O\ I_O\ G_O$ (all of these)

5 smaller, consumption, \$1, decrease, decrease, 16, 80, decrease, 4, is, 100, 5, is, 20, is

6 Eq. (20) $S + T = -a + s(Y - T_O) + T_O$
Eq. (21) $S + T = -a + sY - sT_O + T_O$
constants, vertical intercept

7 Fig. 9-1A

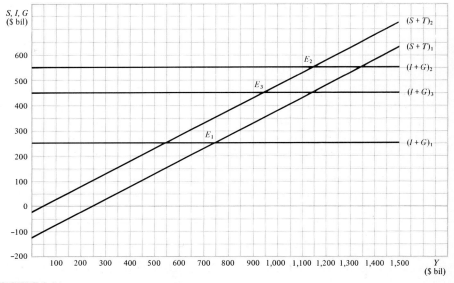

FIGURE 9-1A

8 Eq. (23) $I + G = I_O + G_O$
Fig. 9-1A, 750, Fig. 9-1A, surplus, 25, does not, does
9 decrease, $s\Delta T$, autonomous component, Fig. 9-2A, upward, ΔT, autonomous component, Fig. 9-2A, decrease, expansionary, opposite, $b\Delta T$, AD, Fig. 9-2A

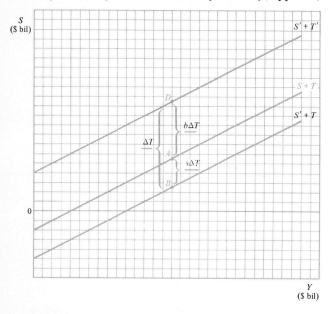

FIGURE 9-2A

10 Eq. (25) $\Delta Y = 1/s(\Delta G) - b/s(\Delta T)$
Eq. (26) $\Delta G = \Delta Y/(1/s)$
increase, 25,
Eq. (27) $\Delta T = -\Delta Y/(b/s)$
decrease, 33, smaller, larger
11 injection, leakage, rise, fall, increase, 400
12 Eq. (28) $S + T = -\$25$ bil $+ 0.50Y$, Fig. 9-1A,
Eq. (29) $I + G = \$550$ bil, Fig. 9-1A, 1,150, is
13 Fig. 9-1A, rise, 200, increase,
Eq. (31) $\$100$ bil $\times 2 = \$200$ bil, does
14 rise, fall,
Eq. (32) $Y = 1/s + bt (a - bT_O + I_O + G_O)$, i.e.,
$$Y = -a + T - sT + sY = I + G$$
$$Y = -a + bT + sY = I_O + G_O$$
$$Y = -a + b(T_O + tY) + sY = I_O + G_O$$
$$Y = -a + bT_O + btY + sY = I_O + G_O$$
$$Y = sY + btY = a - bT_O + I_O + G_O$$
$$Y = Y(s + bt) = a - bT_O + I_O + G_O$$
$$Y = \frac{a - bT_O + I_O + G_O}{s + bt}$$
$$Y = 1/s + bt(a - bT_O + I_O + G_O)$$

15 less than
16 smaller, yes, smaller,
   Eq. $(37)\, S + T = -a + bT_O + (s + bt)Y$
   slope, increased

ANSWERS TO PROBLEMS FOR EXERCISE 9

1 (a) 700, 550 (b) 1,000, 550, balance (c) deflationary, 100 (d) 100, deficit, 100
   (e) $-133\frac{1}{3}$, deficit, $133\frac{1}{3}$ (f) 400, 400
2 (a) 600, 225, 175 (b) surplus, 75 (c) 400, 425, 400 (d) deficit, 125 (e) Government expenditures will only have to be increased by \$275 bil instead of \$400 bil as originally planned
3 Fig. 9-3A

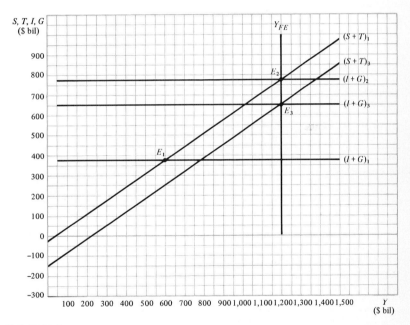

FIGURE 9-3A

4 (a) $Y = \dfrac{1}{s + bt + bh}\,(a - bT_O + bTr_O + I_O + G_O)$

   (b) is, injections into

   (c) $\dfrac{1}{s(1 - t - h) + t + h}$

   (d) $\dfrac{1}{s} > \dfrac{1}{s(1 - t) + t} > \dfrac{1}{s(1 - t - h) + t + h}$

   (e) Transfer payments are inversely related to income, so that as income *increases*, transfer payments *decrease*.

(f) increase, 150, 125, less than, The higher transfer payments increase consumption expenditures through increasing disposable income. As C and Y rise, induced transfer payments decline. yes, 50, deficit, 95, 75, less than, The government budget deficit does not rise by the full amount of the transfer payment increase because, as income increases, induced tax collections also increase to somewhat offset the budget deficit rise.

DETERMINANTS OF INVESTMENT SPENDING:
THE INTEREST RATE

1 The decision on whether to make an investment expenditure during the current time period involves a comparison of the desired or optimal capital stock K^* to the actual capital stock K. When $K^* = K$, all profitable capital projects are being exploited. Thus, except for spending to replace worn-out capital, net investment spending—representing additions to the capital stock—will be (positive, negative, zero).

Whenever K is less than K^*, it is profitable to make additional investment expenditures. Hence, the investment decision involves a revenue-cost comparison. Whenever the expected revenue to be obtained from an investment project is (greater, less) than its cost, the expenditure will be profitable.

2 Because capital goods yield their services over a fairly long period of time, it is necessary to include time as a factor in any attempt to explain investment spending. The role that time plays in investment decisions may be summed up by the observation that an individual would prefer a dollar available (today, next year) to a dollar available (today, next year). This fact is true partly because individuals generally prefer to enjoy goods and services at once rather than defer that enjoyment to the future, and partly because today's dollar can be invested in a productive but time-consuming activity which yields more than a dollar after a year has passed. How much will today's dollar yield next year? This information is given by the market rate of interest. For example, if the interest rate

is 10 percent, a dollar available now will yield $ _____ in one year. The process of computing the future value of today's dollar is called *interest compounding*. Arithmetically, for the preceding problem we have

$$\$1.10 = \$1.00 + \$1.00(0.10)$$

One dollar today plus the 10 percent interest return on a dollar for one year equals $1.10 next year. The value of $5.00 one year from now, lent at an interest rate of 7 percent,

is $ _____ .

Stated in general terms, if the dollar today is denoted by P_O and the interest rate by i, the equation for the above interest compounding problem is

$$(1) \quad P_1 = P_O + P_O(i)$$

where P_1 is the future value of today's dollar. We can rearrange Eq. (1) by factoring out P_O from the terms on the right-hand side.

(2) $P_1 = P_O(1 + i)$

3 Alternatively, we could say in our first example above that $1.10 available next year is worth $ _1.00_ today. The process of computing the present value of a future dollar is called *discounting*. Thus it is said that the present value P_O of $1.10, available next year at an interest rate of 10 percent, is $1.00. The process of discounting is the (same as, opposite from) interest compounding.

The present value of the future sum in Eq. (2) is found by solving the equation for the value of P_O:

(3) $P_O =$ _P_1/1+i_

More generally, the present value of an investment is the amount one would be willing to pay now for the proceeds of the investment which will not be available until some time in the future. If we let R represent the future proceeds of an investment, the present value of a one-year investment may be found by dividing the proceeds by the discount factor $(1 + i)$.

(4) $P_O = \dfrac{R}{(1 + i)}$

Equation (4) is (similar to, different from) Eq. (3). The term R is the future return, net of operating costs but including the return of the original investment. Note that the higher the interest rate, the (larger, smaller) P_O is and thus the (more, less) cost one is willing to incur for an investment yielding R dollars in one year. In general, any fixed payment to be made in the future is worth less if the interest rate rises. Thus, for example, the price of a bond paying $80 per year would (rise, fall) if the market interest rate rises.

4 The expression given in Eq. (4) for the present value of a one-year investment can be extended to cover investments yielding returns over any length of time. If we wish to find the present value of R dollars to be returned two years from now, we can apply the discounting formula twice. If R dollars are available at the beginning of year 2, the present value as of the beginning of year 1 is

(5) $P_1 = \dfrac{R}{(1 + i)}$

Given that P_1 is available at the beginning of year 1, the present value of the R dollars at the beginning of year zero, i.e., the current year, is

(6) $P_O = \dfrac{P_1}{(1 + i)}$

But since the value of P_1 is given by Eq. (5), through substitution we can alternatively express the equation for the present value of a two-year investment as

(7) $P_O =$ _R/(1+i)²_

If R is available only at the end of three years, the present value as of today is

(8) $P_O = \underline{\hspace{3cm}}$

If R is available only at the end of year n, the present value as of today is

(9) $P_O = \underline{\hspace{3cm}}$

5 The present value of a future return is useful to know for individuals or firms who must make investment decisions. Since P_O is the amount that a future payoff is worth, the following decision rule makes sense: *Accept all investment opportunities whose P_O is greater than the cost of the initial investment.* For example, consider an investment project which costs $2,000 and provides a total return of $2,222 after one year. If the market rate of interest is 10 percent, the present value of the investment return is

$ \underline{\hspace{1.5cm}}$. Since P_O is (larger, smaller) than the cost of the investment, a prospective investor would find it profitable to (accept, reject) the opportunity.

6 One-year investment-decision problems can be solved graphically. In Fig. 10-1, the horizontal axis represents income available immediately and the vertical axis represents income available next year. Let us suppose that $2,200 is available next year. This amount is represented by point A. If the rate of interest is 10 percent, the discount factor is $(1 + 0.10)$ or 1.10. The value of the discount factor may be represented as a straight line with a slope of -1.10, signifying that if $1.10 of next year's money is given up, $1.00 of this year's money is gained in exchange. When the line is projected to the horizontal axis, it shows what $2,200 available next year is worth this year. The line meets the horizontal axis at point B, indicating that the present value of next year's

$2,200 is $ \underline{\hspace{1.5cm}}$. It is evident from Fig. 10-1 that if more than $2,200 is available next year, the present value must be (greater than, equal to, less than) $2,000, provided that the interest rate is 10 percent. Specifically, if a prospective investment is expected to pay $2,222 in one year, it would be worth (more than, less than, the same as) $2,000 available immediately, and would be (accepted, rejected) if it cost $2,000 or less.

The present value of any other point along the line AB can be found graphically. Point D represents a return of $1,100. If the vertical axis passed through point D instead of point A, point B would have a value of $2,000 minus $1,000 = $1,000 instead of

$2,000. Thus the present value of the $1,100 is $ \underline{\hspace{1.5cm}}$.

7 Up to now we have been concerned with the justification and illustration of one investment decision rule: *Accept all opportunities whose present value of future returns is greater than the initial cost of the investment.* We now consider an alternative decision rule which, under conditions usually assumed in simple economic models, is equivalent to the first: *Accept all investment opportunities for which the marginal efficiency of capital (MEC) is greater than the market rate of interest.* The MEC is defined as that rate of discount which makes the present value of the future returns of an investment equal to its cost. We have already found that if the future returns are discounted at the market rate of interest, P_O (must be, need not be) equal to the cost of the project. Thus, the rate of discount that actually makes the present values of the investment returns equal to the cost of the project (must be, need not be) equal to the

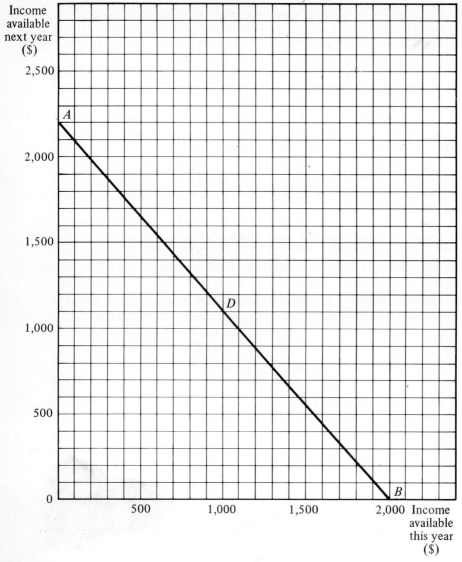

FIGURE 10-1

market rate of interest. For a one-year investment, the MEC, denoted by r, is defined as that value of r which satisfies the following equation:

$$(10) \quad C = \frac{R}{(1 + r)}$$

where C is the known cost of the project and R is the known expected net return. A one-year investment which costs $2,000 and yields $2,222 has a MEC of _____ percent. If the firm had to borrow funds at a market rate interest of 10 percent to finance the project, since their internal rate of return on the investment (exceeds, falls short of, is equal to) the finance charges, the decision would be to (accept, reject, be indifferent to) the investment. A one-year investment which costs $2,000 and yields $2,200 has an MEC

of _____10_____ percent. If the market rate of interest is 10 percent, what would be the investment decision? (accept, reject, be indifferent)   Any MEC which is less than

_____10_____ percent would not be a profitable investment. If, through retained earnings, the firm had the funds on hand to finance the project, it would be (more, less) profitable to lend them out at the market rate of interest, rather than invest them in the firm.

8 For a two-year investment returning R dollars only at the end of two years, the formula for the MEC can be written as (for review, see paragraph 4)

(11) $C = \underline{\quad R/(1+r)^2 \quad}$

Assume, alternatively, that a two-year investment returns R dollars at the end of both the first and second years. The formula for the MEC can be written as:

(12) $C = \underline{\quad R/(1+r) \quad} + \underline{\quad R/(1+r)^2 \quad}$

For example, suppose that the investment costs $1,000, returns $100 at the end of the first year and $1,100 at the end of the second year. The formula for the MEC is

(13) $\underline{\$1000\quad} = \underline{\quad \$100/(1+r) \quad} + \underline{\quad 1100/(1+r)^2 \quad}$

Which of the following is the correct value for r? (0, 0.10, 0.20)

If $i = 10$ percent, what is the present value of the returns from this investment?

$ _____1000_____ . The P_O (is, is not) equal to the investment cost, implying that the equality of C and P_O occurs when r is (greater than, less than, equal to) i.

Compare Eq. (7), the general formula for the P_O of a two-year investment, with Eq. (11), the general formula for the MEC of a two-year investment. The P_O can exceed the cost of the investment only if r is (greater than, less than, equal to) i. Conversely, the cost can exceed the P_O only if r is (greater than, less than, equal to) i. This result (is, is not) changed if the period of the investment is extended beyond two years. Evidently, the decision rule that investments should be accepted if the present value of their returns exceeds their cost and the decision rule that investments should be accepted if their marginal efficiencies of capital exceed the market rate of interest (are, are not) the same under the assumptions used in this exercise.

9 If an investor has several opportunities before him, he will accept all those projects with a MEC greater than i and reject all those projects with a MEC less than i. If one-year investments are under consideration, the decision process can be illustrated graphically. Seven investment opportunities are presented in Fig. 10-2. They are arranged in order of productivity, so that opportunity A is the most productive and opportunity G is the least productive. Each project is assumed to cost $5 mil, and

to return amounts varying from $ _____15_____ mil for opportunity A to $ _____ mil for opportunity G. Complete Table 10-1 by finding the dollar return from each opportunity and by calculating each MEC.

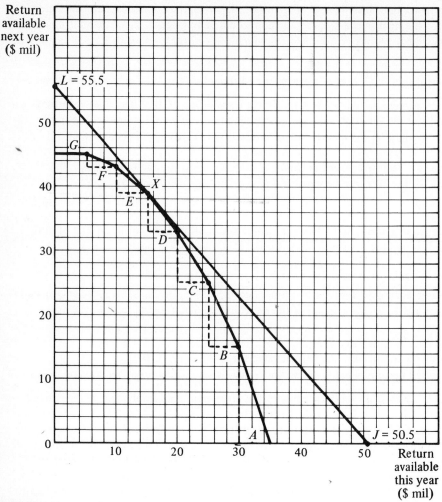

FIGURE 10-2

If $i = 10$ percent, which opportunities will be accepted? _____

What is the total amount of investment spending? $_____ mil. The market interest

rate may be represented on Fig. 10-2 by a straight line with a slope of _____. (For
review, see paragraph 6 above.) Such a line is drawn tangent to the investment opportunity curve at point X. The tangency indicates that to the right of X the slope of the interest
rate line is (greater, less) than the slope of the investment opportunity curve, and (greater,
less) to the left of X. Since the slope of the investment opportunity line is equal to the
market rate of interest at point X, then to the right of X, i is (greater, less) than r.

The present value (P_O) of the investments can be found in Fig. 10-2 by reading the
horizontal intercept of the line passing through point X. Following paragraph 6 above,
if the vertical axis passed through point X instead of point L, the value of the horizontal

Table 10-1

Investment opportunity	Cost	Return	MEC
A	$5 mil	$ 15 mil	180 percent
B	$5 mil	$ 10 mil	100 percent
C	$5 mil	$ 8 mil	60 percent
D	$5 mil	$ 6 mil	20 percent
E	$5 mil	$ 4 mil	-20 percent
F	$5 mil	$ 2 mil	-60 percent
G	$5 mil	$ 0 mil	-100 percent

intercept would be $50.5 mil minus $ _____ mil = $ _____ mil. Is it possible to obtain a higher P_O with this set of investment opportunities (yes, no)? We can therefore state that point X (does, does not) represent the maximum P_O for the opportunities available. Naturally, if all individual opportunities for which the P_O exceeds cost are rejected, the total P_O, net of total cost, must be at a maximum.

10 Suppose that the interest rate rose from 10 to 50 percent. Of the investment opportunities listed in Table 10-1, which ones would still be profitable? __A B C__ .

What would be the total amount of investment spending under these conditions? $ 15 mil. This result indicates that if the interest rate rises, investment spending (rises, falls, remains unchanged). In Fig. 10-3 plot the information calculated above for total investment spending at interest rates of 10 and 50 percent. Label the curve I. The I curve has a (positive, negative) slope which indicates that investment and the interest rate are

__inversely__ related. Because the I curve represents the amount of desired investment spending at each interest rate, it is known as the *investment demand* curve. The general form of this function is

(14) $I = f(i)$

As pointed out in the introduction to Part 3, however, the interest rate is not the only variable which affects investment.

PROBLEMS FOR EXERCISE 10

1 The cost and return are indicated for the one-year investments listed below. Find the MEC for each investment. Find the P_O, assuming a market rate of interest of 10 percent, and indicate whether the investment should be accepted or rejected.

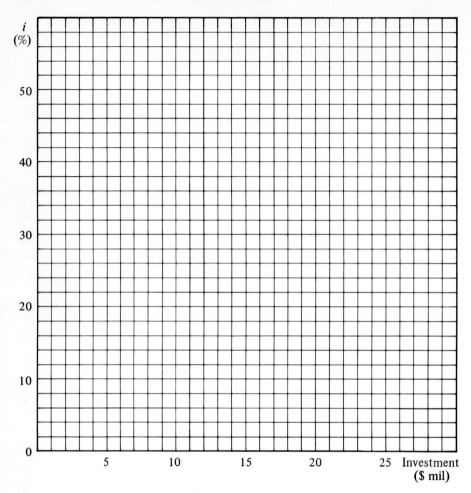

FIGURE 10-3

Project	Cost	Return	MEC	P_O	Investment decision
A	$1,000	$1,090	_____ %	$ _____	_____
B	1,200	1,400	_____	_____	_____
C	2,000	3,000	_____	_____	_____
D	350	390	_____	_____	_____
E	750	800	_____	_____	_____

Which projects initially accepted would be dropped if the interest rate rose to 20 percent?

_____ .

2 The cost and return for each year are indicated for the two-year investments listed below. Find the MEC for each investment; they will be either 0.05, 0.10, or 0.20. Indicate whether each investment should be accepted or rejected, assuming that the market interest rate is 15 percent.

Project	Cost	Return (1)	Return (2)	MEC	Investment decision
A	$1,100	$440	$847	_____ %	_____
B	1,100	525	661.5	_____	_____
C	1,100	480	1,008	_____	_____
D	1,400	660	968	_____	_____
E	1,400	600	1,296	_____	_____

Which projects initially rejected would be added if the interest rate fell to 7 percent?

_____

ANSWERS FOR EXERCISE 10

1 zero, greater

2 today, next year, 1.10, 5.35

3 1.00, opposite from, Eq. (3) $P_O = P_1/1 + i$, similar to, smaller, less, fall

4 Eq. (7) $P_O = R/(1 + i)^2$
Eq. (8) $P_O = R/(1 + i)^3$
Eq. (9) $P_O = R/(1 + i)^n$

5 2,020, larger, accept

6 2,000, greater than, more than, accepted, 1,000

7 need not be, need not be, 11.1, exceeds, accept, 10, be indifferent, 10, more

8 Eq. (11) $C = R/(1 + r)^2$
Eq. (12) $C = R/(1 + r) + R/(1 + r)^2$
Eq. (13) $1,000 = $100/(1 + r) + $1,100/(1 + r)^2$
0.10, 1,000, is, equal to, greater than, less than, is not, are

9 15, zero,

Investment opp.	A	B	C	D	E	F	G
Return	15	10	8	6	4	2	0
MEC	180	100	60	20	-20	-60	-100

A B C D, 10, –1.10, less, greater, less, greater, 15, 35.5, no, does
10 A B C, 15, falls, Fig. 10-3A, negative, inversely

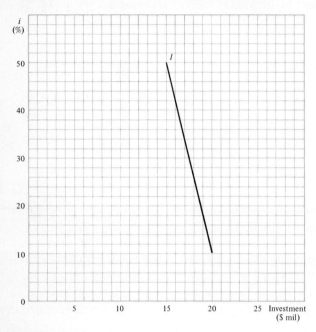

FIGURE 10-3A

ANSWERS TO PROBLEMS FOR EXERCISE 10

1 A   9.0   990.9   reject
   B 16.7   1,272.7   accept
   C 50.0   2,272.2   accept
   D 11.4   354.5   accept
   E   6.66   727.2   reject
   B and D
2 A 10.0   reject
   B   5.0   reject
   C 20.0   accept
   D 10.0   reject
   E 20.0   accept
   A and D

DETERMINANTS OF INVESTMENT SPENDING: THE STOCK OF CAPITAL

1 When a firm purchases investment goods, it does so for one of two reasons: to replace worn-out capital stock or to expand capacity. In either case, the size of the capital stock will enter into the investment decision. The more capital currently in place, the more will wear out each year. Also, a decision to expand capacity cannot be made without consideration of the amount of capacity already available. It is convenient to begin study of the relationship between investment and the capital stock by *ignoring* depreciation. This simplifying assumption enables us to concentrate on decisions to *add* to the capital stock.

Our expenditure-decision model views investment as a process of elimination of a gap between the amount of capital actually in place—*actual* capital stock—and the amount of capital the firm would like to have—*desired* capital stock. If the entire gap is to be eliminated in one year, this model can be described as

(1) $I_t = K_t^* - K_t$

where I_t is the desired net investment spending in the current year, and K_t^* is the desired capital stock at the beginning of the current year, and K_t is the actual capital stock at the beginning of the current year. The larger the actual capital stock, the (larger, smaller) investment spending will be during the year.

What determines the desired capital stock? Presumably, capital is used to produce income (output): Hence, the more income that is to be produced, the more capital stock that is needed to produce it. Suppose that one dollar of capital is required to produce two dollars of output. Then, given the level of output, the desired amount of capital is

(2) $K_t^* = 2Y_t$

This expression can be substituted into Eq. (1)

(3) $I_t = $ _____

2 The expression for investment demand, Eq. (3), can be transformed to reveal another interesting fact about investment. First, we note that in the absence of depreciation, next year's actual capital stock equals this year's actual capital stock plus this year's

_____ . Thus

(4) $K_{t+1} = K_t + I_t$

where K_t is the actual capital stock at the beginning of the year and I_t is the necessary investment made during the year to eliminate the gap. Recalling the assumption made in the introduction to Part 3 that the entire desired-actual capital stock gap is eliminated in one year

(5) $K_{t+1} =$ _____

And, from Eq. (2), since $K_t^* = 2Y_t$, by substituting this expression into Eq. (5), we have

(6) $K_{t+1} =$ _____

Hence, *next year's* actual capital stock, K_{t+1}, is dependent on *this year's* income level. It then follows that *this year's* actual capital stock, K_t, is dependent on the (current, previous) year's income level. This relationship can be expressed as

(7) $K_t =$ _____

Substitute Eq. (7) into Eq. (3).

(8) $I_t =$ _____

By factoring out the term 2, we have

(9) $I_t = 2(Y_t - Y_{t-1})$

The term $(Y_t - Y_{t-1})$ represents the (level of, change in) income. If income does not change from year to year, investment is $ _____ bil. If investment is to be positive, income must be (constant, growing).

3 Suppose, for example, that income has been $1,000 bil for several years. Under the assumptions used in paragraphs 1 and 2, the desired and actual capital stock must be

$ _____ bil, and investment $ _____ bil. If by the end of the next year income rises to $1,100 bil, the desired capital stock will be $ _____ bil. Since the actual capital stock is equal to the desired stock of the (current, previous) year, the actual stock at the end of the next year will (increase to $2,200 bil, remain at $2,000 bil). Desired

net investment will be $ _____ bil. Complete Table 11-1. (Assume that the first year's income has prevailed for several years.) Table 11-1 confirms the point made above that if investment is to be maintained at a constant level, income (must be growing, need only be maintained at a constant level). If income ceases to grow, investment (falls to zero, falls to a positive level). Investment is shown to be a(n) (stable, unstable) component of GNP.

4 In this exercise, no mention has been made of the interest rate as a determinant of investment. For simplicity of exposition, it was assumed that the desired capital stock depends only on income. If this assumption is dropped, it is possible to include the

Table 11-1

Year	Income ($ bil)	Desired capital stock ($ bil)	Actual capital stock ($ bil)	Investment ($ bil)
1	1,000	————	————	————
2	1,100	————	————	————
3	1,200	————	————	————
4	1,200	————	————	————
5	1,300	————	————	————

interest rate as an additional determinant of the desired capital stock and of investment for the reasons given in Exercise 10. Hence, a somewhat more realistic investment demand equation would be

(10) $I_t = f(i, Y_t - Y_{t-1})$

As written, Eq. (10) does not distinguish between positive changes of income and negative changes. It is unlikely that the economy would respond to a negative change in the same way. While the capital stock can be increased on demand, it cannot be reduced on demand unless it is physically destroyed. An individual firm can sell its unwanted capital, but the nation as a whole cannot, unless it can dispose of the capital abroad. The nation must wait until the excess capital wears out, a process that may take much more time than did the creation of the capital.

PROBLEMS FOR EXERCISE 11

1 Let us drop the restrictive assumption used in Exercise 11 that capital never wears out. Instead, assume that 10 percent of the capital stock wears out each year. With this single exception, the model used in Exercise 11 will be unchanged. The symbol I_t refers to *gross* investment. Equation (4) of Exercise 11 must be modified as follows:

(4a) $K_{t+1} = K_t + I_t - D_t$

The symbol D_t represents depreciation. The investment equation can be found in the same way that Eq. (8) was derived. Use the logic of paragraph 2 to complete the following expressions:

(5a) $K_{t+1} =$ _____

(6a) $K_{t+1} =$ _____

(7a) $K_t =$ _____

(8a)　$I_t =$ _____

(9a)　$I_t =$ _____

And, given the assumption that 10 percent of the capital stock wears out each year, Eq. (9a) can be rewritten as

(9b)　$I_t = 2(Y_t - Y_{t-1}) + 0.10K_{t-1}$

If income does not change, gross investment is (positive, zero), while net investment is (positive, zero).

2 Using the model derived in Eq. (9b), complete Table 11-2. Assume that the first year's income has prevailed for several years.

Table 11-2

Year	Income ($ bil)	Desired capital stock ($ bil)	Actual capital stock ($ bil)	Depreciation ($ bil)	Gross investment ($ bil)	Net investment ($ bil)
1	1,000	_____	_____	_____	_____	_____
2	1,100	_____	_____	_____	_____	_____
3	1,200	_____	_____	_____	_____	_____
4	1,300	_____	_____	_____	_____	_____
5	1,300	_____	_____	_____	_____	_____
6	1,200	_____	_____	_____	_____	_____

ANSWERS FOR EXERCISE 11

1 smaller, Eq. (3) $I_t = 2Y_t - K_t$

2 investment, Eq. (5) $K_{t+1} = K_t^*$, Eq. (6) $K_{t+1} = 2Y_t$, previous, Eq. (7) $K_t = 2Y_{t-1}$, Eq. (8) $I_t = 2Y_t - 2Y_{t-1}$, change in, zero, growing

3 2,000, zero, 2,200, previous, remain at $2,000 bil, 200,

Year	Desired capital stock	Actual capital stock	Investment
1	2,000	2,000	0
2	2,200	2,000	200
3	2,400	2,200	200
4	2,600	2,400	200
5	2,600	2,600	0

must be growing, falls to zero, unstable

ANSWERS TO PROBLEMS FOR EXERCISE 11

1 Eq. $(5a) K_{t+1} = K_t^* - D_t$, Eq. $(6a) K_{t+1} = 2Y_t - D_t$,
Eq. $(7a) K_t = 2Y_{t-1} - D_{t-1}$, Eq. $(8a) I_t = 2Y_t - 2Y_{t-1} + D_{t-1}$,
Eq. $(9a) I_t = 2(Y_t - Y_{t-1}) + D_{t-1}$, positive, zero

2

Year	Desired capital stock	Actual capital stock	Depreciation	Gross investment	Net investment
1	2,000	2,000	200	200	0
2	2,200	2,000	200	400	200
3	2,400	2,200	200	400	200
4	2,600	2,400	220	420	200
5	2,600	2,600	240	240	0
6	2,400	2,600	260	60	-200

REVIEW TEST FOR PART 3

1 If there is no government sector, equilibrium is attained when $S = I$. With the addition of a government sector G and T, at equilibrium
   (a) government spending must equal tax collections
   (b) saving must still equal investment
   (c) total leakages will equal total injections
   (d) saving minus investment must equal government spending minus taxes
   (e) saving plus investment must equal government spending plus taxes

2 Assume the following: MPC = 0.8; $t = 0.25$. The value of the investment multiplier is
   (a) 2.0
   (b) 2.2
   (c) 2.5
   (d) 5.0
   (e) none of these

3 Using the same values as in question 2, the value of the autonomous tax multiplier is
   (a) 2.0
   (b) 2.2
   (c) 2.5
   (d) 5.0
   (e) none of these

4 A tax decrease will increase income somewhat, even if the MPC = 0.
   (a) true
   (b) false

5 Government expenditures will increase income
   (a) only if the spending is financed through higher taxes
   (b) only if other aggregate demand components are not reduced by a like amount
   (c) by a multiple of the initial increase of G only if MPS = 1

   (d) only if the expenditures are made on capital goods such as highways, school buildings and tanks

   (e) none of these

6 Which of the following financial policies will have the greatest impact on increasing income? Assume a basic multiplier value of $1/(s + bt)$ for each case.

   (a) a $10 bil decrease in autonomous personal income taxes.

   (b) a $10 bil increase in government spending.

   (c) a $10 bil increase in government spending, accompanied by a $20 bil increase in autonomous taxes.

   (d) a $10 bil increase in government spending, accompanied by a $5 bil decrease in autonomous taxes.

7 Fiscal policy describes government activities designed to stabilize aggregate income levels by

   (a) varying government spending and taxes to influence the level of aggregate demand

   (b) altering tax rates to encourage a desirable change in the composition of output

   (c) altering the distribution of income by changing relative tax rates on different factor incomes

   (d) changing the rate of interest to influence investment spending

8 An inflationary gap can be eliminated by

   (a) decreasing government spending or taxes

   (b) decreasing government spending or increasing taxes

   (c) decreasing investment spending

   (d) decreasing disposable income

Answer questions 9 to 13 on the basis of the following model:

$$C = a + bY_d$$

$$T = T_0 + tY$$

$$I = I_0$$

$$G = G_0$$

9 A built-in stabilizer

   (a) is present in the model

   (b) reduces fluctuations in income, compared to a model where taxes are not a function of income

   (c) reduces fluctuations in total taxes that are due to fluctuations in income

   (d) requires a smaller change in government spending to achieve a given change in income, compared to a model where taxes are not a function of income

10 The built-in stabilizer in the model

   (a) reduces fluctuations in investment

   (b) operates through congressional changes in t, the tax rate

   (c)   reduces the size of the investment *and* government expenditure multipliers
   (d)   stabilizes income by stabilizing tax collections
   (e)   stabilizes income by stabilizing disposable income

11 Tax reductions tend to increase
   (a)   income
   (b)   consumption
   (c)   saving
   (d)   government spending

12 An increase in the government budgetary deficit necessarily indicates that the fiscal authorities are pursuing an expansionary fiscal policy program.
   (a)   true
   (b)   false

13 An increase in autonomous taxes of $20 bil will lead to
   (a)   an increase in income
   (b)   ultimately an increase in tax collections of more than $20 bil
   (c)   a lower tax rate
   (d)   lower government spending
   (e)   none of these

14 Assuming a basic multiplier of $1/s$, if the government decreases both its expenditures and tax collections by $25 bil,
   (a)   income will fall by $25 bil
   (b)   income will fall by more than $25 bil
   (c)   income will fall by less than $25 bil
   (d)   any of the above is possible
   (e)   answer is indeterminate without additional information

15 Government spending and investment multipliers are larger than the tax multiplier because there is no assurance that a tax reduction will lead to a change in spending.
   (a)   true
   (b)   false

16 Given a tax function of the form $T = T_O + tY$, an equivalent decrease in G_O and T_O will lead to a larger government deficit (or a smaller surplus).
   (a)   true
   (b)   false

17 A government surplus always indicates that fiscal policy measures are being taken to reduce or eliminate an inflationary gap.
   (a)   true
   (b)   false

18 An investment opportunity should be accepted if the
   (a) P_O is greater than the MEC

(b) MEC is greater than the cost of the project
(c) MEC is greater than the market rate of interest
(d) P_O is greater than the cost of the project

19 From the preceding question, it could be concluded that investment might be encouraged by
    (a) lower market interest rates
    (b) higher market interest rates
    (c) a lower MEC
    (d) a lower P_O

20 A project costing $1,500 has an MEC of 0.20, a project costing $700 has an MEC of 0.08, and a project costing $1,100 has an MEC of 0.12. What is total investment spending if the market rate of interest is 9 percent?
    (a) $1,800
    (b) $2,200
    (c) $700
    (d) $2,600
    (e) $1,500

21 Project A has an MEC of 0.07, while project B has a P_O of $200. Which is the preferable project?
    (a) A
    (b) B
    (c) they are equal
    (d) indeterminant from information given

22 Project A costs $1,000 and has a P_O of $975, project B costs $850 and has a P_O of $1,100, and project C costs $350 and has a P_O of $400. Assuming no shortage of funds, which project(s) will be accepted?
    (a) A and B
    (b) B only
    (c) B and C
    (d) all of them
    (e) indeterminant from information given

23 If the desired capital stock depends only on income, net investment must rise if
    (a) the interest rate falls
    (b) the capital stock rises
    (c) the capital stock falls
    (d) income rises

24 If income rises at a steady rate, using the model of question 20,
    (a) investment remains constant
    (b) investment rises at a steady rate
    (c) investment rises at a diminishing rate
    (d) the capital stock remains constant

25 Depreciation equals gross investment minus net investment.
   (a) true
   (b) false

26 Net investment can be negative, but gross investment cannot.
   (a) true
   (b) false

27 This year's capital stock is equal to last year's capital stock plus
   (a) gross investment
   (b) net investment
   (c) gross investment minus depreciation
   (d) gross investment plus depreciation
   (e) depreciation

28 Investment occurs when the
   (a) desired capital stock is larger than the actual capital stock
   (b) desired capital stock is larger than income
   (c) actual capital stock is larger than the desired capital stock
   (d) actual capital stock is larger than income

29 If the actual capital stock is $1,400, income is $800, the desired capital stock is two times income, and depreciation is 5 percent of the actual capital stock,
   (a) gross investment is $200 and depreciation is $70
   (b) gross investment is $270 and depreciation is $70
   (c) net investment is $200 and depreciation is $70
   (d) net investment is -$200 and depreciation is $120
   (e) net investment is -$70 and depreciation is $120

THE DEMAND FOR AND SUPPLY OF MONEY

In this part we turn from consideration of the product market to a simple model of the money market. Some discussion of the money market or financial system is necessary because resources cannot be efficiently transferred from savers to investors without markets in which stocks or bonds can be sold by investors to savers for the purpose of financing physical investment. We will study a simplified model which includes only two financial assets: money and government bonds. The only interest rate is the rate on bonds.

Exercises 12 and 13 are concerned with the demand for and the supply of money. The supply of money is handled simply by assuming that it is controlled by the Federal Reserve System. Thus the money supply is considered to be a policy parameter, as was government purchases of goods and services. Hence, virtually the entire discussion here will be confined to the factors that affect the demand for money.

The explanation of the demand for money centers on the answer to the question, "Why would a rational decision-maker hold money assets?" Money earns no interest under present United States institutional arrangements. While it has the advantage of being virtually risk-free, so are some interest-bearing assets, notably savings accounts and short-term government securities. Thus, it would *seem* that money is definitely an inferior asset to hold from both yield and risk considerations. But four reasonably satisfactory rationales for the holding of cash balances can be identified. First, there is the need to finance transactions. Since expenditures are not synchronized perfectly with income receipts, it is useful to have cash balances available for purchases between paydays. Second, one may wish to speculate on the movement of bond prices and yields. If bond prices are expected to fall in the near future—or yields to rise—a speculator would hold cash now and buy the bonds later at a lower price. Third, one might hold cash to avoid the risk that is attached to other assets. Risk depends not only on individual evaluations of the probability of default risk, but also on adverse changes in capital values in the market place. All securities traded in open markets are subject to this latter risk. Fourth, noncash securities are relatively illiquid. If the need for a cash expenditure should arise on short notice, it may not be possible to convert an interest-bearing security to cash in time. We might consider the fourth point to be a special case of the third: The asset has to be sold so quickly that it brings a price substantially below the true market value, due to the forced-sale nature of the transaction.

As we shall see in the exercises which follow, these four motives for holding money assets lead to the hypothesis that the demand for money is determined by income and the interest rate. A higher income raises the demand for money, while a higher interest rate reduces the demand for money.

THE TRANSACTIONS DEMAND FOR MONEY

1 It has long been recognized that the need to bridge the time gap between the receipt of an income payment and the purchase of goods and services or earning assets is one of the most important motives for holding cash balances. Suppose that an individual has a disposable income of $12,000 per year, paid in 12 monthly installments of $1,000. If he had spent all his previous cash holdings before payday, his total cash balance upon

receipt of the paycheck is $ _____ . Plot this amount in Fig. 12-1 for the time coordinate corresponding to the beginning of the month and label the point D. If all the

money is spent during the month, the closing cash balance is $ _____ . Plot this amount in Fig. 12-1 for the time coordinate corresponding to the end of the month and label the point E. Connect the two points plotted in Fig. 12-1 with a straight line. This line shows the level of cash balances at any point in time during the month, assuming that the funds were spent at a constant rate throughout the month. The average cash

balance during the month is $ _____ . Draw a horizontal line through line DE to indicate the average cash balance. Label the line ACB_1. If the individual repeats the same pattern for the entire year, his average cash balance for the year would be ($500,

$6,000), or _____ percent of his annual income.

2 Suppose that the person who had an income of $12,000 per year receives an increase to $14,400 per year, paid in equal monthly installments of $1,200. Again assume that the cash is spent at a steady rate throughout the month, with the cash balance reaching zero at the end of the month. Plot the line showing the level of cash balances at any point during the month in Fig. 12-1. Label the line $D'E$. The average cash balance for

the month is $ _____ . Plot this amount as a horizontal line in Fig. 12-1 and label it

ACB_2. The average cash balance for the year is $ _____ , or _____ percent of yearly income. It appears that the demand for cash balances is a (constant, variable) proportion of income. If there are no other factors affecting the demand for money, the equation for the demand may be written:

(1) $M_1 = $ _____

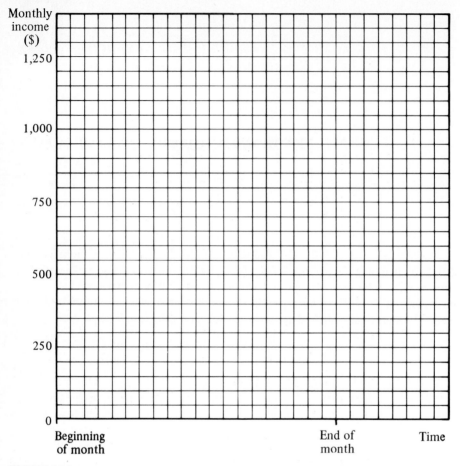

FIGURE 12-1

Plot this demand curve in Fig. 12-2 and label it M_1. Since this demand for money is based on the need to have cash to finance transactions, it is known as the *transactions demand for money*.

The transactions demand for money can be altered by changes in institutional arrangements in the financial system or by changes in individual behavior. Suppose that for the example in paragraphs 1 and 2, the annual salary was paid twice a month instead of once a month. The new demand for cash balances would be

(2) $M_1 =$ _____

Assume that the salary is received once a month and that the individual changed his behavior so that all of his money was spent by the middle of the month. The demand for money would be

(3) $M_1 =$ _____

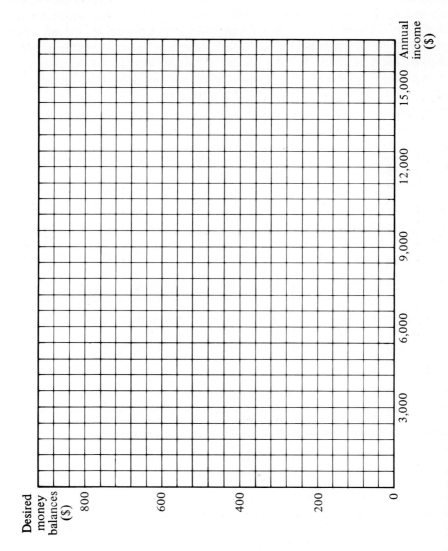

FIGURE 12-2

3 The above discussion of the demand for money is not complete, however, because it ignores the fact that holding idle cash balances is costly. Since cash earns no interest return, one can think of the interest rate as the earnings given up when cash is held rather than bonds. In other words, the interest rate is the cost of holding cash. Presumably, the decision-maker will want to minimize this cost, consistent with other objectives, in his choice of a spending pattern. What is to prevent him from holding the cost at zero merely by keeping all funds in an earning asset, say bonds, until the precise moment of a purchase, then selling the bonds? Such transactions are not cost-free, and the more such transactions there are, the higher the cost will be. It appears, therefore, that large cash balances are costly because of the large amount of foregone interest, and that small cash balances are costly because of the large transactions costs associated with frequent transfers of funds from bonds to cash. Thus, it is evident that there (is, is not) an optimum holding of cash which minimizes the sum of these costs.

4 Let us consider a simple example to illustrate the concept of an optimum cash balance. Suppose an individual receives a monthly salary of Y dollars, which he immediately uses to buy bonds bearing an interest rate i. As the month advances, he withdraws funds from his portfolio—by selling bonds—to buy goods and services. For simplicity, we assume that all the bond-fund withdrawals are the same size, Z dollars, and that they are made at equal intervals during the month. Each withdrawal entails a transactions cost of t dollars, regardless of its size. Since the Y dollars of income are withdrawn Z dollars at a time, the

number of withdrawals is _____ . The total cost of withdrawals is _____ . Since Z dollars are withdrawn each time and spent at an even rate until it is gone, the average

holding of cash is _____ . Thus, the interest cost of holding cash rather than bonds is

_____ . The total cost of the month's financial operation can be expressed as

(4) $F =$ _____ + _____

The individual wishes to choose the level of Z that (maximizes, minimizes) F. Suppose that $Y = \$1,800$ monthly, $t = \$1$, and $i = 4$ percent. This information enables us to

calculate F for various levels of Z. If $Z = \$10$, transactions costs are $ _____ ,

interest cost is $ _____ , and total cost is $ _____ . Complete Table 12-1. The data in Table 12-1 indicate that the minimum total cost of monthly financial

operations F is $ _____ , achieved by selection of _____ withdrawals of $ _____ each. (If the number of withdrawals seems unreasonably large, it is because the assumed cost per withdrawal in this example is undoubtedly too low.) The average cash balance

during the month is $ _____ .

5 Suppose the interest rate rises to 9 percent, while the other magnitudes used in Table 12-1 remain unchanged. Complete Table 12-2.

Table 12-1 Calculation of Optimal Cash Balance When
$i = 4$ Percent, $Y = \$1,800$ per Month, and $t = 1$

Z	tY/Z	$iZ/2$	F	$Z/2$
$10	$ _____	$ _____	$ _____	$ _____
$15	$ _____	$ _____	$ _____	$ _____
$20	$ _____	$ _____	$ _____	$ _____
$25	$ _____	$ _____	$ _____	$ _____
$30	$ _____	$ _____	$ _____	$ _____
$35	$ _____	$ _____	$ _____	$ _____
$40	$ _____	$ _____	$ _____	$ _____
$50	$ _____	$ _____	$ _____	$ _____

The minimum total cost F is now $ _____ , achieved by selection of _____ with-

drawals of $ _____ each. The average cash balance during the month is $ _____ .
This average balance is (more, less) than the balance chosen when the interest rate was 4
percent. This result suggests that the desired level of cash balances (rises, falls, remains
the same) when the interest rate rises.

6 Let us return to the example in paragraph 4, where the rate of interest was 4 percent.
Now change income from $1,800 to $1,250 per month. The cost of a withdrawal
remains at $1 per transaction. Complete Table 12-3.

Table 12-2 Calculation of Optimal Cash Balance When
$i = 9$ Percent, $Y = \$1,800$ per Month, and $t = 1$

Z	tY/Z	$iZ/2$	F	$Z/2$
$10	$ _____	$ _____	$ _____	$ _____
$15	$ _____	$ _____	$ _____	$ _____
$20	$ _____	$ _____	$ _____	$ _____
$25	$ _____	$ _____	$ _____	$ _____
$30	$ _____	$ _____	$ _____	$ _____
$35	$ _____	$ _____	$ _____	$ _____
$40	$ _____	$ _____	$ _____	$ _____
$50	$ _____	$ _____	$ _____	$ _____

Table 12-3 Calculation of Optimal Cash Balance When
$i = 4$ Percent, $Y = \$1,250$ per Month, and $t = 1$

Z	tY/Z	iZ/2	F	Z/2
$10	$ _____	$ _____	$ _____	$ _____
$15	$ _____	$ _____	$ _____	$ _____
$20	$ _____	$ _____	$ _____	$ _____
$25	$ _____	$ _____	$ _____	$ _____
$30	$ _____	$ _____	$ _____	$ _____
$35	$ _____	$ _____	$ _____	$ _____
$40	$ _____	$ _____	$ _____	$ _____
$50	$ _____	$ _____	$ _____	$ _____

The minimum total cost F is now $ _____ , achieved by selection of _____ with-drawals of $ _____ each. The average cash balance during the month is $ _____ . The average balance is (more, less) than the balance chosen when income was $1,800 and the interest rate was 4 percent. This result (agrees, disagrees) with the conclusion reached in paragraph 2, namely that the demand for money is positively related to the level of income.

From the above discussion, we can now express the general form of the transactions demand for money as

(5) $M_1 = f(Y, i)$

where Y is income and i is the interest rate.

PROBLEMS FOR EXERCISE 12

1 Let $Y = \$900$ per month, $i = 4$ percent, and $t = \$8$. The minimum monthly financial cost is obtained by choosing Z equal to ($40, $50, $60, $70), producing a total cost of

$ _____ . The optimal number of withdrawals is _____ , and the optimal average

cash balance is $ _____ .

2 Let $Y = \$1,800$, $i = 16$ percent, and $t = \$1$. The minimum monthly financial cost is

obtained by choosing Z to equal ($10, $15, $20, $25), producing a total cost of $ _____ .

The optimal number of withdrawals is _____ , and the optimal average cash balance is

$ _____ . (Note: This example is the same as those presented in Tables 12-1 and 12-2, except for a change in the interest rate.) Compute the optimal average cash balance for interest rates of 4 and 9 percent. In Fig. 12-3 plot the optimal average cash balance for interest rates of 4, 9, and 16 percent. Label the curve $Y = \$1,800$. The optimal average cash balance for an income level of $1,250 and interest rates of 4, 9, and 16 percent has been plotted in Fig. 12-3, and labeled $Y = \$1,250$. The functions in Fig. 12-3 indicate that the transactions demand for money balances is (positively, inversely) related to the interest rate and (positively, inversely) related to income levels.

3 (Optional) Students familiar with calculus can find the optimal average cash balance by differentiating Eq. (4) with respect to Z:

$dE/dZ =$ _____ $+$ _____ $= 0$

Solving for Z^2,

$Z^2 =$ _____

If the negative root is ignored,

$Z =$ _____

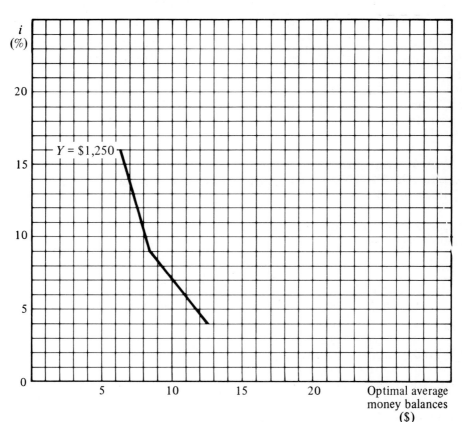

FIGURE 12-3

Find the optimal cash balance if (a) $Y = \$1{,}250$, $i = 9$ percent, $t = \$1$; (b) $Y = \$1{,}250$, $i = 16$ percent, $t = \$1$. Remember that the optimal cash balance is $Z/2$. These examples are identical to those used in Table 12-3, except for the interest rate.

ANSWERS FOR EXERCISE 12

1 1,000, Fig. 12-1A, 0, Fig. 12-1A, 500, Fig. 12-1A, 500, 4.2

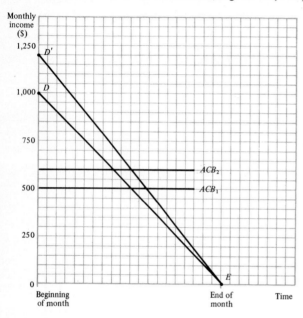

FIGURE 12-1A

2 Fig. 12-1A, 600, Fig. 12-1A, 600, 4.2, constant,
   Eq. (1) $M_1 = 0.042Y$, Fig. 12-2A, Eq. (2) $M_1 = 0.021Y$,
   Eq. (3) $M_1 = 0.021Y$

3 is

4 Y/Z, tY/Z, $Z/2$, $iZ/2$, Eq. (4) $F = tY/Z + iZ/2$
   minimizes, 180, 20, 200,

tY/Z	$iZ/2$	F	$Z/2$
180	20	200	5
120	30	150	7.5
90	40	130	10
75	50	125	12.5
60	60	120	15
51.4	70	121.4	17.5
45	80	125	20
36	100	136	25

120, 60, 30, 15

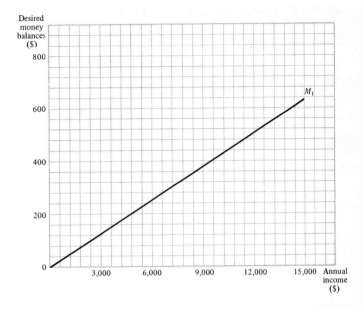

FIGURE 12-2A

5

tY/Z	$iZ/2$	F	$Z/2$
180	45	225	5
120	67.5	187.5	7.5
90	90	180	10
75	112.5	187.5	12.5
60	235	196	15
51.4	157.5	208.9	17.5
45	180	225	20
36	225	261	25

180, 90, 20, 10, less, falls

6

tY/Z	$iZ/2$	F	$Z/2$
125	20	145	5
83.3	30	113.3	7.5
62.5	40	102.5	10
50	50	100	12.5
41.7	60	101.7	15
35.7	70	105.7	17.5
31.3	80	111.3	20
25	100	125	25

100, 50, 25, 12.5, less, agrees

ANSWERS TO PROBLEMS FOR EXERCISE 12

1 60, 240, 15, 30
2 15, 240, 60, 7.5, Fig. 12-3A, inversely, positively
3 $dF/dZ = -tY/Z^2 + i/2 = 0$,
$2tY/i$, $Z = \sqrt{2tY/I}$, 8.33, 6.25, Fig. 12-3A

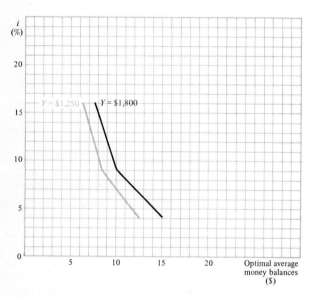

FIGURE 12-3A

THE SPECULATIVE DEMAND FOR MONEY

1 In this exercise we consider two reasons for holding idle cash balances in addition to the transactions motive of Exercise 12—speculation and risk avoidance. The speculative motive is based on the simple premise that if one expects the price of an item to rise, he should buy it now and not wait. Conversely, if one expects the price to fall, he should delay the purchase until later. In the latter case, the person might hold cash so that he will be ready to take action when the price drops. How are these expectations of future prices formed? One possibility is that people tend to form an idea of "normal" prices from the past experience of price fluctuations. If prices are currently above "normal," they are expected to fall. This argument can be made with bond prices as well as with goods prices. In the case of bonds, it is also possible to state the argument using the interest rate instead of the price of a bond. Since higher bond prices are associated with (higher, lower) interest rates, an investor who expects interest rates to fall would also expect bond prices to (rise, fall) and therefore would (buy bonds now, hold cash now and buy bonds later).

2 Suppose that a particular individual believes that the *normal* interest rate is 4 percent. If the rate is currently 4.5 percent, he would expect the rate to (rise, fall) and would (buy bonds now, hold cash now). His demand for money is (zero, 100, between zero and 100) percent of his total assets. If, however, the market interest rate were to fall to 3.5 percent, the investor would expect the rate to (rise, fall) and would (buy bonds now, hold cash now). His demand for money is now (zero, 100, between zero and 100) percent of his total assets. Thus, when the interest rate falls, the demand to hold money assets is likely to (rise, fall). This result is called the *speculative demand for money*. Note that the speculative demand to hold money (reinforces, offsets) the conclusion reached in Exercise 12 about the impact of the interest rate on the transactions demand to hold money.

3 The argument just presented (does, does not) produce a rationale for the speculative demand for money falling *smoothly* as the interest rate rises. Instead, the investor is assumed to abruptly shift his portfolio from 100 percent bonds to 100 percent cash as the interest rate drops below the normal rate expected by this particular individual. When the behavior of the entire economy is under study, the total speculative demand for money is the sum of many individual demands, each of which is conceivably formed by a different expectation of the normal rate of interest. Suppose that there are three individuals, each of whom must make a decision to hold $1,000 of assets either in bonds or cash. Individual A believes that the normal interest rate is 4 percent, B believes that the normal rate is 5 percent, and C believes that it is 6 percent. If the interest rate is currently 4.5 percent, A would expect the rate to (rise, fall), B would expect it to (rise, fall), and C would expect it to (rise, fall). Thus, A would hold (bonds, money), B would hold (bonds, money) and C would hold (bonds, money). The total speculative

demand for money at an interest rate of 4.5 percent would be $ _____ . Complete Table 13-1. Plot the interest rate and speculative demand for money data of Table 13-1 on Fig. 13-1. Label the curve M_2. The total speculative demand for money curve has a (positive, negative) slope.

4 It is unlikely, however, that most people make such decisions to hold all funds in one asset or the other on the basis of a single estimate of the normal asset price. A more realistic view is that individuals have a schedule of price expectations similar to M_2 in Fig. 13-1. Given the possibility of error, when the current interest rate was 4.5 percent, if individual A believed that the normal interest rate was 4 percent, he would hold some bonds and some money assets—in addition to those held for transactions balances. If the market rate then increased to 5.5 percent, and if his expectations were unchanged, A would (increase, decrease) his bond holdings and thereby (increase, decrease) his money holdings. Thus, the speculative demand for money hypothesis suggests that changes in interest rates lead to marginal adjustments in portfolio composition. This extension is (compatible, at variance) with the simple formulation of the speculative demand hypothesis presented in paragraph 3.

5 The speculative hypothesis has the weakness of assuming that rational individuals, sharing common past experiences, would have significantly different expectations about the future. One might postulate, alternatively, that expectations of different individuals would tend to converge, causing them to behave in about the same way. If, for example, the interest rate remained at 4.5 percent for a considerable period of time, most likely individuals A, B, and C would not indefinitely expect the rate to change to 4, 5, and 6

Table 13-1

Interest rate	Individuals choosing to hold money	Total speculative demand for money
3.5%	_____	$_____
4.5%	_____	$_____
5.5%	_____	$_____
6.5%	_____	$_____

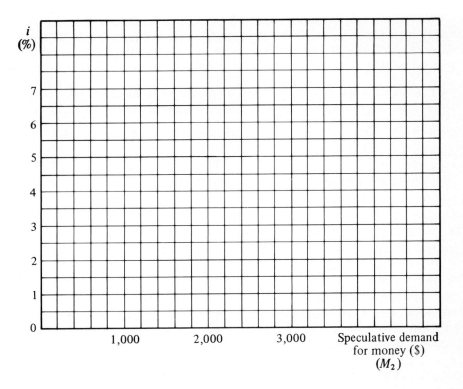

FIGURE 13-1

percent respectively. Thus, the speculative motive may be of more importance for short-term disturbances than for permanent holdings of cash. The speculative motive, however, is sometimes used as a blanket term for all of the factors which make the demand for money interest-elastic. (Recall the interest-elastic transactions demand for money argument of Exercise 12.) If there is a convergence of market expectations over time, this event will result in a (movement along, shift of) the M_2 curve in Fig. 13-1.

6 The final motive for holding cash which will be discussed in this exercise is *risk avoidance*. While it is difficult to quantify risk, it is generally accepted that risk is associated with the variability of the possible outcomes of an investment. The greater the variability of possible outcomes and the greater the likelihood of *unfavorable* outcomes, the riskier is the investment. Since cash has, under normal circumstances, no variability of value and no probability of loss, it may be considered a risk-free investment and consequently may be an attractive investment for those for whom the yields on interest-bearing assets is insufficient to compensate for their risk of capital loss.

7 Suppose there is an available investment, opportunity I, which costs $1,000 and has a 50 percent probability of returning $2,100 and a 50 percent probability of returning $0. If this type of investment was made twice, succeeding once and failing once, the total net profit would be $ _____ or an average of $ _____ per attempt. The expected rate of return on the investment is $ _____ per $1,000, or _____ percent. Another investment, opportunity II, costs $1,000 and has a 50 percent probability of returning $2,000 and a 50 percent probability of returning $0. The average net profit

over a large number of trials of $1,000 invested is $ _____ , or _____ percent. Finally, assume that opportunity III is expected to return $1,000 on a $1,000 investment, with no chance of either a larger or a smaller payment. The average return on

$1,000 invested is $ _____ , or _____ percent. Are any of these opportunities

equivalent to holding cash? (yes, no)   If so, which one(s)? _____ .

Comparing assets II and III, which has the greater risk? _____ . Which has the

greater average yield? _____ . Would a risk-avoiding investor ever choose asset II over

asset I? (yes, no) Why or why not? _____

_____

_____ . Comparing assets I and III, which has the larger yield?

_____ . Which asset has the greater risk? _____   Is there a clear-cut choice between these assets for a risk-avoiding investor? (yes, no)   More specifically, would an investor be irrational if he chose asset III over I, even though asset I is expected to earn 5 percent? (yes, no)   Avoidance of risk, therefore, (does, does not) provide a rationale for holding cash.

8 Suppose that a particular individual decided to diversify his holdings, putting $1,000

in asset I and $1,000 in asset III. In this case, his demand for money is $ _____ when

the expected interest yield on I is _____ percent. Let us now modify asset I such that there is a 50 percent chance of a $2,200 return and a 50 percent chance of a $0

return. The expected rate of return is now _____ percent. If the individual responds to this change by holding $1,500 in asset I and $500 in asset III, then his demand for

money is $ _____ when the interest rate is _____ percent. His demand for money (rises, falls) when the interest rate rises, thus (confirming, denying) the conclusion reached earlier in this exercise and previously in Exercise 12 about the effect of a change in the interest rate on the demand for money.

9 The argument of Exercises 12 and 13 justifies writing the demand for money equation as follows:

(1) $M_d = f(Y, i)$

where M_d is the total demand for money, Y is income and i is the rate of interest. Income has a(n) (direct, inverse) effect on M_d, while i has a(n) (direct, inverse) impact. For simplicity of exposition in later exercises, the demand for money will be treated as if the income effect and the interest effect were completely separable. Moreover, it will be assumed that the income effect is attributable solely to the transactions motive and the interest rate effect to the speculative motive. Finally, the income effect will be assumed to be proportional, despite the conclusion to the contrary reached in Exercise 12, Prob. 3. Thus, Eq. (1) will be written as

(2) $M_d = kY + Li$

where k is a constant and L is a functional notation symbol signifying that the demand for money depends on the interest rate in some unspecified but inverse way.

10   The supply of money is taken to be a policy parameter, determined by the Federal Reserve. While the commercial banking system has much leeway in determining how much demand-deposit money will be created from a given level of reserves, it is convenient—and not completely inaccurate—to assume that the Fed's control of bank reserves gives it effective control of the money supply. Thus, the equation for the money supply is

(3) $M_S = M_O$

where M_O is an arbitrary number *autonomously* determined by the Fed.
     In equilibrium the supply of money must equal the demand for money. Thus, by combining Eqs. (2) and (3), we have

(4) $M_O = kY + Li$

Since it is impossible to determine equilibrium income without knowing in advance the rate of interest, the equality of the supply and demand for money (is, is not) sufficient to determine simultaneously the equilibrium level of income and the interest rate. Determination of these equilibrium values will be explained in Part 5.

PROBLEMS FOR EXERCISE 13

1 Investor A has $500 and believes that the normal interest rate is 4.5 percent. Investor B has $750 and believes that the normal interest rate is 7.0 percent. Investor C has $600 and believes that the normal interest rate is 5.5 percent. What is the total demand for money if the current interest rate is 6.0 percent? $ _____ . What is the total demand for money if the interest rate is 5.0 percent? $ _____ .

2 Suppose that investor C of paragraph 1 above talked to investor A and convinced him that the normal interest rate is really 5.5 percent. When the current interest rate is 5.0 percent, the total demand for money is now $ _____ .

3 Suppose that an investment costing $1,200 has a 2/3 probability of returning $1,500 and a 1/3 probability of returning $900. If an investor accepts the opportunity three times and indeed has two successes and one failure, his total gross return is $ _____ , his net profit is $ _____ , and the rate of return is _____ percent. Now suppose that the probable return from the successful outcomes rose to $1,800, while the probable

return on the unfavorable outcome fell to $300. What is the rate of return on the invest-
ment now? _____ percent. Has the investment become more or less risky? _____ .
Thus, a risk-averting investor would be (more, less) likely to hold cash after the change.

4 If, in the previous example, the probable favorable outcomes paid $2,000, while the
probable unfavorable outcome paid $300, the rate of return would rise to _____ per-
cent. An investor would probably be (more, less) likely to hold cash than if the probable
favorable outcomes paid $1,800 and the probable unfavorable one paid $300.

ANSWERS FOR EXERCISE 13

1 lower, rise, buy bonds now
2 fall, buy bonds now, zero, rise, hold cash now, 100, rise, reinforces
3 does not, fall, rise, rise, bonds, money, money, 2,000,

3.5%	A, B, C	3,000
4.5	B, C	2,000
5.5	C	1,000
6.5	none	0

Fig. 13-1A, negative

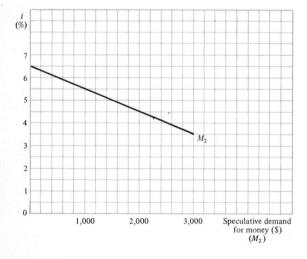

FIGURE 13-1A

4 increase, decrease, compatible
5 shift of
7 100, 50, 50, 5, 0, 0, 0, 0, yes, III, II, neither, no, II has a greater risk than III without
compensating for this factor with a higher yield, I, I, no, no, does

8 1,000, 5, 10, 500, 10, falls, confirming
9 direct, inverse
10 is not

ANSWERS TO PROBLEMS FOR EXERCISE 13

1 1,100, 500
2 0
3 3,900, 300, 8.33, 8.33, more, more
4 19.4, less

REVIEW TEST FOR PART 4

1 If income rises, the demand for money
   (a) rises
   (b) falls
   (c) remains the same

2 The effect of income on the demand for money arises from which motives for holding money?
   (a) transactions demand for money
   (b) speculative demand for money
   (c) risk avoidance

3 If the interest rate rises, the demand for money
   (a) rises
   (b) falls
   (c) remains the same

4 The effect of the interest rate on the demand for money arises from which motive(s) for holding money?
   (a) transactions demand for money
   (b) speculative demand for money
   (c) risk avoidance

5 The assumption that interest rates have a "normal" level to which they tend to return is characteristic of which motive(s) for holding money?
   (a) transactions demand for money
   (b) speculative demand for money
   (c) risk avoidance

6 The argument that the interest rate affects the transactions demand for money arises from the introduction of
   (a) income variation
   (b) risk variation

196

(c) transactions costs

(d) speculation

7 The risk of an investment may be measured by
   (a) the variability of possible returns
   (b) the interest rate
   (c) the probability of incurring losses
   (d) the marginal efficiency of capital

8 A risk-avoiding investor would never choose an investment which
   (a) earns more and has more risk than another investment
   (b) earns the same and has more risk than another investment
   (c) earns more and has the same risk as another investment
   (d) earns less and has the same risk as another investment

9 If people expect interest rates to fall, they would
   (a) buy bonds now
   (b) hold cash and buy bonds later
   (c) expect bond prices to rise
   (d) expect bond prices to fall

10 A person would not hold cash if he were
   (a) a risk seeker rather than a risk avoider
   (b) able to buy and sell bonds without transactions costs
   (c) expecting interest rates to rise
   (d) all of the above
   (e) none of the above

11 If interest rates are extremely high, people would normally hold more bonds and
   less cash because
   (a) the opportunity cost of holding idle cash is higher
   (b) there is a greater chance of a decline in rates in the near future
   (c) there is a larger reward for bearing risk
   (d) as interest rates rise, transactions costs fall
   (e) all of the above

12 The money supply can be considered a policy parameter as a first approximation
   because
   (a) the United States Constitution grants to Congress the power to coin money
   (b) the Federal Reserve has fairly complete control over bank reserves
   (c) the government controls spending on goods and services, which automatically
       provides control over the money supply
   (d) it does not pay the banking system to vary the money supply

13 If the money supply is a policy parameter, then the equilibrium condition that the
   supply of money equal the demand for money is sufficient to determine the interest
   rate and the level of income.
   (a) true
   (b) false

14 If transactions costs were to fall, other things remaining unchanged, the demand for money would
   (a)   rise
   (b)   fall
   (c)   remain unchanged

15 If people's aversion to risk were to increase, other things remaining the same, the demand for money would
   (a)   rise
   (b)   fall
   (c)   remain the same

16 If recent experience with high interest rates were to cause people to conclude that the "normal" rate is higher than they had previously believed, the demand for money at any interest rate would
   (a)   rise
   (b)   fall
   (c)   remain the same

GENERAL EQUILIBRIUM OF THE
PRODUCT AND MONEY MARKETS

The objective of Part 5 is to provide a simple framework for studying the combined effects on aggregate demand of the principal product and monetary variables for a three-sector model—personal, business and government.

One of the difficulties in studying economics, particularly macroeconomics, is the necessity to evaluate all of the effects of an exogenous event in a system in which everything affects everything else. This problem of *general equilibrium analysis* is usually dealt with by dividing the economy into separate sectors which are then studied individually. While one sector is under consideration, the variables in other sectors are held constant and events taking place there are assumed not to affect the sector being studied. Such a framework is provided by the *IS–LM* model, developed in this section.

Analysis of the impact and interaction of macroeconomic variables in determining equilibrium income is approached through a division of the economy into three broad sectors or "markets": product (goods and services), money, and government securities. The usual practice is to study explicitly only the first two sectors, leaving securities in the background. After each of the markets is examined separately, we then consider the effects each has on the other. If one market, money, for example, is in equilibrium, it will not remain so for long if the product market is not in equilibrium. The adjustment process in the product market will produce repercussions in the money market, forcing it out of equilibrium. Thus, no single market can remain in equilibrium unless *all* markets are in equilibrium. When that situation is achieved, the economy is said to be in a state of *general equilibrium*.

The *IS–LM* model also provides a tool for studying the impact of government fiscal and monetary policy actions. Fiscal policy actions in our simple model are restricted to changes in government spending and taxes; monetary policy actions are limited to changes in the money supply. Since each of these three variables has three possible qualitative changes—up, down, no change—there are many possible monetary-fiscal policy combinations. The simple *IS–LM* model is useful for studying the net impact on income of economic policy produced by these different policy tool combinations.

PRODUCT MARKET EQUILIBRIUM

1 The condition for equilibrium in the product market may be stated as an equality between spending leakages and spending injections. In the two-section model – personal and business – total leakages are $(\underline{S}, I, S + I)$ and total injections are $(S, \underline{I}, S + I)$. Hence, the equilibrium condition is ___S___ = ___I___ .

2 Suppose it is found from empirical observation that consumption is related to income by the following equation:

(1) $C = \$100 \text{ bil} + 0.80\,Y$

where C stands for real consumption expenditures and Y stands for real income. Since saving is defined as $S =$ ___$Y-C$___ , the equation for saving corresponding to the above expression for consumption is

(2) $S =$ ___$-100 + 0.2\,Y$___

The MPS is ___.2___ . Plot Eq. (2) m quadrant (B) of Fig. 14-1 and label the curve S.

3 Following Exercise 10, assume that investment is related to the interest rate as follows:

(3) $I = 150 \text{ bil} - 10i$

where I represents real investment and i represents the interest rate. Plot the investment function (3) in quadrant (D) of Fig. 14-1 and label it I.

4 Since saving is measured on the vertical axis of quadrant (B), it can also be measured on the vertical axis of quadrant (A), using the same scale. Since investment is measured on the horizontal axis of quadrant (D), it can also be measured on the horizontal axis of quadrant (A). In quadrant (A), label the vertical axis S and the horizontal axis I. The equilibrium condition $S = I$ can be expressed in quadrant (A) as a $(30°, \underline{45°}, 60°)$ line drawn from the origin. Draw a curve representing this equation in quadrant (A) of Fig. 14-1 and label it $S = I$.

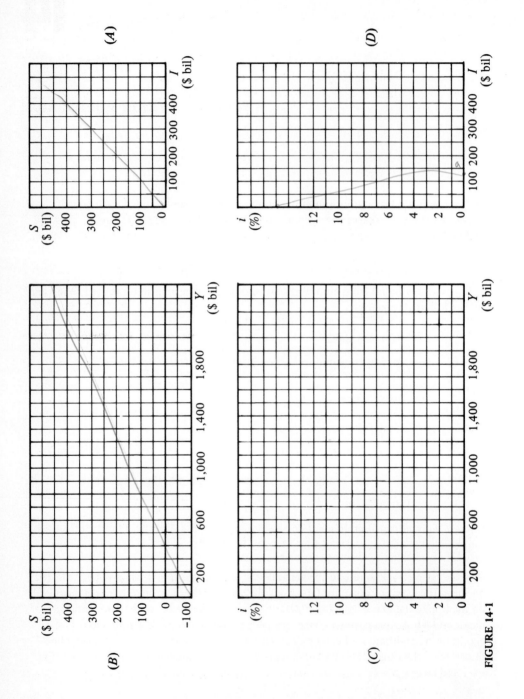

FIGURE 14-1

5 Suppose the rate of interest was zero percent. In quadrant (D) we find that investment would be $ __150__ bil. Label this point a on the investment function. For
equilibrium to occur when I = $150 bil, saving must be $__150__ bil. Find the point in
quadrant (A) which corresponds to these values of S and I. Label this point a. According
to the saving function, saving of $150 bil occurs when income is $_____bil. On the
saving function label with an a the point which corresponds to these levels of saving and
income. Finally, in quadrant (C) label with an a the point corresponding to the values
for income and the interest rate you have found. This point will occur at i = _____
percent and Y = $_____bil. Point a in quadrant (C) represents equilibrium Y in the
(product, money) sector when i = zero percent.

6 Repeat the process of paragraph 5, assuming that the interest rate is 5 percent. Label
the points in the diagram with b's. Repeat the process again, assuming that the interest
rate is 10 percent. Label these points with c's.

7 Connect points a, b and c in quadrant (C) with a straight line and label it IS_1. This
schedule gives all the combinations of income and interest rates for which saving equals
investment—i.e., the equilibrium condition. Alternatively, the IS curve shows the resulting equilibrium income values produced by the structural equations S and I for different
levels of interest rates. The IS curve (does, does not) yield a determinant solution for
equilibrium income unless a unique interest rate is specified.

If i = 7.0 percent, what level of income would equate S and I? $_____bil. If
i = 11.0 percent, equilibrium income would be $_____bil. The change in income
resulting from a change in interest rates represents a (movement along, shift in) the IS
curve. The algebraic equation for the IS_1 curve is:

(4) $Y =$ _____

8 When we add the government sector certain modifications must be made to the foregoing macroeconomic model. Introducing taxes T adds a new (leakage, injection) and
government expenditures G an additional (leakage, injection) to the model.

Since it is generally argued that consumption depends on disposable income Y_d,
with the introduction of taxes the consumption function must be rewritten to account
for the fact that disposable income is not equal to GNP. With the addition of taxes
$Y_d =$ _____. Hence the consumption function in (1) would be rewritten as

(5) $C =$ _____

The equation for saving corresponding to (5) would be

(6) $S =$ _____

As compared to Eq. (2), the MPS (has, has not) changed and hence (2) and (6) (are, are
not) parallel lines.

Equation (6) (does, does not) represent the equation for total leakages, but if we assume initially that taxes are zero, Eq. (6) (does, does not) represent the equation for total leakages. Plot Eq. (6) in quadrant (B) of Fig. 14-2 and label the curve $(S + T)_1$.

9 Assume that investment is related to the interest rate as follows:

(7) $I = \$150 \text{ bil} - 10i$

Plot Eq. (7) in quadrant (D) of Fig. 14-2. Label the curve I.

10 Let government spending be exogenously determined at $150 bil. The equation for total injections would be

(8) $I + G = $ _____

Since G is not functionally related to i, the $I + G$ line (is, is not) parallel to I. Plot Eq. (8) in quadrant (D) of Fig. 14-2 and label it $I + G$.

11 Is the equilibrium equation of quadrant (A) still a 45° line? (yes, no)   Draw the correct line in quadrant (A) of Fig. 14-2. The correct label for this curve is $(S = I, S + T = I + G)$.

12 If the rate of interest were zero, investment would be $_____ bil; total injections would be $_____ bil. For equilibrium to occur, total leakages must be $_____ bil.

In this case, still assuming $T = 0$, saving is $_____ bil. Income must be $_____ bil for total leakages to equal total injections. In quadrant (C) of Fig. 14-2 label with an a the point corresponding to the values for income and the interest rates you have found.

13 Repeat the steps of paragraph 12, assuming that the interest rate is 10 percent. Label with a b the point in quadrant (C) corresponding to the interest rate and income. Connect the points in quadrant (C) with a straight line and label it IS_2. The algebraic expression for the IS_2 curve is:

(9) $Y = $ _____

14 Plot the IS_1 Eq. (4) in quadrant (C) of Fig. 14-2. The IS_1 curve (does, does not) include the effects of government spending. As a result of adding G, the IS curve has

shifted to the (right, left) by an amount equal to $_____ bil for all interest rates. This shift is equal to (3, 4, 5) times the addition of G, which reflects the value of the (C, I, G) multiplier.

Has the slope of the IS curve changed with the addition of G? (yes, no)   Why or why not? _____

_____

15 While maintaining G at $150 bil, raise taxes from zero to $150 bil. The saving function would be

(10) $S = $ _____

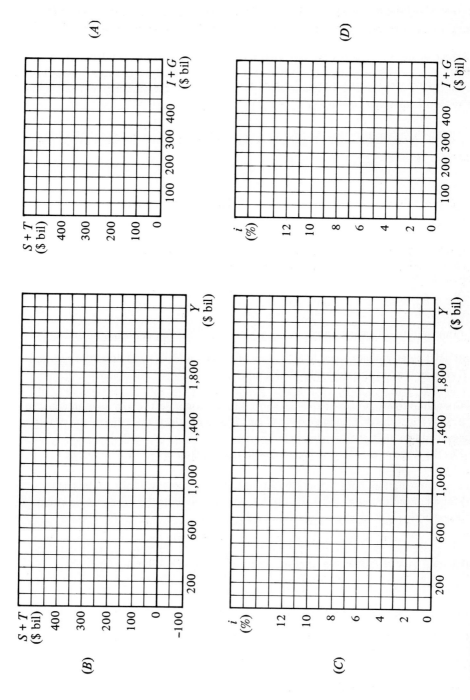

FIGURE 14-2

16 The total leakages equation would be

(11) $S + T =$ _____

The slope of the $S + T$ curve (has, has not) changed because taxes were introduced as an independent variable—that is, T is assumed not to be functionally related to Y. Plot Eq. (11) in quadrant (B) of Fig. 14-2 and label it $(S + T)_2$. Using leakage Eqs. (8) and (11), derive the IS curve and label it IS_3.

17 The algebraic equation for the IS_3 curve is

(12) $Y =$ _____

18 IS_3 shows that when the interest rate is 10 percent, the following amounts are obtained

$S = \$$_____ bil $I = \$$_____ bil

$T = \$$_____ bil $G = \$$_____ bil

Thus, at $i = 10$ percent, total leakages of $\$$_____ bil, equal to total injections of $\$$_____ bil, results in an equilibrium income level of $\$$_____ bil.

19 Compared to IS_2, which (does, does not) include T, the IS_3 curve has shifted to the (right, left) by an amount equal to $\$$_____ bil, which is (2, 3, 4, 5) times the addition of T. The amount of this shift reflects the value of the (I, G, T) multiplier.

20 Compared to IS_1, the IS_3 curve has shifted to the (right, left) by an amount equal to (1, 2, 3, 4) times the original increase in G and T, which reflects the value of the simple balanced budget multiplier developed in Exercise 9.

Has the slope of the IS curve changed with the addition of G and T? (yes, no)

21 If we now increase both G and T by $10 bil, the IS_3 curve will shift to the (right, left) for all interest rates by $\$(10, 30, 40)$ bil, which represents the net algebraic effect of adding both a leakage and an injection to the model.

22 The preceding discussion suggests that a parallel shift to the right of the IS curve is caused by a parallel shift to the (indicate right or left) by the following functions:

S _____ I _____

T _____ G _____

The rightward shift of S and T represents a(n) (increase, decrease) in these functions, which is the (same, opposite) of the I and G functions. The shift in the IS curve will be (greater than, equal to, less than) the initial shift in the structural equation, due to the

_____ .

23 If the government makes transfer payments (Tr) *to* the personal sector, in addition to collecting taxes *from it*, these payments represent an offset to tax leakages $(T - Tr)$.

Consequently, disposable income would be $Y_d =$ _____, and the saving function would be

(13) $S =$ _____

and the total leakages functions would be

(14) $S + T - Tr =$ _____

Thus, the example using taxes equal to $150 bil and transfers equal to zero is precisely equivalent to one in which taxes are zero and transfers are $150 bil.

24 The IS_3 curve and structural Eqs. (8) and (11) are reproduced in Fig. 14-3. Now assume that the investment function changes to

(15) $I = \$150$ bil $- 25i$

This change represents a(n) (increase, decrease) in the interest-elasticity of the investment demand function and results in a (parallel shift, change in the slope) of the total injection function. Plot the new $I + G$ function in quadrant (D) of Fig. 14-3 and label it $(I + G)_2$. Derive the new IS curve and label it IS_4. Has G changed? (yes, no) The IS_4 curve is (steeper, flatter) and thus (more, less) interest-elastic, reflecting the interest elasticity of the I function.

PROBLEMS FOR EXERCISE 14

1 (a) Assume that the following consumption and investment functions are representative in an economy:

$C = \$100$ bil $+ 0.75 Y_d$

$I = \$200$ bil $- 15i$

Government spending and taxes are initially zero. Plot the saving function in quadrant (B) of Fig. 14-4, the investment function in quadrant (D), and the product market equilibrium line in quadrant (C). These are the total leakage and total injection functions.

(b) When $i = 4$ percent, investment is $___140___ bil and total injections are $___140___ bil. In equilibrium, total leakages must be $___140___ bil and saving $___40___ bil. Therefore, income must be $___961___ bil. When $i = 6$ percent, equilibrium income is $___840___ bil. When $i = 8$ percent, equilibrium income is $___720___ bil.

(c) The equation for the IS curve is $Y =$ ___1200___ $-60i$___. Label this total product curve IS_1 on Fig. 14-4.

Using the information developed in paragraph 1, complete questions 2 to 7. Assume that each indicated change remains in effect permanently, so that question 3 depends on what happens in question 2 and so on.

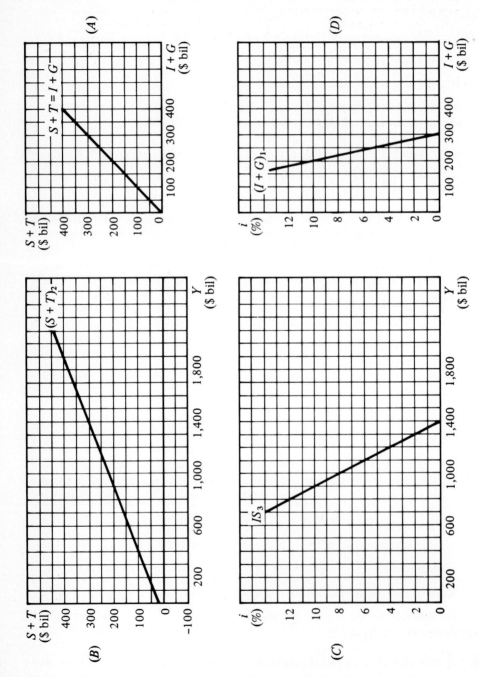

FIGURE 14-3

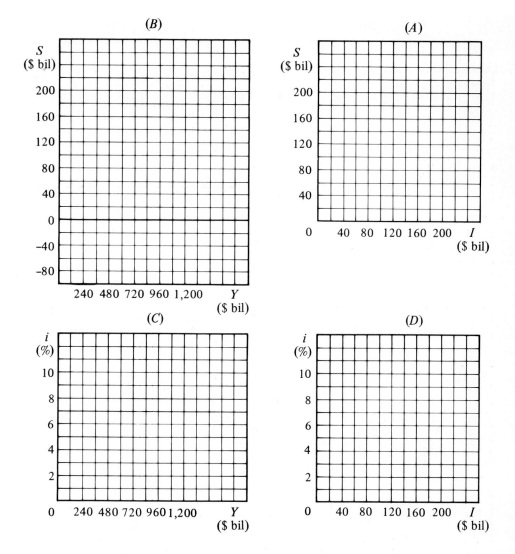

FIGURE 14-4

2 Government spending rises to $30 bil. Show the graphical solution on Fig. 14-5. Label the product market equilibrium curve IS_2. Complete the following, assuming an interest rate of 6 percent:

(a) Investment $_____ bil

(b) Total injections $_____ bil

(c) Equilibrium saving $_____ bil

(d) Equilibrium total leakages $_____ bil

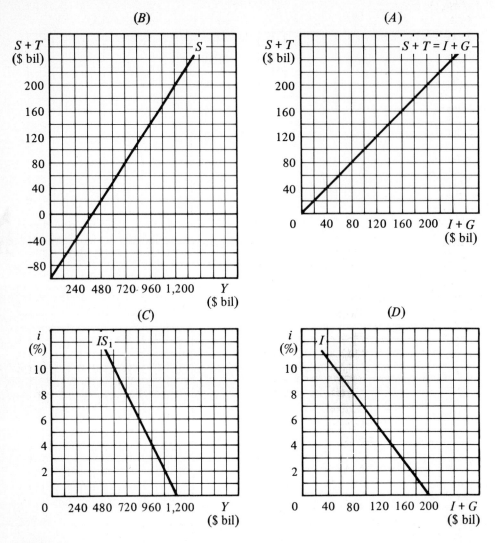

FIGURE 14-5

3 Taxes rise to $80 bil. Show the graphical solution on Fig. 14-5. Label the product market equilibrium curve IS_3. Complete the following, assuming an interest rate of 6 percent:

(a) Investment $_____ bil

(b) Total injections $_____ bil

(c) Equilibrium saving $_____ bil

(d) Equilibrium total leakages $_____ bil

4 The consumption function shifts to $C = \$40$ bil $+ 0.75\,Y_d$. Show the graphical solution on Fig. 14-6. Label the new total leakages function $S' + T$ and the new product market equilibrium curve IS_4. Complete the following, assuming an interest rate of 6 percent:

    (a) Investment $\$$_____ bil

    (b) Total injections $\$$_____ bil

    (c) Equilibrium saving $\$$_____ bil

    (d) Equilibrium total leakages $\$$_____ bil

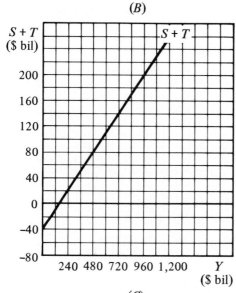

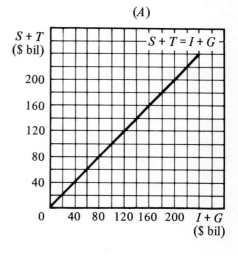

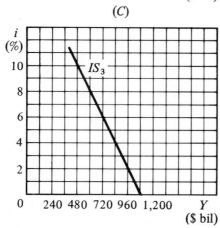

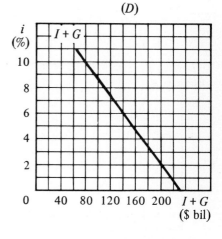

FIGURE 14-6

5 The investment function shifts to $I = \$230$ bil $- 15i$. Show the graphical solution on Fig. 14-6. Label the total injections function $I' + G$ and the new product market equilibrium curve IS_5. Complete the following, assuming an interest rate of 6 percent:

(a) Investment $\$$_____ bil

(b) Total injections $\$$_____ bil

(c) Equilibrium saving $\$$_____ bil

(d) Equilibrium total leakages $\$$_____ bil

6 The investment function shifts to $I = \$230$ bil $- 6i$. Show the graphical solution on Fig. 14-7. Label the new total injections curve $I'' + G$ and the new product market

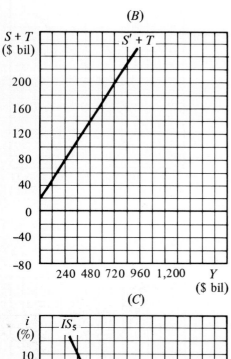

(B)

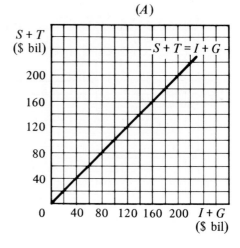

(A)

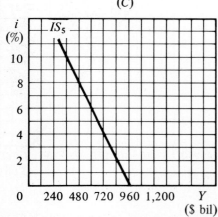

(C)

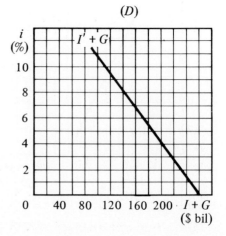

(D)

FIGURE 14-7

equilibrium curve IS_6. Complete the following, assuming an interest rate of 5 percent:

(a) Investment $\$$_____ bil

(b) Total injections $\$$_____ bil

(c) Equilibrium saving $\$$_____ bil

(d) Equilibrium total leakages $\$$_____ bil

7 The consumption function shifts to $C = \$40$ bil $+ 1/6Y_d$. Label the new total injections curve $S'' + T$ and the new product market equilibrium curve IS_7 in Fig. 14.7. Complete the following, assuming an interest rate of 5 percent:

(a) Investment $\$$_____ bil

(b) Total injections $\$$_____ bil

(c) Equilibrium saving $\$$_____ bil

(d) Equilibrium total leakages $\$$_____ bil

ANSWERS FOR EXERCISE 14

1 $S, I, S = I$

2 $Y - C$, $-\$100$ bil $+ 0.20Y$, i.e.:

$$S = Y - C$$
$$C = \$100 \text{ bil} + 0.80Y$$
$$S = Y - (\$100 \text{ bil} + 0.80Y)$$
$$S = Y - \$100 \text{ bil} - 0.80Y$$
$$S = -\$100 \text{ bil} + (1-0.80)Y$$
$$S = -\$100 \text{ bil} + 0.20Y$$

0.20, Fig. 14-1A

3 Fig. 14-1A

4 Fig. 14-1A, $45°$, Fig. 14-1A

5 150, 150, Fig. 14-1A, 1,250, Fig. 14-1A, zero, 1,250, product

6 Fig. 14-1A

7 Fig. 14-1A, does not, 900, 700, movement along, $\$1,250$ bil $- 50i$

8 leakage, injection, $Y - T$, $\$100$ bil $+ 0.80(Y - T)$, $-\$100$ bil $+ 0.20(Y - T)$, has not, are, does not, does, Fig. 14-2A

9 Fig. 14-2A

10 $\$300$ bil $- 10i$, is, Fig. 14-2A

11 yes, Fig. 14-2A, $S + T = I + G$

12 150, 300, 300, 300 (recall that taxes are initially assumed to be zero), 2,000, Fig. 14-2A

13 Fig. 14-2A, $I = \$50$ bil, $I + G = \$200$ bil, $S = \$200$ bil, $Y = \$1,500$ bil, $\$2,000$ bil $- 50i$

14 Fig. 14-2A, does not, right 750, 5, G, no, the slopes of the leakage and injection equations have not changed

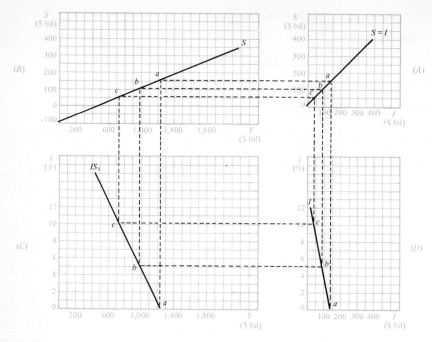

FIGURE 14-1A

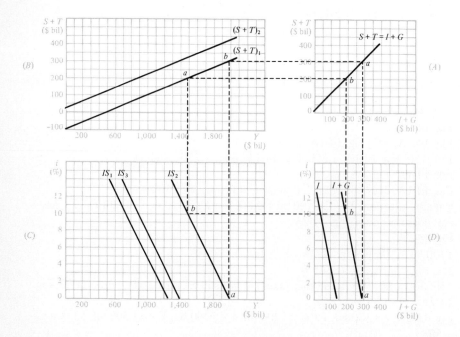

FIGURE 14-2A

15 $S = -\$130$ bil $+ 0.20Y$, i.e.:

$S = -a + s(Y - T)$

$S = -a + sY - sT$

$S = (-a - sT) + sY$

$S = (-\$100$ bil $- \$30$ bil$) + 0.20Y$

$S = -\$130$ bil $+ 0.20Y$

16 $S + T = +\$20$ bil $+ 0.20Y$, i.e.:

$S + T = -a + s(Y - T) + T$

$S + T = -a + sY - sT + T$

$S + T = -a + T - sT + sY$

$S + T = -a + T(1 - s) + sY$

$S + T = (-a + bT) + sY$

$S + T = [-\$100$ bil $+ (0.80)(\$150$ bil$)] + 0.20Y$

$S + T = +\$20$ bil $+ 0.20Y$,

has not

17 Fig. 14-2A, $\$1,400$ bil $- 50i$

18 $S = \$50$ bil, $I = \$50$ bil, $T = \$150$ bil, $G = \$150$ bil, 200, 200, 900

19 does not, left, 600, 4, T

20 right, 1, no

21 right, 10

22 right, right, right, right, decrease, opposite, greater than, multiplier

23 $Y - T + Tr$, $-\$100$ bil $+ 0.20(Y - T + Tr)$,

$S + T - Tr = (-\$100$ bil $+ 0.80T - 0.80Tr) + 0.20Y$, i.e.:

$S + T - Tr = -a + s(Y - T + Tr) + T - Tr$

$S + T - Tr = -a + sY - sT + sTr + T - Tr$

$S + T - Tr = -a + T - sT - Tr + sTr + sY$

$S + T - Tr = -a + T(1 - s) - Tr(1 - s) + sY$

$S + T - Tr = (-a + bT - bTr) + sY$

24 increase, change in the slope, Fig. 14-3A, no, flatter, more

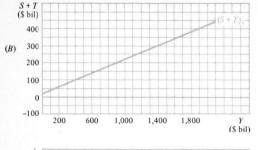

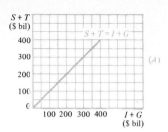

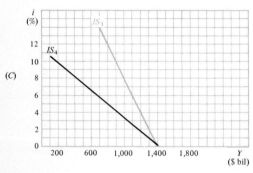

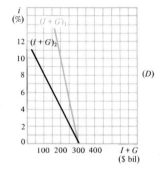

FIGURE 14-3A

ANSWERS TO PROBLEMS FOR EXERCISE 14

1 (a) Fig. 14-4A
   (b) 140, 140, 140, 140, 960, 840, 720
   (c) $1,200 bil − 60$i$
2 Fig. 14-5A, (a) 110, (b) 140, (c) 140, (d) 140
3 Fig. 14-5A, (a) 110, (b) 140, (c) 60, (d) 140
4 Fig. 14-6A, (a) 110, (b) 140, (c) 60, (d) 140
5 Fig. 14-6A, (a) 140, (b) 170, (c) 90, (d) 170
6 Fig. 14-7A, (a) 200, (b) 230, (c) 150, (d) 230
7 Fig. 14-7A, (a) 200, (b) 230, (c) 150, (d) 230

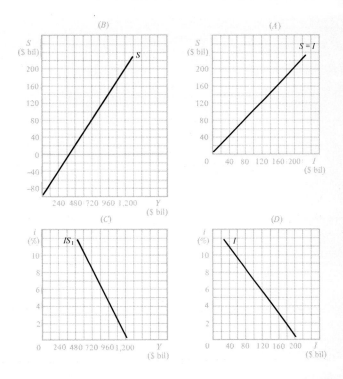

FIGURE 14-4A

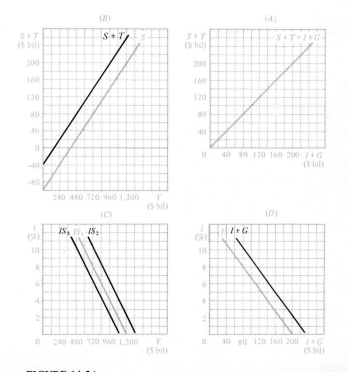

FIGURE 14-5A

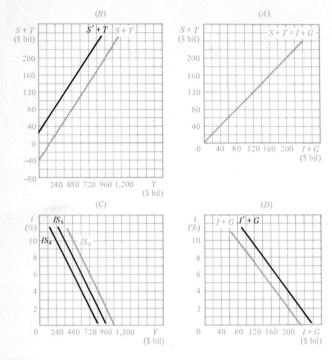

FIGURE 14-6A

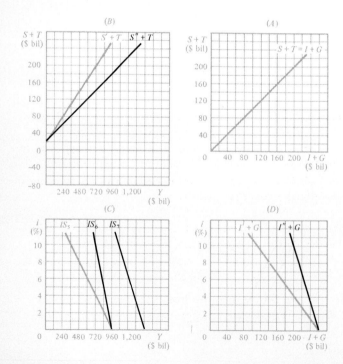

FIGURE 14-7A

MONEY MARKET EQUILIBRIUM

1 The demand for money is separated into two parts, transactions demand M_1 and speculative demand M_2. If the supply of money is denoted by M_S, then equilibrium in the money market requires that $M_S = $ _____ $M_1 + M_2$ _____ . (If necessary, the student should review the principal elements of the theory of interest and money developed in Exercise 12.)

2 Let us assume that intended transactions demand for money is always equal to one quarter of income:

$$(1) \quad M_1 = 0.25Y$$

Plot this relationship in quadrant (B) of Fig. 15-1 and label it M_1. Assure also that intended speculative demand for money is related to the interest rate as follows:

$$(2) \quad M_2 = \$275 \text{ bil} - 25i$$

Plot this function in quadrant (D) of Fig. 15-1 and label it M_2.

3 Since the quantity of money held for transactions purposes is measured on the vertical axis of quadrant (B), it (can, cannot) also be measured on the vertical axis of quadrant (A), using the same scale. Since the quantity of speculative balances is plotted on the horizontal axis of quadrant (D), it (can, cannot) also be plotted on the horizontal axis of quadrant (A). Hence, the *total* demand for money, $M_1 + M_2$, can be represented in quadrant (A) by a straight line whose points have the characteristic that the sum of their vertical distance and their horizontal distance is constant.

4 Complete Table 15-1. The greater the amount of money used for transactions balances, the (more, less) is available for speculative balances, since the money supply is assumed in this problem to be a (constant, variable). In quadrant (A) of Fig. 15-1, draw a line whose points have coordinates adding up to $400 bil. Such a line has a slope of

_____ . Label the line M_S. We will assume that the money supply is autonomously determined by the Federal Reserve. For the preceding example, the equation for the money supply would be

$$(3) \quad M_S = \$400 \text{ bil}$$

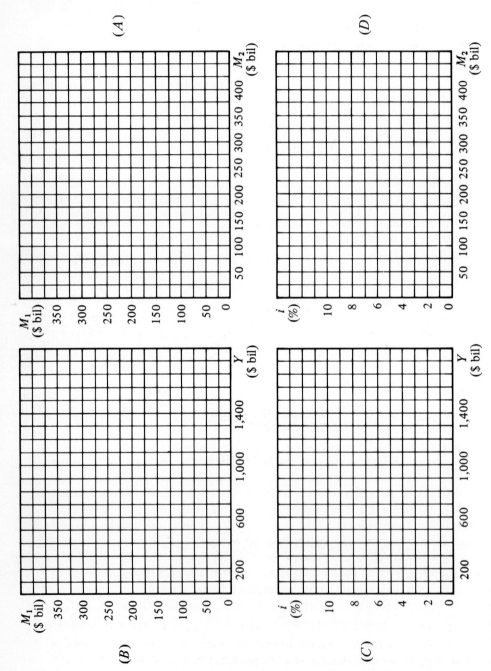

FIGURE 15-1

Table 15-1 Hypothetical Data for
Money Demand and Money Supply
(Billions of Dollars)

M_S	M_1	M_2
$400	$ 0	$_ 400_
400	50	_350_
400	150	_250_
400	300	_100_
400	400	_0_

5 Suppose the rate of interest were 2 percent. The speculative demand for money

would be $_225_ bil. Label this point with an *a* in quadrant (*D*) of Fig. 15-1. Since

the total supply of money is $_____ bil, and if $225 bil of money assets are used for
speculative balances when the interest rate is 2 percent, transactions balances must be

$_____ bil to satisfy the equilibrium condition: $M_S =$ _____ + _____ . Plot this
transaction balance point in quadrant (*A*), labeling it with an *a*. For the transactions
demand to be the required amount to satisfy money market equilibrium, income must

be $_____ bil. Plot this point in quadrant (*B*), labeling the point with an *a*. Finally, in
quadrant (*C*), label with an *a* the point corresponding to the values for income and the
interest rate which you have found.

6 Repeat the process of paragraph 4, using an interest rate of 5 percent. Label the points

in the diagrams with *b*'s. $M_2 = $$_____ bil; $M_1 = $$_____ bil; $Y = $$_____ bil.
Repeat the process again, assuming that the interest rate is 8 percent. Label these points

with *c*'s. $M_2 = $$_____ bil; $M_1 = $$_____ bil; $Y = $$_____ bil.
    Connect the points in quadrant (*C*) with a straight line and label it LM_1. This line

gives all the combinations of _____ and _____ for
which the supply of money equals the demand for money. If $i = 7$ percent, what level
of income would equate money supply with money demand? $_____ bil. The
algebraic expression for the LM_1 or *money market equilibrium* curve is

(4) $Y =$ _____

7 Suppose the Federal Reserve now reduced the money supply from $400 bil to $350
bil. The M_1 line in Fig. 15-1, quadrant (*B*), would shift (to the right, to the left, not
at all). The M_2 line in quadrant (*D*) would shift (to the right, to the left, not at all).
The line in quadrant (*A*), representing the total money supply, would shift (toward the

origin, away from the origin, not at all). Draw the new money supply line and label it M'_S. The M'_S line is (parallel, nonparallel) to M_S. The new equation for the money supply would be:

(5) $M'_S =$ _____

8 Derive a new money market equilibrium curve in Fig. 15-1, using M'_S and label it LM_2. The LM_2 curve has shifted to the (right, left) and is (parallel, nonparallel) to LM_1, reflect-

ing the parallel shift in the _____curve. At an income level of $900 bil, after the decrease in the money supply, the interest rate will be (higher, lower), indicating a (shift of, movement along) the (M_1, M_2, both M_1 and M_2) curve(s). The money supply has (decreased, not changed) and the intended transactions balance has (decreased, not

changed) because the level of _____has not changed. Thus, there are

$_____$bil (more, fewer) money assets available for speculative balances. Conse-quently, under these conditions, the effect in the money market of portfolio adjust-

ments is that interest rates will rise from _____ percent to _____percent. (If necessary, the student should review Exercise 12, on the relationship between bond prices and interest rates.)

9 If expectations about future interest rates change, people might alter their speculative demand for money. Suppose interest rates were expected to rise in the near future from their previously expected level. People would probably hold (more, less) cash at given interest rates in the present time period. A new equation for speculative balances, reflecting a change in expectations, might be of the form:

(6) $M'_2 = \$325 \text{ bil} - 25i$

Plot Eq. (6) in quadrant (D) of Fig. 15-1. This change represents a (parallel, nonparallel)

shift of the function and says that people now intend to hold $_____$bil (more, less)

speculative balances at _____interest rate level. The M_1 and M_S lines will (both, not) shift.

10 Derive a new money market equilibrium curve in Fig. 15-1, using M'_2, M'_S and M_1, and label it LM_3. The LM_3 curve has shifted to the (right, left) and is (parallel, nonparallel)

to LM_2, reflecting the _____shift of M'_2. If equilibrium income is autonomously determined at $900 bil both before *and* after the change in the intended speculative balances function, the interest rate will (rise, fall). This result follows from the fact that, under the new circumstances, intended speculative balances at $i = 6$ percent

are now $_____bil higher and, since M_S (is constant, has declined) and M_1 (is constant, has declined), attempts to reach the new intended speculative balances position causes the interest rate to rise. (If necessary, review paragraph 9 above.) The entire adjustment to the new equilibrium position was via changes in the (interest rate, speculative balances); (the interest rate, speculative balances) remained constant.

If we assume, alternatively, that *interest rates* are held constant both before *and* after the shift to the M_2' line, this condition implies that (more, less) money assets are being held for speculative purposes and consequently less is available for transactions purposes.

As a result, the "supportable" level of equilibrium income will (rise, fall) from \$_____ bil to \$_____ bil. This change in income represents a (shift of, movement along) the (LM_2, LM_3) curve.

11 An "expectations" change could also alter the slope of the speculative demand for money function. Suppose that the M_2 function changed to

$$(7) \qquad M_2' = \$275 \text{ bil} - 12.5i$$

Plot this function in quadrant (D) of Fig. 15-2. Derive a new money market equilibrium curve in Fig. 15-2, using M_2', and label it LM_2. The LM_2 line is to the (right, left) and is (parallel, nonparallel) to LM_1, reflecting the _____ shift of M_2'. As a result of the change indicated by Eq. (7), intended speculative demand is (more, less) interest-elastic, compared to M_2 and, as a result, the money market equilibrium curve is now (more, less) interest-elastic also.

12 If new banking methods make the use of money assets more efficient, the transactions demand for money will (increase, decrease) for each income level. Suppose that, as a result of such a change, the transactions demand function became

$$(8) \qquad M_1' = 0.125Y$$

Using the M_2 and M_s curves in Fig. 15-2, derive a new money market equilibrium curve for the M_1' curve and label it LM_3. The LM_3 line is (parallel, nonparallel) to LM_1, reflecting the _____ shift of M_1', and the LM_3 line has shifted to the (right, left).

13 We can conclude from paragraphs 7 to 10 above that a decrease in the money supply has the same directional shift effect on the *LM* curve as a(n) (increase, decrease) in M_1 or a(n) (increase, decrease) in M_2. The examples in paragraphs 11 and 12 indicate that changes in the slope of $(M_1, M_2, \text{both } M_1 \text{ and } M_2)$ will change the slope of the *LM* curve.

PROBLEMS FOR EXERCISE 15

1 Assume the following transactions and speculative demand functions are representative for the economy:

$$M_1 = 0.5Y$$

$$M_2 = \$300 \text{ bil} - 20i$$

$$M_s = \$500 \text{ bil}$$

If the interest rate is 4 percent, equilibrium income is \$_____ bil

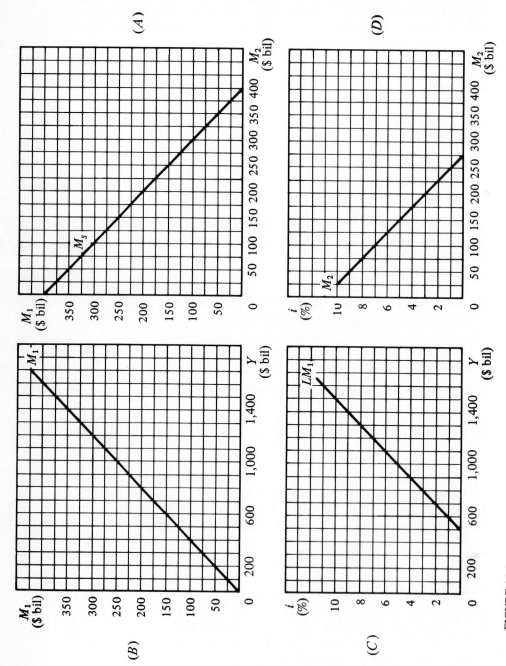

FIGURE 15-2

2 The above equations are plotted in Fig. 15-3. Complete Table 15-2, using the information contained in Fig. 15-3.

Table 15-2

Interest rate (%)	Equilibrium income ($ bil)
0	_____
2	_____
4	_____
6	_____
8	_____
10	_____

The data in Table 15-2 represents the LM or _____

_____ schedule. Plot this schedule in Fig. 15-3 and label it LM_1. The equation for the LM_1 curve is

$Y =$ _____

3 Increase the money supply to $600 bil in Fig. 15-3, label it M_S', and construct the new LM curve. The equation for the LM_2 curve is

$Y =$ _____

4 As a result of the increase in the money supply in paragraph 2, the LM_2 curve has shifted to the (right, left) of LM_1. If the M_S curve had remained unchanged, could the LM curve still have shifted to the right—not necessarily parallel? (yes, no) If *yes*, describe the way(s) this event could occur. If *no*, explain why not.

_____.

5 In Fig. 15-4, draw the new money market equilibrium curves for the following conditions, using LM_1 as the initial equilibrium position before each change.
   (a) Autonomous increase in M_2. Label your answer LM_2.
   (b) Increase in the interest-elasticity of M_2 with no change of the autonomous component. Label your answer LM_3.
   (c) Increase in the transactions demand for money at every income level. Label your answer LM_4.

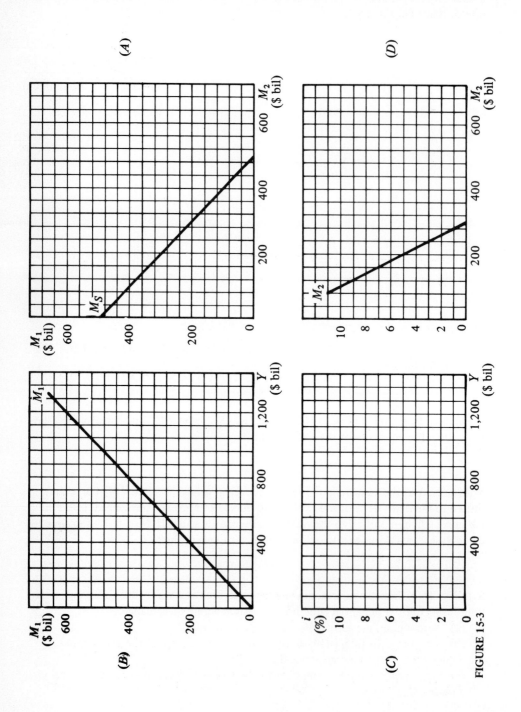

FIGURE 15-3

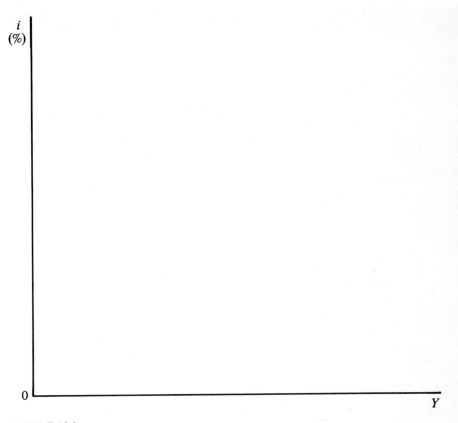

FIGURE 15-4

ANSWERS FOR EXERCISE 15

1 $M_1 + M_2$

2 Fig. 15-1A

3 can, can

4 M_2

    400

    350

    250

    100

     0

    less, constant, Fig. 15-1A, –1

5 225, 400, 175, $M_1 + M_2$, 700

6 150, 250, 1,000, 75, 325, 1,300, income, interest rates, 1,200, $500 bil + 100$i$

7 not at all, not at all, toward the origin, Fig. 15-1A, parallel, $350 bil

8 Fig. 15-1A, left, parallel, M_S, higher, movement along, M_2 decreased, not changed, income, 50, fewer, 4, 6

9 more, Fig. 15-1A, parallel, 50, more, every, not

10 Fig. 15-1A, left, parallel, parallel, rise, 50, is constant, is constant, interest rate,

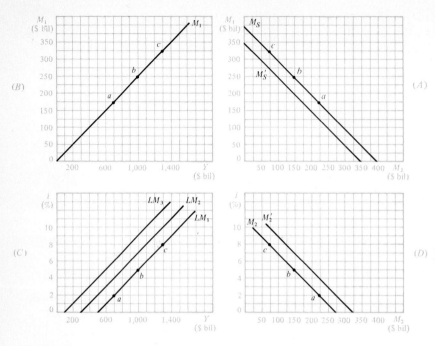

FIGURE 15-1A

speculative balances, more, fall, 900, 700, movement along, LM_3
11 Fig. 15-2A, left, nonparallel, nonparallel, less, less

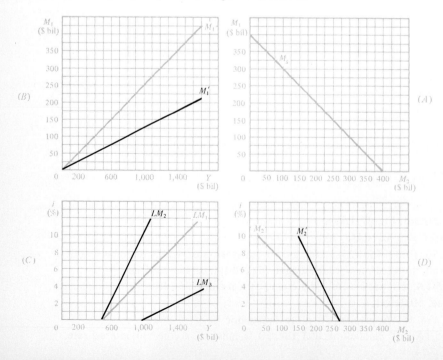

FIGURE 15-2A

12 decrease, Fig. 15-2A, nonparallel, nonparallel, right

13 increase, increase, both M_1 and M_2

ANSWERS TO PROBLEMS FOR EXERCISE 15

1 560

2 400

   480

   560

   640

   720

   800

money market equilibrium, Fig. 15-3A, \$400 bil + 40i

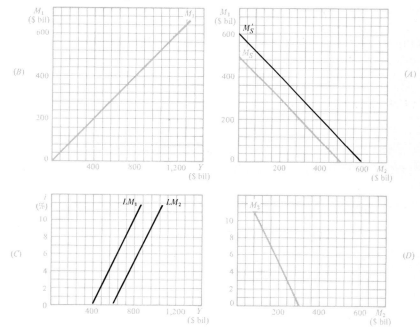

FIGURE 15-3A

3 Fig. 15-3A, \$600 bil + 40i

4 right, yes, decrease—downward shift—in M_1 or M_2

5 Fig. 15-4A

  (a) leftward, parallel shift;

  (b) rightward, nonparallel shift, same origin as LM_1;

  (c) leftward, nonparallel shift, new origin to the left of LM_1 origin.

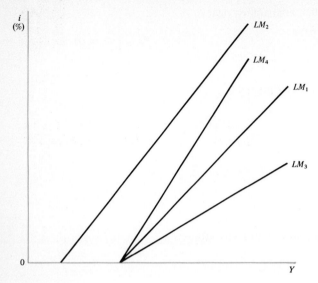

FIGURE 15-4A

EXERCISE **16**

GENERAL EQUILIBRIUM OF THE
PRODUCT AND MONEY MARKETS

1 Assume that the following relationships hold for an economy:

$C = \$100 \text{ bil} + 0.75Y_d$ $M_S = \$300 \text{ bil}$

$I = \$275 \text{ bil} - 25i$ $M_1 = 0.25Y$

$G = 0$ $M_2 = \$275 \text{ bil} - 25i$

$T = 0$

The IS, LM and commodity market equations are plotted in Fig. 16-1. Label the IS curve IS_1 and the LM curve LM_1. The equilibrium level of income is \$_____ bil and the equilibrium interest rate is _____ percent. These amounts will obtain because _____

_____.

Find the following equilibrium values: consumption \$_____ bil; saving \$_____ bil; investment \$_____ bil; transactions demand for money \$_____ bil; speculative demand for money \$_____ bil. Is saving equal to investment? (yes, no) Why or why not? _____

2 Let G increase by \$200 bil. The IS curve shifts (rightward, leftward, not at all). The LM curve shifts (rightward, leftward, not at all). Derive the new IS curve and label it IS_2.

Equilibrium income now is \$_____ bil and equilibrium interest rate is _____ percent.

Income has increased by \$_____ bil. According to our earlier studies, if the MPC = 0.75 and taxes are autonomously determined, the government expenditures multiplier would be _____. Since government spending in the present model has increased by \$200 bil, the government expenditures multiplier is _____. Why is it not equal to 4?

_____

The increase in G, which indirectly decreased I by increasing i, is often called the "crowding out" effect. In the present case, government expenditures have "crowded

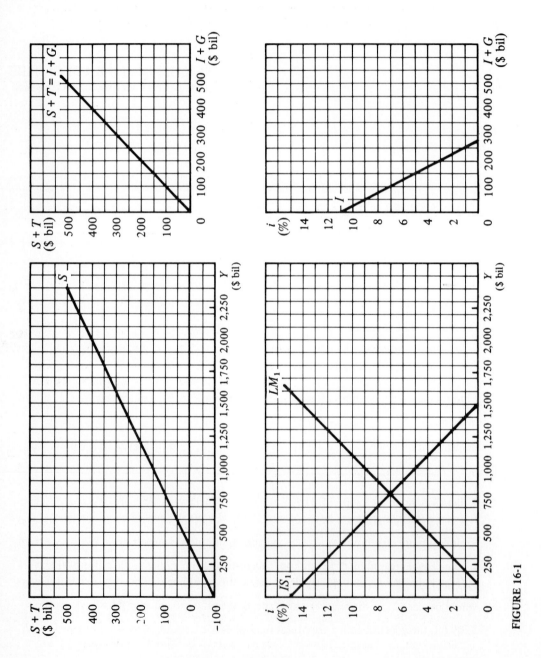

FIGURE 16-1

out" some investment expenditures, so that total expenditures $I + G$ do not increase by the full amount of the government expenditure increase. This "interest-rate drain effect" (increases, decreases) the size of the expenditure multiplier.

Indicate whether the following equilibrium values have increased, decreased, or remained unchanged as a result of the increase in government spending:

Saving	_____
Investment	_____
Taxes	_____
Transactions demand	_____
Speculative demand	_____
Money supply	_____

Is saving equal to investment? (yes, no) Why or why not? _____

_____

_____

3 Let taxes increase by $200 bil. Retain $G = \$200$ bil. Derive the new IS curve in Fig. 16-1 and label it IS_3. Equilibrium income now is $_____ bil and the interest rate is

$_____percent. Income has declined from the IS_2 model because taxes represent a (leakage, injection) which has an effect which is (similar to, different from) that of saving.

Indicate whether the following equilibrium values have increased, decreased, or remained unchanged as a result of the increase in taxes (assuming the economy was initially at IS_2):

Saving	_____
Investment	_____
Taxes	_____
Transactions demand	_____
Speculative demand	_____
Money supply	_____

Is saving equal to investment? (yes, no) Why or why not? _____

_____.

In our earlier studies, we found that if both G and T increased or decreased by equivalent amounts, income changed by the same amount. This was called the _____

_____ multiplier effect and the value of the multiplier was equal to _____
In the present model, both spending and taxes have increased by $200 bil and the value

of the balanced budget multiplier is _____ . Why is it not equal to 1? _____
_____ .

4 Let us return to the original product and money market equilibrium conditions given in paragraph 1 above. The IS, LM and money market equations are plotted in Fig. 16-2. Label the IS curve IS_1 and the LM curve LM_1. If the money supply increased by $200 bil, it (will, will not) change the transactions demand for money schedule; the speculative demand for money schedule (does, does not) change. Since the money supply has increased to $_____ bil, the sum of M_1 and M_2 must be $_____ bil in equilibrium. This condition may be represented in the upper right-hand quadrant by a line with slope of _____ , whose coordinates add up to $_____ bil. This line represents a _____ _____ _____ of $_____ bil. Label it M_S'.

5 Derive the new LM curve and label it LM_2. The LM curve has had a (parallel, non-parallel) shift to the (right, left) by a horizontal amount equal to $_____ bil. Equilibrium income now is $_____ bil and equilibrium interest rate is _____ percent. As a result of the increase in the money supply of $_____ bil, income has increased by $_____ bil. Explain how the money supply increase was transmitted to an income increase. _____

_____ . Explain why income has not increased by the full amount of the LM curve shift. _____

_____

6 Now assume that government expenditures are increased by $200 bil. Derive the new IS curve in Fig. 16-2 and label it IS_2. (See paragraph 2 above.) Can we assume that this government expenditure increase could be financed by the money supply increase in paragraph 5? (yes, no) Since the answer to the preceding question was _____ , equilibrium income is $_____ bil and equilibrium interest rate is _____ percent.

7 There are at least five different cases covered in paragraphs 1 to 6 above:

(a) no government spending or taxes.
(b) government spending, but no taxes.
(c) government spending financed by taxes.
(d) no government spending or taxes, but a money supply increase.
(e) government spending financed entirely by a money supply increase.

Which case has the most expansionary impact on income? **(a, b, c, d, e)** Which case generates the highest interest rate? **(a, b, c, d, e)** Which case produces the largest

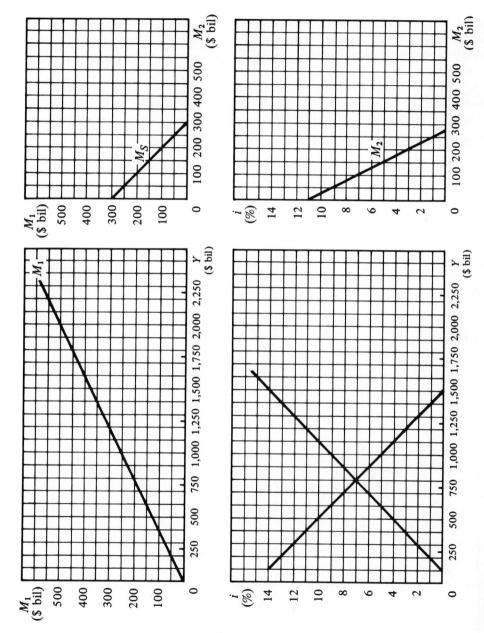

FIGURE 16-2

amount of investment? **(a, b, c, d, e)** Which case produces the largest amount of consumption? **(a, b, c, d, e)**

8 In Fig. 16-3, show how the monetary authorities, by increasing the money supply, can increase income without decreasing the interest rate. Now show how they can stimulate investment spending by decreasing the interest rate without changing the aggregate income level.

Now assume that coordinated fiscal and monetary policy can be used to increase income from Y_1 to Y_2. Assume further that the discretionary variables available to the government officials are G and M_s. Could this coordinated policy raise income without changing the interest rate? **(yes, no)** Explain. _____

_____

Draw the proper graph(s) in Fig. 16-3 to depict your answer. Is your answer similar to any of the cases in paragraph 7? **(yes, no)** If yes, which one(s)? _____

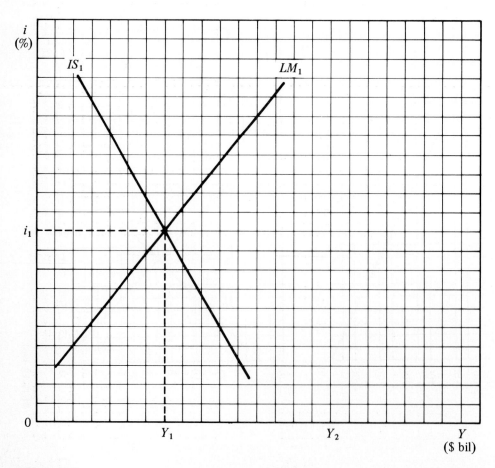

FIGURE 16-3

PROBLEMS FOR EXERCISE 16

1 In the following problem, show on Fig. 16-4 the directional shift that the described event will have on the *IS* and/or *LM* curve(s). Assume that the *IS–LM* shifts are parallel, unless the problem specifically requires a change in the slope of a function. Assume also that general equilibrium initially exists in the product and money markets and that each

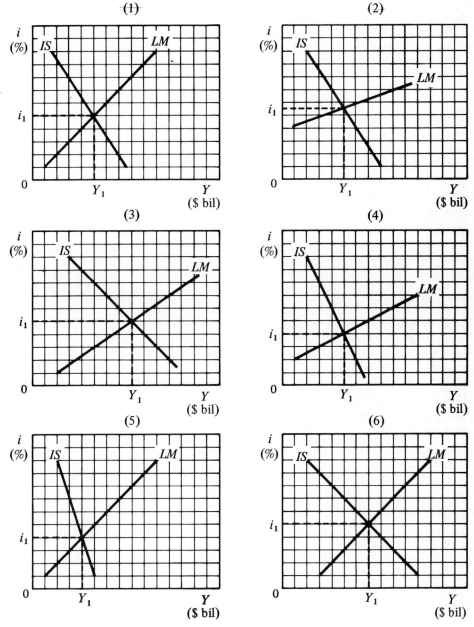

FIGURE 16-4

(7)

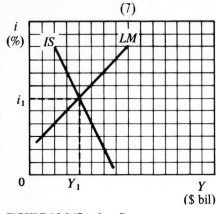

(8)

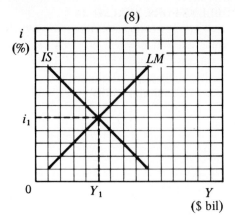

FIGURE 16-4 (Continued)

case is an independent event. For your answer, use the panel number corresponding to the problem number. Label the new curve(s) IS' and LM'.

(a) As a result of a successful savings bond sales campaign by the government, consumers reduce their spending to buy bonds. (Assume no change of MPC.) The new income level is (higher, lower, unchanged). The new interest rate is (higher, lower, unchanged).

(b) As a part of an anti-inflation program, a Price Commission had been established. The commission had instituted a profit control plan. As a result of the reduced inflationary pressure, profit-limitation controls were lifted. The business community generally expects profits to rise as a result. The new income level is (higher, lower, unchanged). The new interest rate is (higher, lower, unchanged).

(c) The Federal Reserve Open Market Committee sells, on balance, government bonds in the open market. The bonds are purchased primarily by commercial banks and large private pension funds. The new income level is (higher, lower, unchanged). The new interest rate is (higher, lower, unchanged).

(d) A government expenditure increase is financed entirely by the sale of government bonds to the non-bank public. The new income level is (higher, lower, unchanged). The new interest rate is (higher, lower, unchanged).

(e) A fiscal policy program calls for an increase in income while maintaining a balanced government budget. Due to other policy constraints, however, the current interest rate level must remain constant. The new income level is (higher, lower, unchanged). The interest rate is (higher, lower, unchanged).

(f) Assume that a community's desired *proportions* of wealth—money, common stock, bonds, and real assets—remains constant, but that, over time, the *level* of common stock, bonds and real assets rises. The new income level is (higher, lower, unchanged). The new interest rate is (higher, lower, unchanged).

(g) There is a sharp increase in the availability and acceptance of new forms of credit and payment, such as Mastercharge cards and an increased use of savings accounts for holding speculative balances. The new income level is (higher, lower, unchanged). The new interest rate is (higher, lower, unchanged).

(h) A fiscal policy program is designed to redistribute income through a transfer payment plan. The transfer payments are financed by selling government securities. The new income level is (higher, lower, unchanged). The new interest rate is (higher, lower, unchanged).

2 In the following problem you are asked to compute the values of the principal macroeconomic variables. Let us assume that the following relationships are representative for an economy:

$$C = \$26 \text{ bil} + 0.9Y_d \qquad M_1 = 0.2Y$$

$$I = \$80 \text{ bil} - i \qquad M_2 = \$64 \text{ bil} - 4i$$

G, T and M_S are autonomously determined variables. We wish to study the following five combinations of G, T and M_S:

Case 1 $G = 0$; $T = 0$; $M_S = \$240$ bil
Case 2 $G = \$30$ bil; $T = \$30$ bil; $M_S = \$240$ bil
Case 3 $G = \$33$ bil; $T = \$33$ bil; $M_S = \$240$ bil
Case 4 $G = \$33$ bil; $T = \$30$ bil; $M_S = \$243$ bil
Case 5 $G = \$33$ bil; $T = \$30$ bil; $M_S = \$240$ bil

Find the following values for each of the above five cases:

Case	IS curve
1	$Y =$ _____
2	$Y =$ _____
3	$Y =$ _____
4	$Y =$ _____
5	$Y =$ _____

Case	LM curve
1	$Y =$ _____
2	$Y =$ _____
3	$Y =$ _____
4	$Y =$ _____
5	$Y =$ _____

Variable (\$ bil exc. i = %)	Case 1	Case 2	Case 3	Case 4	Case 5
Y	___	___	___	___	___
i	___	___	___	___	___
C	___	___	___	___	___
S	___	___	___	___	___
I	___	___	___	___	___
M_1	___	___	___	___	___
M_2	___	___	___	___	___

ANSWERS FOR EXERCISE 16

1 800, 7, only this income and interest rate permit equilibrium in both the product and money markets, 700, 100, 100, 200, 100, yes, saving is the only leakage and investment is the only injection

2 rightward, not at all, Fig. 16-1A, 1,200, 11, 400, 4, 2, the interest rate has risen which reduced investment spending, decreases, increased, decreased, unchanged, increased,

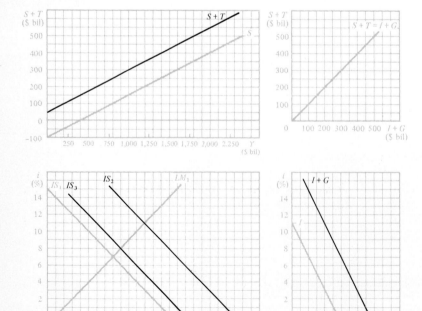

FIGURE 16-1A

decreased, unchanged, no, government spending is an added injection so that saving now equals investment plus government spending

3 Fig. 16-1A, 900, 8, leakage, similar to, decreased, increased, unchanged, decreased, increased, unchanged, yes, because $T = G$ and $S + T = I + G$ so that $S = I$, balanced budget, 1, ½, government expenditures have "crowded out" some investment spending

4 will not, does not, 500, 500, −1, 500, money supply, 500

5 Fig. 16-2A, parallel, right, 800, 1,200, 3, 200, 400, the M_S increase led to an i decrease which increased I and therefore Y, as Y increased M_1 increased and because M_S was constant at the new amount it caused i to increase and somewhat dampen I and Y

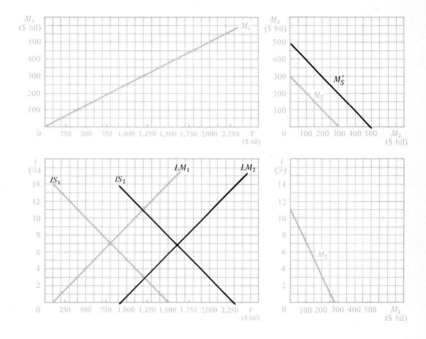

FIGURE 16-2A

6 Fig. 16-2A, yes, yes, 1,600, 7
7 e, b, d, e
8 cannot be done, cannot be done, yes, simultaneously increase both G and M_S so that the IS and LM curves both shift to the right and intersect at the initial interest rate, Fig. 16-3A, yes, case e

ANSWERS TO PROBLEMS FOR EXERCISE 16

1 (a) Fig. 16-4A, lower, lower
   (b) Fig. 16-4A, higher, higher
   (c) Fig. 16-4A, lower, higher

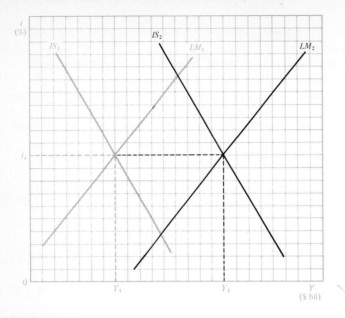

FIGURE 16-3A

(d) Fig. 16-4A, higher, higher
(e) Fig. 16-4A, higher, unchanged
(f) Fig. 16-4A, lower, higher
(g) Fig. 16-4A, higher, lower
(h) Fig. 16-4A, higher, higher

2 Case	IS curve	Case	LM curve
1	$Y = \$1,060$ bil $- 10i$	1	$Y = \$880$ bil $+ 20i$
2	$Y = \$1,090$ bil $- 10i$	2	$Y = \$880$ bil $+ 20i$
3	$Y = \$1,093$ bil $- 10i$	3	$Y = \$880$ bil $+ 20i$
4	$Y = \$1,120$ bil $- 10i$	4	$Y = \$895$ bil $+ 20i$
5	$Y = \$1,120$ bil $- 10i$	5	$Y = \$880$ bil $+ 20i$

Variable ($bil exc. i = %)	Case 1	Case 2	Case 3	Case 4	Case 5
Y	1,000.0	1,020.0	1,022.0	1,045.0	1,040.0
i	6.0	7.0	7.1	7.5	8.0
C	926.0	917.0	916.1	939.5	935.0
S	74.0	73.0	72.9	75.5	75.0
I	74.0	73.0	72.9	72.5	72.0
M_1	200.0	204.0	204.4	209.0	208.0
M_2	40.0	36.0	35.6	34.0	32.0

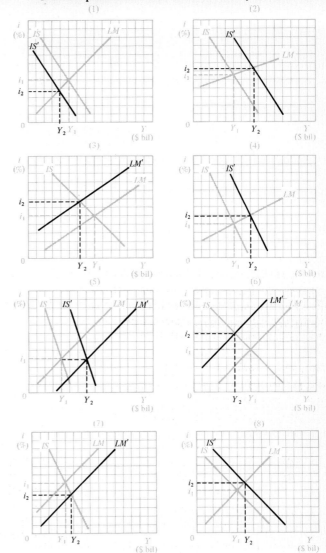

FIGURE 16-4A

1 In the three-sector model—personal, business and government—the *IS* schedule gives all combinations of income and interest rates for which $S = I$.
   (a) true
   (b) false

2 In the three-sector model—personal, business and government—the condition for equilibrium in the product market is
   (a) $Y = C + I$
   (b) $S = I$
   (c) $S + T = I + G$
   (d) $Y = C + S$

3 In the three-sector model—personal, business and government—equilibrium in the product market can be stated as
   (a) $S + T = I + G$
   (b) total leakages = total injections
   (c) $S = I + (G - T)$
   (d) $IS = (I - S) + (G - T)$

4 In the simple three-sector model—personal, business and government—equilibrium in the product market requires that intended saving equal intended investment.
   (a) true
   (b) false

5 If government expenditures increase
   (a) the *IS* curve will shift to the right
   (b) the *IS* curve will shift to the left
   (c) the intended saving schedule will shift to the right
   (d) the $I + G$ schedule will shift to the right, but the *IS* curve will not shift

6 An increase in taxes will shift the
   (a) *IS* curve to the right
   (b) *IS* curve to the left

(c) $I + G$ curve to the right

(d) $S + T = I + G$ curve to the left

7 In the IS model, changes in government expenditures will normally change income by a greater magnitude than an equivalent change in autonomous investment spending.

(a) true

(b) false

8 Equilibrium income will be at full employment only when government expenditures equal taxes.

(a) true

(b) false

9 The larger the MPC, the more interest-elastic (flatter) will be the IS curve.

(a) true

(b) false

10 The more interest-elastic the investment function, the more interest-elastic will be the IS curve.

(a) true

(b) false

11 In the IS model of Exercise 14, an autonomous increase in government spending will shift the IS curve to the right by a horizontal distance equal to the expenditure increase.

(a) true

(b) false

12 In the IS model of Exercise 14, an equivalent increase in both G and T will lead to an equivalent horizontal shift to the right of the IS curve.

(a) true

(b) false

13 If the transactions demand for money schedule shifts upward

(a) the IS curve will shift to the left

(b) the LM curve will shift to the left

(c) the LM curve will shift to the right

(d) the money supply will decline

14 The LM curve

(a) gives all possible equilibrium income levels at which the $S = I$ condition holds true

(b) gives all combinations of income and interest rates for which there is money market equilibrium

(c) gives information about general equilibrium income levels if we assume that prices are constant

(d) shifts to the right when the money supply is increased

15 The slope of the *LM* curve is determined by
   (a) the supply of money
   (b) the speculative demand for money
   (c) the transactions demand for money
   (d) both **(b)** and **(c)** are correct
   (e) none of these

16 One reason that the *LM* curve slopes upward is that, as income rises, the transactions demand for money assets expands.
   (a) true
   (b) false

17 Equilibrium in the money sector requires that the demand for money for transactions purposes equal the supply of money.
   (a) true
   (b) false

18 Equilibrium in the money market
   (a) requires that the transactions demand equal the speculative demand for money assets
   (b) will only be maintained if the product market is in equilibrium
   (c) requires that the demand equal the supply for money assets
   (d) is necessary to maintain an equilibrium in the product market

19 The interest rate is an important determinate of both aggregate saving and the speculative demand for money assets.
   (a) true
   (b) false

20 The *IS* curve can be thought of as an aggregate demand function and the *LM* curve as an aggregate supply function.
   (a) true
   (b) false

21 A rightward shift in the speculative demand for money assets curve will cause a movement along the *LM* curve to a higher equilibrium income level.
   (a) true
   (b) false

22 If the equilibrium level of income declined, while the money supply remained unchanged
   (a) the speculative demand for money assets will rise
   (b) the equilibrium interest rate will remain unchanged
   (c) the transactions demand for money assets will increase
   (d) total leakages will exceed total injections

23 The *LM* curve suggests that there are a number of interest rate levels which are consistent with monetary equilibrium.
   (a) true
   (b) false

24 In the *IS-LM* model, saving and investment are the demand components through which money market variables affect aggregate demand.
   (a) true
   (b) false

25 According to the *IS-LM* model, government expenditures will increase aggregate income only if it is
   (a) in addition to what would have otherwise been spent in the personal and business sectors
   (b) spent on physical capital projects, not government services
   (c) financed by selling bonds to the Federal Reserve
   (d) financed by increased taxes

26 There can only be one interest rate and one income level at which general equilibrium occurs in both the product and money markets.
   (a) true
   (b) false

27 The *IS* curve, but not the *LM* curve, can be shifted for public stabilization policy purposes.
   (a) true
   (b) false

28 The size of the government expenditures multiplier in the *IS-LM* model is influenced by the money demand and supply functions.
   (a) true
   (b) false

29 In terms of the *IS-LM* model, the income tax surcharge of 1968 and the tight money policy that began at the end of 1967 were designed to slow the rate at which the *IS* and *LM* curves were shifting rightward.
   (a) true
   (b) false

Answer questions 30 to 76, based on the *IS–LM* model developed in Exercise 16, choosing from the following possible answers:
   (a) increase
   (b) decrease
   (c) no change
   (d) indeterminate from information available

In answering the questions, assume the following:
(1) General equilibrium initially exists in the product and money markets.
(2) Each question is an independent case.
(3) An increase in *IS* or *LM* refers to a rightward shift; a decrease is a leftward shift.
(4) The *IS* curve is negatively sloped and the *LM* curve is positively sloped.

There is a decrease in intended saving at all income levels.

30 *IS* curve   _____

31 *LM* curve   _____

32 Equilibrium interest rate   _____

33 Equilibrium income   _____

34 Aggregate investment   _____

35 Aggregate saving   _____

The Federal Reserve increases the money supply through open market operations.

36 *IS* curve   _____

37 *LM* curve   _____

38 Equilibrium interest rate   _____

39 Equilibrium income   _____

40 Aggregate investment   _____

41 Aggregate saving   _____

The demand for money to hold for transactions purposes becomes less income-elastic; the autonomous component of the function remains unchanged.

42 *IS* curve   _____

43 *LM* curve   _____

44 Equilibrium interest rate   _____

45 Equilibrium income   _____

46 Aggregate investment   _____

47 Aggregate saving   _____

Due to the institution of a new investment tax credit program, there is an increase in intended investment at all interest rates.

48 *IS* curve   _____

49 *LM* curve   _____

50 Equilibrium interest rate   _____

51 Equilibrium income _____

52 Aggregate investment _____

53 Aggregate saving _____

In pursuit of a fiscal policy program to reduce inflationary pressures, taxes are increased and the additional revenue is used to reduce the federal debt.

54 Equilibrium income _____

55 Aggregate investment _____

56 Aggregate saving _____

57 Total leakages _____

Government expenditures are increased. The Treasury finances the additional expenditures by selling bonds to the Federal Reserve.

58 Equilibrium interest rate _____

59 Equilibrium income _____

60 Aggregate investment _____

61 Total injections _____

Government expenditures are increased. The Treasury increases personal income taxes by just enough to finance the additional expenditures.

62 Equilibrium interest rate _____

63 Equilibrium income _____

64 Total leakages _____

65 Aggregate investment _____

The investment demand function becomes more interest-elastic with no change in the autonomous component.

66 *IS* curve _____

67 *LM* curve _____

68 Equilibrium interest rate _____

69 Equilibrium income _____

70 Aggregate investment _____

71 Government expenditures _____

The marginal propensity to consume increases; the autonomous component of the consumption function remains unchanged.

72 *IS* curve   _____

73 *LM* curve   _____

74 Equilibrium income   _____

75 Government expenditures multiplier   _____

76 Total leakages   _____

PART SIX

EXTENSIONS OF THE *IS–LM*
MODEL: AGGREGATE DEMAND

The usefulness of the *IS–LM* framework, while accepted (with varying degrees of enthusiasm) by the vast majority of economists, has been challenged by able thinkers who have provided a quite different viewpoint about how the economy works. In Exercise 17 we examine alternative models proposed by two strongly opposed schools of thought. One group, the Quantity Theorists, contend that interest rates have a minimal impact on the demand for money. If this theory is correct, we must change drastically our analysis of economic stabilization policy; fiscal policy becomes completely ineffective as a tool for keeping income at full employment levels. The other group, who might be termed (with some risk of inaccuracy) Orthodox Keynesians, contend that fiscal policy is by far the more important policy tool.

The orthodox Keynesian view can be supported by four different arguments. One was emphasized by Keynes himself: It is possible that if interest rates reach a sufficiently low level, people would be so inclined to expect an increase that they would not want to hold securities among their assets. Instead, they would try to keep all of their assets in cash while waiting to buy securities at more favorable terms. Their efforts to sell securities to add to cash balances would keep interest rates from falling any further. Any increase in the money supply would immediately be added to speculative balances. Keynes termed this condition the "liquidity trap." The liquidity trap, also called the Keynesian Trap, like the quantity theory, forces us to reconsider our understanding of stabilization policy; in this case, however, it is monetary policy rather than fiscal policy that becomes ineffective. The second argument for the primacy of fiscal policy, derived primarily from the theory of inventory control, asserts that the transactions demand itself is interest-elastic. Third, it is asserted that institutions involved in the creation of the money supply are responsive to interest-rate changes, thus making the money *supply* interest-elastic. The final argument against the view that monetary policy is important to stabilization policy points to the fact that monetary policy has its impact on income through its effect on interest rates, which in turn affect the investment expenditure component of total income. If interest rates do not significantly affect investment spending decisions, as many analysts have contended, then monetary policy cannot affect income.

Although most economists reject the possibility that the economy is permanently under the influence of either the quantity theory or the liquidity trap, they are willing to acknowledge that either could appear if certain economic conditions exist. The speculative demand for money could disappear if interest rates become extremely high, producing the quantity theory results. At lower interest rates, some people will hold speculative balances because they expect interest rates to rise. If the money supply is unchanged, transactions demand will be smaller, and income must be less. Finally, if the interest rate reaches an extreme low, the speculative demand will become insatiable: people would be willing to hold whatever amount of money the authorities are willing to supply within a wide range of income levels. Under these conditions the liquidity trap exists.

The *IS-LM* framework, while useful for assessing the impact on income and interest rates of various types of behavior in the product and money markets, makes two assumptions which limit its predictive power under "real-world" conditions. These assumptions are

1 The aggregate price level for goods and services is constant
2 The business sector passively adjusts its production to aggregate demand, and has no independent influence on output and income

Exercise 18 of this part will remove the first assumption; the second will be removed in Part 7.

The consequence of assuming that prices are variable is the necessity for rethinking our understanding of the *IS-LM* model. As long as prices are constant, there is no need to distinguish between *real* (deflated) income and *nominal* income, or between the real money supply and the nominal money supply. Theories of investment, consumption, government spending, money demand and money supply must be revised to specify whether real or nominal magnitudes are to be used. Once that is done, we must face the implication of adding a new variable to the equilibrium model: the system no longer determines a unique equilibrium level of income. There is a different equilibrium income for each price level. In Part 7 we will remove the indeterminancy by introducing a model of producer behavior.

THE EFFECT OF INVESTMENT AND THE DEMAND
FOR MONEY ON STABILIZATION POLICY

1 Assume, as in Exercise 16, paragraph 1, that the following relationships hold for an economy:

$C = \$100$ bil $+ 0.75Y_d$ $M_s = \$300$ bil

$I = \$275$ bil $- 25i$ $M_1 = 0.25Y$

$G = 0$ $M_2 = \$275$ bil $- 25i$

$T = 0$

The IS, LM, and money market equations, already plotted in Fig. 16-2, are reproduced in Fig. 17-1. The equilibrium level of income is $_____$ bil and the equilibrium interest rate is $_____$ percent.

2 If interest rates have no effect on the demand for money, as is argued by quantity theorists, then the demand for money consists entirely of $_____$ balances. $_____$ balances are always zero. In terms of Fig. 17-1, the speculative demand for money curve may be represented by $_____$. Plot this new curve in Fig. 17-1 and label it M_2'. In order for the total demand for money to equal the supply of money, the transactions demand must be $\$_____$ bil. This implies that income must be $\$_____$ bil. The LM curve may be described as $_____$. Plot this curve in Fig. 17-1 and label it LM_2. The algebraic equation for LM_2 is $Y = \$_____$ bil. Equilibrium income is $\$_____$ bil and the equilibrium interest rate is $_____$ percent.

3 Let us assume that government spending rises from zero to $\$200$ bil with no increase in M_s or T. Plot the new IS curve in Fig. 17-1 and label it IS_2. (If necessary, refer to Exercise 16, paragraph 6.) If the speculative demand for money is again represented by M_2, the increase in government spending causes income to (increase, decrease, remain

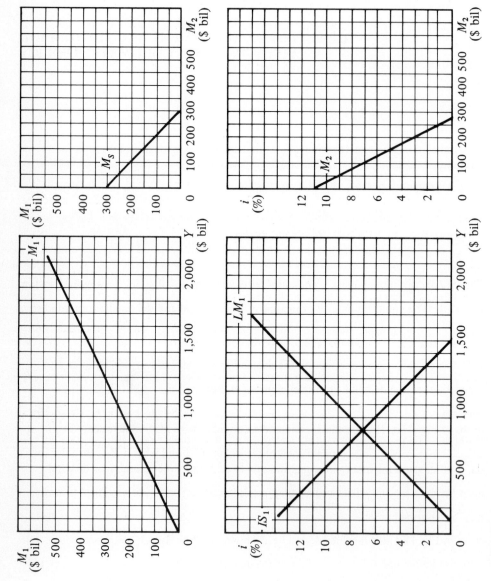

FIGURE 17-1

the same). On the other hand, if the quantity th   vails, the increase in government
spending causes income to (rise, fall, remain the s   Hence, if the quantity theory is
correct, fiscal policy (can, cannot) affect income.

4 If, in the case of the quantity theory, an increase in government spending does not
increase total income, at least one other expenditure component must fall in order to

allow G to rise. In this case, consumption falls by $_____ bil and investment by

$_____ bil. This is an extreme example of "crowding out" of private spending by
government spending. (See Exercise 16, paragraph 2.) Explain why "crowding out" is
not complete if the demand for money does not follow the quantity theory.

_____

_____

_____ .

5 In contrast, under the quantity theory conditions described by LM_2, an increase in the
money supply would shift the (IS, LM) curve to the (right, left), indicating that monetary
policy is (effective, ineffective) as a means to change the level of income. Thus, an
increase in government spending would increase income if it were financed by an increase
in (taxes, the money supply). Tax changes, like changes in government spending, have
(some, no) impact on equilibrium income. A tax increase would initially (reduce, increase)
private consumption demand, but this would be offset as (falling, rising) interest rates
(encouraged, discouraged) investment spending.

6 The quantity theory holds that interest rates have no effect on the demand for money.
At the opposite extreme is a situation in which interest rates completely dominate the
demand for money. This case is called the "liquidity trap" or "Keynesian trap." If the
demand for speculative balances is insatiable, that is, infinitely elastic with respect to i,

it may be represented in Fig. 17-1 as _____ .
Plot this curve in Fig. 17-1 and label it M_2''. In the liquidity trap example, the supply of

money is equal to the demand for money when the interest rate is _____ percent and

income is _____ . The LM curve can be described as _____

_____ . Plot this curve in Fig. 17-1 and label it LM_3. The algebraic

expression for this curve is _____ . Under the liquidity trap and IS_1

conditions, equilibrium income is $_____ bil and equilibrium interest is _____
percent.

7 Now let government spending increase by $200 bil, shifting the IS curve from IS_1 to
IS_2. Equilibrium income (rises, falls, remains the same) under LM_3 conditions. Income

has changed by $_____ bil, which is _____ times the change in government spending.
The value of the government spending multiplier is (more than, less than, equal to) the

simple multiplier 1/MPS. Why? _____

_____

_____.

Is there any "crowding out" of private spending by government spending? (yes, no)

8 If the economy was initially in the liquidity trap, an increase in the money supply (would, would not) shift the horizontal *LM* curve. This is so because the new money would be added to speculative balances (with no change, only with a decrease) in interest rates, regardless of the level of income. Thus, monetary policy is (effective, ineffective) in the liquidity trap.

9 Although most economists doubt that the economy is permanently under the influence of either the quantity theory or the liquidity trap, they are willing to admit that either condition could appear as a special case under the proper conditions. For example, if interest rates reach extreme highs, speculators might conclude that rates had nowhere to go but down. Their speculative portfolios would contain (no, some, exclusively) cash balances. Cash balances would be held only for (speculative, transactions) purposes. Assuming this behavior were to exist only when the interest rate is above 11 percent, in Fig. 17-2 draw the speculative demand for money curve for rates above 11 percent.

10 At interest rates below 11 percent, there will be some people who will expect interest rates to rise, and will therefore hold positive amounts of (speculative, transactions) balances in the expectation that securities' prices will (rise, fall) later. Assuming that interest rates are less than 11 percent and greater than 3 percent, the speculative demand for money is of the form:

(1) $M_2 = \$275 \text{ bil} - 25i$

Draw this segment of the speculative demand curve in Fig. 17-2.

11 Finally, assume that at an interest rate of 3 percent, everyone expects interest rates to rise. Speculative portfolios would consist of (all, some, no) cash and (all, some, no) securities. The speculative demand curve has an elasticity of (zero, infinity, between zero and infinity) when i is 3 percent and income is less than $_____ bil. Draw this segment of the speculative demand curve in Fig. 17-2. Label the speculative demand curve M_2.

12 Derive the *LM* curve corresponding to M_2 and label it LM_1. The LM_1 curve has (one, two, three) distinct segments, and can be described as follows: when Y is zero, i is

_____ percent. As Y increases, the LM_1 curve is (horizontal, positively sloped) until

Y is $_____ bil, whereupon the curve becomes (horizontal, positively sloped, vertical). The initial section corresponds to the (vertical, horizontal, intermediate) range of the speculative demand for money curve, and thus may be identified with the (quantity theory, liquidity trap, intermediate) demand for money conditions. Label this segment of the LM_1 curve with the answer you have just chosen.
   As Y continues to increase beyond $400 bil, monetary equilibrium can only be

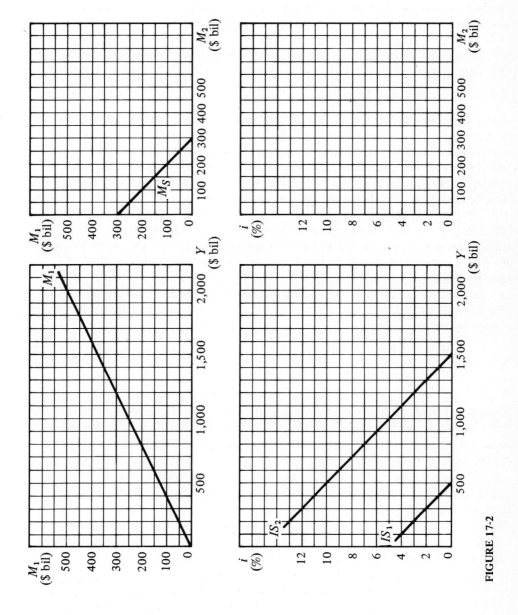

FIGURE 17-2

maintained if interest rates (rise, fall, remain the same). This segment of the LM_1 curve extends to the point where i = _____ percent and Y = \$_____ bil, after which the curve becomes (horizontal, vertical). The second section of the LM_1 curve corresponds to the (vertical, horizontal, intermediate) range of the speculative demand for money curve, and thus may be identified with the (quantity theory, liquidity trap, intermediate) demand for money conditions. Label this segment of the LM_1 curve with the answer you have just chosen.

13 Suppose that the money supply were to increase to \$350 bil. Label the new curve M_s'. In Fig. 17-2, find the new *LM* curve and label it LM_2. If IS_2 describes current conditions in the product market, the new equilibrium income is \$_____ bil and the interest rate is _____ percent. Thus, monetary policy is (effective, ineffective). If IS_1 prevails, a money supply increase will cause income to (rise, fall, remain constant), thereby showing that monetary policy is (effective, ineffective). The fact that most economists reject the proposition that the demand for money has an elasticity of either zero or infinity means that they assume that the *IS* curve will intersect the *LM* curve in the (liquidity trap, intermediate, quantity theory) range of the *LM* curve.

14 The quantity theory and its associated policy conclusions have been challenged not only on the grounds that the demand for money is thought to be interest-elastic, but also because it is possible that both the transactions demand for money and the supply of money are affected by interest rates.

Let us modify the model presented in paragraph 1 above in the following way: eliminate the speculative demand for money, and assume that the transactions demand takes the following form:

(2) $M_1 = 0.25Y + \$275 \text{ bil} - 25i$

The speculative demand may be represented in Fig. 17-3 as _____

_____. In drawing the transactions demand we must remember that there is a different curve for each rate of interest. Draw the curves assuming that i is 0 percent, 5 percent, and 11 percent. Find the three points on the *LM* curve that correspond to these interest rates, and connect them with a straight line. Label this line LM_1. Is this the same curve as LM_2 in Fig. 17-1? (yes, no) This example shows that the absence of a speculative demand (does, does not) necessarily produce the quantity theory conditions.

15 Let us now modify the model presented in paragraph 1 in a different way: eliminate the speculative demand for money, keep the transactions demand unchanged, and assume that the supply of money is interest-elastic. One such money supply function is:

(3) $M_s = \$25 \text{ bil} + 25i$

In Fig. 17-4, draw the money supply lines corresponding to i = 0 percent, i = 5 percent, and i = 11 percent. Find the three points on the *LM* curve that correspond to these interest rates and connect them with a straight line. Label this line LM_1. Is this the

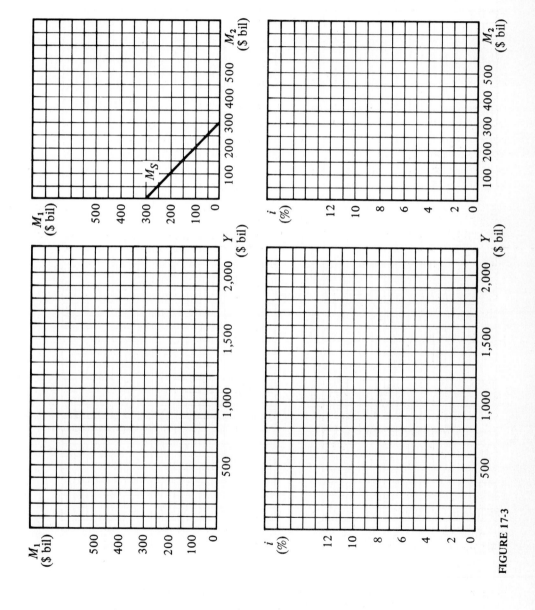

FIGURE 17-3

261

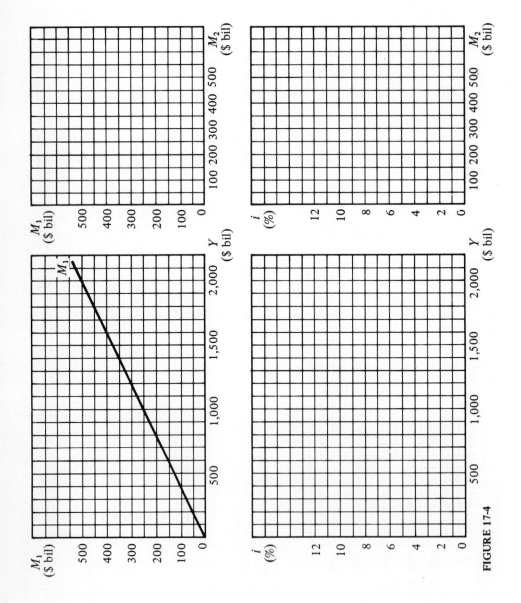

FIGURE 17-4

same curve as LM_1 in Fig. 17-1? (yes, no) This example also shows that the absence of a speculative demand (does, does not) necessarily produce the quantity theory conditions.

16 Since monetary policy has its impact on income through its effect on interest rates and investment spending, monetary policy cannot affect income if investment spending has an interest elasticity of zero. Let us modify the model of paragraph 1 so that investment is not affected by interest rates:

(4) $I = \$150$ bil

Draw Eq. (4) in Fig. 17-5, derive and label the *IS* curve. The *IS* curve may be described

as _____ . Its algebraic equation is

$Y = \$$_____ . If the money supply were to be increased, the *LM* curve would shift (to the right, to the left, not at all). Equilibrium income would (increase, decrease, remain unchanged). Thus, monetary policy in this case is shown to be (effective, ineffective).

PROBLEMS FOR EXERCISE 17

Each problem below is to be solved by reference to the corresponding pair of diagrams in Fig. 17-6. Each pair, for example 1*a* and 1*b*, represents a variety of possible assumptions about economic behavior: the quantity theory, the liquidity trap, and the intermediate case in the monetary system; an interest-elastic and an interest-inelastic demand for investment goods in the product market. In each problem, show on Fig. 17-6 the directional shift that the described event will have on the *IS* and/or *LM* curves pictured. Assume that the *IS–LM* shifts are parallel—in the amount of a two-space horizontal shift—unless the problem specifically requires a change in the slope of a function. Label the new curves you have drawn as IS_1', LM_1', and so on. Label the new equilibrium points as E_1', E_2', and so on. Assume that general equilibrium initially exists in the product and money markets. Each case is an independent event.

1 Consumers expect enactment of a federal sales tax. Which initial equilibrium situation(s) will produce the largest change in income? _____ . The smallest? _____ . The largest change in interest rates? _____ . The smallest? _____

2 Businessmen expect profits to rise. Which initial equilibrium situation(s) will produce the largest change in income? _____ . The smallest? _____ _____ . The largest change in interest rates? _____ . The smallest? _____

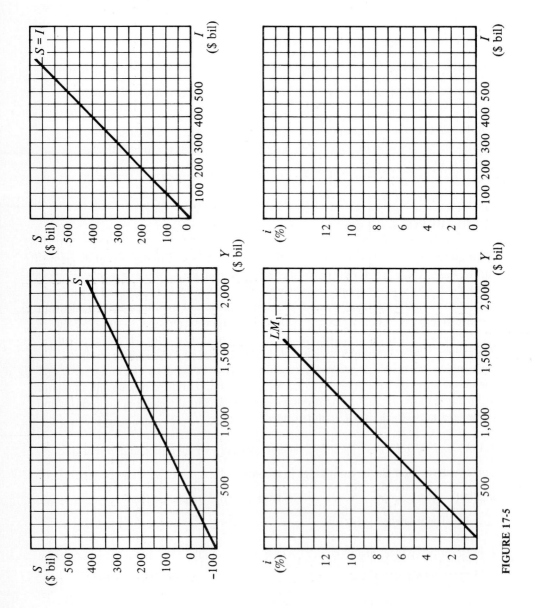

FIGURE 17-5

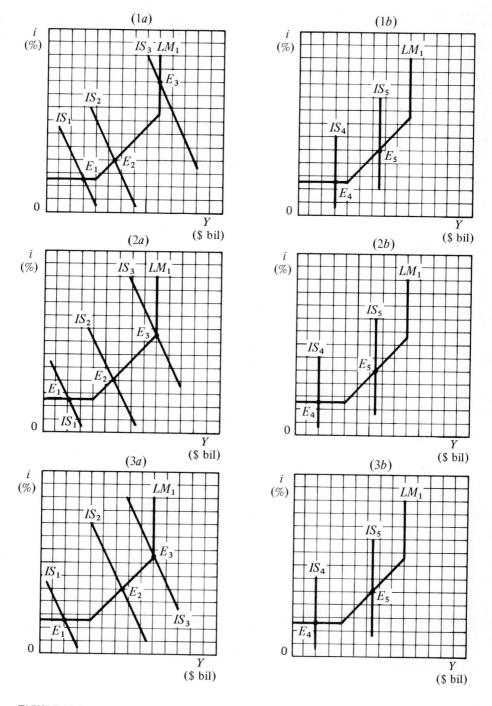

FIGURE 17-6

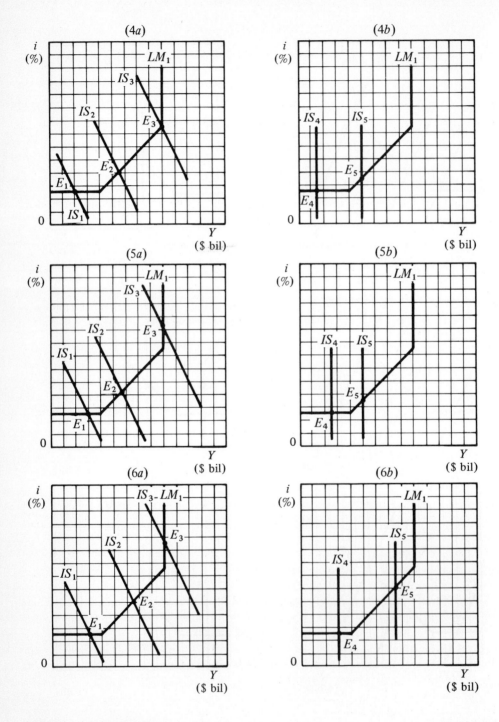

FIGURE 17-6 (Continued)

3 The Federal Reserve sells government bonds to commercial banks. Which initial equilibrium situation(s) will produce the largest change in income? _____.
The smallest? _____. The largest change in interest rates? _____. The smallest? _____

4 A government spending increase is financed entirely by an increase of the money supply. Which initial equilibrium situation(s) will produce the largest change in income? _____. The smallest? _____. The largest change in interest rates? _____. The smallest? _____

5 An increased use of credit cards reduces the need for consumers to keep cash balances. Which initial equilibrium situation(s) will produce the largest change in income? _____. The smallest? _____. The largest change in interest rates? _____. The smallest? _____

6 A federal government investment credit program initially enacted to stimulate investment spending is repealed. Which initial equilibrium situation(s) will produce the largest change in income? _____. The smallest? _____. The largest change in interest rates? _____. The smallest? _____

ANSWERS FOR EXERCISE 17

1 800, 7
2 transactions, speculative, the vertical axis, Fig. 17-1A, 300, 1,200, a vertical line at $Y = \$1,200$ bil, Fig. 17-1A, 1,200, 1,200, 3
3 Fig. 17-1A, increase, remain the same, cannot
4 zero, 200, reduction of speculative balances provides funds to keep interest rates from rising enough to choke off an equivalent amount of private investment (if necessary, the student should review Exercise 16)
5 *LM*, right, effective, the money supply, no, reduce, falling, encouraged
6 a horizontal line (at $i = 3$ percent in this exercise), Fig. 17-1A, 3, at any level, a horizontal line at $i = 3$ percent, Fig. 17-1A, $i = 3$ percent, 1,200, 3
7 rises, 800, 4, equal to, in the liquidity trap speculative balances change enough to finance the full expansion of income with no change in interest rates needed, no
8 would not, with no change, ineffective
9 no, transactions, Fig. 17-2A
10 speculative, fall, Fig. 17-2A

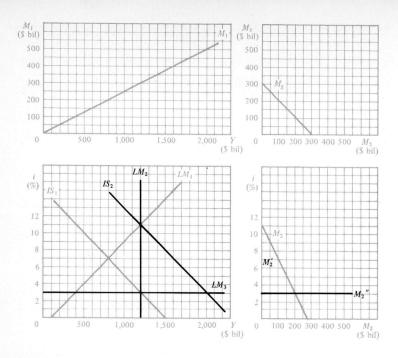

FIGURE 17-1A

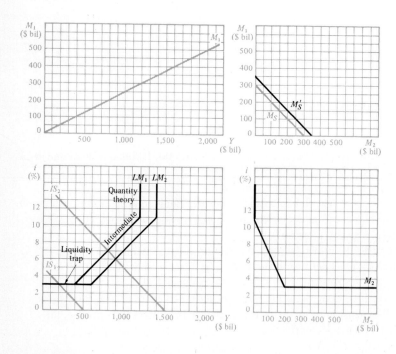

FIGURE 17-2A

11 all, no, infinity, 400, Fig. 17-2A

12 Fig. 17-2A, three, 3, horizontal, 400, positively sloped, horizontal, liquidity trap, Fig. 17-2A, rise, 11, 1,200, vertical, intermediate, intermediate, Fig. 17-2A, vertical, money supply, vertical, quantity theory, Fig. 17-2A

13 Fig. 17-2A, 900, 6, effective, remain constant, ineffective, intermediate

14 the vertical axis, Fig. 17-3A, no, does not

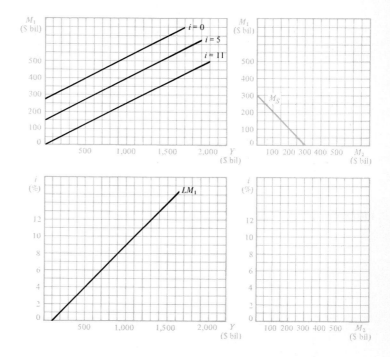

FIGURE 17-3A

15 Fig. 17-4A, yes, does not

16 Fig. 17-5A, a vertical line, $Y = \$1,000$ bil, \$100 bil, to the right, remain unchanged, ineffective

ANSWERS TO PROBLEMS FOR EXERCISE 17

1 Fig. 17-6A, $E_1, E_4, E_5 ; E_3 ; E_3 ; E_1, E_4$

2 $E_1, E_4, E_5 ; E_3 ; E_3 ; E_1, E_4$

3 $E_3 ; E_1, E_4, E_5 ; E_3 ; E_1, E_4$

4 E_1, E_2, E_3, E_4, E_5 ; same; same; same

5 $E_3 ; E_1, E_4, E_5 ; E_3 ; E_1, E_4$

6 $E_1, E_4, E_5 ; E_3 ; E_3 ; E_1, E_4$

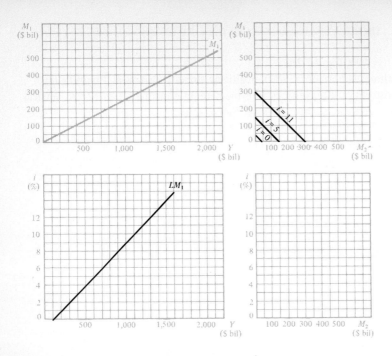

FIGURE 17-4A

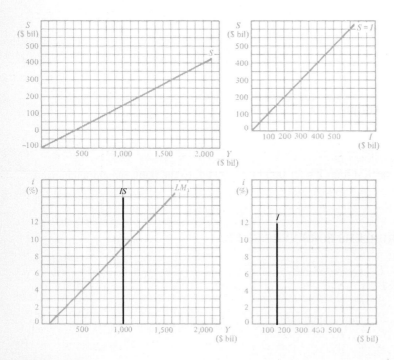

FIGURE 17-5A

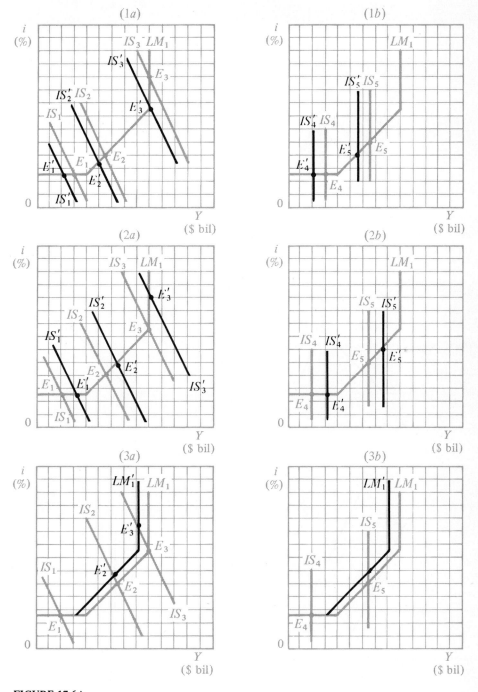

FIGURE 17-6A

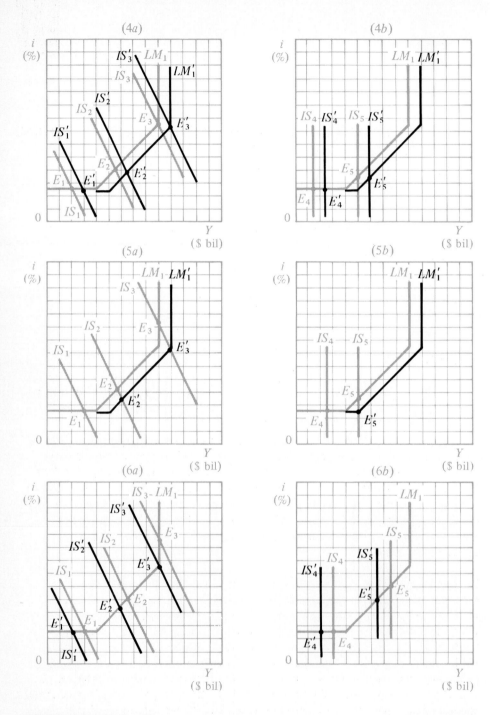

FIGURE 17-6A (Continued)

THE EFFECT OF PRICE CHANGES ON AGGREGATE DEMAND

Let us assume that the following relations hold in a hypothetical economy:

$$\frac{C}{P} = \$100 \text{ bil} + 0.75 \frac{Y_d}{P} \qquad M_S = \$400 \text{ bil}$$

$$\frac{I}{P} = \$275 \text{ bil} - 25i \qquad \frac{M_1}{P} = 0.25 \frac{Y}{P}$$

$$G = \$0$$

$$\frac{M_2}{P} = \$275 \text{ bil} - 25i \qquad \text{for } 3\% \leqslant i \leqslant 11\%$$

$$T = \$0$$

$$\frac{M_2}{P} = \$0 \qquad \text{for } i \geqslant 11\%$$

$$i \geqslant 3\%, \text{ i.e., a liquidity trap at } i = 3\%$$

The consumption and investment demand schedules are the same as those used in Exercise 17, paragraph 1, except that C, I, and Y are divided by P, the price index. Here, we are introducing the distinction between current dollar, or *nominal*, values of income and its components, and deflated, or *real*, values. Deflation of nominal values is done so that we may focus our attention on changes of physical output rather than the effects of price inflation. A rise of $10 bil in income will not produce higher employment if the income change is due to inflation rather than to increased physical production.

1 The consumption and investment demand functions stated above assume that (nominal, real) consumption depends on (nominal, real) income and that (nominal, real) investment depends on the interest rate. If nominal income and price both doubled in value and the interest rate remained constant, real consumption would (double, rise by less than double, remain the same), while investment would (double, rise by less than double, remain the same). Hence, under these assumptions, changes in nominal values such as nominal income and the price level (affect, do not affect) real spending for consumption and investment. This tendency to ignore proportional changes of nominal income and prices is called the absence of "money illusion." If an *IS* curve is drawn using real income and the interest rate, it will be (the same as, different from) the one for income and interest in Fig. 17-1. The *IS* curve is plotted in Fig. 18-1. Label the curve *IS*.

2 In the monetary sector both the transactions and the speculative demand for money are shown to depend only on (nominal, real) variables. Thus, the monetary sector may be said (to exhibit, not to exhibit) money illusion. The transactions and speculative demand for money curves are plotted in Fig. 18-1. Label these curves M_1 and M_2 respectively. These functions are (the same as, different from) those using income and interest in Fig. 17-2.

In the present model, the supply of money is assumed to be determined by the Federal Reserve in (nominal, real) terms; i.e., the Fed decides the number of dollars that will comprise the money supply in the economy, and does not directly control the purchasing power of those dollars. In order to find the equilibrium conditions in the money market, we must set the demand for real money balances equal to the supply of (nominal, real) money balances. Therefore, in representing the money supply in Fig. 18-1, we must use the (nominal, real) money supply. As a result, the money supply will appear as (a single line representing $400 bil, several lines depending on the price level). We (can, cannot) determine the *LM* curve without knowing the price level.

3 Given the nominal money supply, the real money supply can be determined once the price level is known. It is then possible to derive the *LM* curve. In the model presented above, the nominal money supply is $_____ bil; therefore, if the price index is 0.80, the real money supply is $_____ bil. Locate the real money supply curve in Fig. 18-1 and label it $P = 0.80$ to indicate that it is the real money supply curve associated with a price index of 0.80. Now locate the *LM* curve associated with this price level and label it $P = 0.80$. Find the equilibrium real income and interest rate, and complete row 1 of Table 18-1.

Table 18-1 Determination of Real Income and Interest Rate Levels for a Nominal Money Supply of $400 bil and a Variable Price Level

Price index, P	Real money supply, M_S/P	Real income, Y/P	Interest rate, i
0.80	$_____ bil	$_____ bil	_____%
1.00	$_____ bil	$_____ bil	_____%
2.00	$_____ bil	$_____ bil	_____%
4.00	$_____ bil	$_____ bil	_____%

Repeat the steps just completed for price indexes of 1.00, 2.00, and 4.00. Table 18-1 indicates that a reduction of prices is associated with a(n) (increase, decrease) in the level of real income. This effect is (similar to, different from) an increase in the nominal money supply at a given price level. For a given nominal money supply, as the price level falls, the real money supply (increases, decreases). The impact of price level changes on the real money supply is known as the *Keynes effect*.

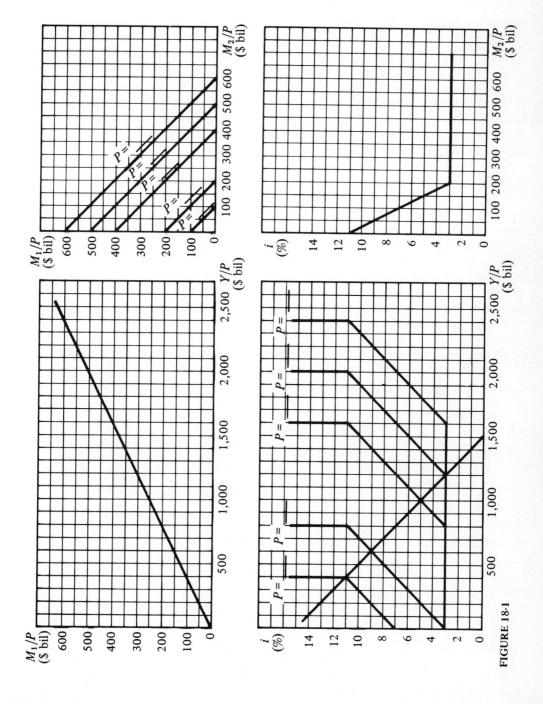

FIGURE 18-1

4 If $i = 3$ percent, the economy is in the (liquidity trap, quantity theory) range of the *LM* curve. In Fig. 18-1 locate and label the real money supply and *LM* curves that are associated with $P = 0.67$. Find the following equilibrium values:

P	M_S/P	Y/P	i
$0.67 = 2/3$	\$_____ bil	\$_____ bil	_____%

A price level decline from 0.80 to 0.67 has (some, no) effect on equilibrium income, whereas under previous conditions price declines (always, never) led to higher income levels. Due to the (liquidity trap, quantity theory) conditions, the Keynes effect is (limited, unlimited) in its ability to raise income.

5 In Fig. 18-2 plot the five points found above which represent the relation between real income and the price level. A sixth point should be plotted, relating real income to a price level of 8.00. Plot a seventh point relating a price index of 0.20 to Y/P. Label the curve AD_1. This curve shows how the price level can affect aggregate demand for goods and services. Because it relates price to quantity demanded, the AD_1 curve appears to have the same properties as a (demand, supply) curve found in price theory. Hence, the curve is usually called an aggregate demand curve. One note of caution is in order when comparing an *aggregate* demand curve with a demand curve for a particular good: in the latter case, all other prices are assumed to be held constant. The *aggregate* demand curve,

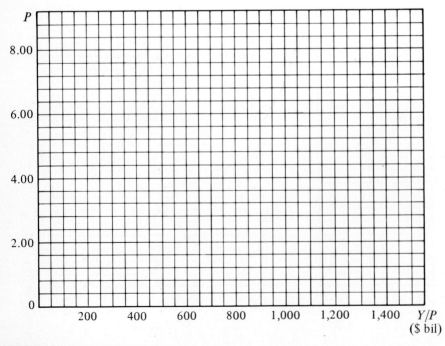

FIGURE 18-2

on the other hand, is derived with a (constant, variable) interest rate and this characteristic (is identical to, differs from) the demand curve for a single good.

6 Suppose that the Federal Reserve increases the nominal money supply to $800 bil. If the price index is 2.00, the real money supply is $_____ bil. This situation would be identical to the previous example wherein a nominal money supply of $400 bil and a price index of _____ produced a real money supply of $400 bil. Referring to Table 18-1, we know that a real money supply of $400 bil is associated with a real income level of $_____ bil. It follows, therefore, that when the nominal money supply is $800 bil and the price index is 2.00, the real income level will be $_____ bil, because the real money supply is (identical, different) in the two cases. Fill in the appropriate amount of real income in Table 18-2 for a price index of 2.00. The information in Table 18-1 also provides the real income levels corresponding to the price levels of 1.60, 4.00, and 8.00 in Table 18-2. Fill in the appropriate amount of real income in Table 18-2 for these price levels.

The first row of Table 18-1 and the discussion in paragraph 4 indicate that the model is in the liquidity trap if the real money supply is greater than $_____ bil. If the nominal money supply is $400 bil, this situation occurs when the price level is (greater than, less than) or equal to 0.80. Similarly, if the nominal money supply is $800 bil, the model is in the liquidity trap if the price level is less than _____. Use this information to complete Table 18-2.

Table 18-2 Determination of Real Income for a Nominal Money Supply of $800 bil and a Variable Price Level

Price index, P	Real income, Y/P
0.20	$_____ bil
0.67 = 2/3	$_____ bil
0.80	$_____ bil
1.00	$_____ bil
1.60	$_____ bil
2.00	$_____ bil
4.00	$_____ bil
8.00	$_____ bil

Repeat the preceding steps and complete Table 18-2. Plot these points in Fig. 18-2 and label the curve AD_2. As a result of the (increase, decrease) in the nominal money supply, the aggregate demand curve has shifted to the (right, left). Does the maximum aggregate demand rise? (yes, no)   The maximum aggregate demand level is controlled by (liquidity trap, quantity theory) conditions and thus indicates that, through the Keynes effect, monetary policy has a(n) (limited, unlimited) ability to increase income.

7 In paragraphs 2 to 6 above, we found that the Keynes effect alters money market equilibrium by changing the real quantity of money. Except for the liquidity trap range, aggregate income is (positively, inversely) related to the price level. We will next explore the possibility that price level changes can affect product market equilibrium. In the following model, price changes might affect the goods and services sector through two expenditure components, consumption and government spending.

$$\frac{C}{P} = \$80 \text{ bil} + 0.75\,\frac{Y_d}{P} + 0.125\,\frac{V}{P} \qquad M_s = \$800 \text{ bil}$$

$$\frac{I}{P} = \$275 \text{ bil} - 25i \qquad\qquad \frac{M_1}{P} = 0.25\,\frac{Y}{P}$$

$$G = \$100 \text{ bil} \qquad\qquad \frac{M_2}{P} = \$275 \text{ bil} - 25i \text{ for } 3\% \leqslant i \leqslant 11\%$$

$$T = \$0 \qquad\qquad \frac{M_2}{P} = \$0 \qquad \text{for } i \geqslant 11\%$$

$$i \geqslant 3\%, \text{ i.e., a liquidity trap at } i = 3\%$$

Except for the larger nominal money supply, the monetary sector shown above is (the same as, different from) the one used at the beginning of this exercise. Hence, the Keynes effect is (present, absent). The consumption function has been altered from our earlier model by the inclusion of the (nominal, real) value of wealth, denoted by V/P. (For justification of including wealth in the consumption function, see Exercise 8, beginning with paragraph 8.) The net wealth of the private sector V includes the physical capital stock K, government securities B, and the money supply M_s. We assume here that the entire money supply is currency issued by the government. If the *real* physical stock, K/P, is fixed at \$160 bil and government securities are \$0, the only variable component of wealth is _____. The consumption function may then be written as follows:

$$\frac{C}{P} = \$80 \text{ bil} + 0.75\,\frac{Y_d}{P} + 0.125\left(\frac{M_s}{P} + \frac{B}{P} + \frac{K}{P}\right)$$

$$\frac{C}{P} = \$80 \text{ bil} + 0.75\,\frac{Y_d}{P} + 0.125\left(\frac{M_s}{P} + \$0 + \$160 \text{ bil}\right)$$

$$\frac{C}{P} = \$100 \text{ bil} + 0.75\,\frac{Y_d}{P} + 0.125\,\frac{M_s}{P}$$

If the Federal Reserve increased the nominal money supply and the price index was held constant, real money balances would (increase, decrease, not change). As a result of the (rise, fall) of household wealth, consumption expenditures would (increase, decrease, not change). If, instead, the Fed held the nominal money supply constant at a time when the price index was falling, real money balances would (rise, fall), causing consumption to (rise, fall). It makes (a, no) difference whether the money supply is doubled and the price index held constant or the money supply is held constant and the price index halved. This fact establishes that, other things being equal, a change of the price level (does, does not) affect real consumption spending in this model. This effect of price changes on real consumption is known as the *Pigou effect*, after the English economist A. C. Pigou.

8 Government purchases of goods and services are assumed to be fixed in (nominal, real) terms. This assumption is (similar to, different from) that in paragraph 2 above, under which the Federal Reserve is said to determine the (nominal, real) money supply. Thus, if the price level should fall, *real* government spending would (rise, fall, remain unchanged). Price changes are assumed to have (some, no) effect on real investment spending. From what has been established about the impact of price changes on the components of total spending, we can conclude that total intended spending on goods and services (rises, falls) when the price level falls. In the *IS-LM* framework, this effect may be represented by a (rightward, leftward) shift of the (*IS, LM*) curve. When both the Pigou effect and the Keynes effect are operating, (the *IS* curve, the *LM* curve, both curves) shift(s) to the right when the price level falls. The Pigou effect shifts the (*IS, LM*) curve while the Keynes effect shifts the (*IS, LM*) curve. Equilibrium real income and the interest rate (can, cannot) be determined without knowledge of the price level.

9 Derivation of the *IS* curve requires that we know how real government spending and consumption vary with the price level. In the model in paragraph 7 above, nominal

government spending is $_____ bil. Find the level of real government spending for the price indexes specified in Table 18-3.

Table 18-3 Determination of Real Government Spending for Nominal *G* = $100 bil and a Variable Price Level

Price index, P	Real government spending, G/P
1.00	$_____ bil
1.33 = 4/3	$_____ bil
2.00	$_____ bil
4.00	$_____ bil

Use the relationships in the model in paragraph 7 above to identify and label the $I/P + G/P$ curves in Fig. 18-3 which correspond to the price levels listed in Table 18-3. As the price level falls, the sum of intended investment and real government spending (rises, falls).

10 In the model in paragraph 7, the price level affects real consumption and saving through the effects of prices on _____. Thus, if we are to know how much saving will occur at a particular income level, we must know the real money supply. Find the saving level that corresponds to a real disposable income of $1,000 bil and a nominal money supply of $800 bil at the various price levels specified in Table 18-4.

Table 18-4 Determination of Real Saving When Real Disposable Income Is $1,000 bil and the Nominal Money Supply Is $800 bil

Price index, P	Real saving, S/P	$0.25Y_d$	$0.125M_s/P$
1.00	$_____ bil	= −$100 bil + $250 bil	−$_____ bil
1.33 = 4/3	$_____ bil	= −$100 bil + $250 bil	−$_____ bil
2.00	$_____ bil	= −$100 bil + $250 bil	−$_____ bil
4.00	$_____ bil	= −$100 bil + $250 bil	−$_____ bil

Identify and label in Fig. 18-3 the saving curves corresponding to these price levels. In this example the real saving function shifts (upward, downward) as the price level falls. This effect is identical to an (upward, downward) shift of the consumption expenditure curve.

11 In Fig. 18-3 identify and label the *IS* curves corresponding to the price levels used in Table 18-4. The *LM* curves are drawn on the assumption that the nominal money supply is $800 bil. Locate the intersection of the *IS* and *LM* curves corresponding to each price level, and complete the following table of equilibrium values for Y/P and i:

Table 18-5 Determination of Real Income and Interest Rates by Combining the Keynes and Pigou Price Effects

Price index, P	Real income, Y/P	Interest rate, i
1.00	$_____ bil	_____ %
1.33 = 4/3	$_____ bil	_____ %
2.00	$_____ bil	_____ %
4.00	$_____ bil	_____ %

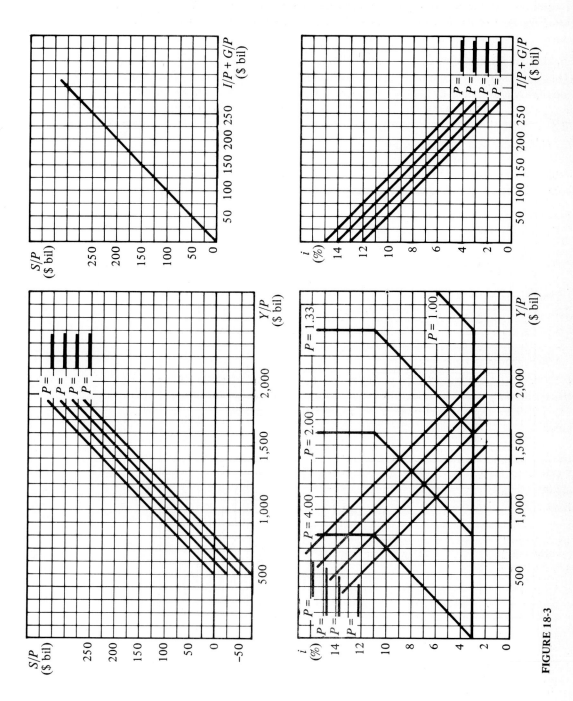

FIGURE 18-3

Plot these four points of the aggregate demand curve in Fig. 18-4. Does the interest rate remain constant when price and real income change? (yes, no)   Six other points on the same aggregate demand curve are already plotted. (These coordinates are marked with small x's.) Connect the ten points and label the curve AD_1. The economy is in the

liquidity trap range at $P =$ _____. When P falls from 1.00 to 0.80, aggregate demand (rises, does not rise), demonstrating that the liquidity trap (does, does not) place a limit on the aggregate demand for goods and services as it did in Fig. 18-2. Why is this the

case? _____

_____

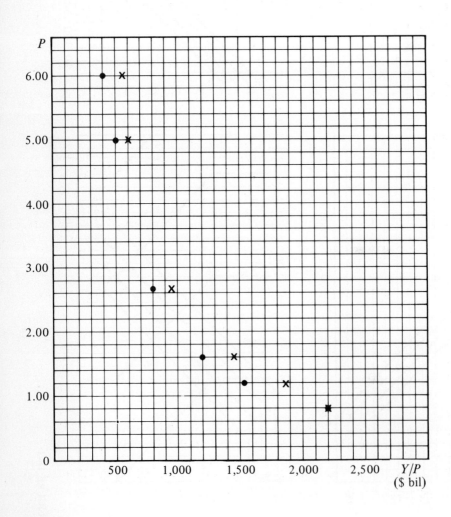

FIGURE 18-4

12 Suppose the Federal Reserve decided to reduce the money supply from $800 bil to $600 bil through an open market operation. A sale of $200 bil of government securities from the Fed's portfolio to the nonbank public would (increase, decrease) the public's holdings of securities while (increasing, decreasing) its holdings of money. Since the

public's total wealth consists of _____ , _____

_____ , and _____ , the above transaction would cause total wealth of the household sector to (rise by $200 bil, fall by $200 bil, remain unchanged). This effect on wealth would cause the saving function to shift (to the right, to the left, not at all), which in turn causes the *IS* curve to shift (to the right, to the left, not at all). The *IS* curves are drawn in Fig. 18-5 and labeled with the proper price indexes.

13 The reduction of the money supply by $200 bil will produce (a rightward, a leftward, no) shift of the *LM* curve. This result is due to the fact that the real money supply is (higher, lower, unchanged) at each price level. Identify and label the real money supply and *LM* curves in Fig. 18-5 with the correct price indexes. Find the equilibrium interest rate and real income that corresponds to each price level. Complete the following table:

Table 18-6 Determination of Real Income and Interest Rate Levels for a Nominal Money Supply of $600 bil and a Variable Price Level

Price level, P	Real income, Y/P	Interest rate, i
0.80	$_____ bil	_____%
1.00	$_____ bil	_____%
1.33 = 4/3	$_____ bil	_____%
2.00	$_____ bil	_____%
4.00	$_____ bil	_____%

Plot these points of the aggregate demand curve in Fig. 18-4. Connect these points and the five other points, designated with small circles, already plotted. Label the new aggregate demand curve AD_2. At most price levels, the new *AD* curve has shifted to the (right, left) of the old one. Why does the aggregate demand curve fail to shift at prices

equal to and lower than 0.80? _____

_____

_____ .

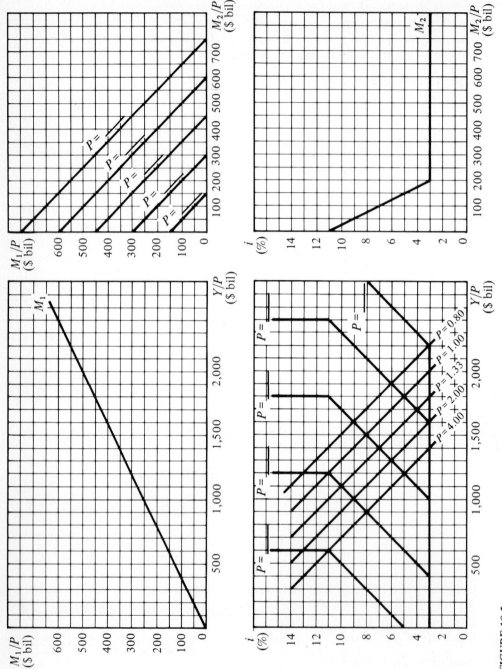

FIGURE 18-5

PROBLEMS FOR EXERCISE 18

1 A series of *IS* and *LM* curves are drawn in Fig. 18-6. For each of the following problems, show the directional shift that the described event will have on the *IS* and/or *LM* curve. Use the panel number in Fig. 18-6 corresponding to the problem number below. Assume that all shifts are parallel and are horizontally two squares in magnitude. Label the new curve(s) IS_2 and LM_2.

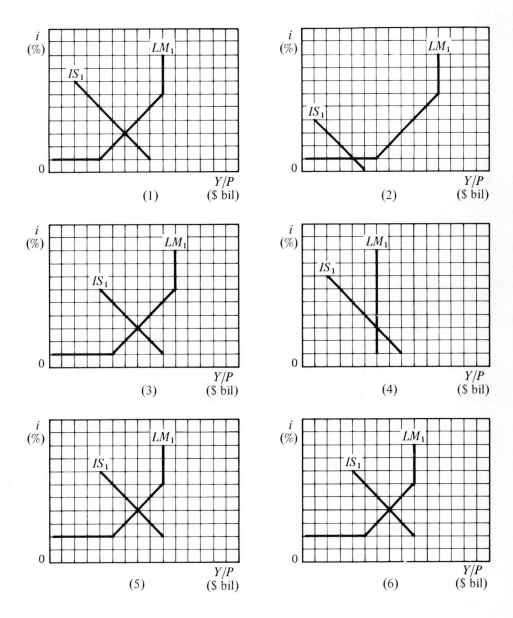

FIGURE 18-6

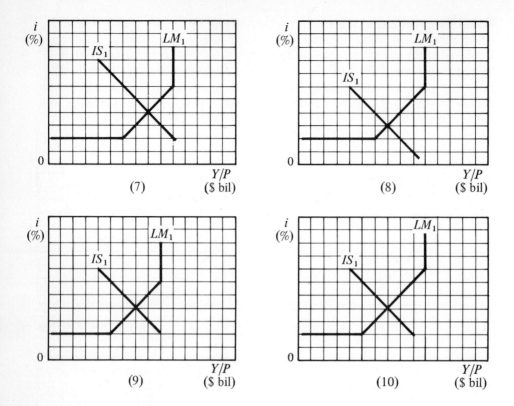

FIGURE 18-6 (Continued)

In each problem, you are asked to indicate the direction the aggregate demand curve shifts after a policy or parameter change. It should be kept in mind that the initial position of the *IS* and *LM* curves assumes a given price level, and that the initial shift of the curves assumes no change of this price level if the shifts are caused by a policy change or a change in behavioral parameters. In effect, the change in aggregate demand at a single price level is being determined; therefore, (only one, all) point(s) of the aggregate demand curve will be shifted. We can assume that in general the rest of the *AD* curve follows the pattern of that one point, provided that we are not in the horizontal portion of the *LM* curve. The process can be illustrated by Figs. 18-3 to 18-5. In Fig. 18-4 two *AD* curves are drawn, one for a money supply of $800 bil and one for a money supply of $600 bil in the former case and $1,000 bil in the latter. Figure 18-3 presents *IS* and *LM* curves for the larger money supply. Note that for *P* = 2.00, the curves intersect at *Y/P* = $1,200 bil In Fig. 18-5, when *P* = 2.00, the curves intersect at *Y/P* = $1,000 bil. This indicates that at *P* = 2.00, the *AD* curve shifts to the left by $200 bil when the money supply falls by $200 bil. The rest of the curve shifts also, except when the price level is low enough to put the economy in the liquidity trap.

(a) The Federal Reserve increases the money supply through an open market operation. The AD curve shifts (right, left, not at all). The new interest rate is (higher, lower, unchanged).

(b) The Federal Reserve increases the money supply through an open market operation. The AD curve shifts (right, left, not at all). The new interest rate is (higher, lower, unchanged).

(c) The government sector increases its purchases of goods and services, financing the increase by selling bonds. The AD curve shifts (right, left, not at all). The new interest rate is (higher, lower, unchanged).

(d) The government sector increases its purchases of goods and services, financing the increase by selling bonds. The AD curve shifts (right, left, not at all). The new interest rate is (higher, lower, unchanged).

(e) The government sector increases its purchases of goods and services, financing the increase by issuing money. The AD curve shifts (right, left, not at all). The new interest rate is (higher, lower, unchanged).

(f) The price level rises. The AD curve shifts (right, left, not at all). The new interest rate is (higher, lower, unchanged).

(g) The business sector reduces investment spending. The AD curve shifts (right, left, not at all). The new interest rate is (higher, lower, unchanged).

(h) The household sector reduces its demand for speculative money balances. The AD curve shifts (right, left, not at all). The new interest rate is (higher, lower, unchanged).

(i) The household sector increases its saving at each income level. The AD curve shifts (right, left, not at all). The new interest rate is (higher, lower, unchanged).

(j) The government sector raises taxes and uses the proceeds to retire bonds. The AD curve shifts (right, left, not at all). The new interest rate is (higher, lower, unchanged).

2 (Optional) It is possible to find algebraic expressions for the IS, LM, and AD curves from the models used in these exercises. Let us use the model of Exercise 18, paragraph 7.

$$\frac{C}{P} = \$80 \text{ bil} + 0.75 \frac{Y_d}{P} + 0.125 \frac{V}{P} \qquad M_s = \$800 \text{ bil}$$

$$\frac{I}{P} = \$275 \text{ bil} - 25i \qquad \frac{M_1}{P} = 0.25 \frac{Y}{P}$$

$$G = \$100 \text{ bil} \qquad \frac{M_1}{P} = \$275 \text{ bil} - 25i \qquad \text{for } 3\% \leqslant i \leqslant 11\%$$

$$T = \$0 \qquad \frac{M_2}{P} = \$0 \quad \text{for } i \geqslant 11\%$$

$$B = \$0 \qquad i \geqslant 3\%, \text{ i.e., a liquidity trap at } i = 3\%$$

$$K = \$160 \text{ bil}$$

The IS curve is found by setting the equation for real personal saving equal to the sum of the expressions for real government spending and real _____, as follows:

$$(1) \quad \frac{S}{P} = \frac{I}{P} + \frac{G}{P}$$

(2) $-\$\underline{\hspace{1cm}}$ bil + $\underline{\hspace{1cm}} \dfrac{Y}{P} - \dfrac{\$\underline{\hspace{1cm}} \text{bil}}{P} = \$\underline{\hspace{1cm}}$ bil $- \underline{\hspace{1cm}} i$

$\quad + \dfrac{\$\underline{\hspace{1cm}} \text{bil}}{P}$

Simplify Eq. (2) and solve for Y/P:

(3) $0.25\dfrac{Y}{P} = \$\underline{\hspace{1cm}}$ bil $+ \dfrac{\$\underline{\hspace{1cm}} \text{bil}}{P} - \underline{\hspace{1cm}} i$

(4) $\dfrac{Y}{P} = \$\underline{\hspace{1cm}}$ bil $+ \dfrac{\$\underline{\hspace{1cm}} \text{bil}}{P} - \underline{\hspace{1cm}} i$

When $P = 2.00$ and $i = 7.0$ percent, $Y/P = \$\underline{\hspace{1cm}}$ bil. Verify this result by checking Fig. 18-3A.

To find the *LM* curve, we must equate the real supply of money with $\underline{\hspace{3cm}}$

$\underline{\hspace{5cm}}$. Since there are three different expressions for the speculative demand for money according to whether the interest rate is 3 percent, between 3 percent and 11 percent, and greater than 11 percent, three separate expressions for the *LM* curve must be found. If $i > 11$ percent, the speculative demand for money is

$\$\underline{\hspace{1cm}}$ bil. Thus, monetary equilibrium is

(5) $\dfrac{M_S}{P} = \dfrac{M_1}{P}$

(6) $\dfrac{\$\underline{\hspace{1cm}} \text{bil}}{P} = \underline{\hspace{1cm}} \dfrac{Y}{P}$ for $i \geqslant 11$ percent

Solving Eq. (6) for real income,

(7) $\dfrac{Y}{P} = \dfrac{\$\underline{\hspace{1cm}} \text{bil}}{P}$ for $\geqslant 11$ percent

If i is between 3 percent and 11 percent, monetary equilibrium can be written as

(8) $\dfrac{M_S}{P} = \dfrac{M_1}{P} + \dfrac{M_2}{P}$

(9) $\dfrac{\$\underline{\hspace{1cm}} \text{bil}}{P} = \underline{\hspace{1cm}} \dfrac{Y}{P} + \$\underline{\hspace{1cm}}$ bil $- \underline{\hspace{1cm}} i$

Solving Eq. (9) for Y/P:

(10) $\dfrac{Y}{P} = \dfrac{\$\underline{\hspace{1cm}} \text{bil}}{P} - \$\underline{\hspace{1cm}}$ bil $+ \underline{\hspace{1cm}} i$ for $3\% \leqslant i \leqslant 11\%$

The third segment of the *LM* curve is where the interest rate is 3 percent. If $P = 2.00$ and $i = 7.0$ percent, $Y/P = \$\underline{\hspace{1cm}}$ bil. Verify the results of this latter statement and Eqs. (6) and (10) by checking with Fig. 18-3A.

The aggregate demand curve can be found by solving the *IS* and *LM* curves to eliminate the variable i. Since there are three segments of the *LM* curve, there will be three segments of the AD curve. Let us proceed by first solving for i and then substituting the value found into either the IS or LM equation. If 3 percent $\leqslant i \leqslant$ 11 percent, then

(11) $IS = LM$

(12)   \$_____ bil + $\dfrac{\$_____ \text{bil}}{P}$ − _____ $i = \dfrac{\$_____ \text{bil}}{P}$ − \$_____ bil

$\quad$ + _____ i

Simplifying Eq. (12) we have:

(13) $200i = \$_____ \text{bil} - \dfrac{\$_____ \text{bil}}{P}$

(14) $i = \$_____ \text{bil} - \dfrac{\$_____ \text{bil}}{P}$

or, ignoring the money units,

(15) $i = 13 - \dfrac{12}{P}$

Therefore, if i is to be greater than or equal to 3 percent, P must be greater than or equal to _____ . If i is to be less than or equal to 11 percent, P must be less than or equal to _____ . Using this information, we can substitute the expression for i into the IS curve to find one segment of the AD curve:

(16) $\dfrac{Y}{P} = \$1{,}500 \text{ bil} + \dfrac{\$800 \text{ bil}}{P} - \$100 \left(13 - \dfrac{12}{P}\right) \text{bil}$

(17) $\dfrac{Y}{P} = \$_____ \text{bil} + \dfrac{\$_____ \text{bil}}{P} \quad$ for $1.20 \leqslant P \leqslant 6.00$

If the liquidity trap is in effect, the interest rate is _____ percent. This interest rate can be substituted directly into the IS curve to find the AD curve in that range:

(18) $\dfrac{Y}{P} = \$_____ \text{bil} + \dfrac{\$_____ \text{bil}}{P} - \$100 (_____) \text{bil}$

(19) $\dfrac{Y}{P} = \$_____ \text{bil} + \dfrac{\$_____ \text{bil}}{P} \quad$ for $P \leqslant 1.20$

If the interest rate is above 11 percent, the economy is in the (liquidity trap, quantity theory) range of the LM curve. We have already found that i will be above 11 percent if the price level is above _____ . In the quantity theory range, the LM curve (does, does not) contain i as a variable. Therefore, it (is, is not) necessary to solve the IS curve and the LM curve together to eliminate the variable. The aggregate demand curve is the (IS, LM) curve in the quantity theory range:

$\dfrac{Y}{P} = \dfrac{\$_____ \text{bil}}{P}$

Given the aggregate demand curve, complete the following table:

Table 18-7

Price index, P	Real output, Y/P
6.00	$_____ bil
5.00	_____ bil
4.00	_____ bil
2.67 = 8/3	_____ bil
2.00	_____ bil
1.60	_____ bil
1.33 = 4/3	_____ bil
1.20	_____ bil
1.00	_____ bil
0.80	_____ bil

Refer to Fig. 18-4A to verify that the data in Table 18-7 represents AD_1 in that figure.

ANSWERS FOR EXERCISE 18

1 real, real, real, remain the same, remain the same, do not affect, the same as, Fig. 18-1A

2 real, not to exhibit, Fig. 18-1A, the same as, nominal, real, real, several lines depending on the price level, cannot

3 400, 500, Fig. 18-1A,

P	M_S/P	Y/P	i
0.80	500	1,200	3
1.00	400	1,000	5
2.00	200	600	9
4.00	100	400	11

increase, similar to, increases

4 liquidity trap, Fig. 18-1A, $P = 0.67$, $M_S/P = 600$, $Y/P = 1,200$, $i = 3$, no, always, liquidity trap, limited

5 Fig. 18-2A, demand, variable, differs from

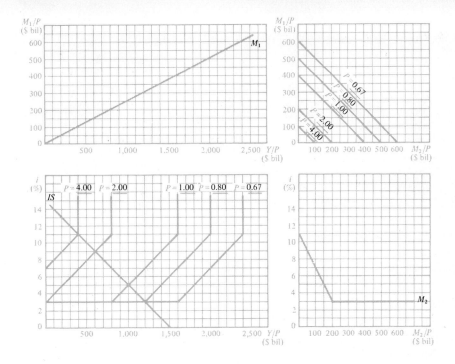

FIGURE 18-1A

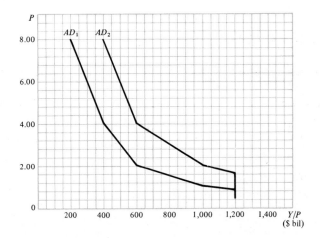

FIGURE 18-2A

6 400, 1.00, 1,000, 1,000, identical

P	Y/P
0.20	1,200
0.67	1,200
0.80	1,200
1.00	1,200
1.60	1,200
2.00	1,000
4.00	600
8.00	400

Fig. 18-2A, increase, right, no, liquidity trap, limited

7 inversely, the same as, present, real, the money supply, increase, rise, increase, rise, rise, no, does

8 nominal, similar to, nominal, rise, no, rises, rightward, *IS*, both curves, *IS*, *LM*, cannot

9 100,

P	G/P
1.00	100
1.33	75
2.00	50
4.00	25

Fig. 18-3A, rises

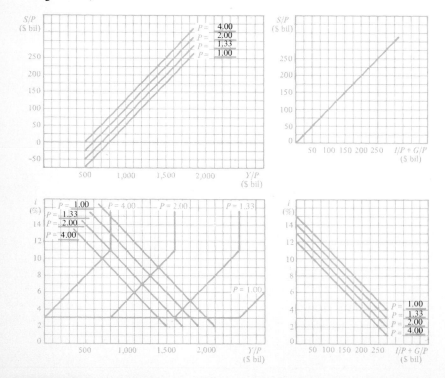

FIGURE 18-3A

10 the real money supply,

P	S/P	0.125 M_S/P
1.00	50	100
1.33	75	75
2.00	100	50
4.00	125	25

Fig. 18-3A, downward, upward

11 Fig. 18-3A,

P	Y/P	i
1.00	2,000	3
1.33	1,700	4
2.00	1,200	7
4.00	700	10

Fig. 18-4A, no, Fig. 18-4A, 1.00, rises, does not, The Pigou effect causes the *IS* curve to shift along the horizontal *LM* curve

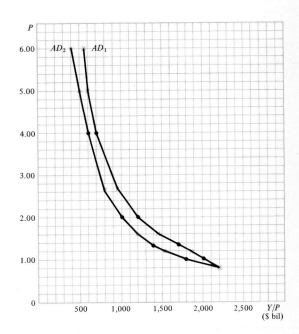

FIGURE 18-4A

12 increase, decreasing, physical capital, government securities, money, remain unchanged, not at all, not at all, Fig. 18-5A

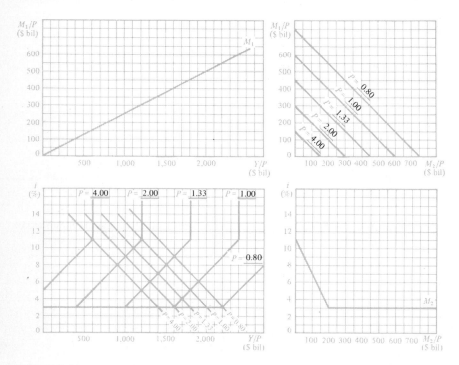

FIGURE 18-5A

13 leftward, lower, Fig. 18-5A,

P	Y/P ·	i
0.80	2,200	3
1.00	1,800	5
1.33	1,400	7
2.00	1,000	9
4.00	600	11

Fig. 18-4A, left, the liquidity trap prevents the money supply change from having any effect on the economy at low prices

ANSWERS TO PROBLEMS FOR EXERCISE 18

1 only one,
    (a) Fig. 18-6A, panel (1), right, lower
    (b) Fig. 18-6A, panel (2), not at all, unchanged

(c) Fig. 18-6A, panel (3), right, higher
(d) Fig. 18-6A, panel (4), not at all, higher
(e) Fig. 18-6A, panel (5), right, unchanged
(f) Fig. 18-6A, panel (6), not at all, unchanged (i.e., this represents a movement *along* the *AD* curve)
(g) Fig. 18-6A, panel (7), left, lower
(h) Fig. 18-6A, panel (8), right, lower
(i) Fig. 18-6A, panel (9), left, lower
(j) Fig. 18-6A, panel (10), left, lower

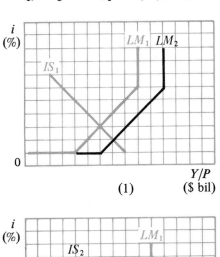

(1)

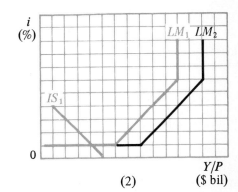

(2)

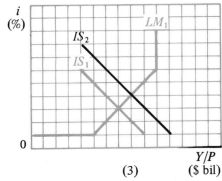

(3)

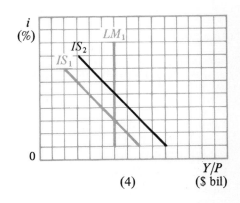

(4)

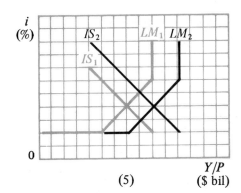

(5)

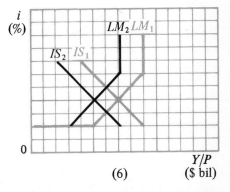

(6)

FIGURE 18-6A

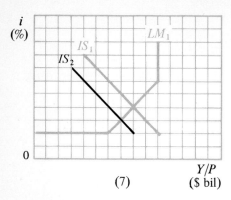

(7)

Y/P ($ bil)

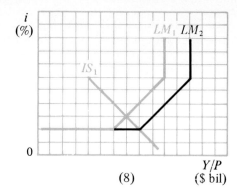

(8)

Y/P ($ bil)

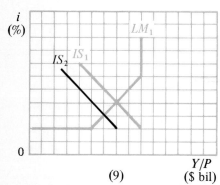

(9)

Y/P ($ bil)

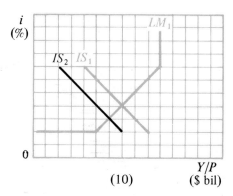

(10)

Y/P ($ bil)

FIGURE 18-6A (Continued)

2 investment,

Eq. (2) $-\$100$ bil $+ 0.25Y/P - \$100$ bil$/P = \$275$ bil $- 25i + \$100$ bil$/P$

Eq. (3) $0.25Y/P = \$375$ bil $+ \$200$ bil$/P - 25i$

Eq. (4) $Y/P = \$1,500$ bil $+ \$800$ bil$/P - 100i$

1,200, real demand for money, 0,

Eq. (6) $\$800$ bil$/P = 0.25Y/P$

Eq. (7) $Y/P = \$3,200$ bil$/P$

Eq. (9) $\$800$ bil$/P = 0.25Y/P + \$275$ bil $- 25i$

Eq. (10) $Y/P = \$3,200$ bil$/P - \$1,100$ bil $+ 100i$

1,200

Eq. (12) $\$1,500$ bil $+ \$800$ bil$/P - 100i = \$3,200$ bil$/P - \$1,100$ bil $+ 100i$

Eq. (13) $200i = \$2,600$ bil $- \$2,400$ bil$/P$

Eq. (14) $i = \$13$ bil $- \$12$ bil$/P$

1.20, 6.00,

Eq. (17) $Y/P = \$200$ bil $+ \$2,000$ bil$/P$

3,

Eq. (18) $Y/P = \$1,500$ bil $+ \$800$ bil$/P - \$100(3)$ bil

Eq. (19) $Y/P = \$1,200$ bil $+ \$800$ bil$/P$

quantity theory, 6, does not, is not, *LM*

$Y/P = \$3200$ bil$/P$

P: 6.00, 5.00, 4.00, 2.66, 2.00, 1.60, 1.33, 1.20, 1.00, 0.80

Y/P: 533.33, 600, 700, 950, 1,200, 1,450, 1,700, 1,866.66, 2,000, 2,200

1 The liquidity trap occurs when people expect
  (a) commodity prices to rise
  (b) securities prices to rise
  (c) interest rates to rise
  (d) securities prices to fall
  (e) interest rates to fall

2 According to the quantity theory of money
  (a) the supply of money is a function of income
  (b) the demand for money has an interest-elasticity of infinity
  (c) the demand for money has an interest-elasticity of zero
  (d) the demand for money always equals the supply of money
  (e) interest rates are primarily determined by liquidity preference

3 Monetary policy is ineffective if
  (a) investment is interest-inelastic
  (b) the transactions demand for money is interest-elastic
  (c) the economy is in the liquidity trap
  (d) the quantity theory of money is operative

4 Fiscal policy is ineffective if
  (a) investment is interest-inelastic
  (b) the transactions demand for money is interest-elastic
  (c) the economy is in the liquidity trap
  (d) the quantity theory of money is operative

5 The quantity theory is invalid if the
  (a) speculative demand for money exists
  (b) transactions demand for money is interest-elastic
  (c) supply of money is interest-elastic
  (d) supply of money is controlled by the Federal Reserve
  (e) economy is on the gold standard

6 "Crowding out" of private expenditures by government expenditures refers to
   (a) reduction of consumption spending as taxes rise
   (b) production controls and rationing in a national emergency
   (c) reduction of investment expenditures as interest rates rise
   (d) effects of price and wage controls

7 The supply of money would be interest-elastic if
   (a) the liquidity trap exists
   (b) commercial banks have an interest-elastic demand for reserves
   (c) government spending is countercyclical
   (d) the Federal Reserve responds to interest rates when setting monetary policy
   (e) individuals reduce cash balances when interest rates rise

8 Most economists believe that the quantity theory is most likely to be valid when the economy is
   (a) near full employment
   (b) in deep depression
   (c) in a condition intermediate between full employment and depression
   (d) none of these

9 If the quantity theory is valid, tax cuts are more effective for stimulating income than government spending increases.
   (a) true
   (b) false

10 If the quantity theory is valid, autonomous increases in investment or consumption will increase income while increases in government spending will have no effect on income.
   (a) true
   (b) false

11 If the quantity theory is valid, changes in government spending can affect income only if they are financed by changes in
   (a) taxes
   (b) government securities
   (c) the money supply
   (d) all of these

12 If the economy is in the liquidity trap, changes in private expenditures cannot increase income while changes in government expenditures can.
   (a) true
   (b) false

13 Most economists believe that the liquidity trap is most likely to appear when the economy is
   (a) near full employment
   (b) in deep depression

(c) in a condition intermediate between full employment and depression

(d) none of these

14 Can the Federal Reserve set whatever interest rate it wants to?

(a) yes

(b) no

(c) yes, unless the economy is in the liquidity trap range and there is no other range

(d) yes, unless the quantity theory is valid

(e) no, unless investment is interest-inelastic

15 Can the Federal Reserve set both the interest rate and the money supply at any level they want to?

(a) yes

(b) no

(c) yes, unless the economy is in the liquidity trap

(d) yes, unless the quantity theory is valid

(e) no, unless investment is interest-inelastic

16 A change of the price level affects aggregate demand by changing the real value of

(a) the money supply

(b) bonds

(c) government spending

(d) taxes

(e) all of the above

17 If there is no "money illusion" in the economy,

(a) real values and nominal values are the same

(b) real spending decisions depend only on real values

(c) the money supply is the sole determinant of income

(d) consumers are irrational

18 The Keynes effect is a name for the effect of changing

(a) prices on the real money supply

(b) prices on real government spending

(c) prices on real wages

(d) interest rates on the demand for money

19 The Pigou effect refers to the effect of changing

(a) prices on the real money supply

(b) prices on real consumption spending

(c) prices on real wages

(d) income on the demand for money

20 The Keynes effect is ineffective

(a) if wages are rigid

(b) in the quantity theory range of the *LM* curve

(c) in the liquidity trap range of the *LM* curve

   (d) if taxes and government spending are zero
   (e) none of the above

21 The Pigou effect is ineffective
   (a) if wages are rigid
   (b) in the quantity theory range of the *LM* curve
   (c) in the liquidity trap range of the *LM* curve
   (d) if taxes and government spending are zero
   (e) none of the above

22 The price level is
   (a) positively related to real aggregate demand
   (b) inversely related to real aggregate demand
   (c) not related to aggregate demand

23 If prices fall,
   (a) the Keynes effect shifts the *IS* curve to the right
   (b) the Keynes effect shifts the *IS* curve to the left
   (c) the Pigou effect shifts the *IS* curve to the right
   (d) the Pigou effect shifts the *IS* curve to the left

For questions 24 to 29, assume that the *IS* curve always intersects the *LM* curve in the intermediate range.

24 If prices fall,
   (a) the Keynes effect shifts the *LM* curve to the right
   (b) the Keynes effect shifts the *LM* curve to the left
   (c) the Pigou effect shifts the *LM* curve to the right
   (d) the Pigou effect shifts the *LM* curve to the left

25 If government spending rises, financed by a sale of bonds,
   (a) the *IS* curve shifts to the right
   (b) the *IS* curve shifts to the left
   (c) the *LM* curve shifts to the right
   (d) the *LM* curve shifts to the left
   (e) the *AD* curve shifts to the right
   (f) the *AD* curve shifts to the left

26 If government spending rises, financed by printing money,
   (a) the *IS* curve shifts to the right
   (b) the *IS* curve shifts to the left
   (c) the *LM* curve shifts to the right
   (d) the *LM* curve shifts to the left
   (e) the *AD* curve shifts to the right
   (f) the *AD* curve shifts to the left

27 If the Fed sells government bonds to the public,
   (a) the *IS* curve shifts to the right
   (b) the *IS* curve shifts to the left
   (c) the *LM* curve shifts to the right
   (d) the *LM* curve shifts to the left
   (e) the *AD* curve shifts to the right
   (f) the *AD* curve shifts to the left

28 If consumers decide to save more at current income levels,
   (a) the *IS* curve shifts to the right
   (b) the *IS* curve shifts to the left
   (c) the *LM* curve shifts to the right
   (d) the *LM* curve shifts to the left
   (e) the *AD* curve shifts to the right
   (f) the *AD* curve shifts to the left

29 If the price level falls,
   (a) the *IS* curve shifts to the right
   (b) the *IS* curve shifts to the left
   (c) the *LM* curve shifts to the right
   (d) the *LM* curve shifts to the left
   (e) the *AD* curve shifts to the right
   (f) the *AD* curve shifts to the left

30 If the economy is in the liquidity trap,
   (a) monetary policy will not work
   (b) fiscal policy will not work
   (c) the Keynes effect is inoperative
   (d) the Pigou effect is inoperative

PART SEVEN

AGGREGATE SUPPLY

In Exercise 18 we found that with the introduction of variable prices the aggregate demand model cannot determine a unique equilibrium real income. This difficulty can be removed if we drop the assumption that production reacts passively to demand, and add to the model a simple theory of producer behavior. As one might anticipate, such a theory will enable us to associate an intended level of output with each possible price level. This relationship between intended aggregate production and the price level is known as the *aggregate supply* curve. The intersection of the aggregate supply curve with the aggregate demand curve determines the equilibrium level of real income (output) and the equilibrium price level.

Two theories of aggregate supply—the Keynesian and the Classical systems—are presented in this part. They have two features in common: (1) a simple model of the labor market, which determines the amount of labor that will be employed; (2) a production function, which shows how much real output can be obtained from a given amount of labor input. Both models are short-run in the sense that capital is fixed. Therefore, labor is the only variable factor of production. The Keynesian and classical theories do not differ in their analysis of the demand side of the labor market. Both assume that the demand for labor at a given real wage is determined by the value of the product and by the marginal physical product of labor, that is, the amount of *additional* output that will be forthcoming from a small increment of labor input. Presumably, producers will not hire more labor unless the value of the marginal output of labor is worth more than the marginal expense, that is, the wage rate. Both theories also assume that output markets are competitive.

The difference between the two theories of aggregate supply of output is found in the treatment of the supply of labor. The Keynesian system—Exercise 19—assumes that labor supply adjusts passively to the demand for labor. The money wage rate is considered to be fixed by government legislation, institutional arrangements and social convention. The business sector can hire all the labor it wants if it is willing to pay this wage. If conditions change so that more workers are needed, they can be added without an increase of the wage. If fewer workers are needed, some will be dismissed and become unemployed. They are willing to work at the going wage, but they cannot obtain jobs by bidding down the wage rate. In this sense, they are involuntarily unemployed.

The classical system—Exercise 20—assumes that the labor supply is governed by the real wage rate. The higher the real wage, the more labor will be supplied. The supply and demand for labor determine the equilibrium real wage and employment. Given that the supply curve of labor is positively sloped, all workers who lack jobs are unemployed because they insist on a wage rate that is higher than the equilibrium wage. Thus, in the classical system, all unemployment is voluntary. No one who is willing to accept the going wage will be unemployed.

The Keynesian and classical systems lead to different conclusions about the desirability of government efforts to stabilize the economy through the use of monetary and fiscal policy. The issue is somewhat one of effectiveness. The classical system generates an equilibrium level of employment which uniquely determines real output. In the Keynesian system, conversely, employment is determined by the demand for labor, with labor supply reacting passively. Government policy *can* affect the demand for labor by changing the demand for the goods and services labor produces.

An additional issue raised by the two systems is, in part, a matter of a social-ethics judgment. In the classical system, those who lack jobs are unemployed because they demand more than the going wage, while in the Keynesian system, the unemployed are willing to work at the going wage but the economic system fails to provide jobs. It is easy to see that, to an adherent of the classical model, unemployment is not a societal responsibility but rather is a product of individual choice. Under the Keynesian system, alternatively, unemployment is a social responsibility because the economic system has failed to provide jobs for those who are willing to work under existing conditions.

AGGREGATE SUPPLY IN THE KEYNESIAN MODEL

1 In the Keynesian model there are three basic elements required to determine the amount of goods and services producers are willing to supply:

   (a) the production function, a schedule giving the maximum output for a given amount of labor and capital input (capital assumed fixed)

   (b) the demand for labor schedule, which is based on the proposition that labor is hired only if its daily output can be sold for an amount of revenue at least as high as the existing daily wage rate

   (c) the supply of labor schedule, which is assumed to be controlled by union pressure, government regulation, and custom such that all of the labor in the economy is available at a fixed money—not real—wage rate.

   These elements may be represented by the following model of producer behavior:

   (1) $Y/P = 4ON - 1/4\,N^2$

   (2) $w = P \cdot MPP_N$

   (3) $w = w_O$

N is employment, P is the price index, w is the wage rate, and MPP_N is the marginal physical product of labor. It is assumed here that labor is the only variable factor of production. The marginal physical product of labor is the amount of output that is added when a small addition is made to the labor force. In order to find how much this added output can be sold for, we multiply it by the price of the output. Since we are evaluating aggregate output we use P, the price index. The value of the marginal physical product must equal the wage rate in order for producers to be in equilibrium. If the value of the marginal physical product is greater than the wage rate, (more, less) labor will be hired. If the value of the marginal physical product is less than the wage rate, employment will (rise, fall). Only when the two values, w and $P \cdot MPP_N$, are equal will producers be satisfied with the size of the employed labor force. Thus, Eq. (2) is a(n) (production maximum, equilibrium) condition.

   The production function, Eq. (1), is plotted in quadrant (2) of Fig. 19-1 for selected values of employment N ranging between zero and 80 mil. When N is 80 mil, Y/P is

$ _____ bil. When N is 81 mil, Y/P is approximately $ _____ bil. This result suggests that $1,600 bil (is, is not) the maximum possible production in this model.

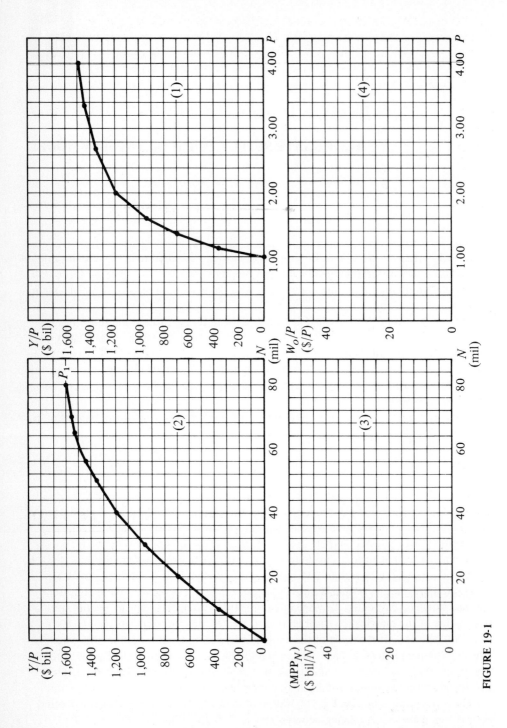

FIGURE 19-1

2 The marginal physical product of labor, MPP_N, is equal to the value $\Delta(Y/P)/\Delta N$, where Δ indicates change in the amounts of Y/P and N. For computational purposes, it is assumed that the changes are small. To find an expression for measuring the marginal physical product, in Eq. (1), we can replace N by the term $N + \Delta N$ and Y/P by the term $Y/P + \Delta(Y/P)$.

(4) $\quad \dfrac{Y}{P} + \Delta \dfrac{Y}{P} = 40(N + \Delta N) - \dfrac{1}{4}(N + \Delta N)^2$

If the term $(N + \Delta N)^2$ is calculated, Eq. (4) can be stated as

(5) $\quad \dfrac{Y}{P} + \Delta \dfrac{Y}{P} =$ _____

The parentheses can be disposed of by performing the indicated multiplications:

(6) $\quad \dfrac{Y}{P} + \Delta \dfrac{Y}{P} =$ _____

Since, according to Eq. (1) $Y/P = 40N - 1/4\,N^2$, Eq. (6) can be simplified by subtracting Eq. (1) from Eq. (6):

(7) $\quad \Delta \dfrac{Y}{P} =$ _____

The marginal physical product of labor can now be found by dividing Eq. (7) by ΔN.

(8) $\quad \Delta \dfrac{Y}{P}/\Delta N =$ _____

If ΔN is very small, its value in Eq. (8) can be ignored. The expression for measuring the marginal physical product of labor then becomes

(9) $\quad \Delta \dfrac{Y}{P}/\Delta N = MPP_N =$ _____

Plot Eq. (9) in quadrant (3) of Fig. 19-1 for the following selected employment values: $N = 0, N = 20, N = 40, N = 60, N = 80$. The MPP_N measures the (slope, maximum values) of the production function plotted in quadrant (2) of Fig. 19-1. As employment rises, the MPP_N (rises, falls).

3 If the money wage is known and determined autonomously, i.e., $w = w_o$, there (is, is not) a unique relation between the real wage, w_o/P, and the price level P. Assuming that $w_o = \$40$ per day, complete Table 19-1 and plot the points in quadrant (4) of Fig. 19-1. Label the curve $w_o = \$40$.

4 We have so far established the following relationships:
   (a) For some given $w = w_o$, P determines w_o/P
   (b) Since $w_o/P = MPP_N$ for producers' equilibrium
   (c) P is related to the MPP_N
   (d) The MPP_N is related to N
   (e) N determines Y/P

Table 19-1

Price index (P)	Real wage (w_O/P)
1.00	_____
1.14 = 8/7	_____
1.33 = 4/3	_____
1.60	_____
2.00	_____
2.67 = 8/3	_____
3.33 = 10/3	_____
4.00	_____

This argument establishes that, through the intermediate steps *b* to *d* above, there (must be, may be, cannot be) a unique relationship between Y/P and P. The function relating real output to price is known as the aggregate supply curve. This function can be constructed in Fig. 19-1. If the price level is 1.14, from quadrant (4) we know that the

real wage will be _____ . Mark this point with an *a* on the $w_O = \$40$ function.

According to quadrant (3) this real wage level will result in employment of _____ mil. Mark this point with an *a* on the MPP_N line. This employment level will lead to

real output of \$ _____ bil. The real output information is obtained in quadrant

_____ . Mark this point with an *a* on the production function. On the function graphed in quadrant (1) locate the \$375 bil level of real output and mark it with an *a*.

This point is associated with a price level of _____ , which (is, is not) the price index we started with.

Repeat the preceding steps for a price level of 2.00, marking the points with *b*'s. If this process were repeated for other price levels, the function drawn in quadrant (1) would

represent the _____ curve described earlier in this paragraph. Label this curve AS_1 .

5 The aggregate supply curve derived in Fig. 19-1 has been replotted in Fig. 19-2 with the axes reversed. An additional point has been plotted for a $P = 6.00$ and $Y/P = \$1,556$ bil. Label this curve AS_1 . The aggregate demand curve AD_1 derived earlier in Fig. 18-3 also has been drawn here. Label this curve AD_1 .

Compute the equilibrium values in Table 19-2. (Note: The model used to derive AD_1 is given on page 271 and graphed on page 273.) Does $G/P + I/P$ equal S/P? (yes, no)

Table 19-2

Real output	$ _____ bil
Price level	_____
Interest rate	_____ percent
Real investment expenditures	$ _____ bil
Real government expenditures	$ _____ bil
Real saving	$ _____ bil

Equilibrium employment is _____ mil. Is this necessarily full employment? (yes, no) What is the annual real wage bill in this economy, assuming a year contains 200 working

days? $ _____ bil. Since equilibrium real income is $ _____ bil, what happens to

the remainder of the national income? _____

(Note: In reality wages are about 75 percent of national income and 60 percent of GNP.)

6 One of the classic controversies in macroeconomics is whether or not full employment can be achieved through reduction of the money wage in the absence of active fiscal and monetary policy. Let us reduce the money wage in the present model to $20 per day. The w_O curve in Fig. 19-1 shifts (to the right, to the left, not at all). The marginal physical product of labor (rises, falls, remains unchanged) at each level of employment, and the production function shifts (upward, downward, not at all) at each level of employment. Complete Table 19-3 and plot the points in quadrant (4) of Fig. 19-1. Label the new function $w_O = \$20$.

Derive the new aggregate supply curve in quadrant (1) and label it AS_2. Transcribe the aggregate supply curve to Fig. 19-2 and label it AS_2. The curve has shifted (to the right, to the left, not at all), thus showing that the money wage decrease, in the absence of other effects, (does, does not) increase real income. What is the approximate equilibrium

real income and price level? $ _____ bil and _____ . The equilibrium level of

employment is _____ mil. Assuming a year contains 200 working days, the total real

wage bill is $ _____ bil, which is (more, less) than the real wage bill when the wage rate was $40 per day. Thus, in this example, a lower money wage rate does increase income and employment, but redistributes income from (labor to capital owners, capital owners to labor). If the two groups have different consumption propensities, this redistribution of income could cause secondary changes in aggregate income, prices, and so on.

7 The total effect of the foregoing aggregate supply curve shift can be summarized in Fig. 19-3. The aggregate supply and demand curves of Fig. 19-2 are reproduced in the upper half of the graph and the *IS-LM* curves in the lower half. The horizontal scales of the two diagrams are identical because they both represent the (price level, real

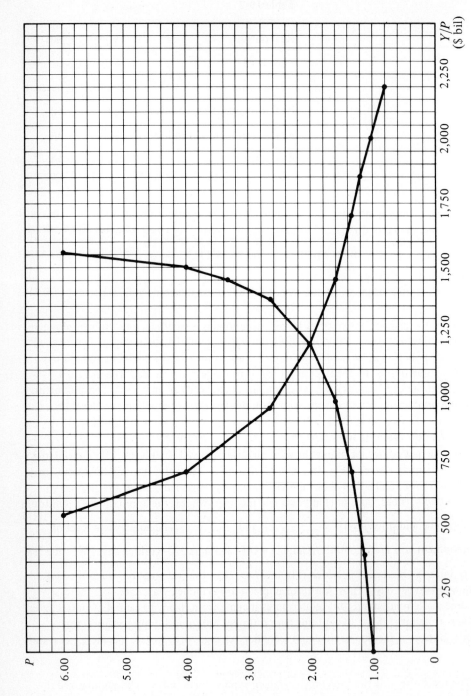

FIGURE 19-2

Table 19-3

Price index (P)	Real wage (w_O/P)
0.50	_____
0.57 = 4/7	_____
0.67 = 2/3	_____
0.80	_____
1.00	_____
1.33 = 4/3	_____
1.60	_____
2.00	_____
2.67 = 8/3	_____
4.00	_____

income, interest rate) prevailing in the economy. The two sets of curves (must, need not) intersect at the same income level.

Before introduction of the money-wage decrease of paragraph 6, the equilibrium price level was _____ and the equilibrium interest rate was _____ percent. The lower money wage rate shifted the *AS* curve in Fig. 19-3 to the (right, left), with (some, no) effect on the *AD* curve. The new equilibrium position has a (higher, lower) real income and a (higher, lower) price level. The changed price level shifts the *IS* curve to the (right, left) and the *LM* curve to the (right, left). These shifts originate in price effects, such as the _____ effect on the *IS* curve and the _____

_____ effect on the *LM* curve examined in Exercise 18. The net result of the shifts of the *IS* and *LM* curves in our example is to (raise, lower) the equilibrium interest rate. It should be pointed out that the lower interest rate is due to the particular model specification used here and might not occur with a different model. If the price sensitivity of the Pigou effect is greater than that of the Keynes effect, the (*IS, LM*) curve will shift rightward relatively more than the (*IS, LM*) curve for a price decline, resulting in an interest rate (increase, decrease) under the same conditions described above. However, the higher income and lower price level (would, would not) occur regardless of the model specification.

8 If technical progress occurs, the economy can enjoy more output from the same amount of input. Technical change can take two forms: that which alters the marginal physical product of labor at each level of employment, and that which does not. First,

let us assume that it becomes possible to produce $250 bil of additional output at each amount of labor input, so that the production function becomes

(10) $\dfrac{Y}{P} = \$ \underline{\hspace{1.5cm}} \text{bil} + 40N - \dfrac{1}{4}N^2$

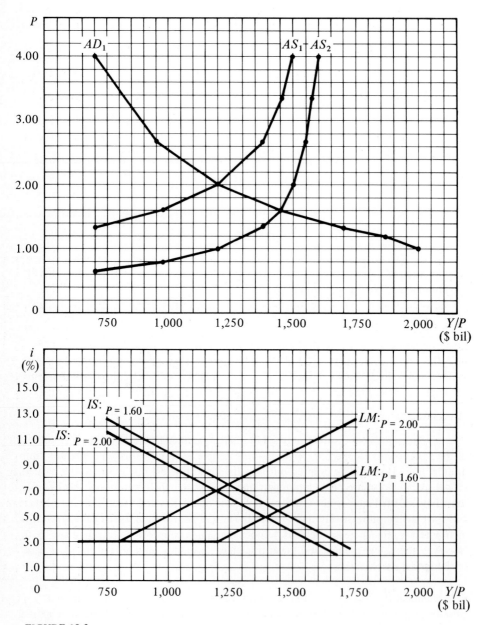

FIGURE 19-3

This production function is plotted in Fig. 19-4. It is labeled P_2. Compared to P_1 (i.e., the production function of quadrant (2) of Fig. 19-1), the marginal physical product of labor (increases, decreases, does not change) at each level of employment. As a result of the (upward, downward) shift of the production function, we would expect the aggregate supply curve to shift (rightward, leftward, not at all).

The new aggregate supply curve, reflecting P_2 conditions, is plotted in Fig. 19-5. It is labeled AS_2. The curve has shifted to the (right, left) from AS_1. Assuming the money wage W_O is again $40 per day, and given that P is now approximately _____ (see Fig. 19-5) the real wage is approximately _____. We can determine from Fig. 19-1, quadrant (3), that employment is approximately _____ mil. The total real wage bill is approximately $ _____ bil. (Assume a year contains 200 working days.) Compared to AS_1, examined in paragraph 5, does technical progress in this example alter the labor/capital shares of income? (yes, no) If yes, in what way? If no, why not? _____

_____

_____.

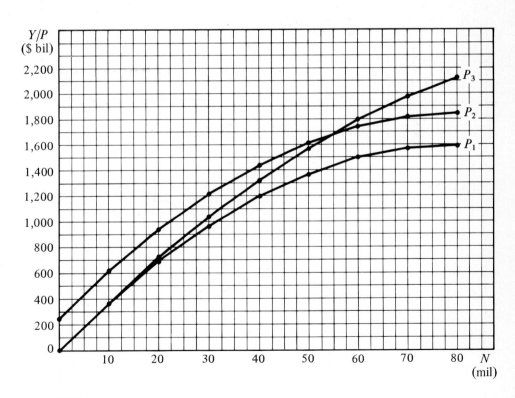

FIGURE 19-4

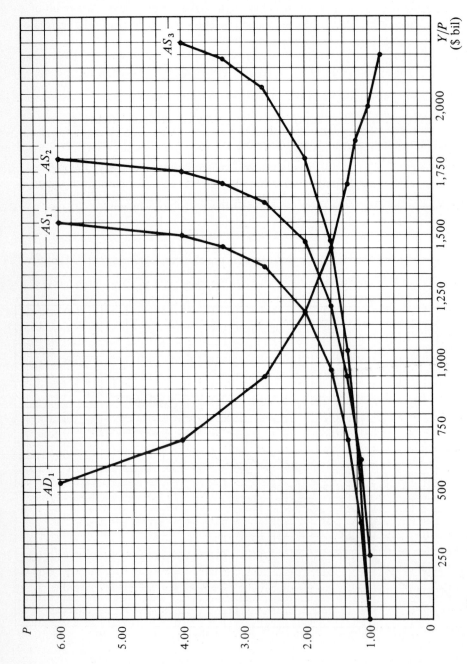

FIGURE 19-5

9 Due to a different form of technical change, now let the production function shift to

$$(11) \quad \frac{Y}{P} = 40N - 1/6\,N^2$$

The marginal physical product of labor is

$$(12) \quad MPP_N = 40 - \frac{1}{2}N$$

This function is also plotted in Fig. 19-4. This production function is labeled P_3. Compared to P_1 and P_2, the marginal physical product of labor has (increased, decreased, not changed) at each level of employment. As a result of the (upward, downward) shift of the production function from P_1, we would expect the aggregate supply curve in Fig. 19-5 to shift (rightward, leftward, not at all) from AS_1.

The new aggregate supply curve, reflecting P_3 conditions, is plotted in Fig. 19-5. It is labeled AS_3. The curve has shifted to the (right, left) from AS_1. The price level is now

_____ . If the money wage is $40 per day, the real wage is _____ . Use Eq. (12)

to find the new level of employment: _____ mil. The total real wage bill is approxi-

mately $ _____ bil. (Assume a year contains 200 working days.) Compared to AS_1, does technical progress in this example alter the labor/capital shares of income? (yes, no)

If yes, in what way? If no, why not? _____

_____

_____ .

10 Refer now to Fig. 19-6. The initial aggregate demand conditions are represented by IS_1 and LM_1 in the lower half of the graph. These demand conditions reflect a nominal money supply of $800 bil and a price index of 2.00. Mark the initial equilibrium point E_1 in this graph. The intersection of the IS and LM curves (must, need not) be at the same income level as the intersection of the AD and AS curves. In the upper half of Fig. 19-6 we assume that the initial aggregate supply conditions are represented by AS_1. Label the correct aggregate demand curve AD_1 and mark the initial equilibrium point E_1. The

equilibrium price level is _____ , which (is, is not) the price level assumed in the aggregate demand conditions represented by IS_1 and LM_1.

Now assume that the Federal Reserve carries out an open market operation to reduce the nominal money supply by selling bonds to the household sector. The money supply falls from $800 bil to $600 bil, while the household sectors' holdings of government

securities (rise, fall) by $ _____ bil. Initially assume that prices are held constant. The

IS curve would shift (to the right, to the left, not at all). Why? _____

_____

_____ .

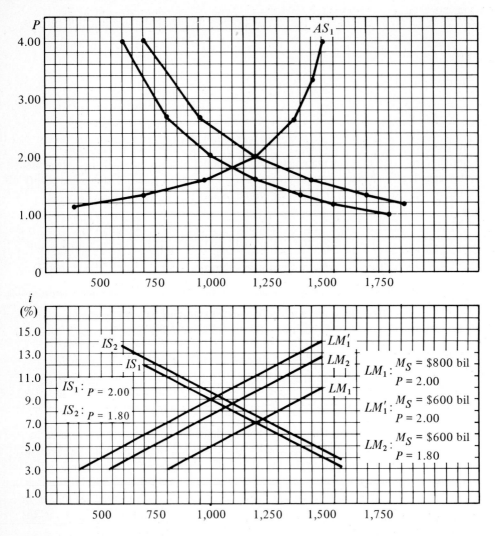

FIGURE 19-6

If prices are held constant, the *LM* curve would shift (to the right, to the left, not at all).
Mark the new *IS-LM* equilibrium point E_2. This result implies that the aggregate demand
curve would shift (to the right, to the left, not at all) at all price levels. The aggregate
supply curve shifts (to the right, to the left, not at all). Label the new aggregate demand
curve AD_2 and mark the new *AD-AS* equilibrium point E_3. The effect of the Fed's
action on aggregate demand and supply is (a higher, a lower, the same) real income and
(a higher, a lower, the same) price level. Thus, it can be seen that the resulting price
change causes the *LM* curve to (shift again, remain at LM_2) and the *IS* curve to (shift,
remain at IS_1). The *IS* curve shifts to the (right, left) and the *LM* curve shifts to the
(right, left). The new intersection of the *IS* and *LM* curves (must, need not) be at the
same income level as the intersection of the *AD* and *AS* curves. Mark the new *IS-LM*

equilibrium point E_3. Assuming that the induced price change does not completely offset the initial shift of the *IS* and *LM* curves, the new equilibrium interest rate (must be higher than the old, must be lower than the old, may be either higher or lower than the old depending on the model).

11 It is not necessary to explicitly work through a detailed model to determine the *direction* of change in income, interest rates and prices caused by a change in a policy parameter or a behavioral assumption. The first step is to determine the effect of the policy change on the *IS* and/or *LM* curves under the initial assumption that prices do not change. This step gives the direction of change in aggregate demand unless, of course, the *IS-LM* curves shift in opposite directions. If aggregate demand changes at one price level, it may be assumed to change at other price levels. The shift of the aggregate demand curve determines the new equilibrium price level, which, in turn, further shifts the *IS* and *LM* curves. The secondary shift of *IS-LM*, however, usually does not offset the initial shift. Thus, if the initial change shifts the *LM* curve to the left, the secondary shifts will not completely negate the tendency for interest rates to (rise, fall). If, of course, the *IS* and *LM* curves initially do not shift in the same direction, the ultimate effect on the principal macroeconomic variables is ambiguous without full empirical specification of the model.

These ideas can be tested on the following example: assume that government spending is increased, financed by selling government bonds to the household sector. The initial impact in the absence of price changes is to shift the *IS* curve (to the right, to the left, not at all) and the *LM* curve (to the right, to the left, not at all). The *AD* curve shifts to the (right, left), producing (higher, lower) income and a (higher, lower) price level. The resultant price change causes a secondary shift of (the *IS*, the *LM*, both *IS* and *LM*) curve(s) to the (right, left). If these secondary shifts do not offset the initial shift of the *IS* curve, the interest rate will ultimately (rise, fall).

PROBLEMS FOR EXERCISE 19

1 Six initial equilibrium situations for an economy are presented in Fig. 19-7. Each problem is represented by two sets of diagrams: the upper half gives the aggregate demand and aggregate supply curves and the lower half gives the corresponding *IS* and *LM* curves. As demonstrated above, both pairs of curves must intersect at the same real income level. The initial equilibrium is represented by the curves AD_1, AS_1, IS_1, and LM_1. The initial equilibrium point is labeled E_1. In each of the six problems listed below, a change is introduced into the economy. You are to make the necessary shifts of the curves and find the new equilibrium point. Label the new curve(s) AD_2, AS_2, IS_2, and LM_2. Assume that all shifts are parallel and that the initial shifts are of two horizontal squares. Note that if, for example, the change given in a problem requires that the *LM* curve be shifted two squares, the shift of the point on the *AD* curve corresponding to the original equilibrium price will be determined by the new intersection of the *IS* and *LM* curves, and will not necessarily be two squares. When the equilibrium price changes, the *IS* and *LM* curves will undergo a secondary shift. *Do not* draw these *IS* and *LM* curves.

(a) The Federal Reserve increases the money supply by means of an open market operation. The initial effect is to shift (the *IS* curve, the *LM* curve, both curves) to the (right, left) at the old equilibrium price. Draw the new curve(s) in the lower half of panel (1) in Fig. 19-7. The (*AD* curve, *AS* curve, both curves) shift to the (right, left). Draw the new curve(s) in the upper half of panel (1) in Fig. 19-7 and label the new equilibrium point E_2. The equilibrium income (rises, falls, remains the same). The price change causes the *IS* and *LM* curves to shift to the (right, left). Assuming that the secondary shift of *IS-LM*, due to the price effect, has a smaller effect on the interest rate than the initial change, *i* will be (higher than, lower than, the same as) it was initially.

(b) The government increases its spending, financing it by selling securities. The initial effect is to shift the (*IS* curve, *LM* curve, both curves) to the (right, left) at the old equilibrium price. Draw the curve(s) in the lower half of panel (2), Fig. 19-7. The (*AD* curve, *AS* curve, both curves) shift to the (right, left). Draw the new curve(s) in the upper half of panel (1), Fig. 19-7, and label the new equilibrium point E_2. The equilibrium income (rises, falls, remains the same) and the equilibrium price (rises, falls, remains the same). The price change causes the *IS* and *LM* curves to shift to the (right, left). Assuming that the secondary shift of *IS-LM*, due to the price effect, has a smaller effect on the interest rate than the initial change, *i* will be (higher than, lower than, the same as) it was initially.

(c) An increase in government spending is financed by printing money. The initial effect is to shift the (*IS* curve, *LM* curve, both curves) to the (right, left) at the old equilibrium price. Draw the new curve(s). The (*AD* curve, *AS* curve, both curves) shift to the (right, left). Draw the new curve(s) and label the new equilibrium point E_2. The equilibrium income (rises, falls, remains the same) and the equilibrium price (rises, falls, remains the same). The price change causes the *IS* and *LM* curves to shift to the (right, left). Assuming that the secondary shift of *IS-LM*, due to the price effect, has a smaller effect on the interest rate than the initial change, *i* will be (higher than, lower than, the same as) it was initially.

(d) The money wage rate rises. The initial effect is to shift (both *IS-LM*, neither *IS-LM*) curves to the right at the old equilibrium price. The initial effect is to shift the (*AD* curve, *AS* curve, both curves) to the (right, left). Draw the new curve(s) and label the new equilibrium point E_2. The equilibrium income (rises, falls, remains the same), and the equilibrium price (rises, falls, remains the same). The price change causes the *IS* and *LM* curves to shift to the (right, left). Assuming that the price sensitivity of the Pigou effect is greater than that of the Keynes effect, *i* will be (higher than, lower than, the same as) it was initially.

(e) An improvement in technology raises the marginal physical product of labor. The initial effect is to shift (both *IS-LM*, neither *IS-LM*) curves to the right at the old equilibrium price. The initial effect is to shift the (*AD* curve, *AS* curve, both curves) to the (right, left). Draw the new curve(s) and label the new equilibrium E_2. The equilibrium income (rises, falls, remains the same), and the equilibrium price (rises, falls, remains the same). The price change causes the *IS* and *LM* curves to shift to the (right, left). Assuming that the price sensitivity of the Pigou effect is less than that of the Keynes effect, *i* will be (higher than, lower than, the same as) it was initially.

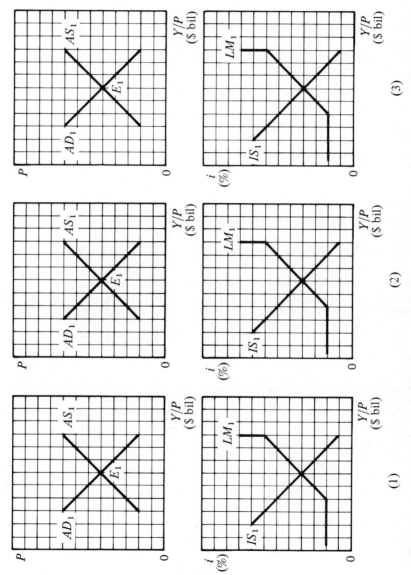

FIGURE 19-7

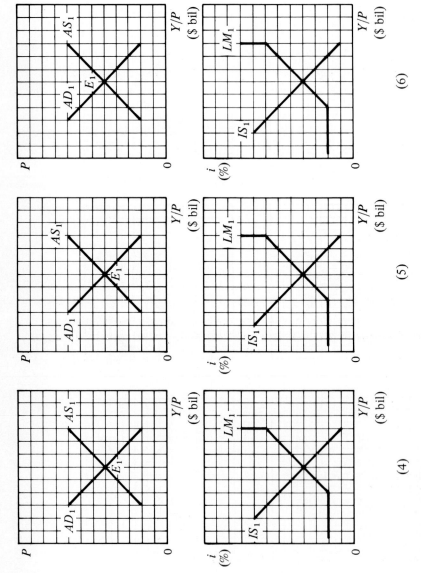

FIGURE 19-7 (Continued)

(f) The government raises taxes and uses the revenue to buy government bonds. The initial effect is to shift the (*IS* curve, *LM* curve, both curves) to the (right, left) at the old equilibrium price. Draw the new curve(s). The (*AD* curve, *AS* curve, both curves) shift to the (right, left). Draw the new curve(s) and label the new equilibrium point E_2. The equilibrium income (rises, falls, remains the same), and the equilibrium price (rises, falls, remains the same). The price change causes the *IS* and *LM* curves to shift to the (right, left). Assuming that the secondary shift of *IS-LM*, due to the price effect, has a smaller effect on the interest rate than the initial change, *i* will be (higher than, lower than, the same as) it was initially.

2 (Optional) It is possible to derive the algebraic expression for the aggregate supply curve of Exercise 19, paragraph 1. First, let us recall that the marginal physical product of labor is

$$(12) \quad MPP_N = 40 - \frac{1}{2} N$$

The demand for labor is determined by the requirement that the marginal physical product of labor equal _____ : therefore,

$$(13) \quad 40 - \frac{1}{2} N = \underline{\hspace{2cm}}$$

The demand for labor, N_d, can be found by solving for N:

$$(14) \quad N_d = \underline{\hspace{2cm}} - \underline{\hspace{2cm}}$$

If the money wage rate is fixed at $w = w_0$, there is a unique relationship between the demand for labor and the price level. Given that the production function tells us how much output can be produced with each level of employment, we can substitute the equilibrium demand for labor—Eq. (14)—into the production function to find the aggregate supply curve. Since the production function is

$$(15) \quad \frac{Y}{P} = 40N - \frac{1}{4} N^2$$

this substitution yields the following equation:

$$(16) \quad \frac{Y}{P} = 40(\underline{\hspace{1.5cm}} - \underline{\hspace{1.5cm}}) - \frac{1}{4} (\underline{\hspace{1.5cm}} - \underline{\hspace{1.5cm}})^2$$

If the square is completed and the indicated multiplications performed, Eq. (16) can be stated as

$$(17) \quad \frac{Y}{P} = \underline{\hspace{1.5cm}} - \frac{w_0}{P} - \underline{\hspace{1.5cm}} + \frac{w_0}{P} - \frac{w_0^2}{P^2}$$

By collecting terms, we can rearrange Eq. (17) as follows:

$$(18) \quad \frac{Y}{P} = \underline{\hspace{1.5cm}} - \underline{\hspace{1.5cm}}$$

If w_O is $40 per day, the aggregate supply curve is

(19) $\quad \dfrac{Y}{P} = \underline{\hspace{2cm}} - \underline{\hspace{1.5cm}}$

Complete the following table:

Table 19-4

Price index (P)	Real output (Y/P)
1.00	$ _____ bil
1.60	$ _____ bil
2.00	$ _____ bil
4.00	$ _____ bil

Verify that these points are on AS_1 in Fig. 19-2.

ANSWERS FOR EXERCISE 19

1 more, fall, equilibrium, 1,600, 1,600, is

2 Eq. (5) $Y/P + \Delta(Y/P) = 40(N + \Delta N) - 1/4(N^2 + 2N\Delta N + \Delta N^2)$
   Eq. (6) $Y/P + \Delta(Y/P) = 40N + 40\Delta N - 1/4N^2 - 1/2N\Delta N - 1/4\Delta N^2$
   Eq. (7) $\Delta(Y/P) = 40\Delta N - 1/2N\Delta N - 1/4\Delta N^2$
   Eq. (8) $MPP_N = \Delta(Y/P)/\Delta N = 40 - 1/2N - 1/4\Delta N$
   Eq. (9) $MPP_N = \Delta(Y/P)/\Delta N = 40 - 1/2N$

N	0	20	40	60	80
MPP_N	40	30	20	10	0

   slope, falls

3 is, 40, 35, 30, 25, 20, 15, 12, 10, Fig. 19-1A

4 must be, 35, 10, 375, 2, 1.14, is, Fig. 19-1A, aggregate supply, Fig. 19-1A

5 Fig. 19-2A, 1,200, 2.00, 7, 100, 50, 150, yes, 40, no, 160, 1,200, it is paid to owners of capital

6 to the left, remains unchanged, not at all, 40, 35, 30, 25, 20, 15, 12, 10, 7, 5, Fig. 19-1A, Fig. 19-2A, to the right, does, 1,450, 1.60, 55, 137.5, less, labor to capital owners

7 real income, must, 2.00, 7.0, right, no, higher, lower, right, right, Pigou, Keynes, lower, *IS, LM,* increase, would

8 Eq. (10) $Y/P = \$250$ bil $+ 40N - 1/4N^2$, does not change, upward, rightward, right, 1.80, 23, 34, 156, yes, the total wage bill declines absolutely *and* relative to the capital share of income

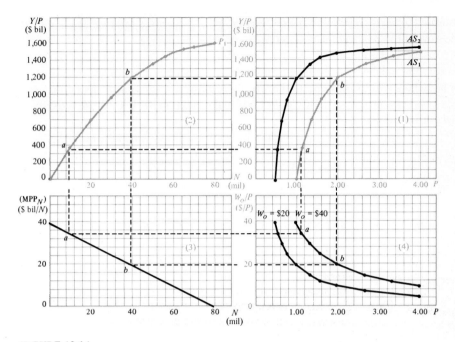

FIGURE 19-1A

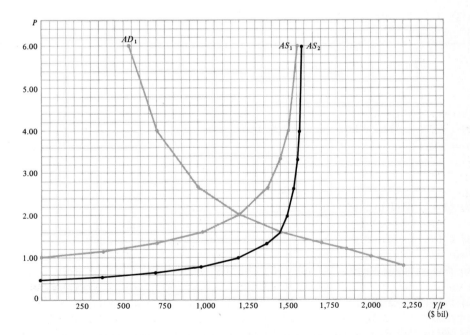

FIGURE 19-2A

9 increased, upward, rightward, right, 1.60, 25, 45, 225, yes, the total real wage bill increases absolutely and relative to the capital share of income

10 Fig. 19-6A, must, Fig. 19-6A, 2.00, is, rise, 200, not at all, there is no wealth effect on consumption because the offsetting changes in money and bonds keep the level of household wealth constant, to the left, Fig. 19-6A, to the left, not at all, Fig. 19-6A, lower, a lower, shift again, shift, right, right, must, Fig. 19-6A, must be higher than the old

11 rise, to the right, not at all, right, higher, higher, both *IS* and *LM*, left, rise

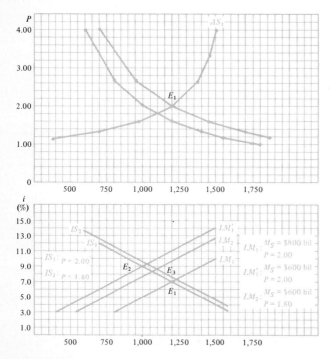

FIGURE 19-6A

ANSWERS TO PROBLEMS FOR EXERCISE 19

1 (a) *LM* curve, right, Fig. 19-7A, *AD* curve, right, Fig. 19-7A, rises, rises, left, lower than

(b) *IS* curve, right, Fig. 19-7A, *AD* curve, right, Fig. 19-7A, rises, rises, left, higher than

(c) both curves, right, Fig. 19-7A, *AD* curve, right, Fig. 19-7A, rises, rises, left, the same as.

(d) neither *IS-LM*, *AS* curve, left, Fig. 19-7A, falls, rises, left, higher than

(e) neither *IS-LM*, *AS* curve, right, Fig. 19-7A, rises, falls, right, lower than

(f) *IS* curve, left, Fig. 19-7A, *AD* curve, left, Fig. 19-7A, falls, falls, right, lower than
2 the real wage,

Eq. (13) $40 - 1/2 N = w/P$,

Eq. (14) $N_d = 80 - 2w/P$,

Eq. (16) $Y/P = 40(80 - 2w_0/P) - 1/4 (80 - 2w_0/P)^2$ (in billions of real dollars),

Eq. (17) $Y/P = 3,200 - 80w_0/P - 1,600 + 80w_0/P - w_0^2/P^2$ (in billions of real dollars),

Eq. (18) $Y/P = 1,600 - w_0^2/P^2$ (in billions of real dollars),

Eq. (19) $Y/P = 1,600 - 1,600/P^2$ (in billions of real dollars),

0, 975, 1,200, 1,500

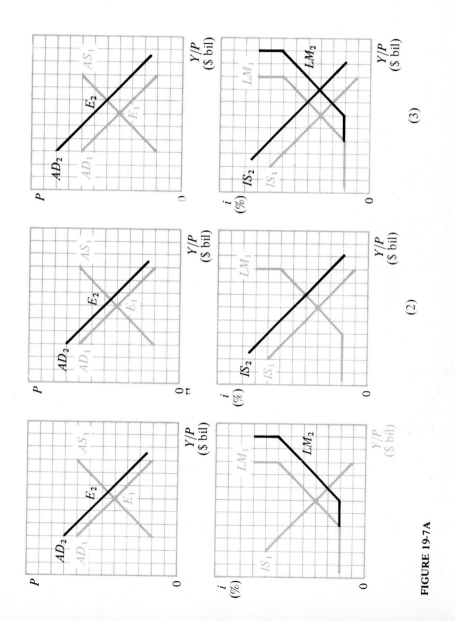

FIGURE 19-7A

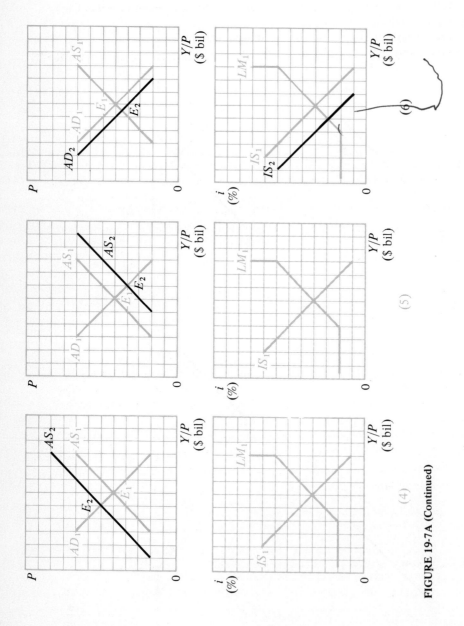

FIGURE 19-7A (Continued)

THE CLASSICAL AGGREGATE SUPPLY CURVE

1 We assumed in Exercise 19 that certain institutional factors in the economy prevent the money wage from adjusting in response to changed conditions. In this exercise, we assume that the labor market is governed by the underlying forces of demand and supply. The demand for and supply of labor determine employment and the wage rate. This model dominated economic thinking before the 1930s; hence, economic models based upon competitively determined wage rates are known as "classical" models. We will use the same production function and marginal product of labor curve as in Exercise 19:

(1) $\quad \dfrac{Y}{P} = 40N - \dfrac{1}{4}N^2$

(2) $\quad MPP_N = \dfrac{w}{P} = 40 - \dfrac{1}{2}N$

These equations are plotted in Fig. 20-1. Label the production function P_1 and the marginal product of labor curve N_d. Labeling the marginal product curve N_d signifies that it is the demand curve for labor. It is a demand curve because it gives the amount of labor that will be hired at each possible real wage rate.

In previous exercises, we assumed that whatever amount of labor was demanded would be supplied at the fixed money wage w_o up to the point of full employment. In this exercise, it is assumed that workers supply their labor services in response to the real wage rate, offering more labor at higher rates:

(3) $\quad N_s = \dfrac{2w}{P}$

Plot Eq. (3) in Fig. 20-1 and label it N_s. In equilibrium, the supply of labor must be equal to the demand for labor. This condition determines the real wage rate and employment:

$\dfrac{w}{P} = \$ \underline{\qquad}$ per day $\qquad N = \underline{\qquad}$ mil

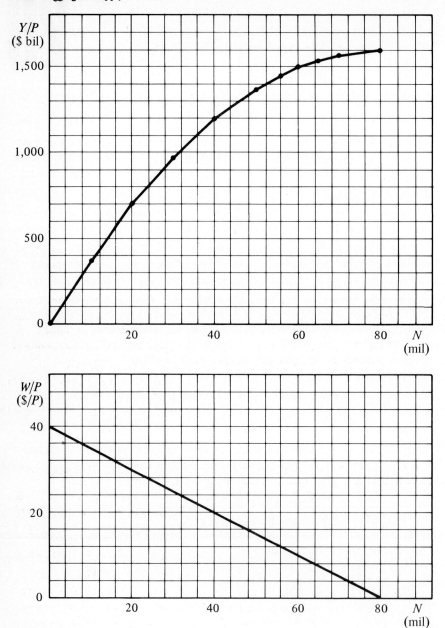

FIGURE 20-1

Since equilibrium employment is determined under the conditions given here, it is evident that producers are willing to supply only one level of output:

(4) $\dfrac{Y}{P} = \$$ _____ bil

The aggregate supply curve is plotted in Fig. 20-2 for $P = 2.00$. It is labeled AS_1. The aggregate supply is (positively sloped, vertical). Real output (is, is not) independent of the price level.

2 The aggregate demand curve derived in Exercise 19, paragraph 4, and drawn in Fig. 19-2 is reproduced in Fig. 20-2 and labeled AD_1. The equilibrium output is $ _____ bil and the equilibrium price level is _____. The IS and LM curves associated with these equilibrium values are drawn in the lower half of Fig. 20-2. These curves are labeled IS_1 and LM_1. They reflect the conditions: $P = 2.00; M_S = \$800$ bil. The equilibrium interest rate is _____ percent.

Now assume that the Federal Reserve carries out the open market sale of government securities described in Exercise 19, paragraph 10, thereby reducing the money supply by $200 bil. If P did not change, the LM curve would shift to the (right, left). The AD curve shifts to the (right, left). The new AD curve is labeled AD_2. The new equilibrium output is (higher, lower, unchanged). The price level is _____. The effect of the lower money supply shifts the IS curve (rightward, leftward, not at all). The price level change induces a secondary shift of the IS and LM curves to the (right, left). Since the new IS-LM equilibrium must be at the same real income level, under the conditions shown in Fig. 20-2 the combined effect of the money supply change and the subsequent price change is to shift the IS curve to the (right, left) and shift the LM curve to the (right, left). The net leftward shift of the LM curve comprises the (rightward, leftward) shift due to the lower money supply and the (rightward, leftward) shift due to the price effect. The interest rate will (rise, fall). The new equilibrium positions of the IS and LM curves are plotted in Fig. 20-2, labeled IS_2 and LM_2.

The new equilibrium interest rate is _____ percent. Thus, while the Fed's action had no effect on total output, it does have an effect on the *composition* of output. Real investment is (higher, lower), real government spending is (higher, lower), and real consumption spending is (higher, lower). The example just studied suggests that, under the classical model assumptions, aggregate demand management is (effective, ineffective) for raising or lowering real income.

3 Suppose that the government increased its spending, paying for it with a sale of bonds. The IS curve would initially shift (to the right, to the left, not at all), the LM curve would initially shift (to the right, to the left, not at all), the AD curve would shift (to the right, to the left, not at all). Real income will (rise, fall, remain the same), the price level would (rise, fall, remain the same), and if the secondary effect of the price change on the interest rate is smaller than that of the initial change, the interest rate will (rise, fall, remain the same). Once again, it appears that demand management by the government affects (total, only the composition of) real income, while having no effect on (total, the composition of) real income. It is clear why the "classical" economists did not believe that depressions could be cured or prevented by active monetary and fiscal policy.

4 It is interesting to add the quantity theory of money to the classical aggregate supply assumptions. If the quantity theory conditions hold, there is no (transactions, specula-

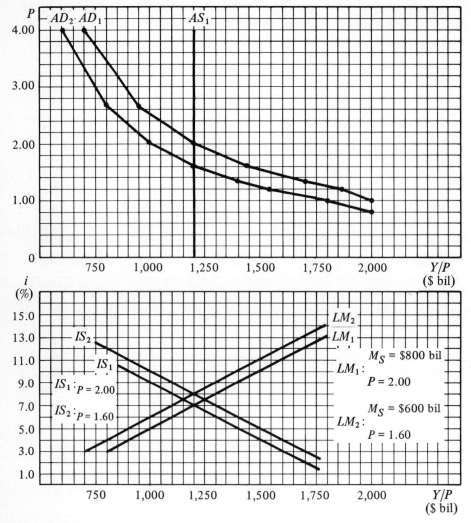

FIGURE 20-2

tive) demand for money. Let us rewrite the pertinent monetary equations:

(5) $M_S = \$800$ bil

(6) $\dfrac{M_1}{P} = \dfrac{1}{3}\dfrac{Y}{P}$

Monetary equilibrium can be found by equating the demand for money with the (real, nominal) supply of money, yielding the following equilibrium condition:

(7) $\dfrac{Y}{P} = \$ \quad \dfrac{}{P} \quad$ bil

Assuming that $P = 2.00$, draw this LM curve in Fig. 20-3 and label the curve LM_1. Does equilibrium income depend on the interest rate? (yes, no) Use the equation just derived to complete the following table of aggregate demand data:

Table 20-1

Price index (P)	Real output (Y/P)
1.60	$ _____ bil
1.80	$ _____ bil
2.00	$ _____ bil
2.40	$ _____ bil
3.00	$ _____ bil
4.00	$ _____ bil

Plot the aggregate demand curve in Fig. 20-3 and label it AD_1. Equilibrium real income is $ _____ bil and the equilibrium price level is _____ . If the same equations hold for the product market, the IS curve will be the same one as used in Fig. 20-1. It is reproduced in Fig. 20-3 and labeled IS_1. The equilibrium interest rate is _____ percent.

5 Again let the Federal Reserve reduce the money supply to $600 bil through an open market operation. The initial impact on the LM curve is a (rightward, leftward) shift. The new equation for monetary equilibrium is (recall the argument used in paragraph 4):

$$(8) \quad \frac{Y}{P} = \$ \ \frac{}{P} \ bil$$

Plot this curve in Fig. 20-3, assuming $P = 2.00$, and label it LM_2. As a result of the lower money supply, the IS curve shifts (to the right, to the left, not at all) and the aggregate demand curve shifts (to the right, to the left, not at all). Complete the following table of aggregate demand data:

Table 20-2

Price index (P)	Real output (Y/P)
1.20	$ _____ bil
1.50	$ _____ bil
1.80	$ _____ bil
2.00	$ _____ bil
2.40	$ _____ bil
3.00	$ _____ bil

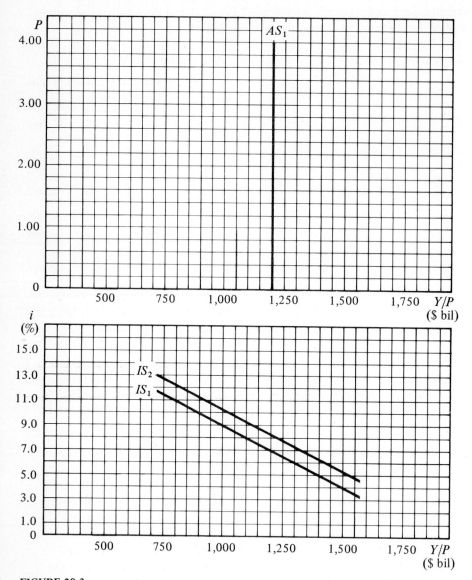

FIGURE 20-3

Draw the new aggregate demand curve in Fig. 20-3 and label it AD_2. The new equilibrium

real income is $ _____ bil, which represents (an increase, a decrease, no change) in real

income. The price level is now _____ , which is (higher, lower) than the initial equilibrium. The price change causes the LM curve to shift (to the right, to the left) from LM_2.
The expression for the LM curve is

(9) $\dfrac{Y}{P} = \$ \dfrac{}{1.5}$ bil

(10) $\quad \dfrac{Y}{P} = \$ \text{_____} \text{ bil}$

which is the same as (LM_1, LM_2, neither LM_1 nor LM_2). In the quantity theory case, therefore, the secondary shift of the LM curve (offsets completely, almost offsets) the initial shift. The IS curve shifts to the right because the lower price level (increases, decreases) the real value of government spending. The new IS curve is labeled IS_2 in Fig. 20-3. The equilibrium interest rate has (increased, decreased) to _____ percent.

6 Quantity theorists before Keynes proposed the following equation:

(11) $\quad MV = P\left(\dfrac{Y}{P}\right)$

or solving for V,

(12) $\quad V = \dfrac{P\left(\dfrac{Y}{P}\right)}{M}$

where V is the "velocity" of money, defined to be nominal income divided by the price level. As written, the equation is a definition, not a theory, but the quantity theorists added an important condition: they contended the V is constant. Let us verify this point by substituting the values given for P, Y/P, and M_S. When $P = 2.00$, $Y/P = 1{,}200$ bil, $M_S = \$800$ bil, then $V =$ _____. When $P = 1.50$, $Y/P = \$1{,}200$ bil, $M_S = \$600$ bil, then $V =$ _____. Thus, under these conditions, V is a (constant, variable). Note that V is the reciprocal of $1/3$, which is the coefficient of income in the transactions demand for money—Eq. (6).

7 Under the classical model assumptions, money was long thought to be a "veil" concealing the determination of real income, employment, interest rates, and relative prices. Money was acknowledged to be useful for facilitating exchanges, but theorists did not think that variations of the quantity of money had any impact on real income, *relative* prices and other real variables; such variations of the money supply were thought to affect only absolute levels of prices and nominal values of income and its components. If the quantity of money affects only the price level and nominal values, money is said to be "neutral." It is useful to know whether or not money is neutral, for if it is, monetary policy is powerless to affect interest rates, real investment, and real income. In the example used in paragraph 5, money (is, is not) neutral. The conditions necessary for neutrality of money are examined in question 2 of the following problem set.

PROBLEMS FOR EXERCISE 20

1 Three initial equilibrium situations for an economy are presented in Fig. 20-4. Each problem is represented by aggregate demand and supply curves and by IS and LM curves, as in the problem set for Exercise 19. The initial equilibrium is represented by the curves AD_1, AS_1, IS_1 and LM_1. The initial equilibrium point is labeled E_1. Make the necessary shift of the curves indicated by the problem. Label the new curve(s) AD_2, AS_2, IS_2, and LM_2. Assume that all shifts are parallel and that the initial shifts are of two horizontal squares. *Do not* draw the IS and LM curves that result from shifts due to price changes.

(a) The government increases spending, financed by a sale of government securities. The initial effect is to shift the (IS curve, LM curve, both curves) to the (right, left) at the old equilibrium price. Draw the new curve(s) in the lower half of panel (1), Fig. 20-4. The (AD curve, AS curve, both curves) shift to the (right, left). Draw the curve(s) in the upper half of panel (1) and label the new equilibrium point E_2. The equilibrium income (rises, falls, remains the same) and the equilibrium price (rises, falls, remains the same). The price change causes the IS and LM curves to shift to the (right, left). Assuming that the secondary shift of IS-LM, due to the price effect, has a smaller effect on the interest rate than the initial change, i will be (higher than, lower than, the same as) it was initially.

(b) The nonbank public reduces its demand for money. The initial effect is to shift the (IS curve, LM curve, both curves) to the (right, left) at the old equilibrium price. Draw the new curves in the lower half of panel (2) in Fig. 20-4. The (AD curve, AS curve, both curves) shift to the (right, left). Draw the curve(s) in the upper half of panel (2) and label the new equilibrium point E_2. The equilibrium income (rises, falls, remains the same) and the equilibrium price (rises, falls, remains the same). The price change causes the IS and LM curves to shift to the (right, left). Assuming that the secondary shift of IS-LM, due to the price effect, has a smaller effect on the interest rate than the initial change, i will be (higher than, lower than, the same as) it was initially.

(c) New technology increases the marginal physical product of labor. The initial effect is to shift (both IS-LM, neither IS-LM) curves to the right at the old equilibrium price. The initial effect is to shift the (AD curve, AS curve, both curves) to the (right, left). Draw the new curve(s) in the upper half of panel (3) in Fig. 20-4 and label the new equilibrium point E_2. The equilibrium income (rises, falls, remains the same) and the equilibrium price (rises, falls, remains the same). The price change causes the IS and LM curves to shift to the (right, left). Assuming that the price sensitivity of the Pigou effect is equal in magnitude to that of the Keynes effect, i will be (higher than, lower than, about the same as) it was initially.

2 (Optional) Money is neutral in the models used in Exercises 19 and 20 under the following conditions:

(a) all prices and wages are flexible

(b) all spending magnitudes, including government spending, are determined in real terms and not in nominal terms

(c) there is no government debt

To establish the validity of this statement, we must make the model conform to these three conditions. The first condition is met by adoption of the classical aggregate supply rather than the Keynesian assumptions. The second condition requires that government spending be fixed in real terms. We will replace our earlier statement $G = \$100$ bil with $G/P = \$50$ bil. The third condition can be met by setting government bonds, $B = \$0$.

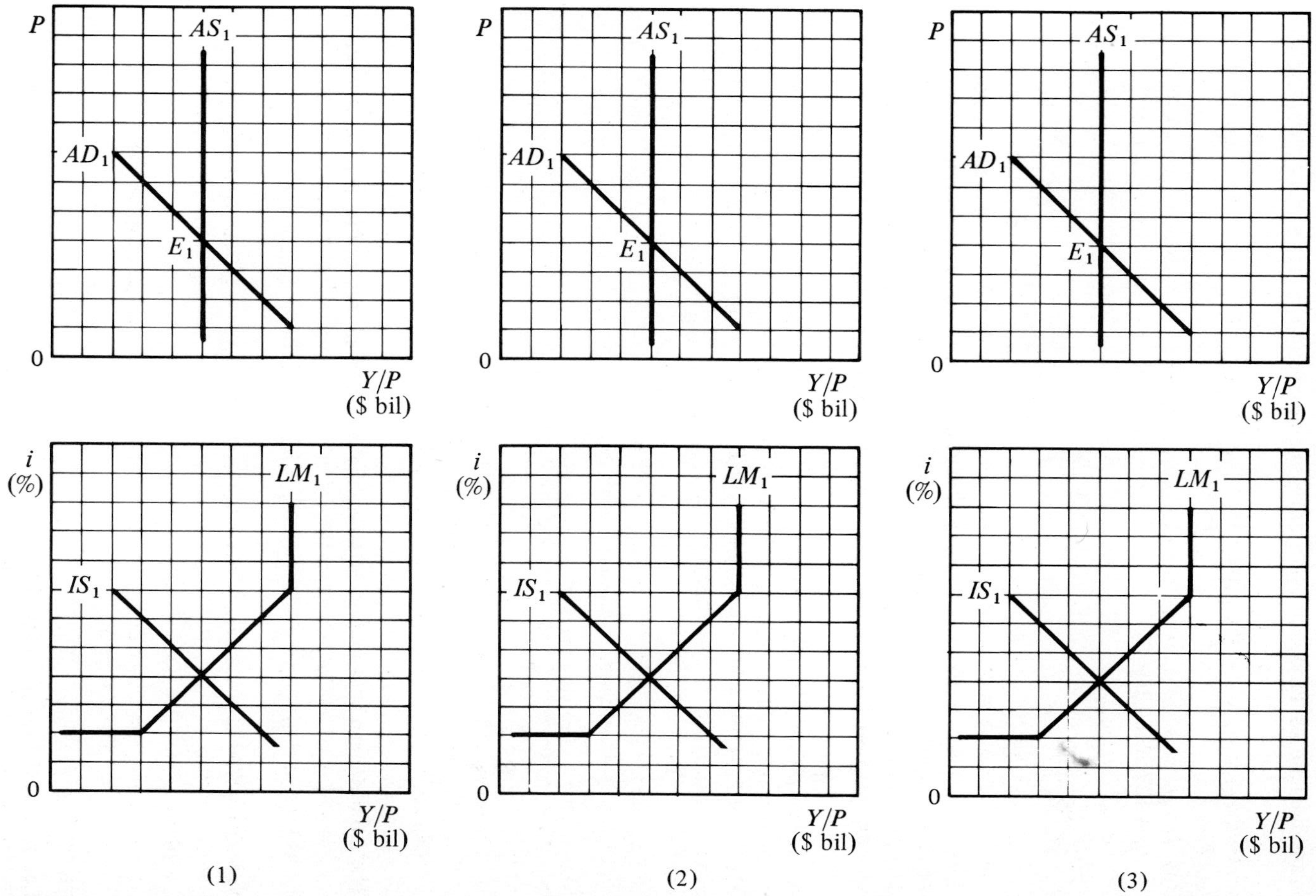

FIGURE 20-4

The demand side of the model is quite similar to that used in Exercise 18, paragraph 7, and Exercise 18, Prob. 2:

$$\frac{C}{P} = \$80 \text{ bil} + 0.75\frac{Y_d}{P} + 0.125\frac{V}{P} \qquad M_S = \$800 \text{ bil} \qquad\qquad T = \$0$$

$$\frac{I}{P} = \$275 \text{ bil} - 25\,i \qquad\qquad \frac{M_1}{P} = 0.25\frac{Y}{P} \qquad\qquad \frac{V}{P} = K + \frac{B}{P} + \frac{M_S}{P}$$

$$\frac{G}{P} = \$50 \text{ bil} \qquad\qquad \frac{M_2}{P} = \$275 \text{ bil} - 25\,i \qquad \frac{B}{P} = \$0$$
$$\qquad\qquad\qquad\qquad\qquad\qquad \text{(for } 3\% \leqslant i \leqslant 11\%)$$

The liquidity trap and quantity theory sections of the demand for money are ignored because in this example the economy always operates in the intermediate range. The aggregate supply side of the model is the classical aggregate supply curve derived above. The production function, demand for labor, and supply of labor equations will not be repeated here; we simply make note of the aggregate supply equation:

(1) $\dfrac{Y}{P} = \$1{,}200 \text{ bil}$

The *IS* curve is found by equating S/P to $I/P + G/P$

(2) $-\$\rule{1.2cm}{0.4pt}\text{bil} + \rule{1.2cm}{0.4pt}\dfrac{Y}{P} - \$\rule{1.2cm}{0.4pt}\dfrac{\text{bil}}{P} = \$\rule{1.2cm}{0.4pt}\text{bil}$

$- \rule{1.2cm}{0.4pt}\,i + \$\rule{1.2cm}{0.4pt}\text{bil}$

Simplifying and solving for Y/P, we find that

(3) $0.25\dfrac{Y}{P} = \$\rule{1.2cm}{0.4pt}\text{bil} + {}^\$\rule{1.2cm}{0.4pt}\dfrac{\text{bil}}{P} - \rule{1.2cm}{0.4pt}\,i$

(4) $\dfrac{Y}{P} = \$\rule{1.2cm}{0.4pt}\text{bil} + {}^\$\rule{1.2cm}{0.4pt}\dfrac{\text{bil}}{P} - \rule{1.2cm}{0.4pt}\,i$

The *LM* curve can be found by equating the supply of money to the demand for money:

(5) ${}^\$\rule{1.2cm}{0.4pt}\dfrac{\text{bil}}{P} = \rule{1.2cm}{0.4pt}\dfrac{Y}{P} + \$\rule{1.2cm}{0.4pt}\text{bil} - \rule{1.2cm}{0.4pt}\,i$

Solving for Y/P

(6) $\dfrac{Y}{P} = {}^\$\rule{1.2cm}{0.4pt}\dfrac{\text{bil}}{P} - \$\rule{1.2cm}{0.4pt}\text{bil} + \rule{1.2cm}{0.4pt}\,i$

for $3\% \leqslant i \leqslant 11\%$

To find the *AD* curve, we must combine the *IS* and *LM* curves to eliminate the variable i. Let us solve the *IS* curve, Eq. (4), for $100i$:

(7) $100i = \$\rule{1.2cm}{0.4pt}\text{bil} + {}^\$\rule{1.2cm}{0.4pt}\dfrac{\text{bil}}{P} - \dfrac{Y}{P}$

This expression can be substituted into that for the *LM* curve, Eq. (6):

(8) $\dfrac{Y}{P} = \dfrac{\$\rule{1cm}{0.4pt}\,\text{bil}}{P} - \$\rule{1cm}{0.4pt}\,\text{bil} + \left(\$\rule{1cm}{0.4pt}\,\text{bil} + \dfrac{\$\rule{1cm}{0.4pt}\,\text{bil}}{P} - \dfrac{Y}{P}\right)$

(9) $\dfrac{Y}{P} = \$\rule{1cm}{0.4pt}\,\text{bil} + \dfrac{\$\rule{1cm}{0.4pt}\,\text{bil}}{P}$

From the aggregate supply curve, Eq. (1), we know that $Y/P = \$\rule{1.5cm}{0.4pt}$ bil. Combine the aggregate supply and demand curves to find equilibrium price: $P = \rule{1.5cm}{0.4pt}$. The equilibrium price and income can be used in the IS or LM curve to determine the equilibrium interest rate: $i = \rule{1.5cm}{0.4pt}$ percent.

Let the Federal Reserve reduce the money supply to $600 bil without selling government bonds. (Presumably they will have to confiscate and burn it.) Total wealth (rises, falls, remains the same), causing the saving function to (shift, remain unchanged). To solve for the IS curve we can make use of the fact that only one change must be made in Eq. (2):

(10) $-\$100\text{ bil} + 0.25\dfrac{Y}{P} - \dfrac{\$\rule{1cm}{0.4pt}\,\text{bil}}{P} = \$275\text{ bil} - 25\,i + \$50\text{ bil}$

The IS curve becomes

(11) $\dfrac{Y}{P} = \$1{,}700\text{ bil} + \dfrac{\$\rule{1cm}{0.4pt}\,\text{bil}}{P} - 100i$

The new LM curve can be found by making one change in Eq. (5):

(12) $\dfrac{\$\rule{1cm}{0.4pt}\,\text{bil}}{P} = 0.25\dfrac{Y}{P} + \$275\text{ bil} - 25\,i$

The new LM curve is

(13) $\dfrac{Y}{P} = \dfrac{\$\rule{1cm}{0.4pt}\,\text{bil}}{P} - \$1{,}100\text{ bil} + 100i$

Again solving the IS curve for $100i$,

(14) $100i = \$\rule{1.5cm}{0.4pt}\text{bil} + \dfrac{\$\rule{1cm}{0.4pt}\,\text{bil}}{P} - \dfrac{Y}{P}$

Substituting into the LM curve,

(15) $\dfrac{Y}{P} = \dfrac{\$\rule{1cm}{0.4pt}\,\text{bil}}{P} - \$1{,}100\text{ bil} + \left(\$\rule{1cm}{0.4pt}\,\text{bil} + \dfrac{\$\rule{1cm}{0.4pt}\,\text{bil}}{P} - \dfrac{Y}{P}\right)$

The aggregate demand curve is

(16) $\dfrac{Y}{P} = \$\rule{1.5cm}{0.4pt}\text{bil} + \dfrac{\$\rule{1cm}{0.4pt}\,\text{bil}}{P}$

Combine the aggregate demand and supply curves to find equilibrium price, real income, and the interest rate

$P = \rule{1.5cm}{0.4pt}$ $\dfrac{Y}{P} = \$\rule{1.5cm}{0.4pt}\text{bil}$ $i = \rule{1.5cm}{0.4pt}$ percent

Real income and the interest rate (have, have not) changed. The other real variables in the model are C/P, I/P, G/P, T/P, B/P, M/P, and w/P. Have any of these variables changed? (yes, no) It thus appears that money (is, is not) neutral under the assumptions given at the beginning of this problem.

If assumption a is relaxed, total real output changes. If either assumption b or c is relaxed, total real output remains constant, but the composition of real expenditures will change. If only assumption c is relaxed, the interest rate rises and I falls, so that, in order to maintain no change in total real output, C/P will rise—due to the wealth effect— to compensate for the I spending decline. If only assumption b is relaxed, both C/P and G/P will rise to compensate for the I decline.

ANSWERS FOR EXERCISE 20

1 Fig. 20-1A, 20, 40, 1,200, vertical, is
2 1,200, 2.00, 7.0, left, left, unchanged, 1.60, not at all, right, right, left, leftward, rightward, rise, 8.0, lower, higher, higher, ineffective
3 to the right, not at all, to the right, remain the same, rise, rise, only the composition of, total

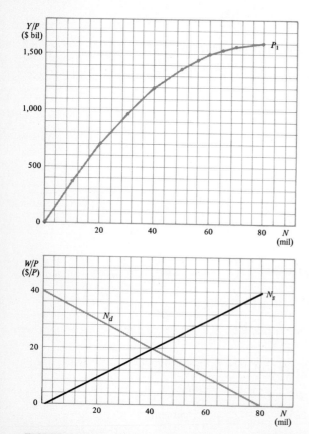

FIGURE 20-1A

4 speculative, real, 2,400, Fig. 20-3A, no, 1,500, 1,333, 1,200, 1,000, 800, 600, Fig. 20-3A, 1,200, 2.00, 7.0

5 leftward, 1,800, Fig. 20-3A, not at all, to the left, 1,500, 1,200, 1,000, 900, 750, 600, Fig. 20-3A, 1,200, no change, 1.50, lower, to the right, 1,800, 1,200, LM_1, offsets completely, increases, increased, 8.33

6 3, 3, constant

7 is not

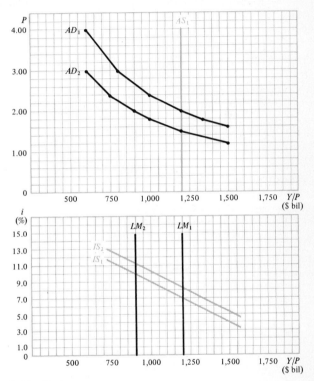

FIGURE 20-3A

ANSWERS TO PROBLEMS FOR EXERCISE 20

1 **(a)** *IS* curve, right, Fig. 20-4A, *AD* curve, right, Fig. 20-4A, remains the same, rises, left, higher than

(b) *LM* curve, right, Fig. 20-4A, *AD* curve, right, Fig. 20-4A, remains the same, rises, left, lower than

(c) neither *IS-LM*, *AS* curve, right, Fig. 20-4A, rises, falls, right, about the same as

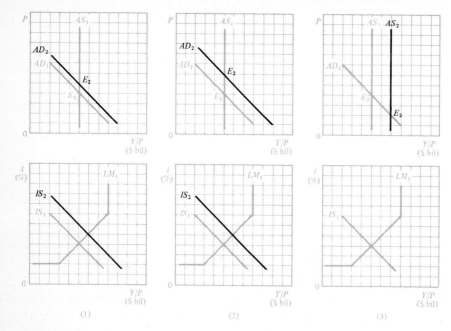

FIGURE 20-4A

2 Eq. (2) –$100 bil + 0.25 Y/P - $100 bil/$P$ = $275 bil – 25$i$ + $50 bil,
   Eq. (3) 0.25 Y/P = $425 bil + $100 bil/$P$ - 25i,
   Eq. (4) Y/P = $1,700 bil + $400 bil/$P$ - 100i,
   Eq. (5) $800 bil/$P$ = 0.25 Y/P + $275 bil - 25$i$,
   Eq. (6) Y/P = $3,200 bil/$P$ - $1,100 bil + 100$i$,
   Eq. (7) 100i = $1,700 bil + $400 bil/$P$ - Y/P,
   Eq. (8) Y/P = $3,200 bil/$\dot{P}$ - $1,100 bil + ($1,700 bil + $400 bil/$P$ - Y/P),
   Eq. (9) Y/P = $300 bil + $1,800 bil/$P$,
   1,200, 2.00, 7.0, falls, shift,
   Eq. (10) the new number is $75 bil,
   Eq. (11) the new number is $300 bil,
   Eq. (12) the new number is $600 bil,
   Eq. (13) the new number is $2,400 bil,
   Eq. (14) 100i = $1,700 bil + $300 bil/$P$ - Y/P,
   Eq. (15) Y/P = $2,400 bil/$P$ - $1,100 bil + ($1,700 + $300 bil/$P$ - Y/P),
   Eq. (16) Y/P = $300 bil + $1,350 bil/$P$,
   2.00, 1,200, 7.0, have not, no, is

1 The amount of output that may be obtained from a given amount of inputs is determined from
    (a) the demand for labor schedule
    (b) the supply of labor schedule
    (c) the production function
    (d) the aggregate demand schedule

2 The marginal physical product of labor is
    (a) the amount of output that can be obtained from a given amount of labor input
    (b) total output divided by labor input
    (c) the amount of output that is added when a small addition is made to the labor force
    (d) set by law or convention in the Keynesian model

3 From Fig. 19-1, it appears that the marginal physical product of labor is zero when
    (a) output is at a maximum
    (b) output is zero
    (c) labor input is at a maximum
    (d) the economy is in equilibrium

4 Producers will hire labor up to the point where
    (a) the value of the average product of labor equals the real wage
    (b) the value of the marginal product of labor equals the real wage
    (c) output is maximized
    (d) labor costs are minimized

5 From question 2, it is evident that the demand curve for labor, which relates quantity demanded to the price of labor, is the same as:
    (a) the marginal physical product curve for labor
    (b) the production function
    (c) the average physical product curve for labor
    (d) a horizontal line at the fixed money wage rate

6 The demand for labor function is the same in the classical model as it is in the Keynesian model
  (a)   true
  (b)   false

7 In the Keynesian model, the supply of labor is
  (a)   fixed
  (b)   infinitely elastic at a fixed money wage (up to the point of the total labor force)
  (c)   determined by individual workers' response to the real wage
  (d)   determined by the production function

8 In the classical model, the supply of labor is
  (a)   fixed
  (b)   infinitely elastic at a fixed money wage
  (c)   determined by individual workers' response to the real wage
  (d)   determined by the production function

9 In the Keynesian model, a lower price level reduces the amount of output producers are willing to supply because
  (a)   a lower price raises the real wage rate
  (b)   a higher real wage makes the previously marginal worker no longer able to earn his wage
  (c)   dismissal of the marginal worker reduces output
  (d)   all of the above

10 In the classical model, a lower price level
  (a)   reduces aggregate supply for the same reasons given in question 9
  (b)   reduces aggregate supply, but for different reasons
  (c)   increases aggregate supply
  (d)   has no effect on aggregate supply

11 Aggregate supply is determined in the classical model by
  (a)   equilibrium employment which is, in turn, determined by the intersection of the supply and demand curves for labor
  (b)   the money supply
  (c)   the money wage rate
  (d)   none of the above

12 Equilibrium price and output are determined by
  (a)   the intersection of the *IS* and *LM* curves
  (b)   the intersection of the *AD* and *AS* curves
  (c)   the intersection of the supply and demand curves for money
  (d)   the intersection of the supply and demand curves for labor

13 The equilibrium interest rate may be found by locating the intersection of
  (a)   any *IS* and *LM* curves
  (b)   the *AD* and *AS* curves

(c) the *IS* and *LM* curves which correspond to the equilibrium price level
(d) the saving and investment curves

In the following questions, assume that the model is Keynesian and that neither the liquidity trap nor the quantity theory appears. A series of changes is introduced into the system, each one of which is to be considered as an isolated event. You are to determine the changes that can be expected in real income, the price level, and the interest rate at the new equilibrium position. Place your answers in the left-hand blank. The possible changes are:

an increase   +
a decrease   −
no change   no
indeterminate change ind

The government sector raises its spending, financing the increase by selling securities:

14 income _____ _____

15 price _____ _____

16 interest rate _____ _____

The government sector raises its spending, financing the increase by printing money:

17 income _____ _____

18 price _____ _____

19 interest rate _____ _____

The government sector raises its spending, financing the increase by raising taxes:

20 income _____ _____

21 price _____ _____

22 interest rate _____ _____

The Federal Reserve sells government bonds to the nonbank public:

23 income _____ _____

24 price _____ _____

25 interest rate _____ _____

The government sector raises taxes, and uses the proceeds to retire bonds:

26 income _____ _____

27 price _____ _____

28 interest rate _____ _____

The business sector reduces investment spending at each interest rate:

29 income _____ _____

30 price _____ _____

31 interest rate _____ _____

The personal sector reduces its intended cash holdings:

32 income _____ _____

33 price _____ _____

34 interest rate _____ _____

The personal sector increases its saving at each income level:

35 income _____ _____

36 price _____ _____

37 interest rate _____ _____

A technical change raises the marginal physical product of labor at each level of output:

38 income _____ _____

39 price _____ _____

40 interest rate _____ _____

A technical change raises the amount of output that can be produced with a given amount of input, but does not raise the marginal product of labor:

41 income _____ _____

42 price _____ _____

43 interest rate _____ _____

The money wage rate is increased:

44 income _____

45 price _____

46 interest rate _____

The government sector sets a maximum price level that is below the current equilibrium price level:

47 income _____

48 price _____

49 interest rate _____

In the following questions, assume that the model is classical.

Workers offer more labor at each real wage level:

50 income _____

51 price _____

52 interest rate _____

Now answer questions 14 to 43 under the assumption that a classical aggregate supply situation is in effect. Place your answers next to the ones found for the Keynesian model. (Questions 44 to 49 are omitted on the grounds that they describe events which are incompatible with the classical model.)

PART **EIGHT**

THE OPEN ECONOMY

Up to this point, we have discussed the national economy as essentially a closed system. The level of national income, employment, and the rate of interest have been discussed as if we were living in isolation. Of course, we do not. No economy does.

Various kinds of economic linkages between different national economies invariably exist. Goods are shipped from one country to another, representing imports when they are bought and exports when they are sold. What one country exports, one or more others must (by definition) import. Services such as insurance, travel, and consulting are exchanged in much the same way. Goods and services are exchanged on the basis of the principles of comparative advantage: buy where the cost/quality ratio is lowest and sell where it is highest. At the same time, there are international capital flows—long-term and short-term, direct and portfolio, private and public—based on a similar principle: borrow or finance where the rate of interest is lowest and lend or invest where it is highest. There are also pension payments, humanitarian relief, government aid, and other unrequited public and private transfers that go on all the time, and that at some point must be matched by a transfer of real resources from one national economy to another.

The best way to measure aggregate international transactions is by the *balance of payments,* a census of all imports, exports, capital inflows, capital outflows, aid grants and receipts, intergovernmental transactions, and all other economic exchanges between countries. But the balance of payments is more than this. It also indicates whether, *on net,* a national economy's monetary receipts from abroad exceed its payments or vice versa; that is, whether a payments *surplus* or *deficit* exists in transactions between one country and the rest of the world. If there is a surplus, the country accumulates *international reserves*—gold and other assets acceptable as international money by the world's governments. If there is a deficit, its stock of reserves is eroded. Chronic surpluses or deficits that go on for long periods of time are called *disequilibria.* A surplus disequilibrium results in accumulation of low-yield international reserves for which the economy has sacrificed real resources, e.g., exports of goods and services, and interest payments on capital inflows. A surplus, in effect, trades high-yield assets for low-yield assets, a questionable proposition at best. A deficit disequilibrium results in a depletion of international reserves, which will eventually impair the nation's ability to conduct international commercial, financial, and governmental transactions. Both are unhealthy, and will sooner or later require policy actions which will have an impact on both domestic and international economic conditions.

A second important element in aggregate economic relations between national economies is the *rate of exchange:* how many units of a foreign country's money one unit of the domestic currency will buy. If $1.00 buys 4.00 Swiss francs (Sfr.), then products we buy from Switzerland are obviously cheaper than if $1.00 bought Sfr. 3.00. Conversely, at the first rate of exchange, American products are more expensive for Swiss residents than at the second exchange rate. So the rate of exchange determines the price of products manufactured at home relative to those produced abroad, and influences the volume of imports and exports, thereby affecting the quantity of domestic output demanded for export and the amount of domestic demand satisfied by imports. Under the existing institutional arrangements, the exchange rate between any two national currencies is determined partly by market forces and partly by government policy.

In this part, we shall examine the linkages that exist between the level of aggregate economic activity and a nation's foreign trade, between its money supply and its international payments, and between the available policy choices for domestic and for foreign economic balance.

THE BALANCE OF PAYMENTS

1 When a transaction occurs between domestic and foreign residents that gives one claim to the other's currency, that transaction enters into the balance of payments of both countries. If the transaction is one which gives foreigners a claim on our domestic currency, that is, one that would *ceteris paribus* deplete our stock of reserve assets, it is a *debit* or minus entry in our balance of payments. If the transaction gives us a claim on foreign currencies, it is a *credit* or plus entry in our balance of payments. Thus, we can enumerate the effects of transactions with the rest of the world as follows:

Type of transaction	Impact on our balance of payments
Sales of goods and services to abroad (exports)	+
Purchases of goods and services from abroad (imports)	−
Interest and dividends received on loans and investments abroad	+
Interest and dividends paid on foreign loans and investments here	−
Gifts from abroad (transfers in)	+
Gifts to abroad (transfers out)	−
Foreign capital investments here (inflow)	+
Our capital investments abroad (outflow)	−
Loans from foreigners (inflow)	+
Loans to foreigners (outflow)	−

2 If, during a given accounting period, all of the credit transactions exceed all of the debit transactions, we have a balance of payments (surplus, deficit). If the debits exceed the credits, we have a balance of payments (surplus, deficit). We can also strike some sub-balances such as merchandise purchases and sales of goods and services, called *balance of merchandise trade,* and long-term loans and investments, called *balance of long-term capital flows.* Once a balance of payments surplus or deficit has emerged, it must be settled. This settlement can be accomplished by transferring reserve assets such as foreign currencies, gold, or "paper gold"–International Monetary Fund Special Drawing Rights

(SDRs)—or anything else acceptable to both debtor and creditor countries. This settlement is called *official reserve transactions*.

3 Table 21-1 presents a typical quarterly United States balance of payments statement.

The balance on the goods and services account is a (surplus, deficit) of $_____ mil. If we add to that the net sum of private and governmental unrequited gifts and grants of

(+, -) $ _____ mil, we get a (surplus, deficit) *balance on current account*, that is, on all

"current" transactions of $ _____ mil. Long-term capital transactions, both public and private, were in (surplus, deficit) during this period. When we combine the current and the long-term capital account, the United States *balance of payments on current account— long-term capital* is a (surplus, deficit) of $ _____ mil. If we add to the preceding balance nonliquid private capital flows, "free" paper gold or SDR disbursements from the IMF, and errors and omissions, we have a *net liquidity balance* (surplus, deficit) of

$ _____ mil.

Table 21-1 United States Balance of Payments, First Quarter, 1971
(Seasonally adjusted, in Millions of Dollars)

Merchandise trade balance	+272	
Military transactions, net	−677	
Travel and transportation, net	−484	
Investment income, net	+1,727	
Other services, net	+213	
Balance on goods and services		(_____)
Remittances, pensions and other transfers	−351	
Balance on goods, services, and remittances		+700
U.S. government grants (excluding military)	−432	
Balance on current account		(_____)
Long-term private capital flows, net	−997	
Long-term U.S. government capital flows, net	−687	
Balance on current account–long-term capital		(_____)
Nonliquid short-term private capital flows	−100	
Allocation of SDRs	+180	
Errors and omissions, net	−1,268	
Net liquidity balance		(_____)
Liquid short-term private capital flows, net	−2,919	
Official reserve transactions balance		(_____)

SOURCE: U.S. Department of Commerce, *Survey of Current Business*, June 1971.

4 When we include the final item, liquid short-term private capital transfers of $2,919 mil, the United States *official reserve transactions balance* is in (surplus, deficit) by

$_____mil. Unless economic events reverse themselves in the next period or shortly thereafter, the United States will have to "settle up" by transferring to foreign central

banks $_____mil of gold, foreign currencies, SDRs, or other acceptable reserve assets. Settlement can be postponed, however, if the foreign official financial institutions we are dealing with are kind enough to hold—lend us—some of the dollars they have acquired as a result of our payments deficit. In any case, the total official reserve transactions must equal +$5,523 mil to exactly balance out our deficit of −$5,523 mil.

5 If, instead of the balance of payments deficit derived from the data in Table 21-1, the United States had ended up with a surplus of the same amount, then our central bank would have accumulated gold, foreign currencies, SDRs, and other reserve assets. Hence, this surplus of +$5,523 mil would have been exactly matched by our official

settlements (accumulation, loss) of (+,−) $_____mil in "international money," which

we could use later on in the event of a subsequent balance of payments _____.
Note that when we obtain or "import" reserves as a result of a payments surplus, the sign is always (+,−) just as when we (export, import) goods and services.

6 The collective "active" items in the balance of payments must *on net* always be (greater than, less than, exactly equal to) the settlement of those items. The balance of payments must always balance in the end. What is important is *how* it balances! Finally, we should note that this discussion is rather simplified. Among other things, countries do not "settle up" at the end of a quarter or a year. Instead, the whole process takes place automatically due to the double-entry system of balance of payments bookkeeping. But the results are the same, as are their implications for economic policy.

PROBLEMS FOR EXERCISE 21

You are given the following balance of payments data for Country *X* for the calendar year 1972:

	Millions of *XC*
Merchandise imports	2,500
Merchandise exports	1,750
Exports of services, including travel and transportation	3,250
Imports of services, including travel and transportation	750
Earnings on loans and investments abroad	120
Earnings on loans and investments in *X* by foreigners	980
Exports of military goods and services	2
Imports of military goods and services	580
Private remittances to abroad (transfers)	21

	Millions of XC
Private remittances from abroad (transfers)	92
Government grants to abroad	8
Government grants from abroad	0
Government loans to abroad	23
Government loans from abroad	12
Direct investments abroad	3
Foreign direct investments in X	64
Portfolio (long-term) investments abroad	28
Foreign portfolio (long-term) investments in X	34
Nonliquid short-term loans and investments abroad	85
Foreign nonliquid short-term loans and investments in X	2
Allocation of SDRs	12
Net errors and omissions	−200
Liquid short-term loans and investment abroad	150
Foreign liquid loans and investments in X	30

Fill in the following balance of payments statement for the year 1972:

		Millions of XC
Merchandise trade balance	(1)	_____
Military transactions (net)	(2)	_____
Services (net)	(3)	_____
Investment income (net)	(4)	_____
Balance on goods and services	(5)	_____
Private remittances (transfers), net	(6)	_____
Balance on goods, services and remittances	(7)	_____
Government grants (net)	(8)	_____
Balance on current account	(9)	_____
Long-term private capital flows (net)	(10)	_____
Long-term government capital flows (net)	(11)	_____
Balance on current account and long-term capital	(12)	_____
Nonliquid short-term private capital flows (net)	(13)	_____
Allocation of SDRs	(14)	_____
Errors and omissions (net)	(15)	_____
Net liquidity balance	(16)	_____

Millions of XC

Liquid short-term capital flows (net) . . . . (17) _____

    Official reserve transactions balance . . . . (18) _____

Change in X's official reserve holdings . . . . (19) _____

20 The last entry represents a (gain, loss) of international reserves.

21 This entry is in settlement of Country *X*'s balance of payments (surplus, deficits).

ANSWERS FOR EXERCISE 21

2 surplus, deficit
3 surplus, 1,051, −, 783, surplus, 268, deficit, deficit, 1,416, deficit, 2,604
4 deficit, 5,523, 5,523
5 accumulation, −5,523, deficit, −, import
6 exactly equal to

ANSWERS TO PROBLEMS FOR EXERCISE 21

1 −750 **2** −578 **3** +2,500 **4** −860 **5** +312 **6** +71 **7** +383 **8** −8 **9** +375
10 +67 **11** −11 **12** +431 **13** −83 **14** +12 **15** −200 **16** +160 **17** −120
18 +40 **19** −40 **20** gain **21** surplus

THE EXCHANGE RATE

1 The price of beef is $1.60 per pound. The price of French francs is $0.20 per franc. The price of one dollar is 10 ounces of beef. The price of one dollar is 5.00 French francs. Note the similarity and the differences in the preceding statements. The beef/dollar exchange rate is a commonly used price, and so is the franc/dollar exchange rate. The dollar/beef exchange rate is never used, but the dollar/franc exchange rate is. The dollar price of a foreign currency is simply that—a price. But the relationship is often stated the other way around—the price of a dollar in terms of the foreign currency.

2 Suppose the price of one French franc, Ffr. 1.00, declined from $0.20 to $0.10. We can now buy (more, less) francs with each U.S. dollar. Consequently, we would be inclined to buy (more, less) French goods because, relative to our own products and those of other countries, they are (more, less) expensive. If we want to buy more French goods, we will need more francs to buy them with. Assume that, at a rate of Ffr. 1.00 = $0.20, we will buy Ffr. 100 mil worth of French products and, at a rate of Ffr. 1.00 = $0.10, we will buy Ffr. 200 mil worth of French goods. In Fig. 22-1, plot the United States demand curve for French francs. Label the demand curve D_f.

The equation for the United States demand curve for French francs can be written as

$$(1) \qquad Q_d = \text{Ffr. 300 mil} - 1{,}000P_f$$

where Q_d is the quantity of francs (mil) and P_f is the price of francs in terms of U.S. dollars.

3 Suppose $0.20 = Ffr. 1.00 is the current market exchange rate. At this rate, $1.00 = Ffr. _____. But if $0.10 = Ffr. 1.00, from the French viewpoint, this exchange rate equals $1.00 = Ffr. _____. Thus, the French will want to buy (more, less) American products under the first exchange rate than under the second because, in terms of francs, these products are (more expensive, cheaper). Assume the French want to buy Ffr. 250 mil worth of American goods at the first rate of exchange, but only Ffr. 50 mil worth at the second rate of exchange. In Fig. 22-1 plot the French supply curve of francs. Label the supply curve S_f.

The equation for the French supply curve of francs can be written as

$$(2) \qquad Q_s = \text{Ffr. } {-150} \text{ mil} + 2{,}000P_f$$

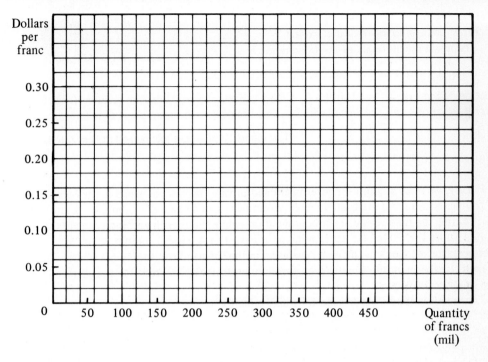

FIGURE 22-1

where Q_s is the quantity of francs (mil) and P_f is the price of francs in terms of U.S. dollars.

4 The equilibrium exchange rate and the equilibrium quantity of francs traded is found by solving for the equilibrium condition equation:

(3) $D_f = S_f$

The equilibrium exchange rate is Ffr. 1.00 = \$_____. An amount of Ffr. _____mil would be traded at this exchange rate. Label the equilibrium point E_1 in Fig. 22-1.

5 Point E_1 would be the equilibrium point *only* if purchases and sales of *goods and services* represented the sole type of transaction between the United States and France. From study of the balance of payments in Exercise 21, we know that trade in goods and services is only *one* type of international transaction giving rise to demand for and supply of foreign exchange. Suppose Americans decided to lend and invest Ffr. 100 mil in France, regardless of the exchange rate, and Frenchmen decided to lend and invest Ffr. 70 mil in the United States. The American decision represents an autonomous (increase, decrease) in the (demand for, supply of) francs; the French decision represents an autonomous (increase, decrease) in the (demand for, supply of) francs.

The new United States demand for francs equation is

(4) $Q_d =$ _____

Plot Eq. (4) in Fig. 22-1 and label it $D_f + K$ to indicate that the function includes foreign exchange demanded for trade *and* capital.

The new French supply of francs equation is

(5) $Q_S =$ _____ .

Plot Eq. (5) in Fig. 22-1 and label it $S_f + K$ to indicate that the function includes foreign exchange supplied for trade *and* capital. Label the new equilibrium point E_2. The new

exchange rate is Ffr. 1.00 = $_____. The quantity of francs exchanged at that rate is

Ffr. _____ mil.

6 Finally, we must account for government and private transfer payments in the balance of payments. Suppose the United States government sent France Ffr. 80 mil in disaster relief during the time period under consideration, while the French government paid the United States Ffr. 50 mil for educational purposes. The American transfer payment represents an autonomous (increase, decrease) in the (demand for, supply of) francs; the French transfer payment represents an autonomous (increase, decrease) in the (demand for, supply of) francs.

The new United States demand for francs equation is

(6) $Q_d =$ _____

Plot Eq. (6) in Fig. 22-1 and label it $D_f + K + T$.

The new French supply of francs equation is

(7) $Q_S =$ _____

Plot Eq. (7) in Fig. 22-1 and label it $S_f + K + T$. Label the new equilibrium point E_3.

The new exchange rate is Ffr. 1.00 = $_____. The quantity of francs exchanged at

that rate is Ffr. _____ mil.

7 The final franc demand and supply positions of Fig. 22-1—Eqs. (6) and (7)—are redrawn in Fig. 22-2. Assume that the two curves include all transactions between the United States and France. Label the demand curve ΣD_f, the supply curve ΣS_f, the equilibrium exchange rate P_f, and the equilibrium quantity of francs exchanged Q_f. At P_f the United States balance of payments with France is in (surplus, deficit, balance).

8 Now assume the United States decides to maintain an equilibrium exchange rate below P_f, say Ffr. 1.00 = $0.10. Mark this rate P'_f.

The quantity of francs demanded for all purposes is now Ffr. _____ mil. Mark this

amount Q_d. The quantity of francs supplied from all sources is now Ffr. _____ mil. Mark this amount Q_s. We now have a (shortage, surplus) of francs on the foreign

exchange market in the amount of Ffr. _____ mil. The only way the United States

government can maintain the exchange rate P'_f is to sell Ffr. _____ mil in the foreign exchange market to supply the demand for francs at exchange rate P'_f. Otherwise the exchange rate will be bid (up, down). The only way the United States government can

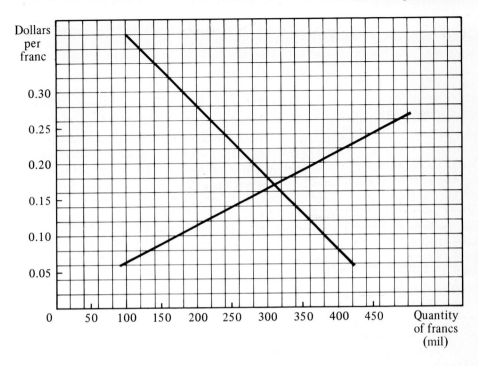

FIGURE 22-2

get the francs is to buy them from France in return for our international reserve assets. We then have a balance of payments (surplus, deficit, balance). In effect, the dollar is (overvalued, undervalued) relative to the franc at P'_f. Or, what is the same thing, the franc is (overvalued, undervalued) relative to the dollar at P'_f.

9 Now repeat the steps of paragraph 8 for a government-imposed exchange rate of Ffr. 1.00 = \$0.24. Mark that rate P''_f in Fig. 22-2.

(a) Quantity of francs demanded = Ffr. _____ mii

(b) Quantity of francs supplied = Ffr. _____ mil

(c) There is a (surplus, shortage) of Ffr. _____ mil

(d) To maintain exchange rate P''_f, the government must (buy, sell) Ffr. _____ mil in the foreign exchange market.

(e) The United States has a balance of payments (surplus, deficit, balance) at P''_f.

(f) At P''_f, the dollar is (overvalued, undervalued) relative to the franc.

10 We can thus see how the exchange rate and the balance of payments are related. The only way a payments surplus or deficit can possibly exist is for a government to "peg" the exchange rate at a level *other than* the equilibrium level, e.g., at P'_f or P''_f in Fig. 22-2, and therefore be prepared to lose or gain reserves. One way to move from a disequilibrium situation to one of equilibrium is to remove the peg and let the dollar price of the franc rise—*appreciate*—or fall—*depreciate*—in response to market forces until equilibrium is reached. *Depreciation* of the franc in terms of the dollar (is, is not) the same thing as *appreciation* of the dollar in terms of the franc. A second way to restore equilibrium is for the government to simply raise the peg to the free market price of the franc—*an upward revaluation*—or, what is the same thing, (appreciation, devaluation) of the dollar.

11 In terms of the information in Fig. 22-2, cutting the exchange rate loose from P_f' would result in a "float" toward equilibrium which would represent a(n) (appreciation, depreciation) of the franc and a(n) (appreciation, depreciation) of the dollar. Conversely, removal of the pegged rate P_f'' would result in a(n) (appreciation, depreciation) of the dollar. Alternatively, at P_f' the United States government could (revalue upward, devalue) the dollar. To remove their balance of payments (surplus, deficit) at exchange rate P_f', the French could (revalue upward, devalue) the franc. If exchange rate P_f' obtained, (France, the United States) is the more likely to undertake revaluation, and if exchange P_f'' obtained, (France, the United States) would be more likely to do so. These tendencies will occur because: _____

_____

_____

_____

12 There are many exchange rates: dollar/franc, dollar/mark, dollar/sterling, sterling/franc, and so on. When a currency depreciates or is devalued, its price changes in terms of *all* other currencies, not just one—unless, that is, some other currencies follow along in a general *realignment* of world currency values. So our examples, while conceptually correct, are greatly oversimplified. Also, it would *appear* reasonable to assume that government policy makers would leave the exchange rate alone to be determined by market forces, thereby avoiding the necessity to deal with fluctuations in the stock of reserve assets. But this course of action apparently is not a costless option. There must be some reason why so many national currencies are pegged in the foreign exchange market. Many countries doubt that the market for foreign exchange is stable under free-market conditions. If it is not, destabilizing consequences would follow for international transactions and for entire economies.

PROBLEMS FOR EXERCISE 22

You are given the following United States demand and supply functions for German marks (DM):

For goods and services:

(1) $Q_d =$ DM 600 mil $- 3,000 P_M$

(2) $Q_s =$ DM -200 mil $+ 1,000 P_M$

For capital transactions:

(3) Q_d = DM 100 mil

(4) Q_s = DM 200 mil

For transfers:

(5) Q_d = DM 50 mil

(6) Q_s = DM 10 mil

1 Write the overall demand and supply functions for German marks:

(7) Q_d = _____

(8) Q_s = _____

2 The equilibrium rate of exchange is $_____ = DM 1.00.

3 United States capital flows to Germany double. The new exchange rate is $_____ = DM 1.00.

4 The dollar has (appreciated, depreciated) in terms of the mark.

5 At the old exchange rate, United States demand for German goods was DM _____ mil worth.

6 At the new exchange rate, United States demand for German goods is DM _____ mil worth.

7 The change in the mark's value has thus been (beneficial, detrimental) to the interests of German exporters and their employees.

8 In response to the above, suppose the German government decides to drive the rate of exchange back to where it was in the first place. It would have to (buy, sell) DM _____ mil in return for dollars.

9 In consequence to paragraph 8, Germany would run a balance of payments (surplus, deficit) at the old rate of exchange, while the United States would run a payments (surplus, deficit).

ANSWERS FOR EXERCISE 22

2 more, more, less, Fig. 22-1A
3 5.00, 10.00, more, cheaper, Fig. 22-1A
4 0.15, 150, Fig. 22-1A

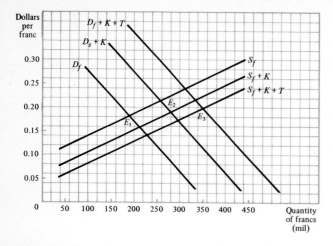

FIGURE 22-1A

5 increase, demand for, increase, supply of
   Eq. (4) Q_d = Ffr. 400 mil − 1,000P_f, Fig. 22-1A,
   Eq. (5) Q_s = Ffr. −80 mil + 2,000P_f, Fig. 22-1A, 0.16, 240
6 increase, demand for, increase, supply of,
   Eq. (6) Q_d = Ffr. 480 mil − 1,000P_f, Fig. 22-1A,
   Eq. (7) Q_s = Ffr. −30 mil + 2,000P_f, Fig. 22-1A, 0.17, 310
7 Fig. 22-2A, balance

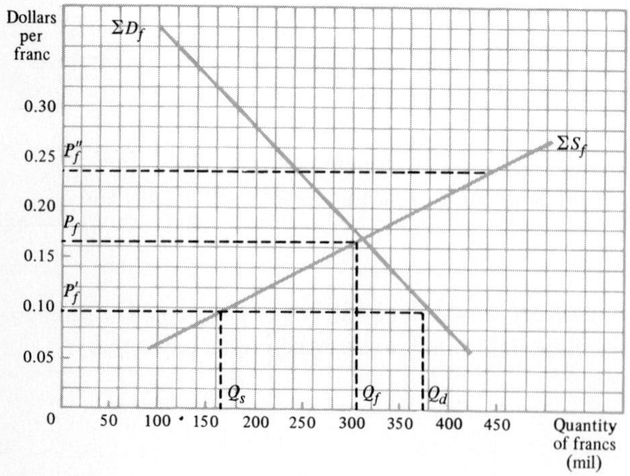

FIGURE 22-2A

8 Fig. 22-2A, 380, Fig. 22-2A, 170, Fig. 22-2A, shortage, 210, 210, up, deficit, overvalued, undervalued

9 Fig. 22-2A, (a) 240, (b) 450, (c) surplus, 210, (d) buy, 210, (e) surplus, (f) undervalued

10 is, devaluation

11 appreciation, depreciation, appreciation, devalue, revalue upward, deficit, devalue,
the United States, France, the deficit country can run out of international reserves
and is under great pressure to restore balance as quickly as possible, but the surplus
country can build up large stocks of reserves over extended periods of time without
its economy suffering materially. Both countries should *cooperate* in the needed
exchange-rate adjustment, but the pressure is always greater on the deficit country.

ANSWERS TO PROBLEMS FOR EXERCISE 22

1 Eq. (7) Q_d = DM 750 mil − 3,000P_M,
Eq. (8) Q_s = DM 10 mil + 1,000P_M

2 0.185

3 0.210

4 depreciated

5 45

6 15

7 detrimental

8 sell, 40

9 surplus, deficit

INCOME DETERMINATION AND THE FOREIGN TRADE SECTOR

1 Like savings, imports represent a(n) (leakage from, injection into) the domestic income stream. Expenditures on imports represent spending on goods and services *not* produced at home, and hence disappear from the domestic spending-responding cycle. Like investment, exports represent a(n) (leakage from, injection into) the domestic income stream— an increase in aggregate demand for home-produced goods and services. Let us consider the basic equilibrium-condition identity, ignoring for the moment the government sector:

(1) $Y = C + I$

If we let X stand for exports and Z for imports, in order to show the effects on income of an economy conducting trade relations with the rest of the world, Eq. (1) would have to be changed to

(2) $Y = $ _____

According to Eq. (2), if exports exceed imports in a given year, then the level of domestic income and output will be (greater, smaller) than if no international trade existed at all.

2 Let us assume that imports are a function of two variables: domestic income Y_D and the prices of domestic goods P_D relative to the prices of competing foreign goods P_F or P_D/P_F. A country's exports (are, are not) identical to foreign countries' imports, and hence they are a function of income abroad Y_F and relative prices P_D/P_F. Thus if domestic income rises, our imports tend to (rise, fall, remain unchanged). If domestic prices rise relative to foreign prices, our expenditures for imports will tend to (rise, fall, remain unchanged). Complete Table 23-1.

3 We now know that imports are a (positive, inverse) function of income. The proportion of its income that a country spends on imports is called the *average propensity to import* (*APZ*).

(3) $APZ = \dfrac{Z}{Y}$

The proportion of any *increase* in income spent on imported goods is called the *marginal propensity to import* (*MPZ*).

(4) $MPZ = \dfrac{\Delta Z}{\Delta Y}$

Table 23-1

Independent variable	Dependent variable	Impact on dependent variable (indicate increase or decrease)
(a) Y_D rises	Z_D	_____
(b) P_D/P_F rises	Z_D	_____
(c) P_D/P_F rises	X_D	_____
(d) Y_F rises	X_D	_____

You are given the following information for two successive years:

	Year 1	Year 2
Y_D	$900 bil	$1,200 bil
Z	$90 bil	$240 bil
P_D	$10/ton	$10/ton
P_F	$8/ton	$8/ton

The *APZ* is _____ in year 1 and _____ in year 2. The *MPZ* between year 1 and year 2 is _____ .

4 Let us proceed to a simple model of income determination in an open economy.

(5) $Y = C + I + X - Z$

(6) $C = \$80$ bil $+ 0.60\,Y$

(7) $I = \$160$ bil

(8) $X = \$180$ bil

(9) $Z = \$20$ bil $+ 0.10\,Y$

In the above model the marginal propensity to consume is _____ , the marginal propensity to save is _____ , and the marginal propensity to import is _____ . Autonomous export expenditures are _____ . Autonomous import expenditures are _____ .

Equation (5), the equilibrium condition, is plotted in Fig. 23-1. Label it $Y = E$, where E represents total expenditures. Plot the line representing aggregate intended expenditures of the closed economy and label it $C + I$. Plot the line representing aggregate intended expenditures of the open economy and label it $C + I + X - Z$. Equilibrium income in the closed economy is $_____$ bil. Equilibrium income in the open economy is $_____$ bil. Why are they different? $_____$

_____

5 Recall that the above model is termed the *total expenditure* model of income determination and applies equally to the open and closed economy. Given equilibrium income, complete Table 23-2.

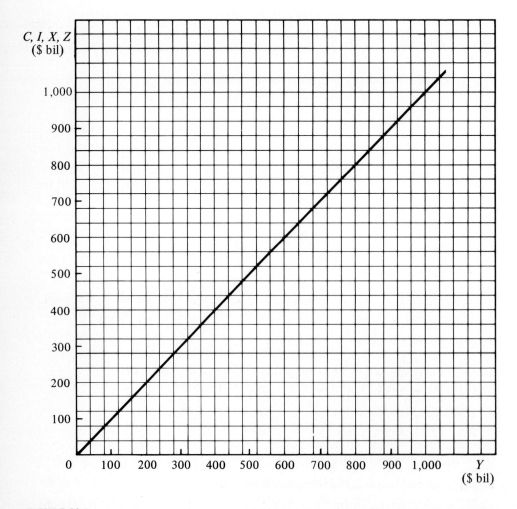

FIGURE 23-1

Table 23-2

	Closed economy	Open economy
Savings (S)	$_____ bil	$_____ bil
Investment (I)	_____	_____
Imports (Z)	_____	_____
Exports (X)	_____	_____
Leakages (S + Z)	_____	_____
Injections (I + X)	_____	_____

6 Now state the model presented in paragraph 4 as a *leakage-injection* model of the open economy. (For review of the leakage-injection model, see Exercise 6, paragraphs 14 to 16.)

(10) _____ = _____ (equilibrium condition)

(11) $S =$ _____

(12) $Z =$ _____

(13) $I =$ _____

(14) $X =$ _____

The total leakage equation can be stated as

(15) $S + Z =$ _____

The total injection equation is

(16) $I + X =$ _____

Plot Eqs. (15) and (16) in Fig. 23-2, labeling them $S + Z$ and $I + X$ respectively. The total leakage and injection equations intersect at $Y = \$$_____ bil, which (is, is not) equal to the equilibrium income derived in Fig. 23-1.

7 Consider an income level of $400 bil. In Fig. 23-1, mark the intended expenditure level A_1 on the aggregate demand function and the corresponding point A_2 on the 45° unit-expenditure line. The distance A_1A_2 represents the (excess, shortfall) of $_____ bil of intended expenditures relative to realized income. Now use the same $400 bil income level and mark the corresponding intended leakages level A_3 and intended injections level A_4 in Fig. 23-2. The difference of $_____ bil represents a(n) (excess, shortfall) of intended injections relative to intended leakages.

The intended-realized gap results in (intended, unintended) inventory (investment, disinvestment) at an income level of $400 bil, thereby driving the level of production (upward, downward), and income in subsequent time periods will (rise, fall, remain the same).

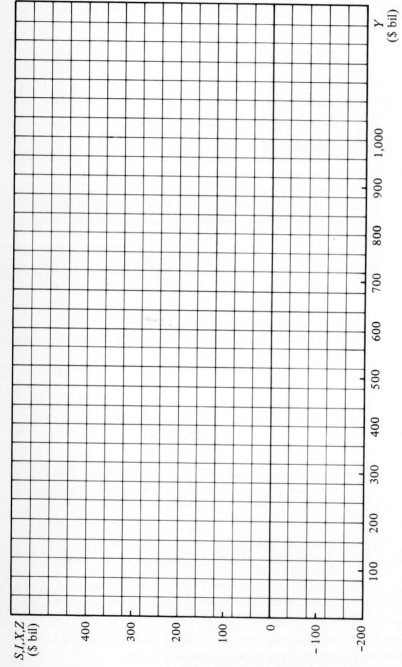

FIGURE 23-2

All of the adjustment from a disequilibrium situation in a model such as that just presented is carried by domestic investment. The other injection into the income stream, exports, does not adjust. Why? _____

_____

8 Now consider an income level of $1,000 bil. Mark the relevant points on the aggregate expenditure function as B_1 and on the $45°$ unit-expenditure line as B_2 in Fig. 23-1, and on the leakage function B_3 and the injection function B_4 in Fig. 23-2. The difference of

$_____ bil in the total-expenditure model represents a(n) (excess, shortfall) of aggregate demand and in the leakage-injection model represents a(n) (different, identical) (excess, shortfall) of intended savings and imports relative to intended investment and exports. As a result of the (intended, unintended) inventory (investment, disinvestment), production and income will (rise, fall) toward equilibrium.

9 We have seen that the foreign trade sector and national income and output are closely linked. Moreover, income determination in the open economy is really no different from that in the closed economy, except that two variables are added. An increase in income will increase imports. The sensitivity of changes in imports to changes in income is

determined by the value of the _____. Since exports and imports are components of aggregate demand, an autonomous shift in either one will affect the level of economic activity. Increases in X and decreases in Z will (raise, lower) the level of income, and decreases in X and increases in Z will (raise, lower) income.

Assume that autonomous exports decrease by $100 bil. Show this change in Fig. 23-2 by shifting the proper curve. The new curve should be labeled $(S + Z') (I + X')$. At the new equilibrium, the balance of trade is in (deficit, surplus, balance).

10 In paragraph 9, as a result of the autonomous change in exports of $100 bil, income

changed by $_____ bil. Thus, the value of the multiplier is _____. Recall that in the closed-economy model a change in autonomous spending leads to a *multiplied* effect on income, due to the circular flow process. (For review, see Exercise 7.) The multiplier value is computed as the reciprocal of the sum of the leakage coefficients in the model. (For review, see Exercise 9, paragraphs 14 and 15.) If we let ΔE stand for a change in autonomous expenditures —consumption, investment, or government—and the marginal propensity to save s is the only leakage coefficient, then

$$(17) \qquad \Delta Y = \text{_____}$$

Recall that $1/s = 1/1 - b$. Hence, if $\Delta E = 10 bil and $b = 0.8$, then income will (increase,

decrease) by $_____ bil.

Imports represent a(n) (leakage from, injection into) the income stream. Thus, they must be taken into account in computing the value of the multiplier. The *rate* at which an increase in income is spent on imported goods is called the (marginal, average, total) propensity to import. From Eq. (17) the multiplier for the closed economy is

$$(18) \qquad k = \text{_____}$$

If we let the term z stand for MPZ, the multiplier value for the open economy is

(19) $k' = $ _____

The value of the multiplier (increases, decreases) when we add imports to the model. If $s = 0.2$, $z = 0.2$, and $\Delta E = \$10$ bil, then $\Delta Y = \$$_____bil. Thus, for a given change in autonomous expenditures, income will rise by $\$$_____bil less in the (open, closed) economy than in the (open) (closed) economy.

11 We will now shift from the "small country case" assumed above to an economy which, through the marginal propensity to import, is interdependent with other national economies. Here, what one country imports, another country—or the rest of the world (ROW)—must by definition export, and vice versa.

An autonomous increase in spending, say ΔI, in the United States results in the following sequence of events: (a) a(n) (increase, decrease) in United States income, which causes (b) a(n) (increase, decrease) in United States imports, which is equivalent to (c) a(n) (increase, decrease) in ROW exports, which causes (d) a (rise, decline) in ROW income, which in turn results in (e) a(n) (increase, decrease) in ROW imports from the United States, which serves to (f) (increase, reduce) United States exports and aggregate demand, thereby (g) partially (offsetting, reinforcing) the initial autonomous change in United States domestic spending. The final change in income in the United States with these *foreign trade repercussions* will be (greater, smaller) than the corresponding income change for the open economy without foreign trade repercussions. Hence, the value of an open-economy multiplier embodying the foreign-repercussions effect must be (larger, smaller) than the standard open-economy multiplier that does not reflect the international feedbacks if the initial disturbance occurs in the foreign sector.

PROBLEMS FOR EXERCISE 23

1 You are given the following functions:

$C = \$100$ bil $+ 0.8\,Y$

$I = \$25$ bil

$X = \$12$ bil

$Z = \$20$ bil $+ 0.1\,Y$

(a) What is the equilibrium level of income of the closed economy? $\$$_____bil.

(b) What is the equilibrium level of income of the open economy? $\$$_____bil.

(c) At the level of income determined in (b);

$C = $ _____

$I = $ _____

$X = $ _____

$Z =$ _____

Balance of trade $X - Z =$ _____

(d) Suppose the equilibrium level of income just brings the domestic economy to a noninflationary state of full employment. Suppose further that income in other countries declines so that they reduce their imports from $X = \$12$ bil to $X = \$6$ bil.

The domestic income level thus (rises, falls) to $\$$_____ bil.

(e) The government could restore full employment equilibrium by (lowering the interest rate, restricting imports, subsidizing increased exports, increased spending, any of these) to increase spending by $\$$_____ bil.

(f) If the government did follow the policy indicated in **(e)**, domestic imports would (increase, decrease) by $\$$_____ bil.

(g) As a result of the activity in **(f)**, the dollar would (appreciate, depreciate) if market-determined exchange rates were permitted.

(h) If the exchange rate obtaining under **(e)** were pegged, the resulting balance of trade (surplus, deficit) for the United States would be $\$$_____ bil (greater, less) under **(e)** than under **(d)**.

(i) Use the following terms to fill in the cause-and-effect relations below: (positively related) (negatively related) (unrelated)

(1) Income → imports _____

(2) Imports → income _____

(3) Exports → income _____

(4) Income → exports _____

(5) Income → interest rate _____

(6) Interest rate → income _____

(7) Interest rate → imports _____

(8) Interest rate → exchange rate _____ (+ = appreciate)

(9) Exchange rate → imports _____ (− = depreciate)

(10) Import → exchange rate _____

(11) Imports → balance of payment _____

(12) Income → balance of trade _____ (+ = surplus)

(13) Exports → balance of trade _____ (− = deficit)

(14) Interest rate → balance of trade _____

ANSWERS FOR EXERCISE 23

1 leakage from, injection into, Eq. (2) $Y = C + I + X - Z$, greater
2 are, rise, rise, (a) increase, (b) increase, (c) decrease, (d) increase
3 positive, 0.10, 0.20, 0.50
4 0.6, 0.4, 0.1, $180 bil, $20 bil, Fig. 23-1A, 600, 800, because at that level of income $X > Z$

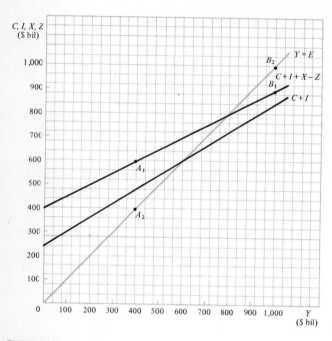

FIGURE 23-1A

5

	Closed economy	Open economy
S	160	240
I	160	160
Z	0	100
X	0	180
$S + Z$	160	340
$I + X$	160	340

6 Eq. (10) $S + Z = I + X$, Eq. (11) $S = \$80$ bil $+ 0.40Y$, Eq. (12) $Z = \$20$ bil $+ 0.10Y$, Eq. (13) $I = \$160$ bil, Eq. (14) $X = \$180$ bil, Eq. (15) $S + Z = -\$60$ bil $+ 0.5Y$, Eq. (16) $I + X = \$340$ bil, Fig. 23-2A, 800, is
7 Fig. 23-1A, excess, 200, Fig. 23-2A, 200, excess, unintended, investment, upward, rise, because exports are autonomously given—they are assumed to depend on the level of income in *other* countries

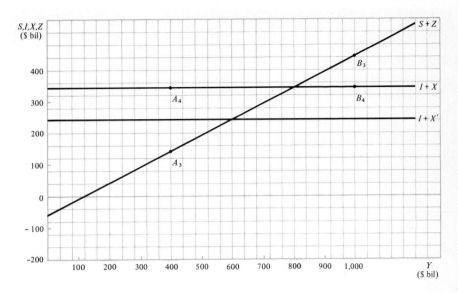

FIGURE 23-2A

8 Fig. 23-1A, Fig. 23-2A, 100, shortfall, identical, shortfall, unintended, disinvestment, fall
9 marginal propensity to import, raise, lower, Fig. 23-2A, $I + X'$, balance
10 200, 2, Eq. (17) $Y = 1/s\Delta E$, increase, 50, leakage from, marginal, Eq. (18) $k = 1/s$, Eq. (19) $k' = 1/(s + z)$, decreases, 25, 25, open, closed
11 increase, increase, increase, rise, increase, increase, reinforcing, greater, larger

ANSWERS TO PROBLEMS FOR EXERCISE 23

1 **(a)** 625
  (b) 390
  (c) $C = \$412$ bil
    $I = \$25$ bil
    $X = \$12$ bil
    $Z = \$59$ bil
    B/T = deficit $47 bil
  (d) falls, 370
  (e) any of these, 6
  (f) increase by $2 bil
  (g) depreciate
  (h) deficit $4 bil greater
  (i) (1) positively related
    (2) negatively related

(3) positively related
(4) unrelated
(5) positively related
(6) negatively related
(7) negatively related
(8) positively related
(9) positively related
(10) negatively related
(11) negatively related
(12) negatively related
(13) positively related
(14) positively related

MAINTAINING INTERNAL AND EXTERNAL BALANCE

1 Recall that "internal balance" refers to full-employment equilibrium of the national economy at stable prices. The term "external balance" refers to equilibrium in the balance of payments—i.e., neither an increase or a decrease in a country's reserve position on average, over a certain period of time. The problem for economic policy makers is to try to maintain *both* internal and external balance, using the tools available to them. Exercise 23 indicated that these goals may not be mutually consistent, because whatever affects the level of activity in the national economy invariably influences the trade sector —and hence the balance of payments. Domestic economic policies will also influence international capital flows, thus providing a second link between internal and external balance. Domestic policies which produce higher rates of interest will tend to induce international capital (inflows, outflows), while lower rates of interest will tend to result in international capital (inflows, outflows). Hence, a monetary policy designed to stimulate the domestic economy will tend to cause (increases, decreases) in a country's reserve position, while policies designed to dampen economic activity at home will tend to cause (increases, decreases) in a country's reserve position.

2 An increase in domestic interest rates, relative to those obtaining abroad, will tend to cause net capital (inflows, outflows). An increase in domestic interest rates will tend to produce a (higher, lower) level of domestic economy activity, and an (increase, decrease) in imports relative to exports. Hence the capital-flow and trade influences of monetary policies on the balance of payments are mutually (offsetting, reinforcing). But this is not necessarily true in the case of fiscal policy. To see why this is so, consider the following example. Let K_o represent capital outflows, K_n represent capital inflows, Z represent imports, Y represent the level of GNP, i represent the rate of interest, and BP represent the net change in a country's reserve position. In Fig. 24-1, trace through the impact of expansionary and contractionary monetary and government-expenditures policy on the balance of payments by indicating the direction of change of each variable ($\uparrow,\downarrow,?$) and the overall BP impact. In which case(s) is the BP impact indeterminate? _____

_____ . Why? _____

_____

_____

(a) Expansionary monetary policy

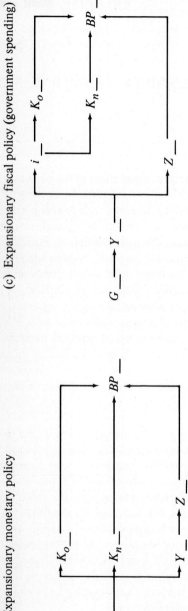

(b) Contractionary monetary policy

(c) Expansionary fiscal policy (government spending)

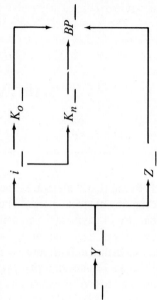

(d) Contractionary fiscal policy (government spending)

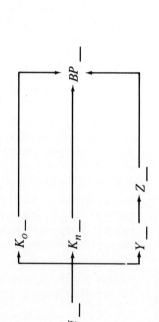

FIGURE 24-1

3 The concept of internal-external balance can be formalized by means of a very simple diagram such as Fig. 24-2. The vertical axis indicates the state of the government budget B in varying amounts of surplus or deficit, as a proxy for stimulative or restrictive fiscal policy. The larger the deficit, the more (stimulative, restrictive) the impact of the government budget on the level of economic activity. The horizontal axis indicates the prevailing rate of interest i, as a proxy for stimulative or restrictive monetary policy. The lower the interest rate, the more (stimulative, restrictive) the impact of monetary policy on the level of economic activity. The XX' function defines all i/B combinations that

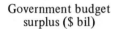

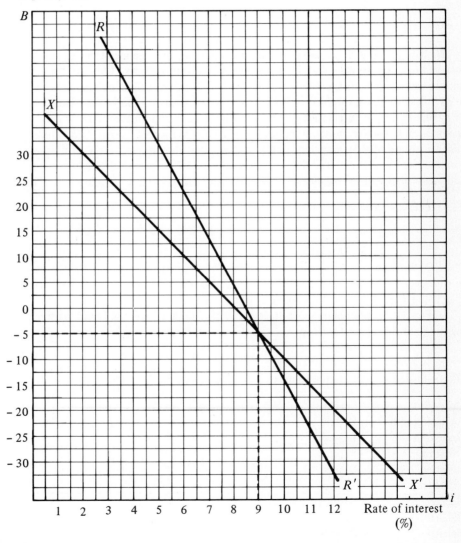

FIGURE 24-2

will yield full employment and stable prices in the national economy—i.e., internal balance, which can be achieved *either* with a combination of high interest rates and large budget deficits, *or* low interest rates and large budget surpluses, or some combination between. Any i/B combination falling to the right of XX' represents domestic (recession, inflation) because _____

_____

_____

Any i/B combination falling to the left of XX' represents domestic (recession, inflation) because _____

_____

_____

   We have seen that fiscal and monetary actions affect the balance of payments as well, both through imports *MPZ* and through international capital flows. Low interest rates tend to cause payments (deficits, surpluses), while stimulative fiscal policy tends to result in payments (deficits, surpluses). Balance of payments balance can be maintained *either* by a combination of stimulative government budgets and high interest rates which results from restrictive monetary policy, *or* by a combination of restrictive government budgets and stimulative monetary policy in the form of low interest rates, or by some combination in between. The RR' function in Fig. 24-2 defines all i/B combinations that will yield balance in the balance of payments. Any i/B combination falling to the right of

RR' represents a payments (surplus, deficit) because _____

_____

The RR' function is steeper than the XX' function because the sensitivity of the balance of payments to the rate of interest—via international capital flows—is relatively greater than is the level of domestic economic activity.

   In Fig. 24-2, mark points representing monetary-fiscal policy combinations embodying the following characteristics:

Internal balance	External balance	Mark point by
Recession	Surplus	*A*
Recession	Deficit	*B*
Recession	Balance	*C*
Inflation	Surplus	*D*
Inflation	Deficit	*E*
Inflation	Balance	*F*
Balance	Surplus	*G*
Balance	Deficit	*H*
Balance	Balance	*I*

Each of the points you have indicated above calls for government policy action in one of three directions: **(a)** expansionary fiscal or monetary policy, **(b)** contractionary fiscal or monetary policy, or **(c)** no action needed. For each of the above points, indicate below the policy action required (expansionary, contractionary, none) to restore internal and external balance, respectively:

Situation	Policy needed for internal balance	Policy needed for external balance
A		
B		
C		
D		
E		
F		
G		
H		
I		

Finally, indicate below in which of the above cases there is or is not a clear policy conflict, and whether any such conflict is or is not immediately serious for the domestic economy.

Situation	Policy conflict (yes or no)	Serious? (yes or no)
A		
B		
C		
D		
E		
F		
G		
H		
I		

For those cases where you have indicated a policy conflict to be serious, explain why:

_____

_____

_____

For those cases where you feel an obvious conflict is not serious, indicate why not:

_____

_____

_____

4 Your analysis of the internal-external balance situations above has clearly indicated that there are two *conflict zones*, where the policy prescription for external balance will worsen internal balance, and vice versa—ignoring instances where one or the other is already in balance. In situation D, a country can attack its inflationary domestic situation by (expansionary, contractionary) monetary or fiscal policies, which will (improve, worsen) its payments surplus. This action may add further (expansionary, contractionary) pressure, but it can afford to run surpluses for a while and accumulate international reserves. In situation B, on the other hand, the country is in serious difficulty. On the one hand, its ability to run payments deficits is limited by its international reserve holdings—which sooner or later will run out—thereby forcing a restoration of external balance at some point. On the other hand, recession in the domestic economy is a serious economic and political matter, demanding priority attention.

What can a country do when it is in a deficit/recession bind and has only monetary and fiscal policy tools to work with? In terms of Fig. 24-2, suppose the interest rate is 6½ percent and the government budget is $12.5 bil in surplus. Mark that point 0 in the diagram. Government officials decide to attack the internal-balance problem using *monetary policy* techniques and payments–balance problems using the tools of *fiscal policy*. Starting from 0, we thus (reduce, raise) interest rates to restore full employment on the XX' function. Mark that point 0_1. Our balance of payments deficit has thus gotten (better, worse). We try to cure it by (increasing, decreasing) the government surplus and moving to the RR' function representing payment balance. Mark that point 0_2. In the process, our domestic economy has moved into (inflation, recession). We cure it by (raising, lowering) interest rates and getting back on the XX' function. Mark that point 0_3. Clearly, by using the policy combination proposed here, we are continually moving (toward, away from) simultaneous internal *and* external balance.

Start again at 0 in Fig. 24-2, but this time reverse your policy ordering, using monetary policy for *external* balance and fiscal policy for *internal* balance. From 0, cure the balance of payments by raising interest rates, thus moving onto the RR' function at a point we will mark 0_4. Our recessionary domestic situation has become (worse, better). We cure it by stimulative fiscal policy, moving back onto the XX' function at a point marked 0_5. Again, our payments balance is in (deficit, surplus), but we can cure that by (raising, lowering) interest rates slightly and moving back onto the RR' function at a point marked 0_6. Clearly, we are now moving (toward, away from) an i/B combination that will yield *both* internal and external balance at point I.

The policy prescription that would appear to follow from the above analysis is that monetary policy should be used for (external, internal) balance, while fiscal policy should be used to achieve (external, internal) balance. Note that this result follows from the difference in the slopes of the RR' and XX' function in Fig. 24-2. RR' is steeper, indicating that the balance of payments is relatively (more, less) sensitive to monetary policy than to fiscal policy changes than in the case of XX', showing that the domestic economy is relatively (more, less) sensitive to monetary policy than to fiscal policy shifts. If the opposite were the case, then the policy prescriptions clearly would be reversed. The point is to use each policy tool to attack that particular policy goal which is relatively the (most, least) sensitive to it.

5 Governments are not, of course, limited to monetary and fiscal policy in the achievement of internal and external balance. Exercise 22 showed that if flexible exchange rates were adopted the balance of payments would cease to be a problem from the standpoint of external economic policy. In terms of Fig. 24-2, the RR' function would (automatically move to whatever i/B combination is closer for internal balance, cease to exist). And so the only remaining concern is internal balance. But flexible exchange rates is not a costless option either. It may entail exchange-rate instability, which can interfere with international trade and capital flows, as well as causing potentially costly readjustments in the allocation of productive resources. The analysis presented here assumes fixed exchange rates. Alternatively, currency devaluation or depreciation may be used to make domestic goods more competitive both at home and in international markets. This action would result in a shift in the RR' function to the (left, right), with once-and-for-all consequences that were (similar to, different from) flexible exchange rates.

Another possible policy option is to apply *exchange controls*—to ration out for imports and other balance of payments disbursements just as much foreign exchange as is obtained through export and other balance of payments receipts. This course of action administratively causes the RR' function to (shift to whatever i/B combination is chosen for internal balance, cease to exist). This alternative is not costless either, because it cuts the national economy off from the rest of the world, and can lead to a serious misallocation of resources nationally and internationally.

Still another policy alternative is to place controls on trade, such as tariffs and quotas, and on international capital flows. If imports and other payments disbursements can thus be restricted, the RR' function can be administratively shifted to the (left, right), and the achievement of internal-external balance is thus facilitated. But the cost, again, is a domestic misallocation of productive resources—a real cost to the national economy.

There is no such thing as a free lunch. For every goal there must be at least one tool that can be used in the implementation of national economic policy. And beyond the dual availability of aggregate monetary and fiscal policy, for every tool that is brought to bear, a goal—such as freer trade and payments—must be sacrificed. Only more flexible exchange rates hold out the promise of bringing a lasting solution to the problems of internal-external balance. And even this, as we have seen in Exercise 22, may not be entirely·costless.

PROBLEMS FOR EXERCISE 24

1 The principal link between the balance of payments and national income is _____ _____ .

2 The principal link between the national monetary sector and the balance of payments is _____ .

3 An autonomous increase in domestic investment tends to cause the payments position to _____ via link number 1.

4 Since this same increase in investment will tend to result in a rise in domestic interest rates, it will tend to cause the payments to _____ via link number 2.

5 Whether *on net* the balance of payments improves or deteriorates depends on _____ _____ _____ .

6 With the balance of payments in equilibrium, and the domestic economy in recession, will monetary or fiscal policy action to restore domestic balance disturb the payments balance *least*? _____

7 Why? _____ _____ _____

8 With the domestic economy in full-employment, noninflationary equilibrium and a balance of payments deficit, will monetary or fiscal policy action restore an external deficit to balance disturbed internal balance least? _____

9 Why? _____ _____ _____

10 Suppose you have four objectives in economic policy: full employment, price stability, payments balance, and rapid economic growth. With monetary and fiscal policy as your only techniques of economic control, how many of these goals could you reasonably be expected to attain? _____

11 Why? _____

_____

_____

12 Does the balance of payments constrain your freedom of action with respect to controlling the domestic economy? _____

13 If so, how? _____

_____

_____

ANSWERS FOR EXERCISE 24

1 inflows, outflows, decreases, increases
2 inflows, lower, decrease, reinforcing, Fig. 24-1A, cases (c) and (d), because the induced increases (or decrease) in incomes cause *both* an increase (or decrease) in imports *and* a net capital inflow (or outflow), thereby offsetting each other.

(a) Expansionary monetary policy

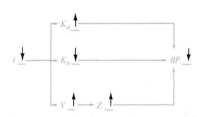

(c) Expansionary fiscal policy (government spending)

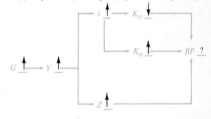

(b) Contractionary monetary policy

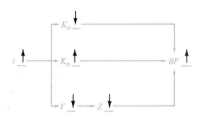

(d) Contractionary fiscal policy (government spending)

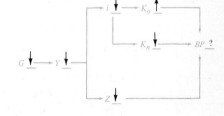

FIGURE 24-1A

3 stimulative, stimulative, recession, the rate of interest is higher than the i/B combination defined as yielding internal balance—or the budget surplus is higher than that needed to get internal balance for any given rate of interest, inflation, the rate of interest is too low or the budget deficit too great to obtain internal balance as defined by XX', deficits, deficits, surplus, the rate of interest and/or government surplus is higher than that combination defined as yielding balance as defined by RR', Fig. 24-2A.

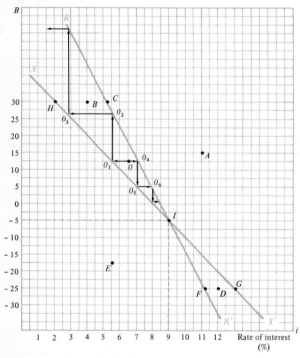

Government budget
surplus ($ bil)

FIGURE 24-2A

Situation	Policy needed for internal balance	Policy needed for external balance
A	expansionary	expansionary
B	expansionary	contractionary
C	expansionary	none
D	contractionary	expansionary
E	contractionary	contractionary
F	contractionary	none
G	none	expansionary
H	none	contractionary
I	none	none

Situation	Policy conflict?	Serious?
A	No	–
B	Yes	Yes
C	Yes	Yes
D	Yes	No
E	No	–
F	Yes	No
G	Yes	No
H	Yes	Yes
I	No	–

B, both payments deficit and domestic recession are high-priority economic issues, and *C*, same as above, since efforts to curb recession will induce deficit in the balance of payments

H, efforts to cure payments deficit will tend to induce domestic recession

In all cases it involves either continuing to run or getting into a payment surplus situation, which can be tolerated easily for a reasonable period of time and in moderate amounts.

4 contractionary, worsen, expansionary, Fig. 24-2A, reduce, worse, increasing, recession, lowering, away from, worse, deficit, raising, toward, external, internal, more, less, most

5 cease to exist, left, similar to, cease to exist, left

ANSWERS TO PROBLEMS FOR EXERCISE 24

1 the marginal propensity to import

2 the interest-elasticity of international capital flows

3 deteriorate

4 improve

5 the size of the marginal propensity to import relative to the elasticity of the transactions demand for money and the interest-elasticity of international capital flows

6 fiscal policy

7 Fiscal expansion will drive the economy upward while tending to raise interest rates, thus drawing in both imports and capital, while monetary policy drives the economy ahead via low interest rates, thus drawing in imports and promoting adverse capital flows

8 monetary policy

9 Monetary constraction immediately raises interest rates and draws in capital while dampening economic activity and pulling in fewer imports; fiscal policy directly reduces incomes and thereby imports while tending at the same time to affect the balance of payments adversely via lower interest rates

10 Three

11 Full employment and price stability may be taken to represent one goal: internal

balance adjusting aggregate demand to aggregate supply. The other goal is payment balance. If internal and external balance are achieved using expansionary fiscal policy and tight credit, then rapid growth—which demands low long-term interest rates—must be sacrificed. To achieve rapid growth one of the other goals may have to be sacrificed

12 Yes
13 It limits your freedom to pursue expansionary economic policy by increasing payments deficit, and contractionary or anti-inflationary policies by increasing large and unhealthy payments surpluses

You are given the following simplified balance of payments data for Country X in 1972:

	Millions of dollars
Exports	
Goods	+ 290.0
Services	+ 116.0
Income from abroad	+ 58.0
Imports	
Goods	− 362.5
Services	− 101.5
Income from foreign investments in X ...	− 87.0
Net unilateral transfers	− 14.5
Net government transactions (grants and loans)	+ 29.0
Net capital movements	− 14.5
Official transactions (gold flows & changes in foreign holdings of X's currency)......	+ 87.0
	−0−

1 In 1972, Country X had a balance of payments surplus of
  (a) $101.5 mil
  (b) $290.0 mil
  (c) $ 14.5 mil
  (d) $ 87.0 mil
  (e) none of these

2 The balance of merchandise trade was
(a) + $101.5 mil
(b) + $290.0 mil
(c) – $ 72.5 mil
(d) – $ 87.0 mil

3 The balance on invisibles trade was
(a) + 14.5 mil
(b) + 10.5 mil
(c) – 14.5 mil
(d) – 87.0 mil
(e) none of these

4 The balance on current account was
(a) – $ 87.0 mil
(b) + $ 87.0 mil
(c) + $ 14.5 mil
(d) + $101.5 mil
(e) none of these

5 The balance on current and unilateral transactions was
(a) – $ 87.0 mil
(b) – $101.5 mil
(c) + $ 14.5 mil
(d) – $ 14.5 mil

6 The balance on long-term capital flows was
(a) – $14.5 mil
(b) + $14.5 mil
(c) + $ 29.0 mil
(d) cannot be determined from data given

7 Which of the following is a true statement?
(a) Foreigners made a larger volume of investment in X than residents of X invested abroad.
(b) International reserves flowed into X.
(c) Government made more grants abroad than it received.
(d) Foreigners made a smaller volume of investment in X than residents of X invested abroad.

8 If X's currency were allowed to vary in terms of the value of other currencies:
(a) the quantity of foreign currencies wanted by X's residents would persistently exceed the amount available
(b) the international value of X's currency would stay the same
(c) gold would automatically flow into X and deflate the price level
(d) the international value of X's currency would depreciate

9 In 1972, X incurred
   (a) a trade surplus but a payments deficit
   (b) a trade surplus and a payments surplus
   (c) a trade deficit and a payments deficit
   (d) a trade deficit but a payments surplus

Questions 10 to 20 refer to the following diagram:

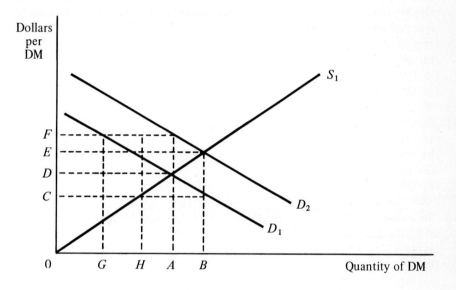

10 The quantity of DM supplied will be greater:
   (a) the lower the dollar price of DM
   (b) the lower the demand for DM
   (c) the higher the dollar price of DM
   (d) the higher the German GNP
   (e) none of these

11 The quantity of DM demanded will be greater:
   (a) the lower the dollar price of DM
   (b) the lower the demand for DM
   (c) the higher the dollar price of DM
   (d) the higher is German GNP
   (e) none of these

12 Given that the supply of and demand for DM are S_1 and D_1, the equilibrium exchange rate is
   (a) OF
   (b) OE
   (c) OD
   (d) OC

13 Given that the supply of and demand for DM are S_1 and D_1, the quantity of *DM* bought and sold is:
  (a) *OG*
  (b) *OH*
  (c) *OA*
  (d) *OB*

14 Suppose D_1 refers only to the United States import demand for German goods and services. Now Americans wish to invest *GA* worth of DM in Germany. The equilibrium exchange rate is now:
  (a) *OF*
  (b) *OE*
  (c) *OD*
  (d) *OC*

15 The amount of DM bought and sold is now:
  (a) *OG*
  (b) *OH*
  (c) *OA*
  (d) *OB*

16 The amount of DM demanded by Americans for purchases of German goods and services is now
  (a) *OG*
  (b) *OH*
  (c) *OA*
  (d) *OB*
  (e) *HB*

17 The amount of DM demanded by Americans for loans and investments in Germany is now
  (a) *OG*
  (b) *OH*
  (c) *OA*
  (d) *OB*
  (e) *HB*

18 The capital flows from the United States to Germany have caused
  (a) depreciation of DM
  (b) depreciation of the dollar
  (c) appreciation of DM
  (d) appreciation of the dollar
  (e) devaluation of the dollar

19 Given that the demand for DM shifts from D_1 to D_2, efforts by the United States government to keep the exchange rate at *C* would result in:
  (a) a United States payments surplus *HB*

(b) a United States payments deficit *HB*
(c) a return flow of capital to United States
(d) none of these

20 It is in the interest of United States exporters
   (a) to let the dollar appreciate
   (b) to let the dollar depreciate
   (c) to keep exchange rates as they are
   (d) to stop international capital flows
   (e) all of these

21 Which of the following would call for "inpayments" to the United States?
   (a) gold flows into the United States
   (b) American imports of Japanese radios
   (c) American firms sell insurance to Norwegian shipping companies
   (d) American unilateral transfers to developing countries

22 The United States balance of payments on current account has in recent years:
   (a) changed from surplus to deficit
   (b) exhibited a surplus which is more than offset by a deficit on long-term capital account
   (c) incurred a chronic deficit
   (d) been balanced
   (e) shown very large deficits

23 Under a system of flexible exchange rates an American trade deficit with France will cause
   (a) an increase in the dollar price of francs
   (b) the United States government to ration francs to American importers
   (c) an increase in the franc price of dollars
   (d) a flow of gold from the United States to France

24 Which is the most desirable means by which the United States might correct a balance of payments deficit?
   (a) monopolize foreign exchange
   (b) increase tariffs on foreign imports to the United States
   (c) subsidize American exporters
   (d) ask other nations to assume a greater share of total aid to developing countries
   (e) increase the level of domestic productivity

25 Which of the following parameters serves as a link between national economies?
   (a) average propensity to consume
   (b) average propensity to save
   (c) marginal propensity to export
   (d) marginal propensity to import

26 If there is an increase in domestic investment spending, imports will eventually
   (a) increase
   (b) decrease
   (c) remain unchanged
   (d) increase, then decrease

27 Refer to the previous question. The foreign repercussions effect will ensure that domestic exports will eventually
   (a) increase
   (b) decrease
   (c) remain unchanged
   (d) increase, then decrease

28 Given an autonomous *domestic* spending increase, the value of the multiplier incorporating the foreign repercussions effect will
   (a) be greater than
   (b) be less than
   (c) be the same as
   (d) bear no relation to
      a comparable multiplier that ignores the foreign repercussions effect

29 If the disturbance represents an autonomous increase in *exports*, the answer to question 28 is
   (a) greater than
   (b) less than
   (c) same as
   (d) no relation

30 Which of the following has generally similar effects on a nation's exports and imports?
   (a) exchange rate appreciation and a decrease in the domestic money stock
   (b) exchange rate depreciation and domestic deflation
   (c) exchange rate depreciation and domestic inflation
   (d) exchange rate appreciation and domestic deflation

31 Given fixed exchange rates, monetary policy will be more effective than fiscal policy in solving domestic unemployment and minimizing balance of payments disturbances.
   (a) true
   (b) false

You are given the following policy options:
   (a) restrictive monetary policy
   (b) expansionary monetary policy
   (c) tax increase
   (d) increase in government spending
   (e) exchange rate devaluation

(f) exchange rate upward revaluation

(g) no monetary, fiscal, or balance of payments policy change

In questions 32 to 37, indicate the initial policy response you would apply to the case given, under fixed exchange rates (no devaluation or upward revaluation permitted):

32 Domestic inflation and payments deficit _____

33 Domestic inflation and payments surplus _____

34 Domestic recession and payments deficit _____

35 Domestic recession and payments surplus _____

36 Domestic balance and payments surplus _____

37 Domestic recession and payments balance _____

Now we permit devaluation and upward revaluation. Answer the above questions again under the new circumstances in questions 38 to 43.

38 Answer to question 32   _____

39 Answer to question 33   _____

40 Answer to question 34   _____

41 Answer to question 35   _____

42 Answer to question 36   _____

43 Answer to question 37   _____

44 A devaluation of a country's currency will always cure its payments deficit.
   (a) true
   (b) false

45 Economic expansion always has a more favorable impact on a country's payments than economic contraction.
   (a) true
   (b) false

46 The more flexible exchange rates, the easier it is to reconcile the need for internal and external balance.
   (a) true
   (b) false

47 Devaluation is costless in terms of real national income.
   (a) true
   (b) false

48 Deflationary policy at home may be a more costly way to restore payments balance than devaluation.
   (a) true
   (b) false

49 Reduced foreign aid will always improve the balance of payments of a country by the amount of the aid reduction.
   (a) true
   (b) false

50 Chronic payments surpluses are not costly for a national economy.
   (a) true
   (b) false

PART **NINE**

ECONOMIC GROWTH

Our discussion so far has focused on income, employment, and price-level determination in an essentially static context—utilization of a *given amount* of productive capacity, assuming that the quantity and quality of resources are given and constant. We have concentrated on the explanation of income in the *short run*. The productive capacity of an economy, of course, is not fixed. The very acts of saving and investing expand the capacity of an economy to produce. So does population growth. So do advances in technology. Sometimes, as a consequence of war, national disaster, or other events, productive capacity actually may shrink. We are thus shooting at a moving target, trying to explain and regulate aggregate demand in the *long* run, so as to absorb whatever productive capacity exists at a point in time.

This part investigates the sources of economic growth and the interrelationships that exist between aggregate demand and aggregate supply. By economic growth is meant growth of capacity to produce, not utilization of existing capacity. An increase in demand that more fully utilizes productive capacity leads to a growth of output, but this event does not necessarily expand capacity to produce. Thus growth is a supply concept, although the characteristics of demand can influence the rate of growth of capacity. The sources of economic growth may be divided into *resources*—or the factors of production—and *productive efficiency,* both of which are important in determining the capacity level of the economy. Exercise 25 discusses what determines productive capacity, and studies the problem of matching aggregate demand to the supply capabilities of a growing economy.

THE ECONOMICS OF GROWTH

1 Suppose we let Y represent *realized* output of real goods and services in a national economy and Y_p represent *potential* output if all of the factors of production are fully utilized, given existing technology. If Y in the United States during 1971 was $1,040 bil and it was estimated that the economy was operating at 80 percent of capacity, then Y_p

is $ _____ bil and the underutilization of productive resources amounted to $ _____ bil. The latter amount represents the *opportunity cost* being incurred by the national economy for operating where it *is* rather than where it *could be*.

Potential or full-employment output is defined as the maximum level of output that could hypothetically be sustained indefinitely, while providing for replacement of depreciating capital. If Y_p above represented 75 percent of maximum conceivable short-run output, termed Y_p^*, then for a short while the economy could operate at a level of

$ _____ bil annually, or _____ percent of long-run, "sustainable" production. To produce at Y_p^*, the economy would have to use up its productive capital, e.g., during wartime.

2 Productive capacity is a function of (a) resources and (b) productivity. The primary resources are labor N, tangible capital K, and natural resources R. Labor inputs may be defined initially as man-hours worked, that is, the total labor time actually devoted to productive activity in a given time period. Indicate below how you think the following variables would ultimately affect the supply of aggregate man-hours, either directly or through the intermediate linkages, assuming all else equal. (Indicate + for increase or – for decrease.)

Variable	Possible intermediate linkage	Change in total man-hours worked
(a) Birth rate rises	Population	_____
(b) Infant mortality rate declines	Population	_____

Variable	Possible intermediate linkage	Change in total man-hours worked
(c) Death rate declines	Population	_____
(d) Income rises	Birth rate	_____
(e) Urbanization grows	Birth rate	_____
(f) Parents' dependence on children, upon retirement, declines	Birth rate	_____
(g) Contraceptive availability rises	Birth rate	_____
(h) Government child support rises	Birth rate	_____
(i) Medical technology grows	Death rate	_____
(j) Labor force participation rate (LPR) declines	–	_____
(k) Percent of population of very old rises	LPR	_____
(l) Percent of population of very young rises	LPR	_____
(m) Increase in average educational expenses	LPR	_____
(n) Participation in labor force by women grows	LPR	_____
(o) Shorter work seek	–	_____
(p) Shorter work day	–	_____
(q) Increased vacation time	–	_____
(r) Immigration (net) rises	–	_____

It is important to note that virtually all of these variables is dependent on economic growth itself. While each of the factors affecting man-hours supplied affects potential output, the level of and rate of change in potential output, in turn, affects each of them. Man-hour inputs thus represent, to a large degree, an (exogenous, endogenous) variable in the economic system.

3 Aside from the *quantity* of labor that is supplied, *quality* is also an important dimension because it determines output per unit of labor input. Indicate below how each of the listed variables affects output through its effect on the quality of labor:

	Quality of labor
(a) Level of education rises	_____
(b) Level of health declines	_____
(c) Acquisitive motivation rises	_____

Note again that each factor is itself affected by economic growth. A society's ability to invest in health and educational facilities, and to forgo the *alternative* services of individuals so that they may be teachers, students, and health-service workers, is a product of a nation's willingness and ability to invest in human capital. The greater a nation's output relative to its population, the more it can afford to do things that will improve the quality of its labor force. Again, the determining variables are (exogenous, endogenous) to the economic system. They affect economic growth and, in turn, are affected by it.

4 The second resource identified above is tangible capital, which includes such social overhead capital as roads, utilities, and communications networks, as well as business plant and equipment. The larger the nation's stock of tangible capital, the larger its potential output of goods and services. Tangible capital is created through investment, although not all investment represents tangible capital, as, for example, investment in inventory and housing. Investment is made possible through reduced consumption or saving. Capital is maintained through provision for depreciation, but we have seen that this is embodied in the definition of "capacity." Tangible capital is a (stock, flow) concept. Additions to the amount of available tangible capital are made possible through net investment, which is a (stock, flow) concept. Indicate below how each of the listed variables can be expected to affect the national stock of tangible capital, assuming demand adjusts accordingly.

	Tangible capital (indicate + or -)
(a) Distribution of income becomes less equal	_____
(b) Efficiency of financial markets rises	_____
(c) Proportion of population who are entrepreneurs grows	_____
(d) Interest rates rise	_____
(e) Average size of family grows	_____
(f) Political stability declines	_____
(g) Direct taxes rise to support military expenditures	_____

5 Let us assume that the potential or full-employment output of an economy is proportional to the stock of capital.

$$(1) \quad Y_p = \sigma K$$

where Y_p represents the productive capacity of the economy, K is the capital stock necessary to support Y_p, and σ (read as "sigma") is termed the "capital coefficient." By solving Eq. (1) for σ, we have

$$(2) \quad \sigma = \frac{Y_p}{K}$$

Equation (2) shows that σ is the (average, marginal, total) *output-capital* ratio and represents the value of the *average productivity* of the capital stock.

Since the capital stock is composed of old and new machines, obsolete buildings and modern productive facilities, σ may not be representative of the *increase* in potential output we can expect from an *increase* in the capital stock. A capacity increase would consist entirely of new capital, which would presumably be more efficient than the average productivity of the present capital stock. Hence, we can also compute the *marginal output-capital ratio.*

$$(3) \quad \sigma' = \frac{\Delta Y_p}{\Delta K}$$

We should expect σ' to be (larger, smaller) than σ if indeed newer tangible capital is more productive than the present capital stock. Suppose the economy is operating at 100 percent of capacity, GNP = $1,200 bil, and the national stock of tangible capital is $3,600 bil. From Eq. (1), the value of the (average, marginal) output-capital ratio is

_____ .

Suppose σ' is 1/2, gross investment is $200 bil, and capital consumption during the year is $50 bil. We can expect capacity to grow by $ _____ bil, to a total of $ _____ bil. Thus, as in the case of labor, we cannot limit ourselves to studying the total stock of capital and changes therein, but must also consider the *quality* of capital and technology embodied in it. Again, both quantity and quality of capital are a *product* of economic growth as well as a *cause* of it, and hence are (exogenous, endogenous) to the system.

6 Consider the following simple, closed-economy model: $C = \$200$ bil $+ 0.80Y$ and $I_n = \$50$ bil, where I_n is defined as net investment. $Y_e = \$$ _____ bil. Assume that Y_e represents internal economic balance, i.e., a fully employed domestic economy with price stability. Hence, $Y_e = Y_p$.

If the average output-capital ratio is 1/3, to support the full-employment level of income, the national stock of tangible capital must be $ _____ bil. (For review, see Eq. (2).) Assume further that the marginal output-capital ratio is 1/2. During the current period, the economy's net addition to its capital stock is $ _____ bil. As a result of this addition, the nation's productive capacity will (rise, fall) by: $Y_p = \$$ _____ bil. (For review, see Eq. (3) ff.) The new productive level is $ _____ bil.

If aggregate demand remains constant, the economy will now experience (unemployed resources, inflationary pressures). In order to get back to full-employment equilibrium, we will thus need a(n) (expansion, contraction) of aggregate demand to $ _____ bil.

If some of the required shift in aggregate demand takes the form of increased investment, then Y_p will (rise, fall, remain unchanged) in the subsequent time period, requiring a (reduction, further increase) in aggregate demand to maintain Y_p. Thus the very act of investment increases productive capacity, which requires an increase in aggregate demand to absorb it. If this latter demand boost takes the form of increased investment, then capacity will again expand and still more aggregate demand will be required to utilize capacity fully. Continued growth of excess capacity can be prevented by _____

_____ .

7 Assume we have the following information for year 1 in our economy:

$C = 0.8Y$

$Y_p = \$1{,}000$ bil

$\sigma' = 1/2$

$G = 0 \quad X = 0 \quad Z = 0$

Since we are studying a long-run income determination model, consumption is assumed to be proportional to income. (This assumption follows the evidence about long-run consumption behavior discussed in Exercise 8.)

At Y_p, consumption is \$ _____ bil and saving is \$ _____ bil. If Y_p is to be maintained, saving must equal (depreciation, consumption, investment). Investment at Y_p will

therefore be \$ _____ bil. Assuming that $I = I_n$, the national capital stock will increase

from \$ _____ bil in year 1 to \$ _____ bil in year 2. Complete Table 25-1. Table 25-1 demonstrates that, under the assumptions specified above, investment must (be constant, continue to rise) if full employment is maintained. In the short-run Keynesian model studied in previous exercises, the capacity-creating effect of investment was (included, not considered) because this effect (is, is not) important in the short run.

8 We can summarize the relationship between demand growth and capacity growth, demonstrated above, with a simple model known as the Harrod-Domar model. We will assume that consumption is proportional to income, all I is net I, $\sigma = \sigma'$, and there is no government or foreign sector. The proposition that the rate of demand growth must

Table 25-1

Year	Y_p	S	I_n	K
1	\$1,000 bil	\$ _____ bil	\$ _____ bil	\$ _____ bil
2	\$ _____ bil	\$ _____ bil	\$ _____ bil	\$ _____ bil
3	\$ _____ bil	\$ _____ bil	\$ _____ bil	\$ _____ bil

equal the rate of capacity growth in order to maintain full employment can be expressed as

(4) $\Delta Y = \Delta Y_p$

Since, in the model presented here, consumption is a function of income and the government and foreign sectors are excluded, *changes* in aggregate income are assumed to depend

solely on *changes* in _____ . Consumption expenditures (do, do not) change through the (autonomous, induced) effect of the multiplier process. Changes in aggregate spending can be expressed as

(5) $\Delta Y =$ _____

If we assume that changes in capacity are proportional to changes in the capital stock, capacity growth can be expressed as

(6) $\Delta Y_p =$ _____

Since the change in the capital stock equals the level of _____ in the current time period, we can state that

(7) $\Delta K =$ _____

By substituting Eq. (7) into Eq. (6), we have

(8) $\Delta Y_p =$ _____

Now substitute Eqs. (5) and (8) into (4).

(9)   _____ = _____

We can rearrange Eq. (9) as follows:

(10) $\dfrac{\Delta I_n}{I_n} = \sigma(1-b)$

Equation (10) indicates that, in equilibrium, full-employment output is maintained when the percentage rate of investment growth $\Delta I_n/I_n$ is equal to the _____ multiplied by the _____ .
This growth rate is called the *warranted rate of growth.*

The warranted rate indicates that the additional capacity produced by the net investment of the current time period is fully utilized by the additional demand created by that net investment. According to the warranted rate, the required growth of investment will be higher the (higher, lower) the marginal propensity to save; required growth will be higher, the (higher, lower) the capital necessary to produce an additional unit of output— that is, the (larger, smaller) the capital coefficient.

The warranted rate describes producers' equilibrium in the sense that intended sales are realized. If, for example, the actual growth rate is less than the warranted rate, excess (demand, capacity) will result in the current time period. Due to the excess capacity condition, investment will *fall* and, through the multiplier effect, the ensuing income (rise, decline) will cause the excess-capacity gap to (narrow, widen).

If actual growth is greater than the warranted rate, conversely, excess (demand, capacity) will result. Attempts to eliminate the capacity shortage will cause income to (rise, fall), which will (alleviate, worsen) this condition.

9 The model of economic growth developed in paragraphs 5 to 8 was based on the assumption that the potential output of the economy is proportional to the stock of capital. This assumption, while useful for many purposes, ignores the fact that other inputs, notably labor, are substitutable for capital in the production process. Thus, it is not accurate to assert that potential output is proportional to the capital stock: In fact, potential output may be achieved with a variety of combinations of inputs. The main effect of this change of assumptions is to reverse the conclusion, stated in paragraph 8, that the economy's growth is inherently unstable. We shall show that the economy tends to move toward an equilibrium growth rate, provided that labor and capital may be substituted for one another.

10* Let us adopt the well-known Cobb-Douglas production function,

$$(11) \quad Y_p = K^a N^{1-a}$$

where Y_p is potential output, K is the capital stock, and N is the labor force. This production function (does, does not) exhibit constant returns to scale, and (does, does not) exhibit diminishing marginal productivities of both capital and labor. We also define the symbol $\dot{K}$:

$$(12) \quad \dot{K} = dK/dt$$

$\dot{K}$ is the time rate of change of the capital stock. It may be interpreted to be the rate of investment at a given instant of time. This follows from the fact that over a given time period, investment net of depreciation is equal to the difference between the ending capital stock and the beginning capital stock.

In equilibrium, saving is equal to investment:

$$(13) \quad sY = \dot{K}$$

where s is the proportion of income saved and Y is actual output. It is assumed that saving is a constant proportion of income. If the economy is at full employment, actual output is equal to potential output, and

$$(14) \quad sY_p = \dot{K}$$

$$(15) \quad sK^a N^{1-a} = \dot{K}$$

11 Let us define r to be the capital/labor ratio:

$$(16) \quad r = K/N$$

The time rate of change of r, dr/dt is

$$(17) \quad \dot{r} = \frac{\dot{K}}{N} - \frac{\dot{K}}{N}\left(\frac{\dot{L}}{N}\right)$$

---

*The remaining sections require the use of differential calculus. They may be skipped without loss of continuity.

Therefore, the *percentage* rate of change of r must be

(18) $\quad \dfrac{\dot{r}}{r} =$ _____

Simplifying,

(19) $\quad \dfrac{\dot{r}}{r} =$ _____

Using Eq. (5), we can substitute for K:

(20) $\quad \dfrac{\dot{r}}{r} = \dfrac{sK^aN^{1-a}}{K} - \dfrac{\dot{N}}{N}$

Given that K^aN^{1-a}/K is the (average, marginal) product of capital,

(21) $\quad \dfrac{\dot{r}}{r} = \dfrac{sY_p}{K} - \dfrac{\dot{N}}{N}$

Following Eq. (2), we define $\sigma = Y_p/K$. We also assume that the labor force grows at a constant percentage rate n. Therefore,

(22) $\quad \dfrac{\dot{r}}{r} = s(\sigma) - n$

According to the discussion in paragraph 8, $s(\sigma)$ is the _____ rate of growth. The growth rate of labor n is defined as the *natural* rate of growth. If $\dot{r}/r$ equals zero, the warranted rate of growth equals the natural rate. In the next section, we show that the system approaches an equilibrium position at which $\dot{r}/r$ equals zero.

12 It follows from Eq. (20) that

(23) $\quad \dfrac{\dot{r}}{r} = K^{a-1}N^{1-a} - n$

(24) $\quad \dfrac{\dot{r}}{r} = s(r)^{a-1} - n$

If $\dot{r}/r$ equals zero, equilibrium r is

(25) $\quad r^* =$ _____

Suppose that r were to rise above r^*. Since $a-1$ is (positive, negative, zero), $s(r)^{a-1}$ would (rise, fall, remain the same), and n would (rise, fall, remain the same). From Eq. (24) it follows that $\dot{r}/r$ would be (positive, negative, zero), indicating that K is growing (faster than, slower than, at the same rate as) N. Then r, or K/N, would be (rising, falling, constant), thus (approaching, moving away from, neither approaching nor moving away from) r^*. If, on the other hand, r were to fall below r^*, $s(r)^{a-1}$ would be (larger than, smaller than, the same as) n, and $\dot{r}/r$ would be (positive, negative, zero). Thus, r would be (rising, falling, constant), and would be (approaching, moving away from, neither approaching nor moving away from) r^*. We can conclude that r (does, does not) have an equilibrium value of r^*, and that the equilibrium is (stable, unstable). This result (confirms, denies) the conclusion about stability reached in paragraph 8.

In equilibrium, $\dot{r}$ is equal to _____; therefore, capital and labor tend to grow at the (same, different) rates. This condition is known as *balanced growth*.

PROBLEMS FOR EXERCISE 25

Define the following terms:

1 Actual output _____

_____

2 Potential output _____

_____

3 Opportunity cost _____

_____

4 Capacity _____

_____

5 Labor inputs _____

_____

6 Human capital _____

_____

7 Tangible capital _____

_____

8 Social overhead capital _____

_____

9 Capital-output ratio _____

_____

10 Incremental capital-output ratio _____

_____

11 Efficiency _____

_____

12 Technology _____

_____

13 Production function _____

_____

14 Residual _____

_____

15 Embodied technical change _____

_____

16 Optimum savings rate _____

_____

ANSWERS FOR EXERCISE 25

1 1,300, 260, 1,733, 133

2 (a) +   (e) –   (i) +   (m) –   (q) –
   (b) +   (f) –   (j) –   (n) +   (r) +, endogenous
   (c) +   (g) –   (k) –   (o) –
   (d) –   (h) +   (l) –   (p) –

3 (a) +, (b) –, (c) +, endogenous

4 stock, flow, (a) +, (b) +, (c) +, (d) –, (e) –, (f) –, (g) –

5 average, larger, average, 1/3, 150, 3,750, endogenous

6 1,250, 3,750, 50, rise, 25, 1,275, unemployed resources, expansion, 1,275, rise, further increase, channeling excess supply into increases in consumption or government spending or the foreign sector

7 800, 200, investment, 200, 2,000, 2,200,

Year	Y_p	S	I_n	K
1	1,000	200	200	2,000
2	1,100	220	220	2,200
3	1,210	242	242	2,420

continue to rise, not considered, is not

8 net investment, do, induced, Eq. (5) $\Delta Y = \Delta I_n / 1 - b$,
Eq. (6) $\Delta Y_p = \sigma' \Delta K$, net investment, Eq. (7) $\Delta K = I_n$,
Eq. (8) $\Delta Y_p = \sigma' I_n$, Eq. (9) $\Delta I_n / 1 - b = \sigma' I_n$, output-capital ratio, marginal propensity to save, higher, lower, larger, capacity, decline, widen, demand, rise, worsen

10 does, does

11 Eq. (18): $\dfrac{\dot{r}}{r} = \dfrac{\dfrac{\dot{K}}{L} - \dfrac{K}{N}\left(\dfrac{\dot{N}}{N}\right)}{K/L}$

Eq. (19): $\dfrac{\dot{r}}{r} = \dfrac{\dot{K}}{K} - \dfrac{\dot{N}}{N}$

average, warranted

12 Eq. (25): $r^* = \dfrac{s}{n}\left(\dfrac{1}{1-a}\right)$

negative, fall, remain the same, negative, slower than, falling, approaching, larger than, positive, rising, approaching, does, stable, denies, zero, same

ANSWERS TO PROBLEMS FOR EXERCISE 25

1 GNP, or total production of goods and services over a specified period of time.
2 Maximum amount of goods and services that *could be* produced in a given year if all productive factors were fully utilized.
3 Gap between number 2 and number 1; output lost due to underutilization of available productive resources.
4 Same as number 2; maximum possible output while maintaining the national stock of tangible capital.
5 Man-hours worked during given period of time.
6 Improvement in the quality of labor through education, health and related means.
7 Physical capital stock of productive assets.
8 Tangible capital available to all consumers and producers in an economy, such as roads, sewers, etc.
9 $K \div Q^*$, the stock of tangible capital required to support a given level of potential output; or the amount of potential output that can be supported by a given stock of tangible capital.
10 $\Delta K \div \Delta Q^*$; the incremental amount of tangible capital required to support a given amount of increased potential output; or the additional amount of potential output that can be supported by a given increment in the national stock of tangible capital.
11 If I = inputs and E = efficiency, then $Q^* = I \times E$, or $E = Q^*/I$, or the amount of output produced by a given quantum of inputs.
12 Technology is *any* knowledge that is useful in economic activity and promotes efficiency, as described above.
13 Production functions relate outputs to inputs, and specify how output varies with changes in the inputs.
14 After all of the known variables have been analyzed in terms of their influence on the dependent variable, the residual is what remains unexplained.
15 Technical change that can only be applied in the productive process in conjunction with another factor of production such as capital.
16 That rate of saving which will produce an amount of additional output just absorbed by the resultant additional consumption.

REVIEW TEST FOR PART 9

1 In the simple capital-output/investment growth model, the economy is in dynamic equilibrium only when actual investment equals required investment.
   (a) true
   (b) false

2 If actual economic growth exceeds the warranted rate, aggregate supply falls short of aggregate demand.
   (a) true
   (b) false

3 Equilibrium in the above type of model involves a current investment level which exceeds the saving level in the previous period.
   (a) true
   (b) false

4 Aggregate demand must grow at a faster rate than production capacity for equilibrium economic growth to occur.
   (a) true
   (b) false

5 The additional productive capacity attributable to net investment will be productively used whether or not aggregate demand increases.
   (a) true
   (b) false

6 One way to increase the rate of economic growth is to raise the productivity of physical capital.
   (a) true
   (b) false

7 If old machines are replaced with an equal number of new machines, the average productivity of physical capital in an economy remains unchanged.
  (a) true
  (b) false

8 The difference between embodied and disembodied technical change is that the former raises output while the latter lowers it.
  (a) true
  (b) false

9 Additions to the labor force, measured as man-hours worked, will lower the capital-output ratio.
  (a) true
  (b) false

10 In a stationary economy, new net investment is zero.
  (a) true
  (b) false

11 Technical change normally raises an economy's capital-output ratio.
  (a) true
  (b) false

12 A 1 percent increase in labor inputs contributes the same increase in potential output as a 1 percent increase in capital inputs.
  (a) true
  (b) false

13 Output per man-hour, as a measure of productivity, depends entirely on technical change.
  (a) true
  (b) false

14 The larger the incremental capital-output ratio, the smaller the increased potential output derived from a given amount of new net investment.
  (a) true
  (b) false

15 Government policy is of no importance in determining the rate of economic growth of a country in the long run.
  (a) true
  (b) false

16 A nation cannot grow at a satisfactory rate without adequate local supplies of natural resources.
  (a) true
  (b) false

17 The definition of "productivity" in the context of economic growth theory refers only to the efficiency with which labor is used in the productive process.
  (a) true
  (b) false

18 It is possible, under some circumstances, for change in productive capacity to be negative.
  (a) true
  (b) false

19 The marginal propensity to consume is an unimportant parameter in the determination of the rate of growth.
  (a) true
  (b) false

20 Economic growth tends to have an effect on the supply of labor, just as labor supplies affect economic growth.
  (a) true
  (b) false

21 Which of the following is emphasized in the simple model of economic growth based on the capital-output ratio?
  (a) capital accumulation is an important element in the growth process
  (b) equilibrium growth is not likely to occur automatically
  (c) an economy must grow to avoid a continually increasing volume of unemployed labor and capital
  (d) the path of growth is perilous
  (e) all of the above

22 If full-employment GNP is $1,600 bil in 1976 and this output is realized in an economy with levels of consumption and net investment of $1,480 and $90 bil respectively, and if the capital-output ratio for the economy is 2/1, the full-employment GNP for 1977 will be:
  (a) $1,780 bil
  (b) $1,660 bil
  (c) $1,720 bil
  (d) $1,840 bil

23 Which of the following is a supply factor in economic growth?
  (a) the quantity of labor
  (b) technology
  (c) natural resources
  (d) capital stock
  (e) all of these

24 In the simple theory of economic growth an increase in productive capacity is equal to
   (a) net investment times the average productivity of investment
   (b) the reciprocal of the average propensity to save times the change in net investment
   (c) the amount of net investment in any specific period
   (d) the average propensity to save times net investment
   (e) none of the above

25 In order to maintain a fixed rate of economic growth,
   (a) investment spending must decline to permit the absolute and relative expansion of consumption which growth entails
   (b) investment spending must increase each successive year
   (c) investment spending must remain at a constant level
   (d) saving must increase at a declining rate

26 It is true that
   (a) all net investment increases capacity but only increases in investment raise aggregate demand
   (b) part of the investment goes to replace capital used up in production, while part of it increases capacity
   (c) investment not only increases capacity but adds to the stock of capital equipment
   (d) investment increases aggregate demand when it increases, and decreases aggregate demand when it decreases
   (e) all of the above

27 Disembodied technical change includes:
   (a) the development of digital computing
   (b) the use of nuclear power in the generation of electricity
   (c) improved management
   (d) the introduction of vocational education

28 Assume the economy is in balance (full employment with price stability). Given the size of the labor force, an increase in the productivity of labor
   (a) will cause unemployment if aggregate demand fails to rise
   (b) will result in unemployment regardless of any changes which may occur in aggregate demand
   (c) will cause real GNP to rise even if aggregate demand is unchanged
   (d) none of these

29 Since net investment increases capacity, we need to
   (a) determine the rate of income growth that will utilize the increase in capacity over time
   (b) determine the rate at which capacity should grow over time
   (c) determine the cause of the increase in capacity over time
   (d) all of the above

30 The equilibrium growth rate in the model based on the capital-output ratio depends on
   (a)   the rate of population growth
   (b)   the value of the marginal propensity to save
   (c)   the initial income level
   (d)   the productivity of capital

ANSWERS FOR REVIEW TESTS

ANSWERS TO REVIEW TEST FOR PART 1

1 c; 2 e; 3 b; 4 c; 5 d; 6 e; 7 c; 8 b;
9 a; 10 d; 11 d; 12 a; 13 a; 14 d; 15 c;
16 b; 17 d; 18 d; 19 c; 20 e; 21 d;
22 b; 23 c; 24 c; 25 b; 26 b; 27 c; 28 c;
29 d; 30 a; 31 c; 32 c; 33 d; 34 c; 35 c;
36 c; 37 a; 38 d; 39 c; 40 c; 41 d; 42 d;
43 d; 44 b; 45 e; 46 d; 47 c; 48 b; 49 c;
50 c.

ANSWERS TO REVIEW TEST FOR PART 2

1 a; 2 c; 3 b; 4 b; 5 a,d; 6 c; 7 b; 8 b;
9 b,d; 10 b; 11 b; 12 b; 13 a; 14 c,d;
15 b; 16 b,d; 17 c; 18 a; 19 a; 20 c;
21 b,e; 22 d; 23 c; 24 c; 25 b; 26 a,d;
27 b; 28 a; 29 a; 30 b; 31 b,d; 32 b,c;
33 c; 34 c,d; 35 b; 36 a,c; 37 c,d,e;
38 b; 39 c; 40 a; 41 b; 42 c; 43 d; 44 c;
45 c; 46 d; 47 a; 48 c; 49 a; 50 c; 51 a;
52 a; 53 a,b,d,e; 54 e; 55 b; 56 c; 57 a;
58 b; 59 d; 60 a; 61 a; 62 a; 63 a; 64 b;
65 b; 66 a; 67 b; 68 a,d; 69 a,d,e;
70 b,c; 71 c,d; 72 e; 73 a; 74 b; 75 b,d;
76 b,d,e; 77 a,e; 78 a,b; 79 d; 80 b;
81 a.

ANSWERS TO REVIEW TEST FOR PART 3

1 c,d; 2 c; 3 a; 4 b; 5 b; 6 d; 7 a; 8 b,
c,d; 9 a,b; 10 c,e; 11 a,b,c; 12 b; 13 e;
14 a; 15 b; 16 a; 17 b; 18 c,d; 19 a; 20 d;
21 d; 22 c; 23 c; 24 a; 25 a; 26 a; 27 b,
c; 28 a; 29 b,c.

ANSWERS TO REVIEW TEST FOR PART 4

1 a; 2 a; 3 b; 4 a,b,c; 5 b; 6 c; 7 a,c;
8 b,d; 9 a,c; 10 a,c; 11 a,b,c; 12 b; 13 b;
14 b; 15 a; 16 b.

ANSWERS TO REVIEW TEST FOR PART 5

1 b; 2 c; 3 a,b,c; 4 b; 5 a; 6 b; 7 b; 8 b; 9 a; 10 a; 11 b; 12 a; 13 b; 14 b,d; 15 d; 16 a; 17 b; 18 b,c,d; 19 b; 20 b; 21 b; 22 a; 23 a; 24 b; 25 a; 26 b; 27 b; 28 a; 29 a; 30 a; 31 c; 32 a; 33 a; 34 b; 35 b; 36 c; 37 a; 38 b; 39 a; 40 a; 41 a; 42 c; 43 b; 44 a; 45 b; 46 b; 47 b; 48 a; 49 c; 50 a; 51 a; 52 a; 53 a; 54 b; 55 a; 56 b; 57 a; 58 d; 59 a; 60 d; 61 a; 62 a; 63 a; 64 a; 65 b; 66 b; 67 c; 68 b; 69 b; 70 b; 71 c; 72 a; 73 c; 74 a; 75 a; 76 b.

ANSWERS TO REVIEW TEST FOR PART 6

1 c,d; 2 c; 3 a,c; 4 d; 5 a,b,c; 6 c; 7 b,d; 8 a; 9 b; 10 b; 11 c; 12 b; 13 b; 14 c; 15 b; 16 e; 17 b; 18 a; 19 b; 20 c; 21 e; 22 b; 23 c; 24 a; 25 a,e; 26 a,c,e; 27 d,f; 28 b,f; 29 a,c; 30 a,c.

ANSWERS TO REVIEW TEST FOR PART 7

1 c; 2 c; 3 a; 4 b; 5 c; 6 a; 7 b; 8 c; 9 d; 10 d; 11 a; 12 b; 13 c;

Keynesian assumptions: 14 +; 15 +; 16 +; 17 +; 18 +; 19 ind; 20 + (note: balanced, budget multiplier); 21 +; 22 +; 23 −; 24 −; 25 +; 26 −; 27 −; 28 −; 29 −; 30 −; 31 −; 32 +; 33 +; 34 −; 35 −; 36 −; 37 −; 38 +; 39 −; 40 ind; 41 +; 42 −; 43 ind; 44 −; 45 +; 46 ind; 47 −; 48 −; 49 ind; 50 +; 51 −; 52 ind;

classical assumptions: 14 no; 15 +; 16 +; 17 no; 18 +; 19 + (see note below); 20 no; 21 +; 22 +; 23 no; 24 −; 25 +; 26 no; 27 −; 28 −; 29 no; 30 −; 31 −; 32 no; 33 +; 34 −; 35 no; 36 −; 37 −; 38 +; 39 −; 40 ind; 41 +; 42 −; 43 ind;

(Note on question 19, classical assumptions: We can show in this case that i rises by noting that both G/P and C/P rise. If Y/P remains constant, I/P must fall. Therefore, i must rise.)

ANSWERS TO REVIEW TEST FOR PART 8

1 e; 2 c; 3 a; 4 a; 5 b; 6 d; 7 a; 8 d; 9 c; 10 c; 11 a; 12 c; 13 c; 14 b; 15 d; 16 b; 17 e; 18 b,c; 19 b; 20 b; 21 c; 22 b; 23 a; 24 e; 25 d; 26 a; 27 a; 28 b; 29 a; 30 b; 31 a; 32 a; 33 c; 34 d; 35 b; 36 b or g; 37 d; 38 a; 39 f; 40 e; 41 a; 42 b or f; 43 d; 44 b; 45 b; 46 a; 47 b; 48 a; 49 b; 50 b.

ANSWERS TO REVIEW TEST FOR PART 9

1 a; 2 b; 3 b; 4 b; 5 b; 6 a; 7 b; 8 b; 9 a; 10 a; 11 b; 12 b; 13 b; 14 b; 15 b; 16 b; 17 b; 18 a; 19 b; 20 a; 21 e; 22 b; 23 e; 24 a; 25 b; 26 e; 27 c; 28 a; 29 a; 30 d.